THE PHILOSOPHY OF TIME

The Philosophy of Time

A COLLECTION OF ESSAYS

EDITED BY RICHARD M. GALE

MACMILLAN

LONDON · MELBOURNE

1968

First published in the United States of America 1967
First published in Great Britain 1968

Published by
MACMILLAN & CO LTD
Little Essex Street London WC2
and also at Bombay Calcutta and Madras
Macmillan South Africa (Publishers) Pty Ltd Johannesburg
The Macmillan Company of Australia Pty Ltd Melbourne

Printed in Great Britain by
Lowe & Brydone (Printers) Ltd., London

Dedicated to the memory of my father—

MOE GALE

PREFACE

Works on time invariably have titles like "The Problem of Time" or "The Mystery of Time." No wonder! For time, more than any other subject of philosophical concern, has been a perennial source of puzzlement and perplexity. It is ironic that something with which we are so intimately acquainted should give rise to paradoxes as soon as we attempt to scrutinize it analytically. The brilliant analyses of time by Zeno, Augustine, and McTaggart, which are included in this volume, show how easily time seems to dissolve—to prove itself unreal—under the weight of analysis. Time, of course, is real: ask any woman who has just seen the first wrinkle on her face in the mirror. The fault must lie, therefore, with the analyses of time; and it is the task of philosophers to cure themselves of their homegrown paradoxes and perplexities.

The first step in the achievement of this therapy is to realize that the problem of time is not a single problem, namely that of defining time. Section I of this volume deals with the inevitable failure of such an attempt. Rather, the problem of time is a group of intimately related questions having to do with the nature of the concepts of truth, events, things, knowledge, causality, identification, action, and change. The remaining sections of this volume are devoted to questions concerning the temporal involvements of these concepts, and it turns out that an adequate treatment of any one of these conceptual questions requires an answer to the others as well. It is this organic, across-the-board feature of the problem of time which, in my opinion, makes it the most important and exciting issue in all of philosophy. My introductions to the different sections attempt to show the interconnections between these different conceptual issues.

The thread for interweaving these far-ranging conceptual questions is supplied in Section II. Herein the connection between the temporal relations of precedence and simultaneity, on the one hand, and the tensed distinctions of past, present, and future, on the other, is explored by noting the manner in which these two different kind of temporal determinations are involved in the meaning of the concepts I have mentioned. Section III gives a more detailed account of how tensed distinctions enter into the concepts of truth, knowledge, causality, and identification by dealing with the questions: "Can statements about the future be true now, and, if so, does this entail fatalism?"; "Can our present actions have past effects, and, if not, why not?"; and "Can an individual who does not yet exist be identified now?" Further questions concerning the nature of past, present, and future are taken up in Section IV, where competing answers are given to the question of whether these tensed distinctions are dependent on a *subject* qua perceiver or language-user, and whether they are therefore *subjective*. In the final section the concept of change is examined in the light of Zeno's paradoxes of motion; here the main issue is whether change is discrete or continuous.

My own research on the philosophy of time, which enabled me to put this anthology together, was greatly aided by various fellowships and grants. These were the Samuel S. Fels Foundation Fellowship for 1960–61; the Vassar College Class of '59 Grant-in-Aid for Summer Research for 1963; the National Science Foundation grant No. 387 for 1964–65; and the University of Pittsburgh Post-Doctoral Andrew Mellon Fellowship for 1966–67. I gratefully appreciate the help of these benefactors.

The introductions to the different sections of this volume were written during the summer of 1966 while my wife and I were visiting her parents, Kiyoshi and Mari Mori, in Tokyo. No one was ever blessed with more wonderful in-laws.

CONTENTS

THE PHILOSOPHY OF TIME

Section I

"WHAT, THEN, IS TIME?"

INTRODUCTION

1. The first serious attempt to analyze the concept of time occurs in Aristotle's *Physics*. He raises the question, "In what sense, if any, can time be said to exist?" For Aristotle, only individual substances, which are compounds of form and matter, can be said to exist in an unqualified sense, everything else being attributes of these substances. Time is defined as the "number of movement in respect of 'before' and 'after.'" Motion is an attribute of a substance, and time in turn is an attribute of motion. Time is not motion, but the number or measure of motion. Motion is *potentially* time and becomes such in *actuality* only when its temporal succession is noted and measured by some sentient creature. Thus time is not a substantial entity which is capable of existing separately from other things: it has no reality independently of the changes that substances undergo. It has being only as an attribute of an attribute of substance.

Aristotle deduces the continuity of time—its infinite divisibility—from the continuity of motion, which in turn is deduced from the continuity of the space traversed. Since the space traversed is continuous, motion must be continuous, and since the motion, therefore the time that measures it, because there is a one-to-one correspondence between each point of the trajectory and a moment of time. (Kant later reversed this by starting with the logical priority of time as a form of our sensibility, and then argued from the continuity of time to the continuity of change.) Time is made continuous by the indivisible, present now-moment, which links the past to the future by serving as the termination of the past and the beginning of the future, just as a mathematical point dissects a line by serving as the end of one segment and the beginning of the other. Time is not made up of now-moments any more than a line is made up of mathematical points. Rather it is the case that time, like a line, is made up of parts each of which has a finite length and is therefore divisible *ad infinitum.*

2. Plotinus, in the Third *Ennead,* raises many objections to Aristotle's analysis of time, his main criticism being that Aristotle's definition of time as the "number of movement in respect of the before and after" suffers from the fatal defect of circularity. Time, obviously, cannot be a number, but is *what* is numbered. Before and after, if they are to refer to temporal relations, must mean before and after *in time,* rather than in the space traversed. Furthermore, motion presupposes time since motion is defined as the occupation, by one entity, of a continuous series of places at a continuous series of *times.* Time is defined in terms of motion and motion in terms of time. Thus we have a circular chain of definitions, and Aristotle tells us only how we measure time, not what time is. Plotinus assumes that time must be something apart, a "kind to itself," a thing "within itself." All motion and rest occur within time, but time does not occur in something else.

Unfortunately, Plotinus, in his own positive attempts to define time, does not get any further than Aristotle. He repeats Plato's metaphor of time being a moving image of eternity, but that will hardly do as a definition. Time is identified with the creative activity of the soul. However, the charge of circularity that Plotinus made against Aristotle's notion applies also to his own definition of time as "the Life of the Soul in movement as it passes from one stage of act or experience to another"; for the notion of *passing* from one stage to another involves time, that is, a soul's being in a different qualitative state at different *times.* If we wish to contend, along with Bergson, that we cannot speak of states of consciousness occurring at *different* moments of time because we cannot separate or distinguish one state from another, then we cannot speak of one state of consciousness *passing* into another, since this involves some distinction between them.

Strangely enough, Aristotle was aware of the circularity involved in his definition for he wrote that "we measure the movement by the time and vice versa." What we in fact do is to select some cyclical physical process to serve as our clock, and we define temporal congruence (equal temporal intervals) in terms of the cyclical events comprising our clock. We define temporal congruence so as to introduce the maximum of simplicity in our co-ordination of physical phenomena. A definition of an ideal clock is made within the confines of a physical theory, for example, inertia in Newton's theory and the light rays of relativity theory. It is misleading to say, as Plotinus does, that all motion and rest are in time, for that suggests that time is some sort of a queer companion process by comparison with which we date and measure the motion and rest of things. Rather it is the case that we correlate real numbers with the events comprising our clock, the larger the number the later the event, and we then determine the date and duration of other processes and states by correlating them with the numbered events in our clock.

An operational or scientific definition of time is based on the method by which we measure time. Any such definition is obviously circular. The definition of a clock involves temporal notions, since a clock is defined as a closed material system which will *return* to exactly the same state in which it found itself at some *earlier instant of time*. The *sine qua non* for a temporal measurement is that two different observations —*non-simultaneous* observations—be made of the measuring scale. By "non-simultaneous" we must mean occurring at different *times*. Therefore our definition is circular. If one does not first understand what we mean by time he will not be able to understand these operational definitions.

3. This brief excursion into operational definitions of time serves only to intensify the problem of defining it. After Plotinus the next serious effort to define time is found in Augustine's *Confessions*. Augustine's famous lament, "What, then, is time? If no one asks me, I know: if I wish to explain it to one that asketh, I know not:" summarizes the mystery that time holds for him. We might try to analyze his predica-

ment in the following way. He has an immediate experiential awareness of time; and moreover, he knows how to use ordinary temporal expressions about past, present, and future, and earlier and later than. Yet oddly enough when he tries to give a *verbal* definition of time he is struck dumb; for any definition he may propose winds up being circular, for the reasons given above. But why should this be a cause for alarm? After all there are many words, such as "yellow," which stand for simple unanalyzable (indefinable) properties. There are, however, good reasons why no one ever asked in anguish, "What, then, is yellow . . . ," for at least we can ostensively (demonstratively) define yellow: we can point to an instance of yellow. Time, unfortunately, admits of no such straightforward ostensive definition. Obviously there is nothing we can point to and say, *"This* is the past (or future)." (We must not confuse a photograph or memory with the *past* event it depicts.) Neither is it possible, for Augustine, to point to the present, since it is, as Aristotle claimed, a knife-edge without thickness which serves merely to connect the past with the future.[1]

But why, we might ask, must the present be of zero duration? Augustine's reply is contained in the following dialogue. Suppose we are at a concert and I ask you what the orchestra is playing now, to which you reply "The Eroica Symphony." After a moment of reflection I come back with the query, "But the Eroica has four movements—certainly all four movements are not present *now.*" You then narrow your original claim and say, "Only the first movement is now being played," but this is immediately countered with my question, "How can all 691 measures comprising this movement be present *now?*" You restrict yourself further to the 100th measure, but I then ask how all three beats, each being a quarter note, can be present now? Finally in despera-

---

[1] Even if we denied that the present had no duration it would still be impossible to define it ostensively. Everything that we point to in giving an ostensive definition is present. Thus the learner would never be able to catch on that it was the *present* which was being ostensively defined since it could not be contrasted with something not present.

tion, after I have forced you to pulverize your present down to twelve eighth notes, you give up and say that *strictly* speaking nothing is present now—*the* present is, as Augustine claimed, an indivisible instant.

Because time cannot be ostensively defined, there being nothing which we can point to and say "This is the present (past or future)," Augustine wonders how it is possible to measure time. He claims that we cannot say that a past (or future) time *is* long, because it does not exist now. What we must mean is that when it was (or will be) present it is long; but this is impossible because the present cannot have a finite duration. For Augustine the only way out of this anomaly is to say that time is a "protraction" of the mind, and that when we measure time we really measure a certain expanse in our conscious memory. Time is essentially subjective or psychological: past, present, and future times depend on the mind. There is only a "present of things past, memory; present of things present, sight; present of things future, expectation." If Augustine's analysis is intended as a *definition* of time it suffers from circularity since we cannot define what we mean by memory (or anticipation) without making explicit reference to a *past* (or *future*) event which is remembered (or anticipated).

4. So far we have considered three serious, though unsuccessful, attempts to define time. Thus, we are back where we started, asking the same old question, "What, then, is time?" Since the days of Augustine there has been no shortage of answers—which, in spite of their differences, all presuppose that the question is meaningful. It is for this reason that Ludwig Wittgenstein's later philosophy, which Friedrich Waismann elaborates in the concluding article of Section I, represents a most radical departure; for the first time the very *legitimacy* of the question is doubted. In his *Blue Book* and subsequent *Philosophical Investigations,* Wittgenstein tries to show why "What, then, is time?" is such a queer question. In the first place, it is not a question about natural science. Augustine would not have rested more easily had he known about the Second Law of Thermodynamics (i.e. that entropy

increases with time). Moreover, as Waismann points out, Augustine knows what the word "time" means in the sense of being able (1) to understand it in various contexts and (2) to use it correctly in appropriate contexts. Why, then, should there be any further mystery?

The answer proposed by Wittgenstein is that Augustine has lost his way in language. There are many surface grammatical analogies between temporal expressions and expressions that refer to physical objects and processes. Augustine's "mental discomforts" come from riding these analogies too hard by expecting temporal expressions to behave in the same way—have the same "grammar" or use—as these other expressions. When the conformity of temporal language to other types of language breaks down—when it is discovered that we cannot meaningfully say and ask the same things about time that we can about trains, rivers, and the wind—Augustine begins to feel that time is a very queer sort of thing. The recommended therapy for this mental cramp is to remind ourselves how we actually use temporal expressions in various contexts, and to note how it resembles and also is dissimilar to the way we use other types of language. We can exhibit the "logic" of a temporal expression by matching it against example after example of expressions progressively diverging from it in various respects and directions. Through this method Wittgenstein showed how striking grammatical similarities may go with important but ordinarily unremarked differences, and how we are tempted to lean too heavily on their similarities and hence to be tripped up by their latent differences. For example, there is a surface grammatical analogy between "Don't live in the past" and "Don't live in the Bronx," but similarity covers up a sharp divergence in logical grammar; we can ask *where* the Bronx is and request instructions for getting there, but we cannot ask the same questions about the past.

In particular, Augustine was mystified by time because he operated with a name-substance theory of meaning: the meaning of a word or expression is the object or thing named by it, in the same way that the dog Fido is the meaning of the name "Fido." What is mystifying about time comes from its use as a noun. It is assumed that the word must function semantically as a noun, and so we look about in vain for the entity it names. As Waismann has said, "We are trying to catch the shadows cast by the opacities of speech."[2] Augustine wants to be able to point to something called time, to see it flow by in the same way that a river does. His confusion concerning the impossibility of measuring time rests on the erroneous assumption that temporal-wholes must be the same as object-wholes—that everything we can say and ask about the latter can be said and asked about the former. But, as J. N. Findlay points out in his article in Section II of this collection, the assimilation of temporal-wholes to object-wholes is misleading, since the parts of a temporal-whole, unlike an object-whole, cannot be said to *coexist*. Therefore, it is wrong to demand that we measure temporal-wholes in the same way we measure objects—that is, to demand that we be able to see the beginning and end of what we are measuring. There is an extensive parallel in the language we use to describe temporal and spatial measurements. In both cases we speak of reading off numbers from a scale, of adding and subtracting numbers, etc. But we must not push these similarities too hard or we might become insensitive, as Augustine did, to the significant differences between them.

Close study of the way we use temporal language in various contexts can also be used to dispel Augustine's paradox concerning the instantaneousness of the present. As Findlay points out, we must not assume that there is one and only one correct answer to the question, "What is now present?" How narrow or wide the present will be depends on the context in which the question is asked. To revert to the previous example, if my reason for asking you what the orchestra is playing now is that I know nothing about music, then your reply that it is the Eroica is perfectly in order. But if we were playing in the orchestra and I had lost my place,

[2] Friedrich Waismann, "How I See Philosophy," in *Contemporary British Philosophy*, third series, H. D. Lewis, ed., London, 1956. Complete information given in Bibliography.

I would want a more precise answer, down to the exact measure, though this answer would still not satisfy an atomic physicist. The concept of precision or accuracy is normative; that is, it varies according to the requirements of each situation.

TIME

ARISTOTLE

Next for discussion after the subjects mentioned is Time.

The best plan will be to begin by working out the difficulties connected with it, making use of the current arguments. First, does it belong to the class of things that exist or to that of things that do not exist? Then secondly, what is its nature? To start, then: the following considerations would make one suspect that it either does not exist at all or barely, and in an obscure way. One part of it has been and is not, while the other is going to be and is not yet. Yet time—both infinite time and any time you like to take—is made up of these. One would naturally suppose that what is made up of things which do not exist could have no share in reality.

Further, if a divisible thing is to exist, it is necessary that, when it exists, all or some of its parts must exist. But of time some parts have been, while others have to be, and no part of it *is*, though it is divisible. For what is 'now' is not a part: a part is a measure of the whole, which must be made up of parts. Time, on the other hand, is not held to be made up of 'nows'.

Again, the 'now' which seems to bound the past and the future—does it always remain one and the same or is it always other and other? It is hard to say.

(1) If it is always different and different, and if none of the *parts* in time which are other and other are simultaneous (unless the one contains and the other is contained, as the shorter time is by the longer), and if the 'now' which is not,

FROM Aristotle, *Physics*, Book IV, translated by R. P. Hardie and R. K. Gaye, 218ª–24ª. *The Works of Aristotle*, W. D. Ross, ed., Clarendon Press, Oxford, 1930. Reprinted by permission of the publishers.

but formerly was, must have ceased-to-be at some time, the '*nows*' too cannot be simultaneous with one another, but the prior 'now' must always have ceased-to-be. But the prior 'now' cannot have ceased-to-be in[1] itself (since it then existed); yet it cannot have ceased-to-be in another 'now'. For we may lay it down that one 'now' cannot be next to another, any more than point to point. If then it did not cease-to-be in the next 'now' but in another, it would exist simultaneously with the innumerable 'nows' between the two—which is impossible.

Yes, but (2) neither is it possible for the 'now' to remain always the same. No determinate divisible thing has a single termination, whether it is continuously extended in one or in more than one dimension: but the 'now' is a termination, and it is possible to cut off a determinate time. Further, if coincidence in time (i. e. being neither prior nor posterior) means to be 'in one and the same "now"', then, if both what is before and what is after are in this same 'now', things which happened ten thousand years ago would be simultaneous with what has happened to-day, and nothing would be before or after anything else.

This may serve as a statement of the difficulties about the attributes of time.

As to what time is or what is its nature, the traditional accounts give us as little light as the preliminary problems which we have worked through.

Some assert that it is (1) the movement of the whole, others that it is (2) the sphere itself.[2]

(1) Yet part, too, of the revolution is a time, but it certainly is not a revolution: for what is taken is part of a revolution, not a revolution. Besides, if there were more heavens than one, the movement of any of them equally would be time, so that there would be many times at the same time.

(2) Those who said that time is the sphere of the whole

---

[1] The argument would be clearer if we could say 'during' itself. If the existent perished 'in' itself, it would never exist without perishing.—Trs.

[2] Aristotle is probably referring to Plato and the Pythagoreans respectively.—Trs.

thought so, no doubt, on the ground that all things are in time and all things are in the sphere of the whole. The view is too naive for it to be worth while to consider the impossibilities implied in it.

But as time is most usually supposed to be (3) motion and a kind of change, we must consider this view.

Now (*a*) the change or movement of each thing is only *in* the thing which changes or *where* the thing itself which moves or changes may chance to be. But time is present equally everywhere and with all things.

Again, (*b*) change is always faster or slower, whereas time is not: for 'fast' and 'slow' are defined by time—'fast' is what moves much in a short time, 'slow' what moves little in a long time; but time is not defined by time, by being either a certain amount or a certain kind of it.

Clearly then it is not movement. (We need not distinguish at present between 'movement' and 'change'.)

But neither does time exist without change; for when the state of our own minds does not change at all, or we have not noticed its changing, we do not realize that time has elapsed, any more than those who are fabled to sleep among the heroes in Sardinia do when they are awakened; for they connect the earlier 'now' with the later and make them one, cutting out the interval because of their failure to notice it. So, just as, if the 'now' were not different but one and the same, there would not have been time, so too when its difference escapes our notice the interval does not seem to be time. If, then, the non-realization of the existence of time happens to us when we do not distinguish any change, but the soul seems to stay in one indivisible state, and when we perceive and distinguish we say time has elapsed, evidently time is not independent of movement and change. It is evident, then, that time is neither movement nor independent of movement.

We must take this as our starting-point and try to discover —since we wish to know what time is—what exactly it has to do with movement.

Now we perceive movement and time together: for even
when it is dark and we are not being affected through the
body, if any movement takes place in the mind we at once
suppose that some time also has elapsed; and not only that
but also, when some time is thought to have passed, some
movement also along with it seems to have taken place.
Hence time is either movement or something that belongs to
movement. Since then it is not movement, it must be the
other.

But what is moved is moved from something to something,
and all magnitude is continuous. Therefore the movement
goes with the magnitude. Because the magnitude is continuous, the movement too must be continuous, and if the
movement, then the time; for the time that has passed is
always thought to be in proportion to the movement.

The distinction of 'before' and 'after' holds primarily then,
in place; and there in virtue of relative position. Since then
'before' and 'after' hold in magnitude, they must hold also
in movement, these corresponding to those. But also in
time the distinction of 'before' and 'after' must hold, for time
and movement always correspond with each other. The 'before' and 'after' in motion identical in substratum with motion yet differs from it in definition, and is not identical with
motion.

But we apprehend time only when we have marked motion,
marking it by 'before' and 'after'; and it is only when we have
perceived 'before' and 'after' in motion that we say that time
has elapsed. Now we mark them by judging that A and B are
different, and that some third thing is intermediate to them.
When we think of the extremes as different from the middle
and the mind pronounces that the 'nows' are two, one before
and one after, it is then that we say that there is time, and
this that we say is time. For what is bounded by the 'now'
is thought to be time—we may assume this.

When, therefore, we perceive the 'now' as one, and neither
as before and after in a motion nor as an identity but in relation to a 'before' and an 'after', no time is thought to have
elapsed, because there has been no motion either. On the
other hand, when we do perceive a 'before' and an 'after',

then we say that there is time. For time is just this—number of motion in respect of 'before' and 'after'.

Hence time is not movement, but only movement in so far as it admits of enumeration. A proof of this: we discriminate the more or the less by number, but more or less movement by time. Time then is a kind of number. (Number, we must note, is used in two senses—both of what is counted or the countable and also of that with which we count. Time obviously is what is counted, not that with which we count: these are different kinds of thing.)

Just as motion is a perpetual succession, so also is time. But every simultaneous time is self-identical; for the 'now' as a subject is an identity, but it accepts different attributes.[3] The 'now' measures time, in so far as time involves the 'before and after'.

The 'now' in one sense is the same, in another it is not the same. In so far as it is in succession, it is different (which is just what its being now was supposed to mean), but its substratum is an identity: for motion, as was said, goes with magnitude, and time, as we maintain, with motion. Similarly, then, there corresponds to the point the body which is carried along, and by which we are aware of the motion and of the 'before and after' involved in it. This is an identical *substratum* (whether a point or a stone or something else of the kind), but it has different *attributes*—as the sophists assume that Coriscus' being in the Lyceum is a different thing from Coriscus' being in the market-place. And the body which is carried along is different, in so far as it is at one time here and at another there. But the 'now' corresponds to the body that is carried along, as time corresponds to the motion. For it is by means of the body that is carried along that we become aware of the 'before and after' in the motion, and if we regard these as countable we get the 'now'. Hence in these also the 'now' as substratum remains the same (for it is what is before and after in movement), but what is predicated of it is different; for it is in so far as the 'before and

[3] E. g. if you come in when I go out, the time of your coming in is in fact the time of my going out, though for it to be the one and to be the other are different things.—Trs.

after' is numerable that we get the 'now'. This is what is most knowable: for, similarly, motion is known because of that which is moved, locomotion because of that which is carried. For what is carried is a real thing, the movement is not. Thus what is called 'now' in one sense is always the same; in another it is not the same: for this is true also of what is carried.

Clearly, too, if there were no time, there would be no 'now', and vice versa. Just as the moving body and its locomotion involve each other mutually, so too do the number of the moving body and the number of its locomotion. For the number of the locomotion is time, while the 'now' corresponds to the moving body, and is like the unit of number.

Time, then, also is both made continuous by the 'now' and divided at it. For here too there is a correspondence with the locomotion and the moving body. For the motion or locomotion is made one by the thing which is moved, because *it* is one—not because it is one in its own nature (for there might be pauses in the movement of such a thing)—but because it is one in definition: for this determines the movement as 'before' and 'after'. Here, too, there is a correspondence with the point; for the point also both connects and terminates the length—it is the beginning of one and the end of another. But when you take it in this way, using the one point as two, a pause is necessary, if the same point is to be the beginning and the end. The 'now' on the other hand, since the body carried is moving, is always different.

Hence time is not number in the sense in which there is 'number' of the same point because it is beginning and end, but rather as the extremities of a line form a number, and not as the parts of the line do so, both for the reason given (for we can use the middle point as two, so that on that analogy time might stand still), and further because obviously the 'now' is no *part* of time nor the section any part of the movement, any more than the points are parts of the line—for it is two *lines* that are *parts* of one line.

In so far then as the 'now' is a boundary, it is not time, but an attribute of it; in so far as it numbers, it is number; for boundaries belong only to that which they bound, but number (e. g. ten) is the number of these horses, and belongs also elsewhere.

It is clear, then, that time is 'number of movement in respect of the before and after', and is continuous since it is an attribute of what is continuous.

The smallest number, in the strict sense of the word 'number', is two. But of number as concrete, sometimes there is a minimum, sometimes not: e. g. of a 'line', the smallest in respect of *multiplicity* is two (or, if you like, one), but in respect of *size* there is no minimum; for every line is divided *ad infinitum*. Hence it is so with time. In respect of number the minimum is one (or two); in point of extent there is no minimum.

It is clear, too, that time is not described as fast or slow, but as many or few[4] and as long or short. For as continuous it is long or short and as a number many or few, but it is not fast or slow—any more than any number with which we number is fast or slow.

Further, there is the same time everywhere at once, but not the same time before and after, for while the present change is one, the change which has happened and that which will happen are different. Time is not number with which we count, but the number of things which are counted, and this according as it occurs before or after is always different, for the 'nows' are different. And the number of a hundred horses and a hundred men is the same, but the things numbered are different—the horses from the men. Further, as a movement can be one and the same again and again, so too can time, e. g. a year or a spring or an autumn.

Not only do we measure the movement by the time, but also the time by the movement, because they define each other. The time marks the movement, since it is its number, and the movement the time. We describe the time as much or little, measuring it by the movement, just as we know the number by what is numbered, e. g. the number of the horses by one horse as the unit. For we know how many horses there

[4] E. g. 'many years'.—Trs.

are by the use of the number; and again by using the one horse as unit we know the number of the horses itself. So it is with the time and the movement; for we measure the movement by the time and vice versa. It is natural that this should happen; for the movement goes with the distance and the time with the movement, because they are quanta and continuous and divisible. The movement has these attributes because the distance is of this nature, and the time has them because of the movement. And we measure both the distance by the movement and the movement by the distance; for we say that the road is long, if the journey is long, and that this is long, if the road is long—the time, too, if the movement, and the movement, if the time.

Time is a measure of motion and of being moved, and it measures the motion by determining a motion which will measure exactly the whole motion, as the cubit does the length by determining an amount which will measure out the whole. Further 'to be in time' means, for movement, that both it and its essence are measured by time (for simultaneously it measures both the movement and its essence, and this is what being in time means for it, that its essence should be measured).

Clearly then 'to be in time' has the same meaning for other things also, namely, that their being should be measured by time. 'To be in time' is one of two things: (1) to exist when time exists, (2) as we say of some things that they are 'in number'. The latter means either what is a part or mode of number—in general, something which belongs to number—or that things have a number.

Now, since time is number, the 'now' and the 'before' and the like are in time, just as 'unit' and 'odd' and 'even' are in number, i. e. in the sense that the one set belongs to number, the other to time. But things are in time as they are in number. If this is so, they are contained by time as things in place are contained by place.

Plainly, too, to be in time does not mean to coexist with time, any more than to be in motion or in place means to coexist with motion or place. For if 'to be in something' is to mean this, then all things will be in anything, and the heaven will be in a grain; for when the grain is, then also is the heaven. But this is a merely incidental conjunction, whereas the other is necessarily involved: that which is in time necessarily involves that there is time when *it* is, and that which is in motion that there is motion when *it* is.

Since what is 'in time' is so in the same sense as what is in number is so, a time greater than everything in time can be found. So it is necessary that all the things in time should be contained by time, just like other things also which are 'in anything', e. g. the things 'in place' by place.

A thing, then, will be affected by time, just as we are accustomed to say that time wastes things away, and that all things grow old through time, and that there is oblivion owing to the lapse of time, but we do not say the same of getting to know or of becoming young or fair. For time is by its nature the cause rather of decay, since it is the number of change, and change removes what is.

Hence, plainly, things which are always are not, as such, in time, for they are not contained by time, nor is their being measured by time. A proof of this is that none of them is *affected* by time, which indicates that they are not in time.

Since time is the measure of motion, it will be the measure of rest too—indirectly. For all rest is in time. For it does not follow that what is in time is moved, though what is in motion is necessarily moved. For time is not motion, but 'number of motion': and what is at rest, also, can be in the number of motion. Not everything that is not in motion can be said to be 'at rest'—but only that which can be moved, though it actually is not moved. . . .

'To be in number' means that there is a number of the thing, and that its being is measured by the number in which it is. Hence if a thing is 'in time' it will be measured by time. But time will measure what is moved and what is at rest, the one *qua* moved, the other *qua* at rest; for it will measure their motion and rest respectively.

Hence what is moved will not be measurable by the time simply in so far as it has quantity, but in so far as its *motion* has quantity. Thus none of the things which are neither moved nor at rest are in time: for 'to be in time' is 'to be measured by time', while time is the measure of motion and rest.

Plainly, then, neither will everything that does not exist be in time, i. e. those non-existent things that cannot exist, as the diagonal cannot be commensurate with the side.

Generally, if time is directly the measure of motion and indirectly of other things, it is clear that a thing whose existence is measured by it will have its existence in rest or motion. Those things therefore which are subject to perishing and becoming—generally, those which at one time exist, at another do not—are necessarily in time: for there is a greater time which will extend both beyond their existence and beyond the time which measures their existence. Of things which do not exist but are contained by time some were, e. g. Homer once was, some will be, e. g. a future event; this depends on the direction in which time contains them; if on both, they have both modes of existence. As to such things as it does not contain in any way, they neither were nor are nor will be. These are those non-existents whose opposites always are, as the incommensurability of the diagonal always is—and this will not be in time. Nor will the commensurability, therefore; hence this eternally is not, because it is contrary to what eternally is. A thing whose contrary is not eternal can be and not be, and it is of such things that there is coming to be and passing away.

The 'now' is the link of time, as has been said[5] (for it connects past and future time), and it is a limit of time (for it is the beginning of the one and the end of the other). But this is not obvious as it is with the point, which is fixed. It divides potentially, and in so far as it is dividing the 'now' is always different, but in so far as it connects it is always the same, as it is with mathematical lines. For the intellect it is not always one and the same point, since it is other and other when one divides the line; but in so far as it is one, it is the same in every respect.

So the 'now' also is in one way a potential dividing of time,

[5] 220^a 5 [p. 14 above].

in another the termination of both parts, and their unity. And the dividing and the uniting are the same thing and in the same reference, but in essence they are not the same.

So one kind of 'now' is described in this way: another is when the time is *near* this kind of 'now'. 'He will come now' because he will come to-day; 'he has come now' because he came to-day. But the things in the *Iliad* have not happened 'now', nor is the flood 'now'—not that the time from now to them is not continuous, but because they are not near.

'At some time' means a time determined in relation to the first of the two types of 'now', e. g. 'at some time' Troy was taken, and 'at some time' there will be a flood; for it must be determined with reference to the 'now'. There *will* thus be a determinate time from this 'now' to that, and there *was* such in reference to the past event. But if there be no time which is not 'sometime', every time will be determined.

Will time then fail? Surely not, if motion always exists. Is time then always different or does the same time recur? Clearly time is, in the same way as motion is. For if one and the same motion sometimes recurs, it will be one and the same time, and if not, not.

Since the 'now' is an end and a beginning of time, not of the same time however, but the end of that which is past and the beginning of that which is to come, it follows that, as the circle has its convexity and its concavity, in a sense, in the same thing, so time is always at a beginning and at an end. And for this reason it seems to be always different; for the 'now' is not the beginning and the end of the same thing; if it were, it would be at the same time and in the same respect two opposites. And time will not fail; for it is always at a beginning.

'Presently' or 'just' refers to the part of future time which is near the indivisible present 'now' ('When do you walk?' 'Presently', because the time in which he is going to do so is near), and to the part of past time which is not far from the 'now' ('When do you walk?' 'I have just been walking'). But to say that Troy has just been taken—we do not say that, because it is too far from the 'now'. 'Lately', too, refers to the part of past time which is near the present 'now'. 'When did you go?' 'Lately', if the time is near the existing now. 'Long ago' refers to the distant past.

'Suddenly' refers to what has departed from its former condition in a time imperceptible because of its smallness; but it is the nature of *all* change to alter things from their former condition. In time all things come into being and pass away; for which reason some called it the wisest of all things, but the Pythagorean Paron called it the most stupid, because in it we also forget; and his was the truer view. It is clear then that it must be in itself, as we said before[6] the condition of destruction rather than of coming into being (for change, in itself, makes things depart from their former condition), and only incidentally of coming into being, and of being. A sufficient evidence of this is that nothing comes into being without itself moving somehow and acting, but a thing can be destroyed even if it does not move at all. And this is what, as a rule, we chiefly mean by a thing's being destroyed by time. Still, time does not work even this change; even this sort of change takes place *incidentally* in time.

We have stated, then, that time exists and what it is, and in how many senses we speak of the 'now', and what 'at some time', 'lately', 'presently' or 'just', 'long ago', and 'suddenly' mean.

These distinctions having been drawn, it is evident that every change and everything that moves is in time; for the distinction of faster and slower exists in reference to all change, since it is found in every instance. In the phrase 'moving faster' I refer to that which changes before another into the condition in question, when it moves over the same interval and with a regular movement; e. g. in the case of locomotion, if both things move along the circumference of a circle, or both along a straight line; and similarly in all other cases. But what is *before* is in time; for we say 'before' and 'after' with reference to the distance from the 'now', and the 'now' is the boundary of the past and the future; so that

[6] 221[b] 1 [p. 17].

since 'nows' are in time, the before and the after will be in time too; for in that in which the 'now' is, the distance from the 'now' will also be. But 'before' is used contrariwise with reference to past and to future time; for in the past we call 'before' what is farther from the 'now', and 'after' what is nearer, but in the future we call the nearer 'before' and the farther 'after'. So that since the 'before' is in time, and every movement involves a 'before', evidently every change and every movement is in time.

It is also worth considering how time can be related to the soul; and why time is thought to be in everything, both in earth and in sea and in heaven. Is it because it is an attribute, or state, of movement (since it is the number of movement) and all these things are movable (for they are all in place), and time and movement are together, both in respect of potentiality and in respect of actuality?

Whether if soul did not exist time would exist or not, is a question that may fairly be asked; for if there cannot be some one to count there cannot be anything that can be counted, so that evidently there cannot be number; for number is either what has been, or what can be, counted. But if nothing but soul, or in soul reason, is qualified to count, there would not be time unless there were soul, but only that of which time is an attribute, i. e. if *movement* can exist without soul, and the before and after are attributes of movement, and time is these *qua* numerable.

One might also raise the question what sort of movement time is the number of. Must we not say 'of *any* kind'? For things both come into being in time and pass away, and grow, and are altered in time, and are moved locally; thus it is of each movement *qua* movement that time is the number. And so it is simply the number of continuous movement, not of any particular kind of it.

But other things as well may have been moved now, and there would be a number of each of the two movements. Is there another time, then, and will there be two equal times at once? Surely not. For a time that is both equal and simultaneous is one and the same time, and even those that are not simultaneous are one in kind; for if there were dogs, and horses, and seven of each, it would be the same number. So, too, movements that have simultaneous limits have the same time, yet the one may in fact be fast and the other not, and one may be locomotion and the other alteration; still the time of the two changes is the same if their number also is equal and simultaneous; and for this reason, while the movements are different and separate, the time is everywhere the same, because the number of equal and simultaneous movements is everywhere one and the same.

Now there is such a thing as locomotion, and in locomotion there is included circular movement, and everything is measured by some one thing homogeneous with it, units by a unit, horses by a horse, and similarly times by some definite time, and, as we said,[7] time is measured by motion as well as motion by time (this being so because by a motion definite in time the quantity both of the motion and of the time is measured): if, then, what is first is the measure of everything homogeneous with it, regular circular motion is above all else the measure, because the number of this is the best known. Now neither alteration nor increase nor coming into being can be regular, but locomotion can be. This also is why time is thought to be the movement of the sphere, viz. because the other movements are measured by this, and time by this movement.

This also explains the common saying that human affairs form a circle, and that there is a circle in all other things that have a natural movement and coming into being and passing away. This is because all other things are discriminated by time, and end and begin as though conforming to a cycle; for even time itself is thought to be a circle. And this opinion again is held because time is the measure of this kind of locomotion and is itself measured by such. So that to say that the things that come into being form a circle is to say that there is a circle of time; and this is to say that it is measured by the circular movement; for apart from the measure nothing else to be measured is observed; the whole is just a plurality of measures.

[7] 220[b] 28 [p. 16].

It is said rightly, too, that the number of the sheep and of
the dogs is the same *number* if the two numbers are equal,
but not the same *decad* or the same *ten;* just as the equilateral and the scalene are not the same *triangle,* yet they are
the same *figure,* because they are both triangles. For things
are called the same so-and-so if they do not differ by a differentia of that thing, but not if they do; e. g. triangle differs
from triangle by a differentia of triangle, therefore they are
different triangles; but they do not differ by a differentia of
figure, but are in one and the same division of it. For a figure
of one kind is a circle and a figure of another kind a triangle,
and a triangle of one kind is equilateral and a triangle of
another kind scalene. They are the same figure, then, and
that, triangle, but not the same triangle. Therefore the number of two groups also is the same number (for their number
does not differ by a differentia of number), but it is not the
same decad; for the things of which it is asserted differ; one
group are dogs, and the other horses.

We have now discussed time—both time itself and the matters appropriate to the consideration of it.

TIME AND ETERNITY

PLOTINUS

Existing explanations of Time seem to fall into three
classes:

Time is variously identified with what we know as Movement, with a moved object, and with some phenomenon of
Movement: obviously it cannot be Rest or a resting object
or any phenomenon of rest, since, in its characteristic idea, it
is concerned with change.

Of those that explain it as Movement, some identify it with
any and every Movement, others with that of the All. Those
that make it a moved object would identify it with the orb
of the All. Those that conceive it as some phenomenon of
Movement treat it, severally, either as a period or as a standard of measure or, more generally, as an accompaniment,
whether of Movement in general or of ordered Movement.

Movement Time cannot be—whether a definite act of moving is meant or a united total made up of all such acts—since
movement, in either sense, takes place in Time. And, of
course, if there is any movement not in Time, the identification with Time becomes all the less tenable.

In a word, Movement must be distinct from the medium
in which it takes place.

And, with all that has been said or is still said, one con-

FROM Plotinus, *The Six Enneads,* translated by Stephen
Mackenna, third edition revised by B. S. Page, Pantheon Books,
New York, and Faber & Faber, London, 1962. Reprinted by per-
mission of Pantheon Books, a division of Random House, Inc.,
and Faber & Faber. All rights reserved. Third Ennead, Seventh
Tractate, sections 7–13.

sideration is decisive: Movement can come to rest, can be intermittent; Time is continuous.

We will be told that the Movement of the All is continuous (and so may be identical with Time).

But, if the reference is to the Circuit of the heavenly system, this Circuit takes place in Time, and the time taken by the total Circuit is twice the time taken by half the Circuit; whether we count the whole or only the first half, it is nevertheless the same movement of the heavenly system.

Further, the fact that we hear of the Movement of the outermost sphere being the swiftest confirms our theory. Obviously, it is the swiftest of movements by taking the lesser time to traverse the greater space—the very greatest—all other moving things are slower by taking a longer time to traverse a mere segment of the same extension: in other words, Time is not this movement.

And, if Time is not even the movement of the Cosmic Sphere much less is it the sphere itself, though that has been identified with Time on the ground of its being in motion.

Is it, then, some phenomenon or connexion of Movement?

Let us, tentatively, suppose it to be extent, or duration, of Movement.

Now, to begin with, Movement, even continuous, has no unchanging extent (as Time the equable has), since—to take only motion in space—it may be faster or slower; there must, therefore, be some unit of standard outside it, by which these differences are measurable, and this outside standard would more properly be called Time. And failing such a measure, which extent would be Time, that of the fast or of the slow— or rather which of them all, since these speed-differences are limitless?

Is it the extent of the ordered Movement?

Again, this gives us no unit since the movement is infinitely variable; we would have, thus, not Time but Times.

The extent of the Movement of the All, then?

If this means extent as inherent in the movement itself, we have Movement pure and simple (and not Time). Admittedly, Movement answers to measure—in two ways. First there is space; the movement is commensurate with the area it passes through, and this area is its extent. But this gives us, still, space only, not Time. Secondly, the circuit, considered apart from distance traversed, has the extent of its continuity, of its tendency not to stop but to proceed indefinitely: but this is merely amplitude of Movement; search it, tell its vastness, and, still, Time has no more appeared, no more enters into the matter, than when one certifies a high pitch of heat; all we have discovered is Motion in ceaseless succession, like water flowing ceaselessly, motion and extent of motion.

Succession or repetition gives us Number—dyad, triad, &c. —and the extent traversed is a matter of Magnitude; thus we have Quantity of Movement—in the form of number, dyad, triad, decade, or in the form of extent apprehended in what we may call the amount of the Movement: but, the idea of Time we have not. That definite Quantity is (not Time but) merely something occurring within Time, for, otherwise Time is not everywhere but is something belonging to Movement which thus would be its substratum or basic-stuff: once more, then, we would be making Time identical with Movement; for the extent of Movement is not something outside it but is simply its continuousness, and we need not halt upon the difference between the momentary and the continuous, which is simply one of manner and degree. The extended movement and its extent are not Time; they are in Time. Those that explain Time as extent of Movement must mean not the extent of the movement itself but something which determines its extension, something with which the movement keeps pace in its course. But what this something is, we are not told; yet it is, clearly, Time, that in which all Movement proceeds. This is what our discussion has aimed at from the first: 'What, essentially, is Time?' It comes to this: we ask 'What is Time?' and we are answered, 'Time is the extension of Movement in Time'!

On the one hand Time is said to be an extension apart from and outside that of Movement; and we are left to guess what this extension may be: on the other hand, it is represented as the extension of Movement; and this leaves the difficulty what to make of the extension of Rest—though one thing may continue as long in repose as another in motion, so that we are obliged to think of one thing, Time, that covers both Rest and Movements, and, therefore, stands distinct from either.

What then is this thing of extension? To what order of beings does it belong?

It obviously is not spatial, for place, too, is something outside it.

'A Number, a Measure, belonging to Movement?'

'Measure' is more plausible since Movement is a continuous thing; but let us consider.

To begin with, we have the doubt which met us when we probed its identification with extent of Movement: is Time the measure of any and every Movement?

Have we any means of calculating disconnected and lawless Movement? What number or measure would apply? What would be the principle of such a Measure?

One Measure for movement slow and fast, for any and every movement: then that number and measure would be like the decade, by which we reckon horses and cows, or like some common standard for liquids and solids. If Time is this kind of Measure, we learn, no doubt, of what objects it is a Measure—of Movements—but we are no nearer understanding what it is in itself.

Or: we may take the decade and think of it, apart from the horses or cows, as a pure number; this gives us a measure which, even though not actually applied, has a definite nature. Is Time, perhaps, a Measure in this sense?

No: to tell us no more of Time in itself than that it is such a number is merely to bring us back to the decade we have already rejected, or to some similar abstract figure.

If, on the other hand, Time is (not such an abstraction but) a Measure possessing a continuous extent of its own, it must have quantity, like a foot-rule; it must have magnitude; it will, clearly, be in the nature of a line traversing the path of Movement. But, itself thus sharing in the movement, how can it be a Measure of Movement? Why should the one of the two be the measure rather than the other? Besides, an accompanying measure is more plausibly considered as a measure of the particular movement it accompanies than of Movement in general. Further, this entire discussion assumes continuous movement, since the accompanying principle, Time, is itself unbroken (but a full explanation implies justification of Time in repose).

The fact is that we are not to think of a measure outside and apart, but of a combined thing, a measured Movement, and we are to discover what measures it.

Given a Movement measured, are we to suppose the measure to be a magnitude?

If so, which of these two would be Time, the measured movement or the measuring magnitude? For Time (as measure) must be either the movement measured by magnitude, or the measuring magnitude itself, or something using the magnitude like a yard-stick to appraise the movement. In all three cases, as we have indicated, the application is scarcely plausible except where continuous movement is assumed; unless the movement proceeds smoothly, and even unintermittently and as embracing the entire content of the moving object, great difficulties arise in the identification of Time with any kind of measure.

Let us, then, suppose Time to be this 'measured Movement', measured by quantity. Now the Movement if it is to be measured requires a measure outside itself; this was the only reason for raising the question of the accompanying measure. In exactly the same way the measuring magnitude, in turn, will require a measure, because only when the standard shows such and such an extension can the degree of movement be appraised. Time then will be, not the magnitude accompanying the Movement, but that numerical value by which the magnitude accompanying the Movement is estimated. But that number can be only the abstract figure which represents the magnitude, and it is difficult to see how an abstract figure can perform the act of measuring.

And, supposing that we discover a way in which it can, we still have not Time, the measure, but a particular quantity of Time, not at all the same thing: Time means something very different from any definite period: before all question as to quantity is the question as to the thing of which a certain quantity is present.

Time, we are told, is the number outside Movement and measuring it, like the tens applied to the reckoning of the horses and cows but not inherent in them: we are not told what this Number is; yet, applied or not, it must, like that decade, have some nature of its own.

Or 'it is that which accompanies a Movement and measures it by its successive stages'; but we are still left asking what this thing recording the stages may be.

In any case, once a thing—whether by point or standard or any other means—measures succession, it must measure according to time: this number appraising movement degree by degree must, therefore, if it is to serve as a measure at all, be something dependent upon time and in contact with it: for, either, degree is spatial, merely—the beginning and end of the Stadium, for example—or in the only alternative, it is a pure matter of Time: the succession of early and late is stage of Time, Time ending upon a certain Now or Time beginning from a Now.

Time, therefore, is something other than the mere number measuring Movement, whether Movement in general or ordered Movement.

Further: why should the mere presence of a number give us Time—a number measuring or measured; for the same number may be either—if Time is not given us by the fact of Movement itself, the movement which inevitably contains in itself a succession of stages? To make the number essential to Time is like saying that magnitude has not its full quantity unless we can estimate that quantity.

Again, if Time is, admittedly, endless, how can number apply to it?

Are we to take some portion of Time and find its numerical statement? That simply means that Time existed before number was applied to it.

We may, therefore, very well think that it existed before the Soul or Mind that estimates it—if, indeed, it is not to be thought to take its origin from the Soul—for no measurement by anything is necessary to its existence; measured or not, it has the full extent of its being.

And suppose it to be true that the Soul is the appraiser, using Magnitude as the measuring standard, how does this help us to the conception of Time?

Time, again, has been described as some sort of a sequence upon Movement, but we learn nothing from this, nothing is said, until we know what it is that produces this sequential thing; probably the cause and not the result would turn out to be Time.

And, admitting such a thing, there would still remain the question whether it came into being before the movement, with it, or after it; and, whether we say before or with or after, we are speaking of order in Time: and thus our definition is, 'Time is a sequence upon movement *in Time*'!

Enough. Our main purpose is to show what Time is, not to refute false definition. To traverse point by point the many opinions of our many predecessors would mean a history rather than an identification; we have treated the various theories as fully as is possible in a cursory review: and, notice, that which makes Time the Measure of the All-Movement is refuted by our entire discussion and, especially, by the observations upon the Measurement of Movement in general, for all the argument—except, of course, that from irregularity—applies to the All as much as to particular Movement.

We are, thus, at the stage where we are to state what Time really is.

To this end we must go back to the state we affirmed of Eternity, unwavering Life, undivided totality, limitless, knowing no divagation, at rest in unity and intent upon it. Time was not yet: or at least it did not exist for the Eternal Beings. It is we that must create Time out of the concept and nature of progressive derivation, which remained latent in the Divine Beings.

How Time emerged we can scarcely call upon the Muses to relate since they were not in existence then—perhaps not even if they had been; though the Cosmos itself, when once engendered, could no doubt tell us best how Time arose and became manifest. Something thus the story must run:

Time at first—in reality before that 'first' was produced by desire of succession—Time lay, though not yet as Time, in the Authentic Existent together with the Cosmos itself; the Cosmos also was merged in the Authentic and motionless within it. But there was an active principle there, one set on governing itself and realizing itself (= the All-Soul), and it chose to aim at something more than its present: it stirred from its rest, and the Cosmos stirred with it. 'And we (the active principle and the Cosmos), stirring to a ceaseless succession, to a next, to the discrimination of identity and the establishment of ever new difference, traversed a portion of the outgoing path and produced an image of Eternity, produced Time.'

For the Soul contained an unquiet faculty, always desirous of translating elsewhere what it saw in the Authentic Realm, and it could not bear to retain within itself all the dense fullness of its possession.

A seed is at rest; the nature-principle within, uncoiling outwards, makes way towards what seems to it a large life; but by that partition it loses; it was a unity self-gathered, and now, in going forth from itself, it fritters its unity away; it advances into a weaker greatness. It is so with this faculty of the Soul, when it produces the Cosmos known to sense—the mimic of the Divine Sphere, moving not in the very movement of the Divine but in its similitude, in an effort to reproduce that of the Divine. To bring this Cosmos into being, the Soul first laid aside its eternity and clothed itself with Time; this world of its fashioning it then gave over to be a servant to Time, making it at every point a thing of Time, setting all its progressions within the bournes of Time. For the Cosmos moves only in Soul—the only Space within the range of the All open to it to move in—and therefore its Movement has always been in the Time which inheres in Soul.

Putting forth its energy in act after act, in a constant progress of novelty, the Soul produces succession as well as act; taking up new purposes added to the old it brings thus into being what had not existed in that former period when its purpose was still dormant and its life was not as it since became: the life is changed and that change carries with it a change of Time. Time, then, is contained in differentiation of Life; the ceaseless forward movement of Life brings with it unending Time; and Life as it achieves its stages constitutes past Time.

Would it, then, be sound to define Time as the Life of the Soul in movement as it passes from one stage of act or experience to another?

Yes; for Eternity, we have said, is Life in repose, unchanging, self-identical, always endlessly complete; and there is to be an image of Eternity—Time—such an image as this lower All presents of the Higher Sphere. Therefore over against that higher Life there must be another life, known by the same name as the more veritable Life of the Soul; over against that Movement of the Intellectual Soul there must be the movement of some partial phase; over against that Identity, Unchangeableness and Stability there must be that which is not constant in the one hold but puts forth multitudinous acts; over against that Oneness without extent or interval there must be an image of oneness, a unity of link and succession; over against the immediately Infinite and All-comprehending, that which tends, yes, to infinity but by tending to a perpetual futurity; over against the Whole in concentration, there must be that which is to be a whole by stages never final. The lesser must always be working towards the increase of its Being; this will be its imitation of what is immediately complete, self-realized, endless without stage: only thus can its Being reproduce that of the Higher.

Time, however, is not to be conceived as outside of Soul; Eternity is not outside of the Authentic Existent: nor is it to be taken as a sequence or succession to Soul, any more than Eternity is to the Divine. It is a thing seen upon Soul, inherent, coeval to it, as Eternity to the Intellectual Realm.

We are brought thus to the conception of a Natural-Principle—Time—a certain expanse (a quantitative phase) of the Life of the Soul, a principle moving forward by smooth and uniform changes following silently upon each other—a

Principle, then, whose Act is (not one like that of the Supreme but) sequent.

But let us conceive this power of the Soul to turn back and withdraw from the life-course which it now maintains, from the continuous and unending activity of an ever-existent Soul not self-contained or self-intent but concerned about doing and engendering: imagine it no longer accomplishing any Act, setting a pause to this work it has inaugurated; let this outgoing phase of the Soul become once more, equally with the rest, turned to the Supreme, to Eternal Being, to the tranquilly stable.

What would then exist but Eternity?

All would remain in unity; how could there be any diversity of things? What earlier or later would there be, what futurity? What ground would lie ready to the Soul's operation but the Supreme in which it has its Being? Or, indeed, what operative tendency could it have even to That since a prior separation is the necessary condition of tendency?

The very sphere of the Universe would not exist; for it cannot antedate Time: it, too, has its Being and its Movement in Time; and if it ceased to move, the Soul-Act (which is the essence of Time) continuing, we could measure the period of its Repose by that standard outside it.

If, then, the Soul withdrew, sinking itself again into its primal unity, Time would disappear: the origin of Time, clearly, is to be traced to the first stir of the Soul's tendency towards the production of the sensible Universe with the consecutive act ensuing. This is how 'Time'—as we read— 'came into Being simultaneously with' this All: the Soul begot at once the Universe and Time; in that activity of the Soul this Universe sprang into being; the activity is Time, the Universe is a content of Time. No doubt it will be urged that we read also of 'the orbit of the Stars being Times': but do not forget what follows; 'the stars exist', we are told, 'for the display and delimitation of Time', and 'that there may be a manifest Measure'. No indication of Time could be derived from (observation of) the Soul; no portion of it can be seen or handled, so it could not be measured in itself, especially when there was as yet no knowledge of counting; therefore the Demiurge (in the Timaeus) brings into being night and day; in their difference is given Duality—from which, we read, arises the concept of Number.

We observe the tract between a sunrise and its return and, as the movement is uniform, we thus obtain a Time-interval upon which to support ourselves, and we use this as a standard. We have thus a measure of Time. Time itself is not a measure. How would it set to work? And what kind of thing is there of which it could say, 'I find the extent of this equal to such and such a stretch of my own extent?' What is this 'I'? Obviously something by which measurement is known. Time, then, serves towards measurement but is not itself the Measure: the Movement of the All will be measured according to Time, but Time will not, of its own nature, be a Measure of Movement: primarily a Kind to itself, it will incidentally exhibit the magnitudes of that movement.

And the reiterated observation of Movement—the same extent found to be traversed in such and such a period—will lead to the conception of a definite quantity of Time past.

This brings us to the fact that, in a certain sense, the Movement, the orbit of the universe, may legitimately be said to measure Time—in so far as that is possible at all—since any definite stretch of that circuit occupies a certain quantity of Time, and this is the only grasp we have of Time, our only understanding of it: what that circuit measures—by indication, that is—will be Time, manifested by the Movement but not brought into being by it.

This means that the measure of the Spheric Movement has itself been measured by a definite stretch of that Movement and therefore is something different; as measure, it is one thing and, as the measured, it is another; (its being measure or) its being measured cannot be of its essence.

We are no nearer knowledge than if we said that the foot-rule measures Magnitude while we left the concept Magnitude undefined; or, again, we might as well define Movement—whose limitlessness puts it out of our reach—as the thing measured by Space; the definition would be parallel since we can mark off a certain space which the Movement has traversed and say the one is equivalent to the other.

The Spheral Circuit, then, performed in Time, indicates it: but when we come to Time itself there is no question of its being 'within' something else: it must be primary, a thing 'within itself'. It is that in which all the rest happens, in which all movement and rest exist smoothly and under order; something following a definite order is necessary to exhibit it and to make it a subject of knowledge—though not to produce it—it is known by order whether in rest or in motion; in motion especially, for Movement better moves Time into our ken than rest can, and it is easier to estimate distance traversed than repose maintained.

This last fact has led to Time being called a measure of Movement when it should have been described as something measured by Movement and then defined in its essential nature; it is an error to define it by a mere accidental concomitant and so to reverse the actual order of things. Possibly, however, this reversal was not intended by the authors of the explanation: but, at any rate, we do not understand them; they plainly apply the term Measure to what is in reality the measured and leave us unable to grasp their meaning: our perplexity may be due to the fact that their writings—addressed to disciples acquainted with their teaching—do not explain what this thing, measure or measured object, is in itself.

Plato does not make the essence of Time consist in its being either a measure or a thing measured by something else.

Upon the point of the means by which it is known, he remarks that the Circuit advances an infinitesimal distance for every infinitesimal segment of Time, so that from that observation it is possible to estimate what the Time is, how much it amounts to: but when his purpose is to explain its essential nature he tells us that it sprang into Being simultaneously with the Heavenly system, a reproduction of Eternity, its image in motion, Time necessarily unresting as the Life with which it must keep pace: and 'coeval with the Heavens' because it is this same Life (of the Divine Soul) which brings the Heavens also into being; Time and the Heavens are the work of the one Life.

Suppose that Life, then, to revert—an impossibility—to perfect unity: Time, whose existence is in that Life, and the Heavens, no longer maintained by that Life, would end at once.

It is the height of absurdity to fasten on the succession of earlier and later occurring in the life and movement of this sphere of ours, to declare that it must be some definite thing and to call it Time, while denying the reality of the more truly existent Movement, that of the Soul, which has also its earlier and later: it cannot be reasonable to recognize succession in the case of the Soulless Movement—and so to associate Time with that—while ignoring succession and the reality of Time in the Movement from which the other takes its imitative existence; to ignore, that is, the very Movement in which succession first appears, a self-actuated movement which, engendering its own every operation, creates the sequence by which each instant no sooner comes into existence than it passes into the next.

But: we treat the Cosmic Movement as overarched by that of the Soul and bring it under Time; yet we do not set under Time that Soul-Movement itself with all its endless progression: what is our explanation of this paradox?

Simply, that the Soul-Movement has for its Prior (not Time but) Eternity which knows neither its progression nor its extension. The descent towards Time begins with this Soul-Movement; it made Time and harbours Time as a concomitant to its Act.

And this is how Time is omnipresent: that Soul is absent from no fragment of the Cosmos just as our Soul is absent from no particle of ourselves. As for those who pronounce Time a thing of no substantial existence, of no reality, they clearly belie God Himself whenever they say 'He was' or 'He will be': for the existence indicated by the 'was and will be' can have only such reality as belongs to that in which it is said to be situated: but this school demands another style of argument.

Meanwhile we have a supplementary observation to make.

Take a man walking and observe the advance he has made; that advance gives you the quantity of movement he is employing: and when you know that quantity—represented by the ground traversed by his feet, for, of course, we are supposing the bodily movement to correspond with the pace he has set within himself—you know also the movement that exists in the man himself before the feet move.

You must relate the body, carried forward during a given period of Time, to a certain quantity of Movement causing the progress and to the Time it takes, and that again to the Movement, equal in extension, within the man's soul.

But the Movement within the Soul—to what are you to refer that?

Let your choice fall where it may, from this point there is nothing but the unextended: and this is the primarily existent, the container to all else, having itself no container, brooking none.

And, as with Man's Soul, so with the Soul of the All.

Is Time, then, within ourselves as well?

Time is in every Soul of the order of the All-Soul, present in like form in all; for all the Souls are the one Soul.

And this is why Time can never be broken apart, any more than Eternity which, similarly, under diverse manifestations, has its Being as an integral constituent of all the eternal Existences.

SOME QUESTIONS ABOUT TIME

ST. AUGUSTINE

Lo are they not full of their old leaven, who say to us,
"What was God doing before *He made heaven and earth?*"
"For if (say they) He were unemployed and wrought not,
why does He not also henceforth, and for ever, as He did
heretofore? For did any new motion arise in God, and a new
will to make a creature, which He had never before made,
how then would that be a true eternity, where there ariseth
a will, which was not? For the will of God is not a creature,
but before the creature; seeing nothing could be created,
unless the will of the Creator had preceded. The will of God
then belongeth to His very Substance. And if aught have
arisen in God's Substance, which before was not, that Substance cannot be truly called eternal. But if the will of God
has been from eternity that the creature should be, why was
not the creature also from eternity?"

Who speaks thus, do not yet understand Thee, O Wisdom
of God, Light of souls, understand not yet how the things be
made, which by Thee, and in Thee are made: yet they strive
to comprehend things eternal, whilst their heart fluttereth
between the motions of things past and to come, and is still
unstable. Who shall hold it, and fix it, that it be settled
awhile, and awhile catch the glory of that ever-fixed Eternity,
and compare it with the times which are never fixed, and
see that it cannot be compared; and that a long time cannot
become long, but out of many motions passing by, which
cannot be prolonged altogether; but that in the Eternal nothing passeth, but the whole is present; whereas no time is all

FROM St. Augustine, *Confessions*, translated by E. B. Pusey.
Chicago, Henry Regnery Co., 1948, Book XI, sections x–xxxi.

at once present: and that all time past, is driven on by time to come, and all to come followeth upon the past; and all past and to come, is created, and flows out of that which is ever present? Who shall hold the heart of man, that it may stand still, and see how eternity ever still-standing, neither past nor to come, uttereth the times past and to come? Can my hand do this, or the hand of my mouth by speech bring about a thing so great?

See, I answer him that asketh, "What did God before He *made heaven and earth?*" I answer not as one is said to have done merrily, (eluding the pressure of the question,) "He was preparing hell (saith he) for pryers into mysteries." It is one thing to answer enquiries, another to make sport of enquirers. So I answer not; for rather had I answer, "I know not," what I know not, than so as to raise a laugh at him who asketh deep things and gain praise for one who answereth false things. But I say that Thou, our God, art the Creator of every creature: and if by the name "heaven and earth," every creature be understood; I boldly say, "that before God made heaven and earth, He did not make any thing." For if He made, what did He make but a creature? And would I knew whatsoever I desire to know to my profit, as I know, that no creature was made, before there was made any creature.

But if any excursive brain rove over the images of forepassed times, and wonder that Thou the God Almighty and All-creating and All-supporting, Maker of heaven and earth, didst for innumerable ages forbear from so great a work, before Thou wouldest make it; let him awake and consider, that he wonders at false conceits. For whence could innumerable ages pass by, which Thou madest not, Thou the Author and Creator of all ages? or what times should there be, which were not made by Thee? or how should they pass by, if they never were? Seeing then Thou art the Creator of all times, if any time was before Thou *madest heaven and earth,* why say they that Thou didst forego working? For that very time didst Thou make, nor could times pass by, before Thou madest those times. But if before *heaven and earth* there was no time, why is it demanded, what Thou then didst? For there was no "then," when there was no time.

Nor dost Thou by time, precede time: else shouldest Thou not precede all times. But Thou precedest all things past, by the sublimity of an ever-present eternity; and surpassest all future because they are future, and when they come, they shall be past; *but Thou art the Same, and Thy years fail not.* Thy years neither come nor go; whereas ours both come and go, that they all may come. Thy years stand together, because they do stand; nor are departing thrust out by coming years, for they pass not away; but ours shall all be, when they shall no more be. Thy years are one day; and Thy day is not daily, but To-day, seeing Thy To-day gives not place unto to-morrow, for neither doth it replace yesterday. Thy To-day, is Eternity; therefore didst Thou beget The Coeternal, to whom Thou saidst, *This day have I begotten Thee.* Thou hast made all things; and before all times Thou art: neither in any time was time not.

At no time then hadst Thou not made any thing, because time itself Thou madest. And no times are coeternal with Thee, because Thou abidest; but if they abode, they should not be times. For what is time? Who can readily and briefly explain this? Who can even in thought comprehend it, so as to utter a word about it? But what in discourse do we mention more familiarly and knowingly, than time? And, we understand, when we speak of it; we understand also, when we hear it spoken of by another. What, then, is time? If no one asks me, I know: if I wish to explain it to one that asketh, I know not: yet I say boldly that I know, that if nothing passed away, time past were not; and if nothing were coming, a time to come were not; and if nothing were, time present were not. Those two times then, past and to come, how are they, seeing the past now is not, and that to come is not yet? But the present, should it always be present, and never pass into time past, verily it should not be time, but eternity. If time present (if it is to be time) only cometh into existence, because it passeth into time past, how can we say that either this is, whose cause of being is, that it shall not be; so, namely, that we cannot truly say that time is, but because it is tending not to be?

And yet we say, "a long time" and "a short time;" still, only of time past or to come. A long time past (for example) we call an hundred years since; and a long time to come, an hundred years hence. But a short time past, we call (suppose) ten days since; and a short time to come, ten days hence. But in what sense is that long or short, which is not? For the past, is not now; and the future, is not yet. Let us not then say, "it is long;" but of the past, "it hath been long;" and of the future, "it will be long." O my Lord, my Light, shall not here also Thy Truth mock at man? For that past time which was long, was it long when it was now past, or when it was yet present? For then might it be long, when there was, what could be long; but when past, it was no longer; wherefore neither could that be long, which was not at all. Let us not then say, "time past hath been long:" for we shall not find, what hath been long, seeing that since it was past, it is no more; but let us say, "that present time was long;" because, when it was present, it was long. For it had not yet passed away, so as not to be; and therefore there was, what could be long; but after it was past, that ceased also to be long, which ceased to be.

Let us see then, thou soul of man, whether present time can be long: for to thee it is given to feel and to measure length of time. What wilt thou answer me? Are an hundred years, when present, a long time? See first, whether an hundred years can be present. For if the first of these years be now current, it is present, but the other ninety and nine are to come, and therefore are not yet, but if the second year be current, one is now past, another present, the rest to come. And so if we assume any middle year of this hundred to be present, all before it, are past; all after it, to come; wherefore an hundred years cannot be present. But see at least whether that one which is now current, itself is present; for if the current month be its first, the rest are to come; if the second, the first is already past, and the rest are not yet. Therefore, neither is the year now current present; and if not present as a whole, then is not the year present. For twelve months are a year; of which whatever be the current month is present; the rest past, or to come. Although neither is that current month present; but one day only; the rest being to come, if it be the first; past, if the last; if any of the middle, then amid past and to come.

See how the present time, which alone we found could be called long, is abridged to the length scarce of one day. But let us examine that also; because neither is one day present as a whole. For it is made up of four and twenty hours of night and day: of which, the first hath the rest to come; the last hath them past; and any of the middle hath those before it past, those behind it to come. Yea, that one hour passeth away in flying particles. Whatsoever of it hath flown away, is past; whatsoever remaineth, is to come. If an instant of time be conceived, which cannot be divided into the smallest particles of moments, that alone is it, which may be called present. Which yet flies with such speed from future to past, as not to be lengthened out with the least stay. For if it be, it is divided into past and future. The present hath no space. Where then is the time, which we may call long? Is it to come? Of it we do not say, "it is long;" because it is not yet, so as to be long; but we say, "it will be long." When therefore will it be? For if even then, when it is yet to come, it shall not be long, (because what can be long, as yet is not,) and so it shall then be long, when from future which as yet is not, it shall begin now to be, and have become present, that so there should exist what may be long; then does time present cry out in the words above, that it cannot be long.

And yet, Lord, we perceive intervals of times, and compare them, and say, some are shorter, and others longer. We measure also, how much longer or shorter this time is than that; and we answer, "This is double, or treble; and that, but once, or only just so much as that." But we measure times as they are passing, by perceiving them; but past, which now are not, or the future, which are not yet, who can measure? unless a man shall presume to say, that can be measured, which is not. When time is passing, it may be perceived and measured; but when it is past, it cannot, because it is not.

I ask, Father, I affirm not: O my God, rule and guide me. "Who will tell me that there are not three times, (as we learned when boys, and taught boys,) past, present, and future; but present only, because those two are not? Or are they also; and when from future it becometh present, doth it come out of some secret place; and so, when retiring, from present it becometh past? For where did they, who foretold things to come, see them, if as yet they be not? For that which is not, cannot be seen. And they who relate things past, could not relate them, if in mind they did not discern them, and if they were not, they could no way be discerned. Things then past and to come are."

Permit me, Lord, to seek further. O my hope, let not my purpose be confounded. For if times past and to come be, I would know where they be. Which yet if I cannot, yet I know, wherever they be, they are not there as future, or past, but present. For if there also they be future, they are not yet there; if there also they be past, they are no longer there. Wheresoever then is whatsoever is, it is only as present. Although when past facts are related, there are drawn out of the memory, not the things themselves which are past, but words which, conceived by the images of the things, they, in passing, have through the senses left as traces in the mind. Thus my childhood, which now is not, is in time past, which now is not: but now when I recall its image, and tell of it, I behold it in the present, because it is still in my memory. Whether there be a like cause of foretelling things to come also; that of things which as yet are not, the images may be perceived before, already existing, I confess, O my God, I know not. This indeed I know, that we generally think before on our future actions, and that that forethinking is present, but the action whereof we forethink is not yet, because it is to come. Which, when we have set upon, and have begun to do what we were forethinking, then shall that action be; because then it is no longer future, but present.

Which way soever then this secret fore-perceiving of things to come be; that only can be seen, which is. But what now is, is not future, but present. When then things to come are said to be seen, it is not themselves which as yet are not, (that is, which are to be,) but their causes perchance or signs are seen, which already are. Therefore they are not future but present to those who now see that, from which the future, being fore-conceived in the mind, is foretold. Which fore-conceptions again now are; and those who foretel those things, do behold the conceptions present before them. Let now the numerous variety of things furnish me some example. I behold the day-break, I foreshew, that the sun is about to rise. What I behold, is present; what I foresignify, to come; not the sun, which already is; but the sun-rising, which is not yet. And yet did I not in my mind imagine the sun-rising itself, (as now while I speak of it,) I could not foretel it. But neither is that daybreak which I discern in the sky, the sun-rising, although it goes before it; nor that imagination of my mind; which two are seen now present, that the other which is to be may be foretold. Future things then are not yet: and if they be not yet, they are not: and if they are not, they cannot be seen; yet foretold they may be from things present, which are already, and are seen.

Thou then, Ruler of Thy creation, by what way dost Thou teach souls things to come? For Thou didst teach Thy Prophets. By what way dost Thou, to whom nothing is to come, teach things to come, or rather of the future, dost teach things present? For, what is not, neither can it be taught. Too far is this way out of my ken: *it is too mighty for me, I cannot attain unto it;* but from Thee I can, when Thou shalt vouchsafe it, O sweet light of my hidden eyes.

What now is clear and plain is, that neither things to come nor past are. Nor is it properly said, "there be three times, past, present, and to come:" yet perchance it might be properly said, "there be three times; a present of things past, a present of things present, and a present of things future." For these three do exist in some sort, in the soul, but otherwhere do I not see them; present of things past, memory; present of things present, sight; present of things future, expectation. If thus we be permitted to speak, I see three times, and I confess there are three. Let it be said too, "there be three times, past, present, and to come:" in our incorrect way. See, I object not, nor gainsay, nor find fault, if what is so said be but understood, that neither what is to be, now is, nor what is past. For but few things are there, which we speak properly, most things improperly; still the things intended are understood.

I said then even now, we measure times as they pass, in order to be able to say, this time is twice so much as that one; or, this is just so much as that; and so of any other parts of time, which be measurable. Wherefore, as I said, we measure times as they pass. And if any should ask me, "How knowest thou?" I might answer, "I know, that we do measure, nor can we measure things that are not; and things past and to come, are not." But time present how do we measure, seeing it hath no space? It is measured while passing, but when it shall have passed, it is not measured; for there will be nothing to be measured. But whence, by what way, and whither passes it while it is a measuring? whence, but from the future? Which way, but through the present? whither, but into the past? From that therefore, which is not yet, through that, which hath no space, into that, which now is not. Yet what do we measure, if not time in some space? For we do not say, single, and double, and triple, and equal, or any other like way that we speak of time, except of spaces of times. In what space then do we measure time passing? In the future, whence it passeth through? But what is not yet, we measure not. Or in the present, by which it passes? but no space, we do not measure: or in the past, to which it passes? But neither do we measure that, which now is not.

My soul is on fire to know this most intricate enigma. Shut it not up, O Lord my God, good Father; through Christ I beseech Thee, do not shut up these usual, yet hidden things, from my desire, that it be hindered from piercing into them; but let them dawn through Thy enlightening mercy, O Lord. Whom shall I enquire of concerning these things? and to whom shall I more fruitfully confess my ignorance, than to Thee, to Whom these my studies, so vehemently kindled toward Thy Scriptures, are not troublesome? Give what I love; for I do love, and this hast Thou given me. Give, Father, Who *truly knowest to give good gifts unto Thy children.* Give, because I have taken upon me to know, and trouble is before me until Thou openest it. By Christ I beseech Thee, in His Name, Holy of holies, let no man disturb me. For *I believed, and therefore do I speak.* This is my hope, for this do I live, that *I may contemplate the delights of the Lord.* Behold, *Thou hast made my days* old, and they pass away, and how, I know not. And we talk of time, and time, and times, and times, "How long time is it since he said this;" "how long time since he did this;" and "how long time since I saw that;" and "this syllable hath double time to that single short syllable." These words we speak, and these we hear, and are understood, and understand. Most manifest and ordinary they are, and the self-same things again are but too deeply hidden, and the discovery of them were new.

I heard once from a learned man, that the motions of the sun, moon, and stars, constituted time, and I assented not. For why should not the motions of all bodies rather be times? Or, if the lights of heaven should cease, and a potter's wheel run round, should there be no time by which we might measure those whirlings, and say, that either it moved with equal pauses, or if it turned sometimes slower, otherwhiles quicker, that some rounds were longer, other shorter? Or, while we were saying this, should we not also be speaking in time? Or, should there in our words be some syllables short, others long, but because those sounded in a shorter time, these in a longer? God, grant to men to see in a small thing notices common to things great and small. The stars and lights of heaven, are also *for signs, and for seasons, and for years, and for days;* they are; yet neither should I say, that the going round of that wooden wheel was a day, nor yet he, that it was therefore no time.

I desire to know the force and nature of time, by which we measure the motions of bodies, and say (for example) this motion is twice as long as that. For I ask, seeing "day" denotes not the stay only of the sun upon the earth, (according to which day is one thing, night another;) but also its whole circuit from east to east again; according to which we say, "there passed so many days," the night being included when we say "so many days," and the nights not reckoned apart; —seeing then a day is completed by the motion of the sun and by his circuit from east to east again, I ask, does the motion alone make the day, or the stay in which that motion is completed, or both? For if the first be the day; then should we have a day, although the sun should finish that course in so small a space of time, as one hour comes to. If the second, then should not that make a day, if between one sun-rise and another there were but so short a stay, as one hour comes to; but the sun must go four and twenty times about, to complete one day. If both, then neither could that be called a day, if the sun should run his whole round in the space of one hour; nor that, if, while the sun stood still, so much time should overpass, as the sun usually makes his whole course in, from morning to morning. I will not therefore now ask, what that is which is called day; but, what time is, whereby we, measuring the circuit of the sun, should say that it was finished in half the time it was wont, if so be it was finished in so small a space as twelve hours, and comparing both times, should call this a single time, that a double time; even supposing the sun to run his round from east to east, sometimes in that single, sometimes in that double time. Let no man then tell me, that the motions of the heavenly bodies constitute times, because, when at the prayer of one, the sun had stood still, till he could achieve his victorious battle, the sun stood still, but time went on. For in its own allotted space of time was that battle waged and ended. I perceive time then to be a certain extension. But do I perceive it, or seem to perceive it? Thou, Light and Truth, wilt shew me.

Dost Thou bid me assent, if any define time to be "motion of a body?" Thou dost not bid me. For that no body is moved, but in time, I hear; this Thou sayest; but that the motion of a body is time, I hear not; Thou sayest it not. For when a body is moved, I by time measure, how long it moveth, from the time it began to move, until it left off? And if I did not see whence it began; and it continue to move so that I see not when it ends, I cannot measure, save perchance from the time I began, until I cease to see. And if I look long, I can only pronounce it to be a long time, but not how long; because when we say "how long," we do it by comparison; as, "this is as long as that," or "twice so long as that," or the like. But when we can mark the distance of the places, whence and whither goeth the body moved, or his parts, if it moved as in a lathe, then can we say precisely, in how much time the motion of that body or his part, from this place unto that, was finished. Seeing therefore the motion of a body is one thing, that by which we measure how long it is, another; who sees not, which of the two is rather to be called time? For and if a body be sometimes moved, sometimes stands still, then we measure, not his motion only, but his standing still too by time; and we say, "it stood still, as much as it moved;" or "it stood still twice or thrice so long as it moved;" or any other space which our measuring hath either ascertained, or guessed; more or less, as we use to say. Time then is not the motion of a body.

And I confess to Thee, O Lord, that I yet know not what time is, and again I confess unto Thee, O Lord, that I know that I speak this in time, and that having long spoken of time, that very "long" is not long, but by the pause of time. How then know I this, seeing I know not what time is? or is it perchance that I know not how to express what I know? Woe is me, that do not even know, what I know not. Behold, O my God, before Thee I lie not; but as I speak so is my heart. *Thou shalt light my candle; Thou O Lord my God, wilt enlighten my darkness.*

Does not my soul most truly confess unto Thee, that I do measure times? Do I then measure, O my God, and know not what I measure? I measure the motion of a body in time; and the time itself do I not measure? Or could I indeed measure the motion of a body how long it were, and in how long space it could come from this place to that, without measuring the time in which it is moved? This same time then, how do I measure? do we by a shorter time measure a longer, as by the space of a cubit, the space of a rood? for so indeed we seem by the space of a short syllable, to measure the space of a long syllable, and to say that this is double the other. Thus measure we the spaces of stanzas, by the spaces of the verses, and the spaces of the verses, by the spaces of the feet, and the spaces of the feet, by the spaces of the syllables, and the spaces of long, by the spaces of short syllables; not measuring by pages, (for then we measure spaces, not times;) but when we utter the words and they pass by, and we say "it is a long stanza, because composed of so many verses; long verses, because consisting of so many feet; long feet, because prolonged by so many syllables; a long syllable because double to a short one." But neither do we this way obtain any certain measure of time; because it may be, that a shorter verse, pronounced more fully, may take up more time than a longer, pronounced hurriedly. And so for a verse, a foot, a syllable. Whence it seemed to me, that time is nothing else than protraction; but of what, I know not; and I marvel, if it be not of the mind itself? For what I beseech Thee, O my God, do I measure, when I say, either indefinitely "this is a longer time than that," or definitely "this is double that?" That I measure time, I know; and yet I measure not time to come, for it is not yet; nor present, because it is not protracted by any space; nor past, because it now is not. What then do I measure? Times passing, not past? for so I said.

Courage, my mind, and press on mightily. God is our helper, He *made us, and not we ourselves.* Press on where truth begins to dawn. Suppose, now, the voice of a body begins to sound, and does sound, and sounds on, and list, it ceases; it is silence now, and that voice is past, and is no more a voice. Before it sounded, it was to come, and could not be measured, because as yet it was not, and now it cannot, because it is no longer. Then therefore while it sounded, it might; because there then was what might be measured. But yet even then it was not at a stay; for it was passing on, and passing away. Could it be measured the rather, for that? For while passing, it was being extended into some space of time, so that it might be measured, since the present hath no space. If therefore then it might, then, lo, suppose another voice hath begun to sound, and still soundeth in one continued tenor without any interruption; let us measure it while it sounds; seeing when it hath left sounding, it will then be past, and nothing left to be measured; let us measure it verily, and tell how much it is. But it sounds still, nor can it be measured but from the instant it began in, unto the end it left in. For the very space between is the thing we measure, namely, from some beginning unto some end. Wherefore, a voice that is not yet ended, cannot be measured, so that it may be said how long, or short it is; nor can it be called equal to another, or double to a single, or the like. But when ended, it no longer is. How may it then be measured? And yet we measure times; but yet neither those which are not yet, nor those which no longer are, nor those which are not lengthened out by some pause, nor those which have no bounds. We measure neither times to come, nor past, nor present, nor passing; and yet we do measure times.

"Deus Creator omnium," this verse of eight syllables alternates between short and long syllables. The four short then, the first, third, fifth, and seventh, are but single, in respect of the four long, the second, fourth, sixth, and eighth. Every one of these, to every one of those, hath a double time: I pronounce them, report on them, and find it so, as one's plain sense perceives. By plain sense then, I measure a long syllable by a short, and I sensibly find it to have twice so much; but when one sounds after the other, if the former be short, the latter long, how shall I detain the short one, and how, measuring, shall I apply it to the long, that I may find this to have twice so much; seeing the long does not begin to sound, unless the short leaves sounding? And that very long one do I measure as present, seeing I measure it not till it be ended? Now his ending is his passing away. What then is it I measure? where is the short syllable by which I measure? where the long which I measure? Both have sounded, have flown, passed away, are no more; and yet I measure, and confidently answer (so far as is presumed on a practised sense) that as to space of time this syllable is but single, that double. And yet I could not do this, unless they were already past and ended. It is not then themselves, which now are not, that I measure, but something in my memory, which there remains fixed.

It is in thee, my mind, that I measure times. Interrupt me not, that is, interrupt not thyself with the tumults of thy impressions. In thee I measure times; the impression, which things as they pass by cause in thee, remains even when they are gone; this it is which, still present, I measure, not the things which pass by to make this impression. This I measure, when I measure times. Either then this is time, or I do not measure times. What when we measure silence, and say that this silence hath held as long time as did that voice? do we not stretch out our thought to the measure of a voice, as if it sounded that so we may be able to report of the intervals of silence in a given space of time? For though both voice and tongue be still, yet in thought we go over poems, and verses, and any other discourse, or dimensions of motions, and report as to the spaces of times, how much this is in respect of that, no otherwise than if vocally we did pronounce them. If a man would utter a lengthened sound, and had settled in thought how long it should be, he hath in silence already gone through a space of time, and committing it to memory, begins to utter that speech, which sounds on, until it be brought unto the end proposed. Yea it hath sounded, and will sound; for so much of it as is finished, hath sounded already, and the rest will sound. And thus passeth it on, until the present intent conveys over the future into the past; the past increasing by the diminution of the future, until by the consumption of the future, all is past.

But how is that future diminished or consumed, which as yet is not? or how that past increased, which is now no longer, save that in the mind which enacteth this, there be three things done? For it expects, it considers, it remembers; that so that which it expecteth, through that which it considereth, passeth into that which it remembereth. Who therefore denieth, that things to come are not as yet? and yet, there is in the mind an expectation of things to come. And who denies past things to be now no longer? and yet is there still in the mind a memory of things past. And who denieth that the present time hath no space, because it passeth away in a moment? and yet our consideration continueth, through which that which shall be present proceedeth to become absent. It is not then future time, that is long, for as yet it is not: but a "long future," is "a long expectation of the future," nor is it time past, which now is not, that is long; but a long past, is "a long memory of the past."

I am about to repeat a Psalm that I know. Before I begin,

my expectation is extended over the whole; but when I have begun, how much soever of it I shall separate off into the past, is extended along my memory; thus the life of this action of mine is divided between my memory as to what I have repeated, and expectation as to what I am about to repeat; but "consideration" is present with me, that through it what was future, may be conveyed over, so as to become past. Which the more it is done again and again, so much the more the expectation being shortened, is the memory enlarged; till the whole expectation be at length exhausted, when that whole action being ended, shall have passed into memory. And this which takes place in the whole Psalm, the same takes place in each several portion of it, and each several syllable; the same holds in that longer action, whereof this Psalm may be a part; the same holds in the whole life of man, whereof all the actions of man are parts; the same holds through the whole age of the sons of men, whereof all the lives of men are parts.

But because *Thy loving kindness is better than* all *lives,* behold, my life is but a distraction, and *Thy right hand upheld me,* in my Lord the *Son of man,* the *Mediator betwixt Thee,* The One, and us many, many also through our manifold distractions amid many things, that by Him *I may apprehend in Whom I have been apprehended,* and may be re-collected from my old conversation, to follow The One, *forgetting what is behind, and* not distended but *extended,* not to things which shall be and shall pass away, but *to those things which are before,* not distractedly but intently, *I follow on for the prize of my heavenly calling,* where I may *hear the voice of* Thy *praise,* and *contemplate* Thy *delights,* neither to come, nor to pass away. But now *are my years spent in mourning.* And Thou, O Lord, art my comfort, my Father everlasting, but I have been severed amid times, whose order I know not; and my thoughts, even the inmost bowels of my soul, are rent and mangled with tumultuous varieties, until I flow together into Thee, purified and molten by the fire of Thy love.

And now will I stand, and become firm in Thee, in my mould, Thy truth; nor will I endure the questions of men, who by a penal disease thirst for more than they can contain, and say, "what did God before He *made heaven and earth?*" "Or, how came it into His mind to make anything, having never before made any thing?" Give them, O Lord, well to bethink themselves what they say, and to find, that "never" cannot be predicated, when "time" is not. This then that He is said "never to have made;" what else is it to say, than "in 'no time' to have made?" Let them see therefore, that time cannot be without created being, and cease to *speak* that *vanity.* May they also be *extended towards those things which are before;* and understand Thee before all times, the eternal Creator of all times, and that no times be coeternal with Thee, nor any creature, even if there be any creature before all times.

O Lord my God, what a depth is that recess of Thy mysteries, and how far from it have the consequences of my transgressions cast me! Heal mine eyes, that I may share the joy of Thy light. Certainly, if there be a mind gifted with such vast knowledge and foreknowledge, as to know all things past and to come, as I know one well-known Psalm, truly that mind is passing wonderful, and fearfully amazing; in that nothing past, nothing to come in after-ages, is any more hidden from him, than when I sung that Psalm, was hidden from me what, and how much of it had passed away from the beginning, what, and how much there remained unto the end. But far be it that Thou the Creator of the Universe, the Creator of souls and bodies, far be it, that Thou shouldest in such wise know all things past and to come. Far, far more wonderfully, and far more mysteriously, dost thou know them. For not, as the feelings of one who singeth what he knoweth, or heareth some well-known song, are through expectation of the words to come, and the remembering of those that are past, varied, and his senses divided,—not so doth any thing happen unto Thee, unchangeably eternal, that is, the eternal Creator of minds. Like then as Thou *in the Beginning* knewest *the heaven and the earth,* without any variety of Thy knowledge, so *madest* Thou *in the Beginning heaven and earth,* without any distraction of Thy action. Whoso understandeth, let him confess unto Thee; and whoso understandeth not, let him confess unto Thee. Oh how high art Thou, and yet the humble in heart are Thy dwelling-place; for Thou *raisest up those that are bowed down,* and they fall not, whose elevation Thou art.

ANALYTIC-SYNTHETIC

FRIEDRICH WAISMANN

Friedrich Waismann (1896–1959) was closely associated with "The Vienna Circle" of philosophers and scientists. He fled to England in 1937; his first position was at Cambridge, and two years later he became Reader in the Philosophy of Mathematics at Cambridge. Among his publications are the *Introduction to Mathematical Thinking* and *The Principles of Linguistic Philosophy*.

What is time? Philosophers since the days of St. Augustine have been pondering over this question. The queer thing is that we all seem to know perfectly well "what time is", and yet if we are asked *what* it is, we are reduced to speechlessness. Indeed, what *should* one say? That time is 'the form of becoming', 'the possibility of change', or some such thing? Wouldn't it be extraordinary if someone, instead of saying, "Don't hurry, still plenty of time" were to say, "Don't hurry, still plenty of form of becoming"? Would it be any better to declare, "Time is measurable duration"? Needless to say this will not do either. So what? We can't help feeling *puzzled* by the question, and we are apt to express this puzzlement in Augustine's words: "What is time? If I am not asked, I know; if I am asked, I don't".[1] But what exactly is the difficulty? We know what the word 'time' means in the sense that we are able (1) to understand it in various contexts ("He has come just in time", "What is the right time?" "My time is up, I must go", etc.) and (2) to use it on the proper sort of occasions in the right sort of contexts. But it would not be

FROM Friedrich Waismann, "Analytic-Synthetic," *Analysis*, 2 and 3 (December 1950 and January 1951). Reprinted by permission of the editor and the publisher.

[1] *Confessions, Liber XI, Cap. XV* [p. 40 of this volume].

right to say that we know the meaning of the word in the further sense (3) that we are able to *reduce* its whole immensely variegated use to a simple formula. Knowing how to apply the word in the right sort of way is one, condensing its usage into a single formula, a very different thing.

Here it might be asked: *can* the word be defined? But *why* should I try to find a definition? A definition would enable me to eliminate the word 'time' from any given context and replace it by its *definiens*. But it is *just the point* that there exists in English no other word, nor any combination of words which does the job the noun 'time' does. There is but one word, and no other, to express what I want to express, and that is just the word 'time'. In vain do I look for some paraphrase, or circumlocution, or roundabout mode of expression which can be used *in place* of the word 'time', though, in *particular* cases, such rewording *is* possible. To give some examples: by this time = now; a long time ago = long ago; in times to come = in future; in time = in good season; early enough; behind time = late; at the same time = simultaneously; however; from time to time = now and then; occasionally; time after time = repeatedly; out of due time = prematurely; too late; not in proper season; against time = with all possible speed or haste; in the nick of time = just at the exact moment; in no time = as quick as a wink; time enough = sufficiently long; no need for haste; now is your time = now is your opportunity; had a good time = enjoyed myself; mark time = make no progress; time-honoured = venerable by antiquity; etc. Thus the word 'time' can in fact be eliminated from a great many phrases; but the difficulty is to go on with *one* translation *consistently* for all the phrases in which the word occurs, *i.e.* to make the translation hold *throughout*. The fact is that there is no standard translation that can serve to eliminate the word from any context whatsoever and replace it by the *definiens*.

So to answer the question we look into diverse phrases in which the word occurs, spread out before us, as it were, the whole tortuous usage. We connect this word with others, we put it into various contexts, we trace over the lines of its use, and by doing this we convey its meaning. Indeed, if anyone is able to use the word correctly, in all sort of contexts and on the right sort of occasions, he knows 'what time is', and no formula in the world can make him wiser.

It should be noticed that this is only a *very rough* account of the matter. There is no such thing as a *standard* test to decide infallibly whether, *e.g.*, a child really does grasp the meaning of that word. If the question "What is the right time?" only elicits a blank from him, if he shows not the slightest sign of understanding the most common phrases, we should certainly not be satisfied. On the other hand, we do not require him to know *all* the idioms of speech such as 'in the nick of time', 'the time of one's life', 'hell of a time'. But to ask, "In what moment does he catch the meaning?" is like asking in which moment a man who is learning to play chess turns into a chess player. These are not the right questions to ask.

What, then, are we to say in reply to the question whether a word like 'time' *can* be defined? We are inclined to say that it can not, and the reason for this, I suppose, is that we think of a definition as a *concise* formula covering the word's use. But we have already seen the infiltration of other types of definitions alongside the explicit ones by which the use of a word is explained in certain specified contexts. As there is no limit to the number of these contexts—a good example of this is the definition of irrational numbers in mathematics—there is no limit to the complexity of the pattern woven by this sort of definition. If such accretions are admitted, why not take a bolder step and include the case we are considering too? Admittedly, that would be a departure from the ordinary (traditional) use of the word 'definition'; but why not stretch this usage?

My object in dealing with this sort of question was not to recommend a way of speaking in which spreading out a word's use may be called a definition, but rather make you see that 'definitions in use'[2] gradually shade off into more and more complicated patterns, and that it would be unnatural to say, "So far it is a definition and from there on it is no

[2] [A *definition in use* of a term gives an analysis of a statement containing this term.—Ed.]

longer". On the other hand, if a person feels unhappy about extending the use so far, we can also see that there is a point in this. What troubles him is perhaps this that the use of the word *cannot be formalised.* Indeed, the usage of a word like 'time' is *not only* far more intricate than that of, let us say, 'similar' (in the theory of classes), but also *irregular, loose,* and above all, *incomplete,* the latter in the sense that new figures of speech may come, and in fact have come, into being (such as 'time is money'), without apparently altering the sense of the word. It is therefore not only *difficult,* but *next to impossible* to tabulate all the phrases in which it occurs. *Its use can no longer be distilled into rules.* The more we attend to this peculiarity, the less satisfied we feel with calling such a procedure a definition. Having reached this stage, we are perhaps more inclined to say something like this; it is true, we can make a person understand the word 'time' by producing examples of its use, characteristic examples: but what we cannot do is to present a fixed formula comprising as in a magic crystal the whole often so infinitely complicated and elusive meaning of the word. Accordingly, one may perhaps wish to distinguish between 'definable' in the strict sense, and 'teachable' (or 'learnable'), thus bringing out the difference just considered. . . .

. . . . In forming a concept like 'definition' we are grouping together a cluster of unequal things, held together only by a sort of family likeness. It is important to notice that this family likeness is itself of a *vague* kind, consisting of all sorts of similarities which need have nothing in common, just as, to use an example given by Wittgenstein, members of the same family may be alike in many different ways, *e.g.* may have the same abrupt manner of talking, the same way of smiling with the eyes, of bending the head, of knitting the brows, or the same expression of defiance. Not that all these features need be present: but now this, now that, and at another time some combination of them, thus giving rise to a boundless variety of possible ways of 'looking alike'. As with people, so with definitions. If we group cases of definition together according to their similarity, it is easy to see that the similarity resolves itself into a bundle of relations, holding at times only between the forms (expressions) of the definitions, at other times between the various jobs they perform. And it is also easy to see that many different ways of grouping can be adopted. Thus we have seen some of the reasons for excluding dictionary definitions, or for not classing ostensive definitions with others, etc. There is no *specific* feature to be found that is peculiar to all the situations in which the term 'definition' might be used. It should be noticed that much the same indeterminacy is characteristic of words such as 'explaining', 'describing', 'introducing' (into a notation), 'stating precisely', 'declaring the meaning', 'making intelligible', and scores of others.

My purpose in calling attention to these indeterminacies can now be seen. Any inexactitude in the idea of a definition will be reflected in a similar inexactitude in the conception of analytic: according as the boundary of what is called 'definition' is drawn more broadly or more narrowly, the class of expressions to be included in the range of analytic will become larger or smaller. For example, if *definitions in use* are precluded, it cannot be proved that the statement "If α is similar to β, β is similar to α" is analytic; if *recursive*[3] definitions are precluded, it cannot be proved that a formula like "$7 + 5 = 12$" is analytic (in the sense of being valid on the ground of definitions only); without *implicit* definitions such as those referring to the concept of betweenness it cannot be proved that saying, *e.g.*, "If A, B and C are points on a straight line, and B is between A and C, then B is also between C and A" is analytic. If, on the other hand, *dictionary definitions* are permitted, almost *every* statement might be proved to be analytic. Our trouble is not with the last sort of definition which, for the purposes of the present paper, may be excluded; nor is it with any of the other types of definition just mentioned. Our trouble is with the sort of definition, or explanation, instanced by the word 'time'. Suppose one is asked whether "Time is measurable" is analytic —what ought one to reply? We are, perhaps, first inclined to

[3] [For an explanation of a recursive definition, see S. C. Kleene, *Introduction to Metamathematics*, Amsterdam, 1952.—Ed.]

answer, yes. What tempts us to do this is that it seems to be *part of the meaning* of 'time' that time should be measurable. Yet this claim can hardly be substantiated, *i.e.* there seems to be hardly any way of transforming the given expression step by step into a truth of logic. What we could do is, at the most, to point out some of the uses (such as 'timing', 'timepiece', 'what is the right time?' etc.) which seem to indicate that time is measurable. This, however, will lead only to a scarcely enviable position since there is no sharp line which separates those uses which, as one would say, are *characteristic* of the concept, from those which are not. Here all sorts of questions may be missed: Are you willing to say that the word 'time', before sand-glasses, water-clocks, or sun-dials had come into use, had a meaning different from that which it has now? Would you say that 'mythological time' must be something quite different, because, though Uranus was deposed by Cronus, and Cronus by Zeus, it is not possible to *date* these 'events', any more than it makes sense to ask whether the reign of Uranus lasted as long as that of Cronus? Would you be prepared to say that, in case the world was such that time could not be measured—say, because of the absence of sequences of recurrent events— time would not be what it is now? Here, I suppose, you may be inclined to say that it lies *in the nature* of time that it can be measured. But what do you mean by the expression 'it lies in the nature of time'? That this is part of the *definition* of the word 'time'? But as there is no definition to refer to, but only a use, forming a vast maze of lines, as it were, you will feel that this argument loses its point. On what, then, rests your assurance? Some people may turn to intuition, and take a more or less Kantian point of view. In order to see whether intuition can show the *necessity* of our statement ('time is measurable'), we have to consider some of the facts which underlie the measurement of time. One such fact is the existence of sequences of recurrent events, such as the tides, the seasons, the phases of the moon, the revolution of the starry sky, the oscillations of a pendulum, the vibrations of a spring, etc. That is by no means enough. It is easy to imagine the following case: when I compare two such sequences, I find that they stand in a certain constant ratio to each other which, for a given pair, *e.g.* moon phases and sidereal days, is always the same. But there is nothing impossible in the idea that, if I started from a different series, *e.g.*, the swings of a weather cock, and compared them with the events of another series such as thunderstorms or night frosts, I might *also* find a constant ratio between them, whereas comparing a member of the first group with a member of the second would lead to *no* constant relation. In other words, it makes sense to suppose that all the sequences in the universe should fall into two distinct classes, the members of the same class being correlated by well-defined constant ratios, whereas between members of different classes no such relation holds. Then time would, as it were, bifurcate into two distinct rivers (say, 'star time' and 'storm time'), each flowing at an even rate, and yet irregular when viewed from the other: it would have become impossible to establish a common all-embracing time scale for the whole universe. Experience teaches that all those sequences which are linked by constant ratios in fact fit only in one extensive system; those which fit badly or not at all to the one system, do not fit together in a rival system. But even that must not be taken as an irrefutable fact; there are certain doubts, connected with the moon's irregularity as to whether the ratio-linked sequences really fit together *precisely* in a coherent system, or whether in the long run this may not turn out to be illusory. We can, indeed, imagine that within historical periods 'irregularities' are scarcely noticeable which, on an astronomical scale, may pile up to such an extent as to make a chronology of the universe impossible. Why not, indeed, imagine that events of high frequency (vibration of strings, tuning forks, etc.) should be ratio-linked within short periods of observation, a few minutes or hours only, but incommensurable for longer periods, a few weeks or months? In such a case the 'uniformity' of time's flow would be a very transient thing. A time of this sort may be likened to a space in which no measurement is definable, what is called a 'non-metrical', 'topological' space (*i.e.* the type of space jelly-fish would likely be familiar with if they were doing geometry and living in a world of liquids or jellified objects). Incidentally, time may be non-metric without being disorderly. Recitals of poems would always bring forth words in precisely the same order, though it would not be a proper question to ask whether one stanza lasts *as long* as another. The attempt to measure a period between two events would be like trying to measure the Reign of Terror in terms of thunderstorms or earthquakes.

The fact that only one system exists in which all correlated sequences are linked now assumes a profound significance. It is no less significant that the time scale, based on this system, is in keeping with our natural estimation of the lapse of time (for short intervals anyhow), and further that it leads to the formulation of *simple* laws of nature. That this should be so does not follow from the mere idea of a time scale; it is conceivable that the time scale of the clock should not lead to simple and transparent laws, and that it should first have to undergo some transformation before it could serve the purpose of rendering "the equations of mechanics as simple as possible", to use Poincaré's words.[4] That shows what an enormous variety of cases can be thought of in which time wouldn't be measurable in the way it actually is. I say all this, because looking at things in this light may loosen a position which prevents one from seeing the importance of certain facts. Once you are aware of the vast mass of evidence which is relevant to the case, you will be less inclined to think that time 'must' be measurable.

Consider a somewhat analogous case: can pain be measured? There is a temptation to say just the opposite here, that it lies in the nature of pain that it can*not* be measured. But suppose that psychologists had devised a technique for measuring pain, or at least for assigning numbers to pains in roughly the same way in which hardnesses are ordered according to Mohs' scale. We may imagine that an idiom has come into use in which the doctor asks the nurse "What pain had the patient last night?" and she replies "Pain number 3". Ask yourself whether you would say in such a case

[4] *The Value of Science*, Ch. II.

that the word 'pain' has changed in meaning? Compare this question with the following: Supposing that certain astronomical speculations regarding departures from the constant ratios for the cycles of events had proved true (so that no universal and precise time scale could be set up), would you say that the word 'time' had now a new meaning? Now all this obviously hinges on the absence of a definition of 'time', or, more generally, on the absence of a *precise grammar* of this word. That brings me to the crucial point. When we were asking this sort of question, namely, whether the meaning of 'time' or 'pain' changes when a method of measuring is introduced, we were thinking of the meaning of a word as *clear-cut*. What we were not aware of was that there are no *precise rules* governing the use of words like 'time', 'pain', etc., and that consequently to speak of the 'meaning' of a word and to ask whether it has, or has not changed in meaning, is to operate with too blurred an expression. . . .

Section II

THE STATIC VERSUS THE DYNAMIC TEMPORAL

INTRODUCTION

This section will consider the treatment of time in twentieth-century analytic philosophy, this being a generic term which includes logical atomism, logical positivism, rational reconstruction, and linguistic analysis (ordinary language philosophy). We shall begin our investigation by considering J. M. E. McTaggart's famous argument for the unreality of time, which was first published in 1908. McTaggart's discussion is a key to the views of time held by twentieth-century analytic philosophers, for one can detect in their writings a common underlying concern: almost all of them are attempting to answer McTaggart's paradox. This is not to say that all these writings mention McTaggart by name, or even that their authors always had him consciously in mind; but only that the problems they wrestled with were those bequeathed to them by McTaggart. A person can scratch a mosquito bite without knowing that it is a mosquito bite. McTaggart's argument is fallacious, but it is fallacious in such a deep and basic way that an adequate answer to it must supply a rather extensive analysis of the concept of time, along with a host of neighboring concepts that are themselves of philosophical interest, such as change, substance, event, proposition, truth, and others. What we shall notice is that the answers proposed involve very different analyses of these concepts.

McTaggart's paradox is deeply rooted in two fundamentally different ways in which we conceive of and talk about time. On the one hand, we conceive of time in a dynamic or tensed way, as being the very quintessence of flux and transiency. Accordingly events are represented as being past, present, and future, and as continually changing in respect to these tensed determinations. Thus what is now happening ceases to happen and becomes past as future events become present, so that past events become more past and future events less future. This process of temporal becoming is often referred to by various metaphors and aphorisms—the gnawing tooth of time; the river of time; time flies; here today and gone tomorrow; gather ye rosebuds while ye may; enjoy yourself, it's later than you think; and the rest of them. The dynamic conception of time lies at the basis of the temporalistic view of man which is present in certain religions, philosophies, and works of art, and finds expression in our tensed way of talking.

Yet time, in which all things come to be and pass away, necessarily involves a static structure or order. It is, to use T. S. Eliot's phrase, "a pattern of timeless moments." The very same events which are continually changing in respect to their pastness, presentness, or futurity are laid out in a permanent order whose generating relation is that of *earlier* (or *later*) *than*. This is the static or tenseless way of conceiving time, in which the history of the world is viewed in a God-like manner, all events being given at once in a *nunc stans*. Here there is no gnawing tooth of time—no temporal becoming—but only a democratic equality of all times. The static conception finds expression in our tenseless way of talking, in which temporal relations of precedence and subsequence between events are described by timelessly true or false statements.

The central problem is to relate these two radically different ways of conceiving or talking about time. As we shall see, McTaggart's paradox rests on a seeming incompatibility between the two. Adequately to dispel his paradox, analysts have had to inspect the logic of our tensed and tenseless ways of talking and to see how these two different manners of speaking are related.

McTaggart's argument comprises both a positive and a negative thesis. The positive thesis contains an analysis of the concept of time that McTaggart claims to be the only correct one. The negative thesis attempts to show that this analysis entails a contradiction. The assumption here is that any concept which is contradictory cannot be true of reality.

In his positive thesis, McTaggart analyzes the concept of time in terms of two different types of temporal facts. First, there are facts about temporal relations of precedence and subsequence between events, and, second, there are facts about the pastness, presentness, and futurity of these same events. Corresponding to the first type of temporal fact is a series of events, called the "B-Series," which runs from earlier to later, its generating relation being *earlier* (or *later*) *than;* corresponding to the second type is a series of events, called the "A-Series," which runs from the past through the present and through the present to the future. The relation of *earlier* or *later than* will be referred to as a "B-relation," and the pastness, presentness, or futurity of an event as an "A-determination."

Events can never change their position in the B-Series. Plato's death, for example, cannot through diligence and hard work sneak up on Stalin's death, for if one event is earlier than some other event by so many time-units, then it is always the case that the one is so many time-units earlier than the other. The only change that an event can undergo is a change in its A-determination. Plato's death once was future, became present, and is now retreating into the more distant past. Such change has been referred to above as temporal becoming. McTaggart's B-Series corresponds to what we have called the static temporal and his A-Series to the dynamic temporal.

While time essentially involves both the A- and B-Series, both a dynamic and a static aspect, McTaggart claims that the A-Series is more basic, in that B-relations between events can be reduced to the A-determinations of the related events, but not vice versa. Events can bear B-relations to each other only because each of the related events has a determinate A-determination, just as harmonic relations can hold only between notes having an absolute pitch. Without the A-Series, the B-Series is no longer a temporal series. Therefore, if it can be shown that the A-Series is unreal the unreality of time will *ipso facto* have been established.

In his negative thesis, McTaggart attempts to demonstrate the contradictory and therefore unreal nature of the A-Series, thereby proving the unreality of time. His main argument is as follows. Every event in the A-Series, assuming that there is no first or last event, has all three mutually incompatible A-determinations—past, present, and future—and therefore involves a contradiction. We might try to explain away this seeming contradiction by saying that no event has more than one A-determination *at the same moment of time.* Rather it is the case that an event, such as M, has three A-determinations successively: for example, M has been future, will be past, and is now present. But to say this, McTaggart claims, must mean that M is future at a moment of past time, is past at a moment of future time, and is present at a moment of present time, respectively.

But this reply will not do, since it involves either a vicious circle or a vicious infinite regress. What we have done is to explain away the contradiction of an event in the first-order time-series having all three A-determinations by claiming that it has these determinations successively *at moments of time* in a second-order time-series. But since this second-order time-series is itself a time-series, its members, which are moments of time, must also form an A-Series, which means that every moment of time has all three mutually incompatible A-determinations. Therefore, we have explained away the contradiction inherent in the first-order A-Series only by introducing a second-order A-Series. And this is to reason in a vicious circle, since we must presuppose a second A-Series to rid the first A-Series of contradiction.

If we should try to remove the contradiction in this second-order A-Series, owing to all the moments of time in it having all three A-determinations, by saying that these moments of time are successively future, present, and past at moments of time in some third-order A-Series, we are merely transferring the contradiction to the third-order A-Series. We are launched on a vicious infinite regress, for at any point at which we stop we are left with a contradictory A-Series. The curse of contradiction pursues us down the infinite regress like a sort of baton that each A-Series passes on to the next.

The obvious opening move to make when confronted with an argument for the unreality of time is to appeal to commonsense facts. G. E. Moore pointed out that if time is unreal then there are no temporal facts: nothing is past, present, or future, and nothing is earlier or later than anything else. But, plainly, it is false that there are no temporal facts, for it is a fact that I am *presently* inscribing this sentence and that my breakfast yesterday *preceded* my lunch. Since the conclusion of McTaggart's argument entails a statement known to be false, it follows by the rule of *modus tollens* that his conclusion is false. Therefore, his argument contains either a false premiss or a non sequitur.

Valuable as this opening move is, it is of course nothing but an opening move, for it fails to locate and correct the source of McTaggart's error. The task of the philosopher is not just to remind us that we *were* born and that our breakfast *precedes* our lunch, but to give a coherent account of what we mean by these expressions. The account McTaggart gives seems to result in the absurd conclusion that time is unreal. What must be done is to replace McTaggart's account of time by a more adequate one that will not involve this absurd result. The serious answers to McTaggart's paradox are those which attempted to do just that.

Analysts have given three different types of serious answer: (1) The *B*-Series alone is sufficient to account for time; (2) the *A*-Series alone is sufficient, but the concept of the *A*-Series does not contain a contradiction; and (3) either the *A*- or the *B*-Series alone is sufficient to account for time, but they must not be confused with each other, otherwise paradoxes arise. Answer (1), to be called the "*B*-Theory Answer," attacks McTaggart's positive thesis because it denies that the *A*-Series is necessary for the reality of time. Answer (2), to be called the "*A*-Theory Answer," agrees with McTaggart's positive thesis that the *A*-Series is both necessary and fundamental, but denies his negative thesis that the concept of the *A*-Series is contradictory. Answer (3), to be called the "Either-Way-Will-Work Theory Answer," attempts to show that, whether we affirm or deny McTaggart's positive thesis,

D

we can give an adequate account of time. Each of these answers will now be considered separately, with particular attention to the competing analyses of time contained in the first two.

The B-*Theory Answer*

This answer to McTaggart, along with the theory of time contained in it, which will be called the "*B*-Theory," has been popular with those analysts whose approach to philosophy has been made from the side of mathematical logic and theoretical physics, which includes most logical atomists, logical positivists, and rational reconstructionists. The father of the modern version of the *B*-Theory is Bertrand Russell and among his followers are: R. B. Braithwaite, C. J. Ducasse, A. Grünbaum, A. J. Ayer, W. V. Quine, N. Goodman, D. C. Williams, J. J. C. Smart, and R. D. Bradley. Most of these philosophers would agree to the following four tenets, which together constitute the *B*-Theory of Time:

(1) The *A*-Series is reducible to the *B*-Series since *A*-determinations can be analyzed in terms of *B*-relations between events;

(2) Temporal becoming is psychological since *A*-determinations involve a *B*-relation to a perceiver;

(3) The *B*-Series is objective, all events being equally real; and

(4) Change is analyzable solely in terms of *B*-relations between qualitatively different states of a single thing.

Each of these tenets is vigorously defended in the paper by Donald Williams reprinted below. We shall consider each separately and then show how collectively they contain an answer to McTaggart's argument.

(1) *The A-Series is reducible to the B-Series since A-determinations can be analyzed in terms of B-relations between events.* The main contention of the *B*-Theory of Time is that events are not past, present, and future *simplici-*

ter, but are merely earlier than, simultaneous with,[1] and later than other events. Another way of stating this position is that "is present," "is past," and "is future," grammatical appearances to the contrary, are really tenseless two-place predicates that take event-expressions as their arguments. Nelson Goodman has attempted to reduce *A*-determinations to *B*-relations in this manner:

> The "past", "present", and "future" name no times. Rather the "is past at", the "is present at", and the "is future at" are tenseless two-place predicates that may respectively be translated by the tenseless predicates "is earlier than", "is at", and "is later than".[2]

If such a reduction of *A*-determinations to *B*-relations is sound, then the *A*-Series is reducible to the *B*-Series.

An event is not intrinsically past, present or future; it is merely earlier than, simultaneous with, or later than some other chosen event. The chosen event is usually either a *linguistic* event consisting in the utterance of a tensed statement about the event in question or a *mental* event consisting of a memory, perception, or expectation of it. The first method of reducing *A*-determinations to *B*-relations will be called the "Linguistic Reduction"; the second will be called the "Psychological Reduction," and will be considered under tenet (2). The aim of both reductions is to show that the *A*-Series can be reduced to the *B*-Series and that furthermore the *A*-Series is subjective, since *A*-determinations involve a reference to a subject as either a language-user or a perceiver. If there were no language-users or perceivers in the world there would still be a *B*-Series; however, there would be no *A*-Series. We shall now consider the Linguistic Reduction.

---

[1] We are counting *simultaneous with* as a *B*-relation. Our justification for this is that *simultaneity* (a) expresses a permanent temporal relation between events, as does *earlier than*, and (b) is needed in the construction of the *B*-Series, since *earlier than* relates classes of simultaneous events.

[2] N. Goodman, *The Structure of Appearance*, Cambridge, Mass., 1951, p. 295. Goodman's use of "is at" is synonymous with "is simultaneous with."

The first step in this reduction is to point out that
A-statements, that is, statements asserting that an event
has a given A-determination,[3] are, as Williams contends,
situational in that they reveal the speaker's temporal relation
to the event reported by his statement. To say that an event
occurred or will occur simply means that it occupies a time
earlier or later than my statement about it. More precisely,
an A-statement such as "M is past" means "M is earlier than
this utterance," in which "this utterance" refers to the occurrence of the sentence token within which it occurs, a token
being a pattern of sounds or ink marks, etc. For this reason
A-statements are said to be "token-reflexive."[4] The second
step in the Linguistic Reduction is to claim that the sole
function of tense is to express a B-relation between the reported event and the occurrence of the tensed sentence token
that reports the event. Therefore there is no reason why we
cannot translate the A-statement into a B-statement, that is,
a timelessly true or false statement describing a B-relation
between two events, which makes the relation explicit. "M
is present (past, future)" can be translated without loss of
meaning into the B-statement "M is (tenselessly) simultaneous with (earlier than, later than) the utterance of 'M is
present (past, future).'" This statement is made through the
use of a sentence that is freely repeatable, since it makes a
statement having the same truth-value whenever it is used.
Notice that it mentions rather than uses the tensed sentence
"M is present (past, future)." Thus this statement does not
assert that either M or the linguistic event consisting in the
utterance of the tensed sentence, "M is present (past, future)," is now present (past, future); it merely describes
a timeless B-relation between M and the tensed utterance
about M.

A more common technique for translating A-statements
into B-statements is to eliminate in the tenseless rendering
all reference to the original tensed statement and instead

[3] For a more precise definition of an A-statement, see pp. 295 ff
of my introduction to Section IV.

[4] For a fuller and more critical account of this see pp. 296–97
of my introduction to Section IV.

tenselessly to ascribe a date to the event reported by the original tensed statement; for example, "It is now raining" is rendered by "Rain is (tenselessly) at June 24, 1966." When we tenselessly ascribe a date to an event we show a timeless B-relation between this event and the event which serves as the origin of our calendar. In mathematical logic a date is one among sundry predicates that are tenselessly ascribed to something. The characterizing copula as well as the quantifier is tenseless. When a logician says, "There is a sea battle, which is at June 25, 1966," he is not saying that either the sea battle or the date in question is now present; for both the "is" of the existential quantifier ("There is a") and the "is" of the characterizing copula are tenseless. Quine has claimed that the tenseless mode of existential quantification fits in well with the tenseless space-time talk of Minkowskian geometry employed in relativity theory. In relativity theory, supposedly, a thing is represented as a four-dimensional worm consisting of three-dimensional cross sections strung along the fourth dimension of time. The physicist speaks in a tenseless mode about these spatial cross sections, saying, for example, that a certain cross section is tenselessly earlier or later than some other cross section. Williams' "manifold theory of time" is largely derived from such considerations. The assumption here is that what is good for physics is also good for logic and metaphysics.

Regardless of which technique we use for translating A-statements into B-statements, we are left with tenseless propositions about B-relations that are true or false once and for all, even if the original A-statement was about a contingent event in the future. The fact that language can be detensed without loss of meaning shows that A-determinations are not intrinsic to events.

(2) *Temporal becoming is psychological since* A-*determinations involve a* B-*relation to a perceiver.* The Psychological Reduction can be viewed as a supplement to the Linguistic Reduction. To the claim that A-determinations indicate B-relations between reported events and utterances, the Psychological Reduction adds the claim that A-determina-

tions also *express* the characteristic state of belief of the
utterer—whether he remembers, perceives, or anticipates the
reported event. Russell has argued that A-determinations are
notions derived from psychology, since to understand them
reference must be made to consciousness. To understand
what is meant by "past" we must make one of our past experiences an object of experience, while to understand the
meaning of "present" we must refer to one of our sensations,
since "to be present" means to be the object of a sensation.
Thus, in a world devoid of sentient organisms there no more
would be A-determinations than there would be pains. And
since A-determinations are psychological it follows that temporal becoming is also. The temporal becoming of a physical
event is analyzable in terms of its bearing different B-relations
to a series of mental events consisting of an expectation,
perception, and memory, experienced by a single mind.
Whether becoming is mind-dependent will be one of the
major themes in Section IV on Human Time.

(3) *The B-Series is objective, all events being equally
real.* What is objectively real is the B-Series. The A-determinations of events are subjective in the sense of being relative
to our temporal perspective as either utterer or perceiver.
However, there could be B-relations in a world devoid of
language-users or perceivers, since these relations do not involve reference to a subject; they are objective relations between events, neither of which need be a mental or linguistic
event. Corresponding to our timeless B-statements describing
B-relations between events is a timeless series of events—the
B-Series. All events of history form a *totum simul*. As Williams says, past, present, and future are equally real and
determinate by a necessity of logic, since we can formulate
timelessly true or false propositions about B-relations between
events.

(4) *Change is analyzable solely in terms of B-relations
between qualitatively different states of a single thing.* It is
claimed that the B-Series alone is sufficient to account for
(i) changes *of* time, that is, changes in the A-determi-

nations of events, and (ii) changes *in* time, that is, qualitative and quantitative changes of things. The first type of change is temporal becoming, and we have already seen how it is analyzable in terms of *B*-relations between events, in which one of the relata is either a linguistic event (the Linguistic Reduction) or a mental event (the Psychological Reduction).

Qualitative and quantitative change—change *in* time—is analyzed by Russell solely in terms of the *B*-Series as follows:

> Change is the difference, in respect of truth or falsehood, between a proposition concerning an entity and a time *T* and a proposition concerning the same entity and another time *T'*, provided that the two propositions differ only by the fact that *T* occurs in the one where *T'* occurs in the other.[5]

In expounding this position, Braithwaite said that change *in* time "consists in the fact that a different relation holds between the thing (a substance in the ordinary sense) and a certain property at one of the times than holds at the other time."[6] An empirical thing or substance is reducible to a certain series of successive events, such that the members of any one such series are intimately interconnected by certain spatial and causal relations that do not interconnect members of any two such series. What we mean by the change of a thing *in* time is a sequence of *successive* events all regarded as states of one thing. Such changes are analyzable solely in terms of *B*-relations between events comprising the history of a single thing without invoking the becoming of these events. This view of change underlies Williams' claim that time is nothing but a certain ordered extension of events.

Answer to McTaggart's Paradox. McTaggart, in arguing for the necessity of the *A*-Series, claimed that change, without which there could not be time, required the *A*-Series. It is logically impossible for any features of the *B*-Series to

[5] Bertrand Russell, *The Principles of Mathematics*, Cambridge, 1903, p. 469.
[6] R. Braithwaite, "Time and Change," *Aristotelian Society Supp. Vol.* 8 (1928), 169.

change: there can be no increase or decrease in its membership, no change in the qualities of any event included in it,
and no change in the B-relations between its members.
Therefore, by a process of elimination, the only possible
change is change in the A-determination of an event. The
B-Theory claims that McTaggart considered only changes
in *events* and thus overlooked one possible candidate for the
title of change, namely changes in *things*. And in tenet (4)
of the B-Theory it was argued that such changes in things—
changes *in* time—require only the B-Series. Therefore, the
reality of time does not require that there be an A-Series.
McTaggart's reply to this way of countering his argument is
contained in the passage from his *Nature of Existence* that
is reprinted in this section.

While the B-Theory denies the necessity of the A-Series,
it still cannot countenance McTaggart's claim that the
A-Series is contradictory; for in tenet (1) it claims that the
A-Series is reducible to the B-Series. Such a reduction would
not be possible if the A-Series really harbored a contradiction.
Therefore it behooves B-Theorists to answer McTaggart's
main argument to the effect that the A-Series is contradictory
because every one of its members has all three mutually
incompatible A-determinations. The B-theorists' way of explaining away this alleged contradiction is to claim, in accordance with their Linguistic and Psychological Reductions,
that the A-determinations of past, present, and future are
really disguised B-relations, meaning respectively earlier
than, simultaneous with, and later than. There is no more a
contradiction in an event being past, present, and future
than there is in an event being earlier than, simultaneous
with, and later than. A contradiction would emerge only if
an event had two or more of these temporal relations to one
and the same event; but this McTaggart has never shown to
be the case. By the Linguistic Reduction it is shown that an
event is past, present, and future only in the elliptical sense
of being respectively earlier than a tensed statement that it
did occur, simultaneous with a statement that it is occurring,
and later than a statement that it will occur. And by the
Psychological Reduction it is claimed that an event has these

three A-determinations only in virtue of its being respectively earlier than a memory of it, simultaneous with a perception of it, and later than an expectation of it.

The A-Theory Answer

Another answer to McTaggart is based on what we shall call the "A-Theory of Time." The A-Theory of Time received its most articulate formulation in the work of C. D. Broad, which is reprinted in this section, and it has been prevalent among those philosophers whose main concern is to clarify ordinary language by studying the way words are used in various contexts. Among those holding views in some way similar to Broad's are L. S. Stebbing, J. Wisdom, P. Marhenke, A. N. Prior, D. Pears, W. Sellars, S. Hampshire, P. F. Strawson, and J. N. Findlay. As these men have far less in common than the defenders of the B-Theory, it is more difficult to abstract a set of common tenets from their writings; but I believe that the following four are representative of their work:

(1) The B-Series is reducible to the A-Series since B-relations can be analyzed in terms of A-determinations;

(2) Temporal becoming is intrinsic to all events;

(3) There are important ontological differences between the past and the future; and

(4) Change requires the A-Series.

Each of these tenets is either the contradictory or the contrary of the B-Theory tenet of the same number. As before, we shall discuss each tenet separately and then show how together they constitute an answer to McTaggart.

(1) *The B-Series is reducible to the A-Series since B-relations can be analyzed in terms of A-determinations.* The defenders of the A-Theory agree with McTaggart's positive thesis that the A-Series is both necessary and fundamental. Their arguments attempt to show that B-relations are *temporal* relations only because their relata have A-determinations and change in respect to them.

D*

One argument, which is contained in the Broad selection, states that what makes the *B*-Series a temporal series is that its members form an *A*-Series and change in respect to their *A*-determinations. In the course of his argument Broad makes two claims, one highly controversial and the other acceptable even to those holding the *B*-Theory of Time. The non-controversial claim is that a temporal series differs from a spatial one in that, while both have an intrinsic order, only the temporal has an intrinsic direction or sense. The controversial claim is that the direction of a temporal series is due to the fact that its members undergo temporal becoming.

A linear spatial order of one dimension has an intrinsic order, because, given any three members of this order, one of them will appear to be between the other two regardless of what position they are viewed from. This order, however, does not have an intrinsic direction because whether one member of it is to the right of another will depend on the position from which they are viewed. An observer in the orchestra will see Warren standing to the right of Tebaldi, but an observer backstage will see Warren to the left of Tebaldi. A linear spatial order has a direction only in reference to the right and left hands of an *external* observer; thus its direction is extrinsic to the order itself. The spatial relation *to the right of* is triadic, since it involves a relation to some third position from which one object is to the right of another. In a linear spatial series there is no asymmetric dyadic relation intrinsic to the series.

Like a spatial series of one dimension, a temporal series has an intrinsic order, but in addition it has an intrinsic direction; since its generating relation—*earlier than*—is a genuine dyadic relation. Max Black, who has made an analysis of temporal relations similar to Broad's, states that temporal relations, unlike spatial ones, are not *incomplete relations,* since they do not involve reference to some third term.[7] If we say that X is earlier than Y we do not have to specify some third position from which X and Y are viewed, as we do when we say that X is to the right of Y. When we are told

[7] M. Black, "The 'Direction' of Time," *Analysis,* 19 (1959), 60.

that Warren's singing of a rousing aria was earlier than his dropping dead we do not ask from what third position these events were viewed. Broad claims that temporal betweenness is not fundamental (as is spatial betweenness) because it is definable in terms of the genuinely dyadic relation of *earlier than* taken twice over.

The controversial claim made by Broad is that becoming, what he calls the "transitory aspect of temporal facts," is of the very essence of time, and that without it a temporal series would not have an intrinsic direction, thereby being indistinguishable from a spatial order. It is because and only because the events comprising a *B*-Series undergo temporal becoming that we can distinguish a *B*-Series from nontemporal series. We cannot do this solely in terms of the logical properties of the generating relation of the *B*-Series— its being asymmetric, transitive, and irreflexive—since there are non-temporal relations, such as *larger than*, which have the same logical properties: and yet we know that a numberseries is basically different from a time-series. It is temporal becoming that causes all analogies between space and time to break down. When we represent time by a line we cannot account for the direction of a time-series. If direction is to be introduced into a one-dimensional spatial order this must be done extrinsically, either by reference to motion along the line (and therefore including time, since motion takes time), or by reference to the right and left hands of an external observer. The intrinsic direction of the *B*-Series is therefore essentially bound up with the temporal becoming of its members.[8]

This argument of Broad's, if it can be called such, will not convince any *B*-Theorist. He would agree with Broad that *earlier than* is a dyadic relation and that a time-series is *sui generis*, but would deny that these two facts are dependent upon temporal becoming. What makes a time-series unique, he would contend, is that its generating relation is a *temporal* relation. Certain empirically minded *B*-Theorists would argue, as does Adolf Grünbaum in his article on "The Status of

[8] Cf. C. D. Broad, *Scientific Thought*, London, 1925, pp. 57–58.

Temporal Becoming" in Section IV, that what bestows a direction on a time-series, what makes it irreversible or anisotropic, are certain physical asymmetries, such as increase of entropy, which are intrinsic to the B-Series of physical events. The efforts of such theorists to explicate the direction of time make no reference to temporal becoming, being concerned only with law-like asymmetries and/or boundary condition asymmetries between earlier and later times.

The second argument presented by Broad and other proponents of the A-Theory of Time for the necessity of the A-Series is that B-relations are definable or analyzable in terms of A-determinations. In addition to showing the necessity for the A-Series, this is also an argument for the fundamentality of the A-Series, since it attempts to show that the B-Series is reducible to the A-Series. This argument claims that the meaning of "M is (tenselessly) earlier than N" is "When M is present N is future and when N is present M is past."

Since B-relations are analyzable or definable in terms of A-determinations, it follows that A-statements cannot be translated without loss of meaning into B-statements, that is, freely repeatable statements that describe a B-relation between two events. The main difficulty with all such translations is that the B-statement does not assert, as does the A-statement of which it is a rendering, whether the reported event is past, present, or future. There is an asymmetry in information between A- and B-statements. When I tell you that X is present and Y is future I have already told you that X is earlier than Y; but if instead I had asserted the latter B-statement I would not have told you the X is present or that Y is future. Attempts to detense language by the use of dates fail for the same reason.

We are not able to assimilate tensed existential statements to the tenseless mold of existential quantification, as the B-Theory demands. Ordinary language, as Strawson and Hampshire have argued, is an irreducibly tensed-substance language because of necessity it must contain referring expressions, and only tensed statements can refer successfully to unique objects and events. In order to single out and describe some object in our immediate environment we must speak in a tensed mode, using ourselves as centers of spatio-temporal orientation. When we speak about objects (or events) in ordinary contexts the question of whether they exist (or occur) now is always relevant. For this reason the method of existential quantification employed in mathematical logic cannot do justice to ordinary language.

Broad attacks the first step in the Linguistic Reduction, for he denies that A-statements refer to themselves. Even if it were possible for these statements to be self-referring (token-reflexive), it would still not eliminate a reference to the A-determinations of events, for supposedly the tensed utterance to which I refer when I make a tensed statement differs from all my other utterances in that it is present whilst they are past or future. In other words, if "X is present" means "X is simultaneous with this utterance" there is still a reference to the A-determination of an event, for by "this utterance" I mean "the utterance I am making at present." If my tensed utterances are intrinsically past, present, and future, how is it possible for events bearing B-relations to these utterances not also to be intrinsically past, present, and future?

(2) *Temporal becoming is intrinsic to all events.* A similar argument can be employed against the Psychological Reduction, which said that events have A-determinations only in relation to a perceiver. But once again this does not reduce A-determinations to B-relations, because the series of mental events that runs concurrently with the series of physical events forms an A-Series. I am sure that my own mental events temporally become. If the mental acts of an observer are intrinsically past, present, and future, then the objects of these acts, which are contemporaneous with them, must likewise be intrinsically past, present, and future. Becoming cannot be intrinsic to one series of events without being intrinsic to the other. Grünbaum attempts to refute this argument in his piece on "The Status of Temporal Becoming."

(3) *There are important ontological differences between the past and the future.* The A-Series is objective, not being

dependent upon a language-user or perceiver. Several defenders of the A-Theory have gone on to claim that because temporal becoming is objective there are significant ontological differences between past and future events, consisting in the fact that the future is open, a realm of possibilities, while the past is closed, a realm of actualities. This ontological difference reveals itself in certain logical asymmetries in our ways of talking about the past and future in that (i) statements about the future must be general in logical form while statements about the past can be singular, and (ii) all statements about the past are either true or false while some statements about the future are neither true nor false now. These matters will be discussed at length in Section III.

(4) *Change requires the* A-*Series.* The B-Theory analyzed change *in* time in terms of B-relations between events or states belonging to the history of a single thing. The A-Theory challenges this analysis, for in tenet (1) it claims that B-relations are dependent upon A-determinations. From this it follows that (a) since change *in* time necessarily involves B-relations between events and (b) since B-relations depend upon the A-determinations of the events related, that there can be no change *in* time without the A-Series. Thus the claim that there can be no change in time without the A-Series is a corollary of tenet (1). Only if B-relations were independent of A-determinations could change in time be explained solely in terms of B-relations between events.

Broad claims that change *of* time—temporal becoming—is *sui generis* and that any attempt to represent it in terms of change *in* time is vicious. Though a thing exists both before and after it undergoes some qualitative or quantitative change, an event does not exist both before and after it becomes present. When we represent becoming by analogy with motion along a one-dimensional spatial order we are reducing change of time to change in time. We think of the present as a spotlight that plays along a line of chorus-girl-like events; but this involves us in the pseudoproblem of how fast—how many seconds per second—the spotlight moves. All representations of becoming in terms of some kind of motion (or other change in time) involve a vicious circle, since motion (or any other change in time) presupposes becoming.

Answer to McTaggart. The A-Theory agrees with McTaggart's positive thesis concerning the necessity and fundamentality of the A-Series, but disagrees with his negative doctrine that the A-Series involves a contradiction. McTaggart's inability to combine the static view of time exemplified in his B-Series with the dynamic view contained in his A-Series is due to his substantialization of the events in the B-Series, which causes him to represent temporal becoming as if it were some sort of motion, the A-Series moving up the B-Series. McTaggart substantialized events because he thought—mistakenly—that the events in the B-Series must always coexist since B-relations are permanent. The events in the B-Series are now treated like a line of chorus girls, who exist both before and after they do their brief bit in the spotlight of presentness. But that view involves us in the above difficulties of reducing becoming to movement. Broad claims that there is no incompatibility between becoming and the "permanency" of B-relations between events.

The B-Theory explained away the contradiction inherent in each event's having all three A-determinations by showing that these determinations are reducible to B-relations. The A-Theory cannot avail itself of this way out, since it denies that such a reduction is possible. Rather it claims that since temporal becoming is intrinsic to all events, there is no contradiction to be explained away. A contradiction would arise only if in a single utterance an event was asserted to have two or more A-determinations, but there is nothing in our temporal experiences to warrant making such a statement. A-determinations are unanalyzable. "M is present" entails, but does not mean, according to Stebbing and Wisdom, "M is present at a moment which is present." McTaggart's infinite regress, it follows, is benign: it is a regress of entailings and not meanings. Therefore, there is no need to analyze statements predicating an A-determination of an event in terms of a moment of time in some second-order A-Series at which the event has this A-determination.

The Either-Way-Will-Work Theory Answer

The third answer to McTaggart, which is put forth by J. N. Findlay and J. J. C. Smart, is based on a theory of time that claims that either the *A*- or the *B*-Series alone is a sufficient account of time and change, and paradoxes arise only if one is confused with the other. The essential tenet of this theory is that the tensed and tenseless modes of speaking are both equally workable and legitimate: everything sayable in a language containing only *A*-statements is sayable equally well in a language containing only *B*-statements, and vice versa. Herein the Either-Way-Will-Work Theory is closer to the *B*-Theory than to the *A*-Theory, since one of the essential tenets of the *A*-Theory is a denial that *A*-statements can be rendered without loss of meaning by *B*-statements.

Findlay points out in his article in this section that while the tensed and tenseless modes of speaking are both equally workable and legitimate, there nevertheless are certain practical advantages in speaking tenselessly, since our statements are then timelessly true or false independently of when they are made. The ideal of science is to eliminate tenses so that statements can be freely repeatable. In the tensed mode of speaking we must systematically alter the tense of our statement depending on our *B*-relation to the reported event. McTaggart's paradox results from the attempt to speak at one and the same time in both the tensed and tenseless modes. In certain "moods" we become enamored with the time-independence of our tenseless mode of speaking, and we attempt to apply this ideal to the tensed mode: we are then apt to think that there is something contradictory about tenses since we must continually change the tense of our statements with the passage of time. When McTaggart claims that the *A*-Series is contradictory because every event in it has all three *A*-determinations, he is applying the ideal of the tenseless mode of speaking to the tensed mode. A contradiction results only if we expect tensed statements to have the same logical behavior as tenseless ones, that is, to be freely repeatable.

The brief paper by Smart defends a similar thesis. Smart distinguishes between an objectionable and an unobjectionable sense of spatializing time. In the objectionable sense we conceive of events as being in time in exactly the same way that ordinary empirical substances are in space. We must conceive of them as coexisting substances which endure in some meta-time. In the unobjectionable sense of spatializing time we treat time as a fourth dimension, as in the four-dimensional space-time geometry of Minkowski. Herein time is a dimension in which the three-dimensional spatial cross sections are strung out in accordance with the timeless B-relations between them. A system of solid geometry, regardless of how many dimensions it deals with, has no reference to change or time. In a four-dimensional geometry we do not think of space or the network of spatial relations as enduring or lasting throughout some period of time. When we represent time spatially as a timeless network of B-relations we must not apply tensed concepts of enduring or changing to these relations. If we do, we are spatializing time in the objectionable sense, since we would then need a meta-time for this change or changelessness to be in. This is the start of the famous infinite regress of times changing or enduring within times.[9]

[9] For a fuller and more critical discussion of the material contained in this introduction as well as the introductions to Sections III and IV, see my book, *The Language of Time*, Routledge & Kegan Paul, London, 1967.

TIME

J. M. E. MC TAGGART

JOHN MCTAGGART ELLIS MCTAGGART (1866–1925) was a
Fellow of Trinity College, Cambridge. His major works include *Studies in Hegelian Cosmology, Some Dogmas of Religion,* and *The Nature of Existence.*

It will be convenient to begin our enquiry by asking
whether anything existent can possess the characteristic of
being in time. I shall endeavour to prove that it cannot.

It seems highly paradoxical to assert that time is unreal,
and that all statements which involve its reality are erroneous. Such an assertion involves a departure from the natural
position of mankind which is far greater than that involved
in the assertion of the unreality of space or the unreality of
matter. For in each man's experience there is a part—his own
states as known to him by introspection—which does not even
appear to be spatial or material. But we have no experience
which does not appear to be temporal. Even our judgments
that time is unreal appear to be themselves in time.

Yet in all ages and in all parts of the world the belief in
the unreality of time has shown itself to be singularly persistent. In the philosophy and religion of the West—and still
more, I suppose, in the philosophy and religion of the East—
we find that the doctrine of the unreality of time continually
recurs. Neither philosophy nor religion ever hold themselves
apart from mysticism for any long period, and almost all
mysticism denies the reality of time. In philosophy, time is
treated as unreal by Spinoza, by Kant, and by Hegel. Among

FROM J. M. E. McTaggart, *The Nature of Existence,* Volume
II, Cambridge University Press, 1927, Book V, Chapter 33. Reprinted by permission of the publishers.

more modern thinkers, the same view is taken by Mr Bradley. Such a concurrence of opinion is highly significant, and is not the less significant because the doctrine takes such different forms, and is supported by such different arguments.

I believe that nothing that exists can be temporal, and that therefore time is unreal. But I believe it for reasons which are not put forward by any of the philosophers I have just mentioned.

Positions in time, as time appears to us *primâ facie,* are distinguished in two ways. Each position is Earlier than some and Later than some of the other positions. To constitute such a series there is required a transitive asymmetrical relation, and a collection of terms such that, of any two of them, either the first is in this relation to the second, or the second is in this relation to the first. We may take here either the relation of "earlier than" or the relation of "later than," both of which, of course, are transitive and asymmetrical. If we take the first, then the terms have to be such that, of any two of them, either the first is earlier than the second, or the second is earlier than the first.

In the second place, each position is either Past, Present, or Future. The distinctions of the former class are permanent, while those of the latter are not. If M is ever earlier than N, it is always earlier. But an event, which is now present, was future, and will be past.

Since distinctions of the first class are permanent, it might be thought that they were more objective, and more essential to the nature of time, than those of the second class. I believe, however, that this would be a mistake, and that the distinction of past, present, and future is as *essential* to time as the distinction of earlier and later, while in a certain sense it may . . . be regarded as more *fundamental* than the distinction of earlier and later. And it is because the distinctions of past, present, and future seem to me to be essential for time, that I regard time as unreal.

For the sake of brevity I shall give the name of the A series to that series of positions which runs from the far past through the near past to the present, and then from the present through the near future to the far future, or conversely. The series of positions which runs from earlier to later, or conversely, I shall call the B series. The contents of any position in time form an event. The varied simultaneous contents of a single position are, of course, a plurality of events. But, like any other substance, they form a group, and this group is a compound substance. And a compound substance consisting of simultaneous events may properly be spoken of as itself an event.[1]

The first question which we must consider is whether it is essential to the reality of time that its events should form an A series as well as a B series. It is clear, to begin with, that, in present experience, we never *observe* events in time except as forming both these series. We perceive events in time as being present, and those are the only events which we actually perceive. And all other events which, by memory or by inference, we believe to be real, we regard as present, past, or future. Thus the events of time as observed by us form an A series.

It might be said, however, that this is merely subjective.

[1] It is very usual to contemplate time by the help of a metaphor of spatial movement. But spatial movement in which direction? The movement of time consists in the fact that later and later terms pass into the present, or—which is the same fact expressed in another way—that presentness passes to later and later terms. If we take it the first way, we are taking the B series as sliding along a fixed A series. If we take it the second way, we are taking the A series as sliding along a fixed B series. In the first case time presents itself as a movement from future to past. In the second case it presents itself as a movement from earlier to later. And this explains why we say that events come out of the future, while we say that we ourselves move towards the future. For each man identifies himself especially with his present state, as against his future or his past, since it is the only one which he is directly perceiving. And this leads him to say that he is moving with the present towards later events. And as those events are now future, he says that he is moving towards the future.

Thus the question as to the movement of time is ambiguous. But if we ask what is the movement of either series, the question is not ambiguous. The movement of the A series along the B series is from earlier to later. The movement of the B series along the A series is from future to past.

It might be the case that the distinction of positions in time into past, present, and future, is only a constant illusion of our minds, and that the real nature of time contains only the distinctions of the *B* series—the distinctions of earlier and later. In that case we should not perceive time as it really is, though we might be able to *think* of it as it really is.

This is not a very common view, but it requires careful consideration. I believe it to be untenable, because, as I said above, it seems to me that the *A* series is essential to the nature of time, and that any difficulty in the way of regarding the *A* series as real is equally a difficulty in the way of regarding time as real.

It would, I suppose, be universally admitted that time involves change. In ordinary language, indeed, we say that something can remain unchanged through time. But there could be no time if nothing changed. And if anything changes, then all other things change with it. For its change must change some of their relations to it, and so their relational qualities. The fall of a sand-castle on the English coast changes the nature of the Great Pyramid.

If, then, a *B* series without an *A* series can constitute time, change must be possible without an *A* series. Let us suppose that the distinctions of past, present, and future do not apply to reality. In that case, can change apply to reality?

What, on this supposition, could it be that changes? Can we say that, in a time which formed a *B* series but not an *A* series, the change consisted in the fact that the event ceased to be an event, while another event began to be an event? If this were the case, we should certainly have got a change.

But this is impossible. If *N* is ever earlier than *O* and later than *M*, it will always be, and has always been, earlier than *O* and later than *M*, since the relations of earlier and later are permanent. *N* will thus always be in a *B* series. And as, by our present hypothesis, a *B* series by itself constitutes time, *N* will always have a position in a time-series, and always has had one. That is, it always has been an event, and always will be one, and cannot begin or cease to be an event.

Or shall we say that one event *M* merges itself into another event *N*, while still preserving a certain identity by means of an unchanged element, so that it can be said, not merely that M has ceased and N begun, but that it is M which has become N? Still the same difficulty recurs. M and N may have a common element, but they are not the same event, or there would be no change. If, therefore, M changed into N at a certain moment, then at that moment, M would have ceased to be M, and N would have begun to be N. This involves that, at that moment, M would have ceased to be an event, and N would have begun to be an event. And we saw, in the last paragraph, that, on our present hypothesis, this is impossible.

Nor can such change be looked for in the different moments of absolute time, even if such moments should exist. For the same argument will apply here. Each such moment will have its own place in the B series, since each would be earlier or later than each of the others. And, as the B series depends on permanent relations, no moment could ever cease to be, nor could it become another moment.

Change, then, cannot arise from an event ceasing to be an event, nor from one event changing into another. In what other way can it arise? If the characteristics of an event change, then there is certainly change. But what characteristics of an event can change? It seems to me that there is only one class of such characteristics. And that class consists of the determinations of the event in question by the terms of the A series.

Take any event—the death of Queen Anne, for example— and consider what changes can take place in its characteristics. That it is a death, that it is the death of Anne Stuart, that it has such causes, that it has such effects—every characteristic of this sort never changes. "Before the stars saw one another plain," the event in question was the death of a Queen. At the last moment of time—if time has a last moment—it will still be the death of a Queen. And in every respect but one, it is equally devoid of change. But in one respect it does change. It was once an event in the far future. It became every moment an event in the nearer future. At last it was present. Then it became past, and will always remain past, though every moment it becomes further and further past.[2]

Such characteristics as these are the only characteristics which can change. And, therefore, if there is any change, it must be looked for in the A series, and in the A series alone. If there is no real A series, there is no real change. The B series, therefore, is not by itself sufficient to constitute time, since time involves change.

The B series, however, cannot exist except as temporal, since earlier and later, which are the relations which connect its terms, are clearly time-relations. So it follows that there can be no B series when there is no A series, since without an A series there is no time.

We must now consider three objections[3] which have been made to this position. The first is involved in the view of time which has been taken by Mr Russell, according to which past, present, and future do not belong to time *per se*, but only in relation to a knowing subject. An assertion that N is present means that it is simultaneous with that assertion, an assertion that it is past or future means that it is earlier or later than that assertion. Thus it is only past, present, or future, in relation to some assertion. If there were no consciousness, there would be events which were earlier and later than others, but nothing would be in any sense past, present, or future. And if there were events earlier than any consciousness, those events would never be future or present, though they could be past.

If N were ever present, past, or future in relation to some assertion V, it would always be so, since whatever is ever simultaneous to, earlier than, or later than, V, will always

[2] The past, therefore, is always changing, if the A series is real at all, since at each moment a past event is further in the past than it was before. This result follows from the reality of the A series, and is independent of the truth of our view that all change depends exclusively on the A series. It is worth while to notice this, since most people combine the view that the A series is real with the view that the past cannot change—a combination which is inconsistent.

[3] [The discussion of the second and third of these objections has been omitted from the selection.—Ed.]

be so. What, then, is change? We find Mr Russell's views
on this subject in his *Principles of Mathematics*, Section 442.
"Change is the difference, in respect of truth or falsehood,
between a proposition concerning an entity and the time T,
and a proposition concerning the same entity and the time
T', provided that these propositions differ only by the fact
that T occurs in the one where T' occurs in the other." That
is to say, there is change, on Mr Russell's view, if the proposition "at the time T my poker is hot" is true, and the proposition "at the time T' my poker is hot" is false.

I am unable to agree with Mr Russell. I should, indeed,
admit that, when two such propositions were respectively
true and false, there would be change. But then I maintain
that there can be no time without an A series. If, with Mr
Russell, we reject the A series, it seems to me that change
goes with it, and that therefore time, for which change is
essential, goes too. In other words, if the A series is rejected,
no proposition of the type "at the time T my poker is hot"
can ever be true, because there would be no time.

It will be noticed that Mr Russell looks for change, not in
the events in the time-series, but in the entity to which those
events happen, or of which they are states. If my poker, for
example, is hot on a particular Monday, and never before or
since, the event of the poker being hot does not change. But
the poker changes, because there is a time when this event
is happening to it, and a time when it is not happening to it.

But this makes no change in the qualities of the poker. It
is always a quality of that poker that it is one which is hot
on that particular Monday. And it is always a quality of that
poker that it is one which is not hot at any other time. Both
these qualities are true of it at any time—the time when it
is hot and the time when it is cold. And therefore it seems
to be erroneous to say that there is any change in the poker.
The fact that it is hot at one point in a series and cold at
other points cannot give change, if neither of these facts
change—and neither of them does. Nor does any other fact
about the poker change, unless its presentness, pastness, or
futurity change.

Let us consider the case of another sort of series. The

meridian of Greenwich passes through a series of degrees of latitude. And we can find two points in this series, S and S', such that the proposition "at S the meridian of Greenwich is within the United Kingdom" is true, while the proposition "at S' the meridian of Greenwich is within the United Kingdom" is false. But no one would say that this gave us change. Why should we say so in the case of the other series?

Of course there is a satisfactory answer to this question if we are correct in speaking of the other series as a time-series. For where there is time, there is change. But then the whole question is whether it is a time-series. My contention is that if we remove the A series from the *primâ facie* nature of time, we are left with a series which is not temporal, and which allows change no more than the series of latitudes does.

If, as I have maintained, there can be no change unless facts change, then there can be no change without an A series. For, as we saw with the death of Queen Anne, and also in the case of the poker, no fact about anything can change, unless it is a fact about its place in the A series. Whatever other qualities it has, it has always. But that which is future will not always be future, and that which was past was not always past.

It follows from what we have said that there can be no change unless some propositions are sometimes true and sometimes false. This is the case of propositions which deal with the place of anything in the A series—"the battle of Waterloo is in the past," "it is now raining." But it is not the case with any other propositions.

Mr Russell holds that such propositions are ambiguous, and that to make them definite we must substitute propositions which are always true or always false—"the battle of Waterloo is earlier than this judgment," "the fall of rain is simultaneous with this judgment." If he is right, all judgments are either always true, or always false. Then, I maintain, no facts change. And then, I maintain, there is no change at all.

I hold, as Mr Russell does, that there is no A series. (My reasons for this will be given below, pp. 94–97.) And . . . I regard the reality lying behind the appearance of the A series in a manner not completely unlike that which Mr Russell has adopted. The difference between us is that he thinks that, when the *A* series is rejected, change, time, and the *B* series can still be kept, while I maintain that its rejection involves the rejection of change, and, consequently, of time, and of the *B* series. . . .

We conclude, then, that the distinctions of past, present, and future are essential to time, and that, if the distinctions are never true of reality, then no reality is in time. This view, whether true or false, has nothing surprising in it. It was pointed out above that we always perceive time as having these distinctions. And it has generally been held that their connection with time is a real characteristic of time, and not an illusion due to the way in which we perceive it. Most philosophers, whether they did or did not believe time to be true of reality, have regarded the distinctions of the *A* series as essential to time.

When the opposite view has been maintained it has generally been, I believe, because it was held (rightly, as I shall try to show) that the distinctions of past, present, and future cannot be true of reality, and that consequently, if the reality of time is to be saved, the distinction in question must be shown to be unessential to time. The presumption, it was held, was for the reality of time, and this would give us a reason for rejecting the *A* series as unessential to time. But, of course, this could only give a presumption. If the analysis of the nature of time has shown that, by removing the *A* series, time is destroyed, this line of argument is no longer open.

I now pass to the second part of my task. Having, as it seems to me, succeeded in proving that there can be no time without an *A* series, it remains to prove that an *A* series cannot exist, and that therefore time cannot exist. This would involve that time is not real at all, since it is admitted that the only way in which time can be real is by existing. . . .

Past, present, and future are incompatible determinations. Every event must be one or the other, but no event can be more than one. If I say that any event is past, that implies that it is neither present nor future, and so with the others. And this exclusiveness is essential to change, and therefore to time. For the only change we can get is from future to present, and from present to past.

The characteristics, therefore, are incompatible. But every event has them all.[4] If M is past, it has been present and future. If it is future, it will be present and past. If it is present, it has been future and will be past. Thus all the three characteristics belong to each event. How is this consistent with their being incompatible?

It may seem that this can easily be explained. Indeed, it has been impossible to state the difficulty without almost giving the explanation, since our language has verb-forms for the past, present, and future, but no form that is common to all three. It is never true, the answer will run, that M *is* present, past, and future. It *is* present, *will be* past, and *has been* future. Or it *is* past, and *has been* future and present, or again *is* future, and *will be* present and past. The characteristics are only incompatible when they are simultaneous, and there is no contradiction to this in the fact that each term has all of them successively.

But what is meant by "has been" and "will be"? And what is meant by "is," when, as here, it is used with a temporal meaning, and not simply for predication? When we say that X has been Y, we are asserting X to be Y at a moment of past time. When we say that X will be Y, we are asserting X to be Y at a moment of future time. When we say that X is Y (in the temporal sense of "is"), we are asserting X to be Y at a moment of present time.

Thus our first statement about M—that it is present, will be past, and has been future—means that M is present at a moment of present time, past at some moment of future time, and future at some moment of past time. But every moment, like every event, is both past, present, and future. And so a

----

[4] If the time-series has a first term, that term will never be future, and if it has a last term, that term will never be past. But the first term, in that case, will be present and past, and the last term will be future and present. And the possession of two incompatible characteristics raises the same difficulty as the possession of three.

similar difficulty arises. If M is present, there is no moment of past time at which it is past. But the moments of future time, in which it is past, are equally moments of past time, in which it cannot be past. Again, that M is future and will be present and past means that M is future at a moment of present time, and present and past at different moments of future time. In that case it cannot be present or past at any moments of past time. But all the moments of future time, in which M will be present or past, are equally moments of past time.

And thus again we get a contradiction, since the moments at which M has any one of the three determinations of the A series are also moments at which it cannot have that determination. If we try to avoid this by saying of these moments what had been previously said of M itself—that some moment, for example, is future, and will be present and past— then "is" and "will be" have the same meaning as before. Our statement, then, means that the moment in question is future at a present moment, and will be present and past at different moments of future time. This, of course, is the same difficulty over again. And so on infinitely.

Such an infinity is vicious. The attribution of the characteristics past, present, and future to the terms of any series leads to a contradiction, unless it is specified that they have them successively. This means, as we have seen, that they have them in relation to terms specified as past, present, and future. These again, to avoid a like contradiction, must in turn be specified as past, present, and future. And, since this continues infinitely, the first set of terms never escapes from contradiction at all.[5]

The contradiction, it will be seen, would arise in the same way supposing that pastness, presentness, and futurity were

[5] It may be worth while to point out that the vicious infinite has not arisen from the impossibility of *defining* past, present, and future, without using the terms in their own definitions. On the contrary, we have admitted these terms to be indefinable. It arises from the fact that the nature of the terms involves a contradiction, and that the attempt to remove the contradiction involves the employment of the terms, and the generation of a similar contradiction.

original qualities, and not, as we have decided that they are, relations. For it would still be the case that they were characteristics which were incompatible with one another, and that whichever had one of them would also have the other. And it is from this that the contradiction arises.

The reality of the A series, then, leads to a contradiction, and must be rejected. And, since we have seen that change and time require the A series, the reality of change and time must be rejected. And so must the reality of the B series, since that requires time. Nothing is really present, past, or future. Nothing is really earlier or later than anything else or temporally simultaneous with it. Nothing really changes. And nothing is really in time. Whenever we perceive anything in time—which is the only way in which, in our present experience, we do perceive things—we are perceiving it more or less as it really is not.[6] . . .

[6] Even on the hypothesis that judgments are real it would be necessary to regard ourselves as perceiving things in time, and so perceiving them erroneously. And we shall see later that all cognition is perception, and that, therefore, all error is erroneous perception.

THE MYTH OF PASSAGE

DONALD C. WILLIAMS

DONALD C. WILLIAMS is Professor of Philosophy at Harvard University. He is the author of *The Ground of Induction* and *Principles of Empirical Realism*.

At every moment each of us finds himself the apparent center of the world, enjoying a little lit foreground of the here and now, while around him there looms, thing beyond thing, event beyond event, the plethora of a universe. Linking the furniture of the foreground are sets of relations which he supposes also to bind the things beyond and to bind the foreground with the rest. Noteworthy among them are those queerly obvious relations, peculiarly external to their terms, which compose the systems of space and time, modes of connection exhaustively specifiable in a scheme of four dimensions at right angles to one another. Within this manifold, for all that it is so firmly integrated, we are immediately struck by a disparity between the three-dimensional spread of space and the one dimension of time. The spatial dimensions are in a literal and precise sense perpendicular to one another, and the submanifold which they compose is isotropic, the same in all directions. The one dimension of time, on the other hand, although it has the same formal properties as each of the other three, is at least sensuously different from them as they are not from one another, and the total manifold is apparently not isotropic. Whereas an

FROM Donald C. Williams, *Principles of Empirical Realism*, Charles C. Thomas, Springfield, Illinois, 1966. "The Myth of Passage" appeared first in the *Journal of Philosophy*, 48 (1951). Reprinted by permission of the editor and D. C. Williams. Courtesy of Charles C. Thomas, publisher, Springfield, Ill.

object can preserve the same shape while it is so shifted that its height becomes its breadth, we cannot easily conceive how it could do so while being shifted so that its breadth becomes its duration.

The theory of the manifold, I think, is the one model on which we can describe and explain the foreground of experience, or can intelligibly and credibly construct our account of the rest of the world, and this is so because in fact the universe is spread out in those dimensions. There may be Platonic entities which are foreign to both space and time; there may be Cartesian spirits which are foreign to space; but the homely realm of natural existence, the total of world history, is a spatiotemporal volume of somewhat uncertain magnitude, chockablock with things and events. Logic, with its law of excluded middle and its tenseless operators, and natural science, with its secular world charts, concur inexorably with the vision of metaphysics and high religion that truth and fact are thus eternal.

I believe that the universe consists, without residue, of the spread of events in space-time, and that if we thus accept realistically the four-dimensional fabric of juxtaposed actualities we can dispense with all those dim nonfactual categories which have so bedeviled our race: the potential, the subsistential, and the influential, the noumenal, the numinous, and the nonnatural. But I am arguing here, not that there is nothing outside the natural world of events, but that the theory of the manifold is anyhow literally true and adequate to that world: true, in that the world contains no less than the manifold; adequate, in that it contains no more.

Since I think that this philosophy offers correct and coherent answers to real questions, I must think that metaphysical difficulties raised against it are genuine too. There are facts, logical and empirical, which can be described and explained only by the concept of the manifold; there are facts which some honest men deem irreconcilable with it. Few issues can better deserve adjudication. The difficulties which we need not take seriously are those made by primitive minds, and by new deliberate primitivists, who recommend that we follow out the Augustinian clue, as Augustine did not, that the man who best feels he understands time is he who refuses to think about it.

Among philosophical complainants against the manifold, some few raise difficulties about space—there are subjectivistic epistemologists, for example, who grant more reality to their own past and future than to things spatially beyond themselves. The temporal dimension of the manifold, however, bears the principal brunt. Sir James Jeans regretted that time is mathematically attached to space by so "weird" a function as the square root of minus one,[1] and the very word "weird," being cognate with "werden," to become, is a monument to the uncanniness of our fourth dimension. Maintaining that time is in its essence something wholly unique, a flow or passage, the "time snobs" (as Wyndham Lewis called them) either deny that the temporal spread is a reality at all, or think it only a very abstract phase of real time. Far from disparaging time itself, they conceive themselves thus to be "taking time seriously" in a profounder sense than our party who are content with the vasty reaches of what is, was, and will be.

The more radical opposition to the manifold takes time with such Spartan seriousness that almost none of it is left— only the pulse of the present, born virginally from nothing and devouring itself as soon as born, so that whatever past and future there be are strictly only the memory and anticipation of them in this Now.[2] One set of motives for this view is in the general romantic polemic against logic and the competence of concepts. The theory of the manifold is the logical account of events par excellence, the teeth by which the jaws of the intellect grip the flesh of occurrence. The Bergsonian, who thinks that concepts cannot convey the reality of time because they are "static," the Marxist who thinks that process defies the cadres of two-valued logic, and the Heideggerian who thinks that temporality, history, and existence are

[1] *The Mysterious Universe.* New York, 1930, p. 118.
[2] This I think is a fair description of G. H. Mead's doctrine in *The Philosophy of the Present.* See also, e.g., Schopenhauer: *The World as Will and Idea,* Bk. 4, Sec. 54.

leagued outside the categories of the intellect, thus have incentives for denying, in effect, all the temporal universe beyond what is immanent in the present flare and urge.

To counter their attack, it is a nice and tempting question whether and how concepts are "static," whether and how, in any case, a true concept must be similar to its object, and whether and how history and existence are any more temporal than spatial. But we cannot here undertake the whole defense of the intellect against its most violent critics. We shall rather notice such doubters as trust and use conceptual analysis and still think there are cogent arguments against the manifold. One argument to that effect is an extreme sharpening of the positivistic argument from the egocentric predicament. For if it is impossible for my concepts to transcend experience in general, it may well be impossible for them to transcend the momentary experience in which they are entertained. Conversely, however, anybody who rejects the arguments for instantaneous solipsism, as most people do, must reject this argument for diminishing the manifold. The chief mode of argument is rather the finding of an intolerable anomaly in the statement that what was but has ceased, or what will be but has not begun, nevertheless is. This reflection has been used against the reality of the future, in particular, by philosophers as miscellaneous as Aristotle and neoscholastics, C. D. Broad, Paul Weiss, and Charles Hartshorne. In so far as it is an argument from logic, charging the manifold with self-contradiction, it would be as valid against the past as against the future; but, I have argued, it is by no means valid.[3]

The statement that a sea fight not present in time nevertheless exists is no more contradictory than that one not present in space nevertheless exists. If it seems so, this is only because there happens to be a temporal reference (tense) built into our verbs rather than a spatial reference (as in some languages) or than no locative reference (as in canonical symbolic transcriptions into logic).

[3] "The Sea Fight Tomorrow," Williams, *Principles of Empirical Realism.*

E

I am not to contend now for the reality of the manifold, however, but against the extra *weirdness* alleged for time both by some champions who reject the manifold out of hand and by some who contend anyhow that it is not the whole story, both parties agreeing that the temporal dimension is not "real time," not "the genuine creative flux." If our temporalist means by this that the theory of temporal extension, along with the spatial models provided by calendars, kymographs, and statistical time charts, is in the last analysis fictitious, corresponding to nothing in the facts, he is reverting, under a thin cloak of dissimulation, to the mere rejection which we have agreed to leave aside. If he means, at the other extreme, no more than that the theory and the models themselves are not identical, either numerically or qualitatively, with the actual temporal succession which they represent, he is uttering a triviality which is true of every theory or representation. If he means that the temporal spread, though real and formally similar to a spatial spread, is qualitatively or intuitively very different from it, or lies in a palpably and absolutely unique direction, he says something plausible and important but not at all incompatible with the philosophy of the manifold.

He is most likely to mean, however, another proposition which is never more than vaguely expressed: that over and above the sheer spread of events, with their several qualities, along the time axis, which is analogous enough to the spread of space, there is something extra, something active and dynamic, which is often and perhaps best described as "passage." This something extra, I am going to plead, is a myth: not one of those myths which foreshadow a difficult truth in a metaphorical way, but altogether a false start, deceiving us about the facts, and blocking our understanding of them.

The literature of "passage" is immense, but it is naturally not very exact and lucid, and we cannot be sure of distinguishing in it between mere harmless allegorical phenomenology and the special metaphysical declaration which I criticize. But "passage," it would seem, is a character supposed to inhabit and glorify the present, "the passing present,"[4] "the moving present,"[5] the "travelling *now*."[6] It is "the passage of time as actual . . . given now with the jerky or whooshy quality of transience."[7] It is James' "passing moment."[8] It is what Broad calls "the transitory aspect" of time, in contrast with the "extensive."[9] It is Bergson's living felt duration. It is Heidegger's *Zeitlichkeit*. It is Tillich's "moment that is creation and fate."[10] It is "the act of becoming," the mode of potency and generation, which Hugh King finds properly appreciated only by Aristotle and Whitehead.[11] It is Eddington's "ongoing" and "the formality of taking place,"[12] and Dennes' "surge of process."[13] It is the dynamic essence which Ushenko believes that Einstein omits from the world.[14] It is the mainspring of McTaggart's "A-series" which puts movement in time,[15] and it is Broad's pure becoming.[16] Withal it is the flow and go of very existence, nearer to us than breathing, closer than hands and feet.

So far as one can interpret these expressions into a theory,

[4] W. R. Dennes, in California, University, Philosophical Union, *The Problem of Time*. Berkeley, Calif., 1935, p. 103.

[5] I. Stearns, in *Review of Metaphysics*, 4 (1950), 198.

[6] Santayana: *Realms of Being*, in *Works*, Vol. 14, p. 254.

[7] Lewis: *An Analysis of Knowledge and Valuation*, p. 19. This is pretty surely phenomenology, not metaphysics, but it is too good to omit.

[8] James: *A Pluralistic Universe*, p. 254.

[9] Broad: *An Examination of McTaggart's Philosophy*, Vol. 2, Pt. 1, p. 271 [pp. 122 ff of this volume—Ed.].

[10] Paul Tillich: *The Interpretation of History*. New York, 1936, p. 129.

[11] H. R. King, in *Journal of Philosophy*, 46 (1949), 657–70. This is an exceptionally ingenious, serious, and explicit statement of the philosophy which I am opposing.

[12] Arthur S. Eddington: *Space, Time, and Gravitation*, New York, 1920, p. 51; *The Nature of the Physical World*, New York, 1928, p. 68.

[13] Dennes: *op. cit.*, pp. 91, 93.

[14] Andrew P. Ushenko: *Power and Events*. Princeton, 1946, p. 146.

[15] John M. E. McTaggart: *The Nature of Existence*. Cambridge, 1927, Vol. 2, Bk. 5, Chap. 33.

[16] Broad: *Scientific Thought*, p. 67; *An Examination of McTaggart's Philosophy*, Vol. 2, Pt. 1, p. 277 [pp. 124 ff of this volume—Ed.].

they have the same purport as all the immemorial turns of speech by which we describe time as *moving*, with respect to the present or with respect to our minds. Time flows or flies or marches, years roll, hours pass. More explicitly we may speak as if the perceiving mind were stationary while time flows by like a river, with the flotsam of events upon it; or as if presentness were a fixed pointer under which the tape of happenings slides; or as if the time sequence were a moving-picture film, unwinding from the dark reel of the future, projected briefly on the screen of the present, and rewound into the dark can of the past. Sometimes, again, we speak as if the time sequence were a stationary plain or ocean on which we voyage, or a variegated river gorge down which we drift; or, in Broad's analogy, as if it were a row of house fronts along which the spotlight of the present plays. "The essence of nowness," Santayana says, "runs like fire along the fuse of time."[17]

Augustine pictures the present passing into the past, where the modern pictures the present as invading the future,[18] but these do not conflict, for Augustine means that the *events* which were present become past, while the modern means that *presentness* encroaches on what was previously the future. Sometimes the surge of presentness is conceived as a mere moving illumination by consciousness, sometimes as a sort of vivification and heightening, like an ocean wave heaving along beneath a stagnant expanse of floating seaweed, sometimes as no less than the boon of existence itself, reifying minute by minute a limbo of unthings.

Now, the most remarkable feature of all this is that while the modes of speech and thought which enshrine the idea of passage are universal and perhaps ineradicable, the instant one thinks about them one feels uneasy, and the most laborious effort cannot construct an intelligible theory which admits the literal truth of any of them. The obvious and notorious fault of the idea, as we have now localized it, is this. Motion is already defined and explained in the dimensional manifold

17 *Realms of Being*, in *Works*, Vol. 15, p. 90.
18 *Confessions*, Bk. 11, Chap. 14 [pp. 40–41 of this volume]; cf. E. B. McGilvary, in *Philosophical Review*, 23 (1914), 121–45.

as consisting of the presence of the same individual in different places at different times. It consists of bends or quirks in the world line, or the space-time worm, which is the four-dimensioned totality of the individual's existence. This is motion in space, if you like; but we can readily define a corresponding "motion in time." It comes out as nothing more dramatic than an exact equivalent: "motion in time" consists of being at different times in different places.

True motion then is motion at once in time and space. Nothing can "move" in time alone any more than in space alone, and time itself cannot "move" any more than space itself. "Does this road go anywhere?" asks the city tourist. "No, it stays right along here," replies the countryman. Time "flows" only in the sense in which a line flows or a landscape "recedes into the west." That is, it is an ordered extension. And each of us proceeds through time only as a fence proceeds across a farm: that is, parts of our being, and the fence's, occupy successive instants and points, respectively. There is passage, but it is nothing extra. It is the mere happening of things, their existence strung along in the manifold. The term "the present" is the conventional way of designating the cross section of events which are simultaneous with the uttering of the phrase, and "the present moves" only in that when similar words occur at successively different moments, they denote, by a twist of language essentially the same as that of all "egocentric particulars," like "here" and "this," different cross sections of the manifold.

Time travel, prima facie, then, is analyzable either as the banality that at each different moment we occupy a different moment from the one we occupied before, or the contradiction that at each different moment we occupy a different moment from the one which we are then occupying—that five minutes from now, for example, I may be a hundred years from now.[19]

[19] "He may even now—if I may use the phrase—be wandering on some plesiosaurus-haunted oolitic coral reef, or beside the lonely saline seas of the Triassic Age"—H. G. Wells, *The Time Machine*, epilogue. This book, perhaps the best yarn ever written, contains such early and excellent accounts of the theory of the manifold

The tragedy then of the extra idea of passage or absolute becoming, as a philosophical principle, is that it incomprehensibly doubles its world by reintroducing terms like "moving" and "becoming" in a sense which both requires and forbids interpretation in the preceding ways. For as soon as we say that time or the present or we move in the odd extra way which the doctrine of passage requires, we have no recourse but to suppose that this movement in turn takes time of a special sort: $time_1$ moves at a certain rate in $time_2$, perhaps one $second_1$ per one $second_2$, perhaps slower, perhaps faster. Or, conversely, the moving present slides over so many seconds of $time_1$ in so many seconds of $time_2$. The history of the new moving present, in $time_2$, then composes a new and higher time dimension again, which cries to be vitalized by a new level of passage, and so on forever.

We hardly needed to point out the unhappy regress to which the idea of time's motion commits us, for any candid philosopher, as soon as he looks hard at the idea, must *see* that it is preposterous. "Taking place" is not a formality to which an event incidentally submits—it is the event's very being. World history consists of actual concrete happenings in a temporal sequence; it is not necessary or possible that happening should happen to them all over again. The system of the manifold is thus "complete" in something like the technical logical sense, and any attempted addition to it is bound to be either contradictory or supererogatory.

Bergson, Broad, and some of the followers of Whitehead[20] have tried to soften the paradoxes of passage by supposing that the present does not move across the total time level, but that it is the very fountain where the river of time gushes out of nothingness (or out of the power of God). The past, then, having swum into being and floated away, is eternally real, but the future has no existence at all. This may be a

that it has been quoted and requoted by scientific writers. Though it makes slips, its logic is better than that of later such stories.

[20] Bergson's theory of the snowball of time may be thus understood: the past abides in the center while ever new presents accrete around it. For Broad, see *Scientific Thought*, p. 66, and on Whitehead, see King, *op. cit.*, esp. p. 663.

more appealing figure, but logically it involves the same anomalies of metahappening and metatime which we observed in the other version.

What, then, we must ask, were the motives which drove men to the staggering philosophy of passage? One of them, I believe, we can dispose of at once. It is the innocent vertigo which inevitably besets a creature whose thinking is strung out in time, as soon as he tries to think of the time dimension itself. He finds it easiest to conceive and understand purely geometrical structures. Motion is more difficult, and generally remains vague, while time per se is very difficult indeed, but being now identified as the principle which imports motion into space, it is put down as a kind of quintessential motion itself. The process is helped by the fact that the mere further-along-ness of successive segments, either of a spatial or of a temporal stretch, can quite logically be conceived as a degenerate sort of change, as when we speak of the flow of a line or say that the scenery changes along the Union Pacific.

A rather more serious excuse for the idea of passage is that it is supposed necessary and sufficient for adding to the temporal dimension that intrinsic *sense* from earlier to later in which time is supposed to differ radically from any dimension of space.[21] A meridian of longitude has only a direction, but a river has a "sense," and time is in this like the river. It is, as the saying goes, irreversible and irrevocable. It has a "directed tension."[22] The mere dimension of time, on the other hand, would seem to be symmetrical. The principle of absolute passage is bidden to rectify this symmetry with what Eddington called "time's arrow."

It might be replied that science does not supply an arrow for time because it has no need of it. But I think it plain that time does have a sense, from early to late. I only think that it can be taken care of on much less draconian principles than absolute passage. There is nothing in the dimensional view of time to preclude its being generated by a uniquely asym-

[21] See, for example, Broad: *Scientific Thought,* p. 57.
[22] Tillich, *op. cit.,* p. 245.

metrical relation, and experience suggests powerfully that it is so generated. But the fact is that every real series has a "sense" anyhow. This is provided, if by nothing else, then by the sheer numerical identity and diversity of terms.

In the line of individual things or events, $a, b, c, \ldots z,$ whether in space or in time, the "sense" from a to z is *ipso facto* other than the "sense" from z to a. Only because there is a difference between the ordered couple $a;z$ and the couple $z;a$ can we define the difference between a symmetrical and an asymmetrical relation. Only because there are already two distinguishable "ways" on a street, determined by its individual ends, can we decide to permit traffic to move one way and prohibit it the other. But a sufficient difference of sense, finally, would appear to be constituted, if nothing else offered, by the inevitably asymmetrical distribution of properties along the temporal line (or any other). Eddington has been only one of many scientists who think the arrow is provided for the cosmos by the principle of entropy, and entropy has been only one principle thus advocated.[23]

In so far as what men mean by "the irrevocability of the past" is the causal circumstance that we can affect the future in a way we cannot affect the past, it is just a trait of the physicist's arrow. They often mean by it, however, only the inexorability of fact, that what is the case is the case, past, present, or future; or the triviality that the particular events of 1902, let us say, cannot also be the events of 1952. Very similar events might be so, however, and if very few of them are, this is the fault of the concrete nature of things and not of any grudge on the part of time.[24]

The final motive for the attempt to consummate or supplant the fourth dimension of the manifold with the special perfection, the grace and whiz, of passage is the vaguest but the most substantial and incorrigible. It is simply that we *find* passage, that we are immediately and poignantly involved in the whoosh of process, the felt flow of one moment

[23] *The Nature of the Physical World,* Chap. 3. For the present scientific state of the question, see Adolf Grünbaum: *Philosophical Problems of Space and Time,* New York, 1963.

[24] Dennes argues thus, *loc. cit.*

into the next. Here is the focus of being. Here is the shore whence the youngster watches the golden mornings swing toward him like serried bright breakers from the ocean of the future. Here is the flood on which the oldster wakes in the night to shudder at its swollen black torrent cascading him into the abyss.

It would be futile to try to deny these experiences, but their correct description is another matter. If they are in fact consistent with our theory, they are no evidence against it; and if they are entailed by it, they are evidence in its favor. Since the theory was originally constructed to take account of them, it would be odd if they were inconsistent with it or even irrelevant to it. I believe that in fact they are neither, and that the theory of the manifold provides the true and literal description of what the enthusiastic metaphors of passage have deceptively garbled.

The principal reason why we are troubled to accommodate our experience of time to the intellectual theory of time goes very deep in the philosophy of philosophy. It is that we must here scrutinize the undoctored fact of perception, on the one hand, and must imagine our way into a conceptual scheme, and envisage the true intrinsic being of its objects, on the other hand, and then pronounce on the numerical identity of the first with the second. This is a very rare requirement. Even such apt ideas as those of space and of physical objects, as soon as we contemplate them realistically, begin to embarrass us, so that we slip into the assumption that the real objects of the conceptions, if they exist at all, exist on a different plane or in a different realm from the sensuous spread and lumpiness of experience. The ideas of time and of the mind, however, do not permit of such evasion. Those beings are given in their own right and person, filling the foreground. Here for once we must fit the fact directly into the intellectual form, without benefit of precedent or accustomed criteria. First off, then, comparing the calm conceptual scheme with the turbid event itself, we may be repelled by the former, not because it is not true to the latter, but because it *is* not the latter. When we see that this kind of diversity is inevitable to every concept and its object, and hence is irrele-

E*

vant to the validity of any, we demur because the conceptual scheme is indifferently flat and third-personal, like a map, while the experienced reality is centripetal and perspectival, piled up and palpitating where we are, gray and retiring elsewhere.

But this is only because every occasion on which we compare the world map with experience has itself a single specific location, confronting part of the world, remote from the rest. The perspectivity of the view is exactly predictable from the map. The deception with respect to time is worse than with respect to space because our memories and desires run timewise and not spacewise. The jerk and whoosh of this moment, which are simply the real occurrence of one particular batch of events, are no different from the whoosh and being of any other patch of events up and down the eternal timestretch. Remembering some of the latter, however, and anticipating more, and bearing in mind that while they happen they are all called "the present," we mistakenly hypostatize *the* Present as a single surge of bigness which rolls along the time axis. There is in fact no more a single rolling Now than there is a single rolling Here along a spatial line—a standing line of soldiers, for example, though each of them has the vivid presentment of his own here.

Let us hug to us as closely as we like that there is real succession, that rivers flow and winds blow, that things burn and burst, that men strive and guess and die. All this is the concrete stuff of the manifold, the reality of serial happening, one event after another, in exactly the time spread which we have been at pains to diagram. What does the theory allege except what we find, and what do we find that is not accepted and asserted by the theory? Suppose a pure intelligence, bred outside of time, instructed in the nature of the manifold and the design of the human spacetime worm, with its mnemic organization, its particular delimited but overlapping conscious fields, and the strands of world history which flank them, and suppose him incarnated among us: what could he have expected the temporal experience to be like except just about what he actually discovers it to be? How, in brief, could processes and experiences which endure and succeed each other along the time line appear as anything other than enduring and successive processes and a stream of consciousness?

The theory of the manifold leaves abundant room for the sensitive observer to record any describable difference he may find, in intrinsic quality, relational texture, or absolute direction, between the temporal dimension and the spatial ones. He is welcome to mark it so on the map. The very singleness of the time dimension, over against the amalgamated three dimensions of space, may be an idiosyncrasy with momentous effects; its *fourthness,* so to speak, so oddly and immensely multiplying the degrees of freedom embodied in the familiar spatial complex, was bound to seem momentous too.

The theory has generally conceded or emphasized that time is unique in these and other respects, and I have been assuming that it was right to do so. In the working out of this thesis, however, and in considering the very lame demurrals which oppose it, I have come a little uneasily to the surmise that the idea of an absolute or intrinsic difference of texture or orientation is superfluous, and that the four dimensions of the manifold compose a perfectly homogeneous scheme of location relations, the same in all directions, and that the oddity of temporal distances is altogether a function of features which occupy them—a function of *de facto* pattern like the shape of an arrow, like the difference between the way in and the way out of a flytrap, and like the terrestrial difference between up and down.

Even a person who believes that temporal distances are a categorically peculiar mode of relation, intrinsically different from spatial distance, regardless of how they are filled, must grant that they nevertheless *are* filled differently: things, persons, and events, as a matter of natural fact, are strung along with respect to the time axis in rhythms and designs notably different from those in which they are deployed spacewise. Entropy and the other scientific criteria for the "sense" from past to future distinguish no less the whole temporal direction from the spatial ones. The very concept of "things" or "individual substances" derives from a peculiar kind of coherence and elongation of clumps of events in the time direction. Living bodies in particular have a special organized trend timewise, a *conatus sese conservandi,* which nothing has in spatial section. Characteristic themes of causation run in the same direction, and paralleling all these, and accounting for their importance and obviousness to us, is the pattern of mental events, the stream of consciousness, with its mnemic cumulation and that sad anxiety to *keep going* futureward which contrasts strangely with our comparative indifference to our spatial girth.

The same fact of the grain and configuration of events which, if it does not constitute, certainly accompanies and underlines the "senses" of space and time, has other virtues which help to naturalize experience in the manifold. It accounts for the apparent *rate* of happening, for example; for the span of the specious present; and for the way in which the future is comparatively malleable to our present efforts and correspondingly dark to our present knowledge. An easy interpretation would be that the world content is uniquely organized in the time direction because the time direction itself is aboriginally unique. Modern philosophical wisdom, however, consists mostly of trying the cart before the horse, and I find myself more than half convinced by the oddly repellent hypothesis that the peculiarity of the time dimension is not thus primitive but is wholly a resultant of those differences in the mere *de facto* run and order of the world's filling.

It is conceivable, then, though perhaps physically impossible, that one four-dimensional part of the manifold of events be slued around at right angles to the rest, so that the time order of that area, as composed by its interior lines of strain and structure, runs parallel with a spatial order in its environment. It is conceivable, indeed, that a single whole human life should lie thwartwise of the manifold, with its belly plump in time, its birth at the east and its death in the west, and its conscious stream perhaps running alongside somebody's garden path.[25]

[25] I should expect the impact of the environment on such a being to be so wildly queer and out of step with the way he is put together, that his mental life must be a dragged-out monstrous

It is conceivable too then that a human life be twisted, not 90° but 180°, from the normal temporal grain of the world. F. Scott Fitzgerald tells the story of Benjamin Button who was born in the last stages of senility and got younger all his life till he died a dwindling embryo.[26] Fitzgerald imagined the reversal to be so imperfect that Benjamin's stream of consciousness ran, not backward with his body's gross development, but in the common clockwise manner. We might better conceive a reversal of every cell twitch and electron whirl, and hence suppose that he experienced his own life stages in the same order as we do ours, but that he observed everyone around him moving backward from the grave to the cradle. True time travel, then, is conceivable after all, though we cannot imagine how it could be caused by beings whose lives are extended in the normal way: it would consist of a man's life-pattern, and the pattern of any appliances he employed, running at an abnormal rate or on an abnormal heading across the manifold.

As the dimensional theory accommodates what is true in the notion of passage, that is, the occurrence of events, in contrast with a mythical rearing and charging of time itself, so it accounts for what is true in the notions of "flux," "emergence," "creative advance," and the rest. Having learned the trick of mutual translation between theory and experience, we see where the utter misrepresentation lies in the accusation that the dimensional theory denies that time is "real," or that it substitutes a safe and static world, a block universe, a petrified *fait accompli*, a *totum simul*, for the actuality of risk and change.

Taking time with the truest seriousness, on the contrary, it calmly diagnoses "novelty" or "becoming," for example, as the existence of an entity, or kind of entity, at one time in the world continuum which does not exist at any previous time. No other sort of novelty than this, I earnestly submit,

---

delirium. Professor George Burch has suggested to me that it might be the mystic's timeless illumination. Whether these diagnoses are different I shall not attempt to say.

[26] "The Curious Case of Benjamin Button," in *Tales of the Jazz Age*. New York, 1922.

is discoverable or conceivable—or desirable. In practice, the modern sciences of the manifold have depicted it as a veritable caldron of force and action. Although the theory entails that it is true at every time that events occur at other times, it emphatically does not entail that all events happen at the same time or at every time, or at no time. It does not assert, therefore, that future things "already" exist or exist "forever." Emphatically also it does not, as is frequently charged, "make time a dimension of space,"[27] any more than it makes space a dimension of time.

The theory of the manifold, which is thus neutral with respect to the amount of change and permanence in the world, is surprisingly neutral also toward many other topics often broached as though they could be crucial between it and the extra idea of passage. It is neutral, so far, toward whether space and time are absolute and substantival in the Democritean and Newtonian way, or relative and adjectival in Spencer's and Whitehead's way, or further relativistic in Einstein's way. The theory of space does not, as Bergson pretended, have any preference for discontinuity over continuity, and while a time order in which nothing exists but the present would be fatal to any real continuity, the philosophy of the manifold is quite prepared to accept any verdict on whether space or time or both are continuous or discrete, as it is also on whether they are finite or infinite. Instead of "denying history," it preserves it, and is equally hospitable to all philosophies of history except such as themselves deny history by disputing the objectivity and irrevocability of historical truth. It does not care whether events eternally recur, or run along forever on the dead level as Aristotle thought, or enact the ringing brief drama of the Christian episode, or strive into the Faustian boundless. It is similarly neutral toward theories of causation and of knowledge.

The world manifold of occurrences, each eternally determinate at its own place and date, may and may not be so

[27] See Charles Hartshorne: *Man's Vision of God, and the Logic of Theism,* Chicago, 1941, p. 140, and Tillich, *op. cit.,* pp. 132, 248; and remember Bergson's allegation that the principle of the manifold "spatializes" time.

determined in its texture that what occurs at one juncture has its sufficient reason at others. If it does evince such causal connections, these may be either efficient (as apparently they are) or final (as apparently they are not). The core of the causal nexus itself may be, so far as the manifold is concerned, either a real connection of Spinoza's sort, or Whitehead's, or the scholastics', or the mere regular succession admitted by Hume and Russell. It was a mistake for Spinoza to infer, if he did, that the eternal manifold and strict causation entail one another, as it is a worse mistake for the scholastics, Whitehead, Ushenko, and Weiss to infer the opposite (as they seem to), that "real time" and "real causation" entail one another.[28] The theory is similarly noncommittal toward metaphysical accounts of individual substances, which it can allow to be compounds of form and matter or mere sheaves of properties.

The theory of the manifold makes a man at home in the world to the extent that it guarantees that intelligence is not affronted at its first step into reality. Beyond that, the cosmos is as it is. If there is moral responsibility, if the will is free, if there is reasonableness in regret and hope in decision, these must be ascertained by more particular observations and hypotheses than the doctrine of the manifold. It makes no difference to our theory whether we are locked in an ice pack of fate, or whirled in a tornado of chance, or are firm-footed makers of destiny. It will accept benignly either the Christian Creator, or the organic and perfect Absolute, or Hume's sand pile of sensation, or the fluid melee of contextualism, or the structured world process of materialism.

The service which the theory performs with respect to all these problems is other than dictating solutions of them. It is the provision of a lucent frame or arena where they and their solutions can be laid out and clearheadedly appraised in view of their special classes of evidence. Once under this kind of observation, for example, the theories of change which describe becoming as a marriage of being and not-being, or an

[28] See, for example, Whitehead: *Process and Reality*, p. 363; Paul Weiss: *Nature and Man*, New York, 1947.

interpenetration of the present with the future and the past, become repulsive, not because they conflict especially with the philosophy of the manifold, but because if they are not mere incantations they contradict themselves. When we see that the problem how Achilles can overtake the tortoise is essentially the same as the problem how two lines can intersect one another obliquely, we are likely to be content with the simple mathematical intelligibility of both. When we see that the "change" of a leaf's color from day to day is of the same denomination as its "change" from inch to inch of its surface, we are less likely to hope that mysterious formulas about the actualization of the potential and the perdurance of a substratum are of any use in accounting for either of them.

If then there is some appearance of didactic self-righteousness in my effort here to save the pure theory of the manifold from being either displaced or amended by what I think is the disastrous myth of passage, this is because I believe that the theory of the manifold is the very paradigm of philosophic understanding. It grasps with a firm logic, so far as I can see, the most intimate and pervasive of facts; it clarifies the obscure and assimilates the apparently diverse.

Most of the effect of the prophets of passage, on the other hand, is to melt back into the primitive magma of confusion and plurality the best and sharpest instruments which the mind has forged. Some of those who do this have a deliberate preference for the melting pot of mystery as an end in itself. Others, I suppose, hope eventually to cast from it a finer metal and to forge a sharper point. No hope of that sort is altogether chimerical. But I suggest that if a tithe of the animus and industry invested in that ill-omened enterprise were spent on the refinement and imaginative use of the instrument we have, whatever difficulties still attend it would soon be dissipated.

OSTENSIBLE TEMPORALITY

C. D. BROAD

CHARLIE DUNBAR BROAD is a Fellow of Trinity College, Cambridge, and Professor Emeritus of Moral Philosophy at Cambridge. His chief publications are *Perception, Physics, and Reality; Scientific Thought; The Mind and Its Place in Nature; An Examination of McTaggart's Philosophy;* and *Five Types of Ethical Theory.*

The temporal characteristics of experiences fall into three different, though closely interconnected, sets. (i) Every experience has some duration. It is, in this respect, like a finite straight line and not like a geometrical point. It may be qualitatively variegated or qualitatively uniform throughout its duration, just as a line may vary in color from one end to the other or be uniformly colored throughout.

(ii) Any two experiences of the same person stand to each other in a certain determinate form of a determinable temporal relation. Since experiences are not instantaneous, these determinate forms of temporal relation cannot be reduced to the familiar three, viz., earlier than, simultaneous with, and later than. Many other possibilities must be recognized, e.g., earlier than and *not* adjoined to, earlier than *and* adjoined to, partly preceding and partly overlapping, and so on. It is needless to go into elaborate detail; the total number of possible determinate temporal relations between two experiences is finite and can easily be worked out. If A and B are two experiences of the same person, and no assumption is made about the relative durations of A and B, there are in

FROM C. D. Broad, *An Examination of McTaggart's Philosophy,* Volume II, Part I, Cambridge University Press, Cambridge, 1938. Reprinted by permission of the publisher.

fact just thirteen alternative possible relations in which A may stand to B. Of these, six are independent of the relative duration of A and B; one, viz., exact temporal coincidence without overlap, can hold only if A and B are of equal duration; three can hold from A to B only if A is shorter than B; and the remaining three can hold from A to B only if A is longer than B.

(iii) The third, and much the most puzzling, set of temporal characteristics are those which are involved in facts of the following kind. An experience is at one time wholly in the future, as when one says "I am going to have a painful experience at the dentist's tomorrow." It keeps on becoming less and less remotely future. Eventually the earliest phase of it becomes present; as when the dentist begins drilling one's tooth, and one thinks or says "The painful experience which I have been anticipating has now begun." Each phase ceases to be present, slips into the immediate past, and then keeps on becoming more and more remotely past. But it is followed by phases which were future and have become present. Eventually the latest phase of this particular experience becomes present and then slips into the immediate past. There is the fact which one records by saying "Thank God [on the theistic hypothesis] that's over now!" After that the experience as a whole retreats continually into the more and more remote past.

There is no doubt that the sentences which I have just been quoting record facts, and that such facts are of the very essence of Time. But it is, of course, quite possible that the grammatical form of these sentences is highly misleading. It may dispose people to take for granted a certain view of the structure and the elements of these facts, and this view may be mistaken and may lead to difficulties and contradictions.

The two aspects of duration and temporal relations are very closely interconnected, and it is in respect of them that there is a close analogy between Time and Space. I shall therefore class them together under the name of "the Extensive Aspect of Temporal Facts". The third feature is absolutely peculiar to Time, and bears no analogy to any feature of spatial facts. I will call it "the Transitory Aspect of Temporal Facts". I will first take these two aspects separately, and will then consider the relations between them.

1.1 *The Extensive Aspect of Temporal Facts.* There is evidently a very close analogy between a person's mental history, taken as a whole, and a cord made up of shorter strands arranged in the following way. The shorter strands are all parallel to each other and to the axis of the cord. No strand stretches the whole length of the cord; the strands are of various lengths and the two ends of any one strand are in general at different positions, respectively, from the two ends of any other strand. Any short segment of the cord will contain segments of several overlapping strands; but two short segments of the cord at some distance apart may be composed of segments of wholly different strands. Some strands may be practically uniform in color and texture throughout their length. Others may vary greatly in color or texture from one end to the other. The former correspond to monotonous experiences, and the latter to variegated and exciting experiences.

This spatial analogy is valid and useful up to a point; but I will now indicate some important ways in which it breaks down. (i) The triadic relation "between" occurs both in a linear spatial series and in a temporal series. We can say both that Bletchley is between Euston and Rugby, and that the experience of writing this sentence is between the experience of eating my breakfast and that of eating my dinner. Nevertheless, there is a profound difference. Temporal betweenness is not fundamental; it is analyzable into the relational product of a certain *dyadic* relation taken twice over. The fundamental facts are that eating my breakfast *preceded* writing the sentence, and that writing the sentence *preceded* eating my dinner. The triadic relational fact that writing the sentence is between eating my breakfast and eating my dinner is analyzable into the conjunction of these two dyadic relational facts.

Now in the linear spatial series the exact opposite is the case. No doubt one can say that Euston is south of Bletchley and that Bletchley is south of Rugby, and one can compare this with my breakfast preceding my writing the sentence

and the latter preceding my dinner. But there is a fundamental difference. The relation "south of" tacitly involves a
reference to some third term beside those which are explicitly
mentioned, viz., to the sun or to a compass-needle. But the
relation "earlier than" is a genuinely dyadic relation which
directly relates two experiences of the same person and contains no tacit reference to some third term.

We may sum this up as follows. In a linear spatial series
there is no asymmetric dyadic relation intrinsic to the series.
The only relation which does not involve a tacit reference
to some term outside the series is the partly symmetrical and
partly asymmetrical *triadic* relation of "betweenness". This
is partly symmetrical because, if B is between A and C, then
it is equally between C and A; and conversely. It is partly
asymmetrical because, if B is between A and C, C cannot be
between A and B and A cannot be between B and C. In
the temporal series of experiences which constitutes a person's
mental history there is a genuine dyadic relation which is
intrinsic to the series and involves no reference to any term
outside the latter. This is the relation "earlier than". It is the
fundamental relation here, and *temporal* betweenness is definable in terms of it. In the temporal series there are two
intrinsically opposite directions, earlier-to-later and later-to-
earlier. In the linear spatial series there is no *intrinsic* direction. If direction is to be introduced, this must be done
extrinsically, either by reference to motion along the line
(and therefore to time), or by reference to the right and left
hands of an external observer, or in some other way.

(ii) Spatial extension and the occurrence of spatial relations *presuppose* temporal duration and a certain determinate
form of temporal relation. Shape and size are commonly
ascribed to particulars which persist through periods of time
and have histories of longer or shorter duration. Since, however, one and the same thing can have different determinate
shapes and sizes at different times in its history, we have to
divide its history into short successive phases during each of
which its shape and size are sensibly constant. Thus we reach
the limiting conception of "the shape and size of a certain
thing at a certain moment". If the thing is very rigid and

usually remains practically unchanged in shape and size over long periods, we often drop the reference to a particular moment and refer to the shape and size which it has at every moment throughout such a long period as "*the* shape and size of this thing". Again, if a thing is elastic, there may be a certain shape and size which it will automatically assume whenever it is free from external distorting or compressing forces. We sometimes refer to this as "*the* shape and size" or "the *natural* shape and size" of such a body, even though the body is at most moments in its history subject to external forces which distort or compress it. I think that it is clear from these remarks that the notions of shape and size, as applied to bodies, all involve a tacit or explicit reference to temporal characteristics.

We do not very often apply the notions of shape and size to events or processes, as distinct from material things. But we do, e.g., talk of a "long jagged flash of lightning". I think that we talk in this way only when the event or process is so short as to be sensibly instantaneous.

Lastly, we talk of spatial relations between two events only when each is sensibly instantaneous and the two are simultaneous with each other. And we talk of spatial relations between two material things only when the following conditions are fulfilled. The histories of the two things must go on parallel to each other in time. Then each history must be divided into successive instantaneous states, and we must consider the spatial relations between the two bodies at each pair of simultaneous instants in their respective histories. Thus there is a rather elaborate and complicated temporal relation implied in talking of spatial relations between bodies.

Now contrast all this with the extensive aspect of temporal facts. Temporal relations *directly* relate *events or processes;* they do not directly relate the continuants of which events and processes constitute the histories. Again, it is the events or processes which are temporally extended, i.e., which are longer or shorter in the temporal sense. The continuants, of which these events or processes constitute the histories, *endure through* periods of time. And the period through which a continuant endures is measured by the length of its history.

Lastly, it is evident that a temporal whole may be composed of parts which do not temporally overlap but are completely successive to each other. Consider a variegated process, such as a single rendering of a certain tune on a piano. It can be regarded as a whole composed of adjoined phases, each of shorter duration, such that each phase wholly precedes one, and wholly follows another, phase of the same process.

I think that I have now made it plain that the unlikeness between spatial and temporal facts is almost as striking as the likeness, even when we confine ourselves to the purely extensive aspect. So far as I can see, all spatial illustrations even of the extensive aspect of temporal facts presuppose temporal notions. For our lines, etc., are all things which endure through certain periods and have longer or shorter temporal histories. This is no reason for refusing to use such illustrations, if we find them helpful. But it makes it certain that a point will be reached after which they can give us no further help.

1.2 *The Transitory Aspect of Temporal Facts.* We will now turn to the transitory aspect of temporal facts. Here there are two points to be considered, viz. (i) the characteristics of pastness, presentness, and futurity; and (ii) the fact that every event is continually changing in respect of these characteristics. It continually becomes less and less remotely future, then it becomes present, and then it continually becomes more and more remotely past.

The first remark to be made is concerned primarily with language, but it leads us on to a conclusion which is not purely linguistic. In all the languages with which I am acquainted there are two different ways of recording such temporal facts as we are now considering. The most usual way is by means of differences of tense in inflected languages, or by means of a temporal copula, which can take three different forms, together with certain temporal adverbs. Thus I should most naturally say "I *had* my breakfast *lately*", "I *am* writing *now*", "I *shall be* eating my lunch *soon*" and so on. The other way is by means of a single uniform copula and temporal adjectives, which take three different forms, together with certain adverbs. Thus I might have said, "Eating my breakfast is just past", "My writing is present", "Eating my lunch is slightly future", and so on. Such expressions are rather unnatural; but they are intelligible, and in some contexts they would be quite normal. Thus it sounds quite natural to say "The next glacial period is in the remote future." The various temporal copulas can be combined with the various temporal adjectives in many ways. Thus we can say "The invention of wireless broadcasting was still future when Queen Victoria died", "This spell of writing will be past (or over) when I am eating my lunch", and so on.

I come now to the point which is not purely linguistic. It is this. By using various forms of temporal adjective we may be able to reduce the number of forms of temporal copula needed in recording temporal facts to the single copula "is". We can, e.g., replace the sentence "I *was* eating my breakfast, I *am* writing, and I *shall be* eating my lunch" by the sentence "Eating my breakfast *is* past, this spell of writing *is* present, and eating my lunch *is* future." But the "is" is the temporal copula "is now", which a person would use if he said of me "He is now writing"; it is not the non-temporal copula which would be used if one said "37 is a prime number" or "Scarlet is a determinate form of red."

The following considerations make this quite plain. Suppose that, on a certain occasion, I utter the sentence "The event *e* is present." And suppose that this utterance records a fact. If the word "is" in it were a non-temporal copula, *every* utterance by me of the same sentence would record the same fact, no matter whether it were earlier than, contemporary with, or later than this utterance of mine. But actually the only utterances of this sentence which would record the same fact as this utterance of mine would be those which are *contemporary with* my utterance. Earlier or later utterances of this sentence would simply be false; though an earlier utterance of the sentence "The event *e* is future" would be true, and a later utterance of the sentence "The event *e* is past" would also be true. Similar remarks would apply, *mutatis mutandis,* if we had taken as our example a true utterance of the sentence "The event *e* is future" or a true utterance of the sentence "The event *e* is past." It is clear then that there can be no question of getting rid altogether of temporal copulas, and replacing them by a single non-temporal copula and various temporal predicates. This point is highly relevant in connexion with McTaggart's argument against the reality of Time. . . .

1.22 *Absolute Becoming.* We must now consider the other feature in temporal facts to which there is no spatial analogy, viz., temporal becoming. People have often tried to explain or to represent this in terms of qualitative change or motion. It seems to me quite evident that all such attempts are doomed to failure. Qualitative change and motion presuppose qualitative or substantial persistence, and both presuppose temporal becoming. It will be worth while to consider this point rather more fully.

Let us begin with the attempt to represent temporal becoming by means of motion. Here we are supposed to have a series of event-particles[1] related by the relation of earlier and later. This may be represented by a straight line, which may be uniformly shaded if the process is to be qualitatively uniform, or may be colored with a continuously variable shade from one end to the other if the process is to be one of continuous qualitative change. The characteristic of presentness is then supposed to move along this series of event-particles, in the direction from earlier to later, as the light from a policeman's bullseye might move along a row of palings.

The following fatal objections can at once be raised. (i) If anything moves, it must move with some determinate velocity. It will always be sensible to ask "How fast does it move?" even if we have no means of answering the question. Now this is equivalent to asking "How great a distance will it have traversed in unit time-lapse?" But here the series along which presentness is supposed to move is temporal and not spatial. In it "distance" *is* time-lapse. So the question becomes "How great a time-lapse will presentness have traversed in unit time-lapse?" And this question seems to be meaningless.

[1] [This term is introduced by Broad to stand for an *instantaneous* event, i.e., one having a non-finite duration. Such event-particles are defined in terms of a set of overlapping events of finite duration which converge toward a point.—Ed.]

(ii) Consider any event-particle in the series. At a certain moment this acquires presentness and then loses it again without delay. Before that moment it was future, afterwards it is past. Now the acquisition and the loss of presentness by this event-particle is itself an event-particle of the second order, which happens to the first-order event-particle. Therefore every first-order event-*particle* has a *history* of indefinite length; and, at a certain stage of this there is one outstanding second-order event-particle, viz., the acquisition and the immediately subsequent loss of presentness. Yet, by definition, the first-order event-particle which we have been considering has no duration, and therefore can have no history, in the time-series along which presentness is supposed to move.

The two considerations which I have just mentioned would seem to make the following conclusion inevitable. If there is any sense in talking of presentness moving along a series of events, related by the relation of earlier-and-later, we must postulate a *second* time-dimension in addition to that in which the series is spread out. An event which has zero duration, and therefore no history, in the first time-dimension, will yet have an indefinitely long duration and a history in the second time-dimension. Let e_1 and e_2 be two first-order event-particles, and let e_1 precede e_2 by t units of the first time-dimension. Suppose that the second-order event-particle which is e_1's acquirement of presentness precedes the second-order event-particle which is e_2's acquirement of presentness by t' units of the second time-dimension. Then the velocity with which presentness moves along the original series will be measured by the ratio t/t'. The numerical value of this ratio is of no importance; it could always be given the value $1/1$ by a suitable choice of the units in which we measure time-lapses in the two dimensions. The important point is that, whatever may be the numerical value, the ratio cannot possibly represent a rate of change unless its denominator measures a *lapse of time* and its numerator measures something *other than* a lapse of time in the same time-dimension.

Now let e_1, e_2, e_3, etc., be a series of event-particles of the first order, succeeding each other in the first time-dimension. Consider the following set of second-order event-particles, viz., e_1's acquirement of presentness, e_2's acquirement of presentness, e_3's acquirement of presentness, and so on. These might be denoted respectively by the symbols e_1^2, e_2^2, e_3^2, etc. These will form a series of second-order event-particles which succeed each other in the second time-dimension. Now, just as e_1 was future, became present, and then became past, so e_1^2 (i.e., e_1's acquirement of presentness) was future, became present, and then became past. Again, just as e_1 became present before e_2 became present, so e_1^2 (i.e., e_1's acquirement of presentness) had ceased to be present when e_2^2 (i.e., e_2's acquirement of presentness) had become present. Thus the series of second-order event-particles, e_1^2, e_2^2, e_3^2, etc., in the second time-dimension, is precisely like the series of first-order event-particles, e_1, e_2, e_3, etc., in the first time-dimension, in all those respects which led people to say that presentness "moves along" the first-order series. Such people ought therefore to say, if they want to be consistent, that presentness "moves along" the second-order series too.

Now, if they do say this, we can show by exactly the same arguments as we used at the first stage that a *third* time-dimension must be postulated. Each second-order event-particle, such as e_1^2, must be supposed to endure indefinitely and to have a history in the third time-dimension. And the acquirement of presentness by e_1^2 will be a third-order event-particle in the history of e_1^2. It could be symbolized by e_1^3, which thus stands for "the acquirement of presentness by the acquirement of presentness by e_1". It is easy to see that the argument is quite general, and that there is no stage at which one could consistently stop in postulating further time-dimensions and events of a higher order.

It is a great merit of Mr. J. W. Dunne, in his two books *An Experiment with Time* and *The Serial Universe,* to have insisted on what is substantially the same fact as this. Unfortunately he persuades himself, by false analogies with infinite series which have limits, that the regress is harmless and that it is sensible to postulate what he calls "the Observer at infinity". Actually the series which we have been considering could not have a last term or an upper limit, and so the conception of "the Observer at infinity" is the contradictory notion of the last term or upper limit of a series which, from its nature, could have neither. . . .

When one finds oneself launched on an endless series of this kind it is generally a sign that one has made a false move at the beginning. I think that it is easy to see what the false move is in this case. The phrase "to become present" is grammatically of the same form as the phrase "to become hot" or "to become louder". We are therefore tempted to think that sentences like "This event became present" record facts of the same kind as those which are recorded by sentences like "This water became hot" or "This noise became louder." Now a very little reflection is enough to show that this is a mistake.

Any subject of which we can significantly say that it "became hot" must be a more or less persistent substance, which persisted and had temperature before and after the date at which it became hot. The determinate form of its temperature was coldness for an earlier period and hotness for a later period, and the two periods are adjoined phases in its history. Again, any subject of which we can significantly say that it "became louder" must be a more or less prolonged noise-process, which divides into an earlier phase of less loudness adjoined to a later phase of greater loudness. But a literally *instantaneous* event-particle can significantly be said to "become present"; and, indeed, in the strict sense of "present" *only* instantaneous event-particles can be said to "become present". To "become present" is, in fact, just to "become", in an absolute sense; i.e., to "come to pass" in the Biblical phraseology, or, most simply, to "happen". Sentences like "This water became hot" or "This noise became louder" record facts of *qualitative change.* Sentences like "This event became present" record facts of *absolute becoming.* Now it is clear that qualitative change involves absolute becoming, and it seems to me equally certain that absolute becoming is involved in mere continuance without qualitative change. It is therefore hopeless to expect to treat absolute becoming as if it were a particular case of qualitative change. The endless series of time-dimensions and of orders of events, which such an attempt involves, is the sign and the measure of its futility. I do not suppose that so simple and fundamental a notion as that of absolute becoming can be analyzed, and I am quite certain that it cannot be analyzed in terms of a non-temporal copula and some kind of temporal predicate.

2.23 . . . McTaggart professes to show that a *B*-series of terms which had no *A*-characteristics could not constitute a process of qualitative change in ##310 and 311.[2] His argument is as follows: (*a*) A process of qualitative change could not consist in the annihilation of one event in such a series and the generation of another event in place of it. For any term that is *ever* earlier than another *always* precedes that other, and always precedes it by exactly the same amount. (*b*) A process of qualitative change cannot consist in one event "merging into" another, so that the two have a slice in common. For then the change would involve the annihilation of that phase of the first event which precedes the common slice and the subsequent generation of that phase of the second event which follows the common slice. And such generation and annihilation of terms in a *B*-series is impossible for the reasons already given. (*c*) Having rejected these two alternative analyses of qualitative change in #310, McTaggart assumes in #311 that the only alternative left is that each term in a *B*-series changes in respect of certain characteristics. Since the terms are events, the only characteristics in respect of which they can change are temporal ones. They can only become less and less remotely future, then present, and then more and more remotely past. That is, they must have *A*-characteristics, and they must change in respect of these.

Plainly there are two questions to be raised about this argument. (i) Are the alternative analyses of qualitative change which McTaggart here proposes exhaustive? (ii) Is he justified in rejecting the first two of the three alternatives which he considers?

(i) It will be noticed that, in all the alternatives which

[2] [Pp. 90–91 of this volume.—Ed.]

McTaggart here considers, he confines his attention to *events* and says nothing about *things*. The alternatives which he considers are (*a*) that *events* are generated and annihilated *en bloc*, (*b*) that *events* are continually "losing their tails and growing new heads", and (*c*) that *events* change in respect of A-characteristics. Now *prima facie* it is *things*, and not events, which are the subject of qualitative change. Oddly enough, McTaggart never mentions this apparent alternative until he begins to criticize Russell's analysis of qualitative change in ##314 to 316 inclusive.[3] It will be well to consider what he says about this at once.

Perhaps the most plausible way of stating Russell's theory is the following. Events are neither generated nor annihilated, nor do they change in respect of any of their characteristics. There are certain series of successive events, such that the members of any one such series are intimately interconnected by certain spatial, causal, and other relations, which do not interconnect members of any two such series. Each such series is counted as the history of a different thing. Now successive members of one such series may differ in respect of a certain quality; e.g., one term may have the determinable quality Q in the determinate form q_1 and a later term may have Q in the form q_2. The statement "The thing T changes from q_1 to q_2" is completely analyzable into a statement of the following kind. "There is a certain series of successive events so interrelated that it counts as the history of a certain thing T; e_1 and e_2 are two successive adjoined phases in this series; and e_1 has Q in the form q_1 whilst e_2 has Q in the form q_2." Now what objection has McTaggart to this alternative, which he failed to consider in ##310 and 311? He has two objections. The first is, I think, irrelevant; and the second is, I think, an *ignoratio elenchi*. We will now consider them in turn.

(*a*) In #315 his objection amounts to the following. It is *always* a fact about this series that it contains a term which has q_1 and a term which has q_2 and that the former immediately precedes the latter. Hence this fact cannot be

[3] [Pp. 92–93 of this volume.—Ed.]

what is referred to when we say that T has changed in respect of Q from q_1 to q_2.

Now this seems to me to be irrelevant. Certainly, on this view of qualitative change, no fact and no event changes. It is alleged, instead, by the supporters of this view, that the fact of change consists in a conjunction of facts which neither change nor are about change. To this McTaggart merely makes the counter-assertion that there can be no change unless certain facts about events change, i.e., unless events of the first-order are subjects of events of the second-order. And the only ground which he has given for this is the argument in ##310 and 311, where he *ignored* the present alternative and *assumed* that he had exhausted all the possible alternative views about qualitative change.

(*b*) In #316 he takes a different line. He there admits that such a series *would* constitute a process of qualitative change, provided that the terms in it *could* be related by the relation "earlier than". But he claims to have shown that, unless the terms had A-characteristics and changed in respect of these, they could not be related by this relation, and therefore the series could not be a process of qualitative change.

But how has he shown this? He has done so, if at all, only by using an argument which *ignores* the present alternative and *assumes* that the three alternatives enumerated in ##310 and 311 are exhaustive. Thus he rejects the present alternative only by appealing to an argument which tacitly assumes that it has already been rejected.

(ii) We can now pass to the second question. Was McTaggart justified in rejecting the alternatives which he mentioned in #310? The basis of his rejection is the principle that, if X *ever* precedes Y by a certain amount, then it *always* precedes Y by precisely that amount. This principle is supposed to be incompatible with the view that events are generated and annihilated. Now I think that this principle, though it is obviously true in some sense or other, needs to be rather carefully considered.

Let us take as examples the Battle of Hastings and the Battle of Waterloo. Before either battle had happened it would have been true to say "There will be a battle at Has-

tings and there will be a battle at Waterloo 749 years later",
though perhaps no one would have been in a position to say
it. During the Battle of Hastings it would have been true to
say "There is a battle going on at Hastings and there will be a
battle at Waterloo 749 years later." At any intermediate date
it would have been true to say "There was a battle at Hastings and there will be a battle at Waterloo 749 years later."
During the Battle of Waterloo it would have been true to
say "There is a battle going on at Waterloo and there was a
battle at Hastings 749 years earlier." At any moment after
the Battle of Waterloo it is true to say "There was a battle
at Hastings and there was a battle at Waterloo 749 years
later." These expressions, all of which involve *temporal copulas,* are the natural and the accurate ways of recording
facts about relations of precedence. When both events are
known or confidently believed to have happened it is usual
and convenient to employ such a phrase as "The Battle of
Hastings preced*ed* the Battle of Waterloo by 749 years."
When it is confidently expected that both events will happen
it is usual and convenient to employ such a phrase as "The
degree-ceremony *will be* followed after an interval of half-an-
hour by a luncheon in Trinity."

It will be noticed that, in every case, either a temporal
copula or a verb with tense is used. No one but a philosopher
doing philosophy would say "The Battle of Hastings preced*es*
the Battle of Waterloo by 749 years." Such phraseology
would suggest that the two events are two particulars which
(*a*) somehow *coexist* either timelessly or simultaneously, and
yet (*b*) stand timelessly or sempiternally in a certain *temporal* relation of precedence. This must be nonsense, and it
is most undesirable to use phrases which inevitably suggest
such nonsense. I cannot help suspecting that there is some
muddle of this kind at the back of McTaggart's mind when
he says that events cannot be annihilated or generated because this would be incompatible with the fact that they
always stand in the determinate temporal relation in which
they do stand to each other. I suspect that his thought, if
made explicit, would run somewhat as follows. "In order to
stand in any relation to each other at any moment two re-

lated terms must, in some sense, *coexist*. Therefore, if a certain pair of terms *always* stand in a certain relation to each other, they must *always* coexist in that sense, whatever it may be. But, if two terms always coexist, *each* term must, in some sense, *always exist*. And, if each term always exists, neither term can ever be generated or annihilated."

Now I think that this argument owes any plausibility that it may have to the following confusion. One begins by thinking of relations between timeless terms, like numbers, or of spatial relations between bodies. Numbers "coexist" timelessly, and spatial relations hold between bodies only while the bodies coexist. If the fountain in the Great Court of Trinity were "annihilated", in the perfectly intelligible sense in which it would be if it were blown up by a bomb, it would no longer be between the Great Gate and the Hall. If a statue of Henry VIII were "generated" in its place, in the perfectly intelligible sense in which it would be if the College had one constructed there, it would begin to be between the Great Gate and the Hall. I suspect that one tends to carry over these notions and principles from timeless terms and continuants, where they are intelligible and true, to the perfectly unique case of events, where they are meaningless. The only sense in which an event *e* is "annihilated" is that there was and no longer is an event answering to the description of *e*. The only sense in which an event *e* is "generated" is that there was not and now is an event answering to the description of *e*. In this sense events *are* "generated" and "annihilated", and this is compatible with any two of them "always" standing to each other in any temporal relation in which they "ever" stand.

To sum up. It seems to me that McTaggart's arguments to prove that a *B*-series of terms which had no *A*-characteristics would not constitute a process of qualitative change, and therefore would not be a *B*-series, are thoroughly confused and inconclusive. It does not follow that his conclusion is false, or that it could not be proved in some other way. We will therefore re-consider the question independently.

2.24 *Restatement of the Position*. . . . McTaggart's mind probably moved in the following way in thinking of the connexion between A-characteristics and B-characteristics. I suspect that he thought that the B-relation could be *defined* in terms of the A-characteristics, and that the latter could not be defined in terms of the former; and he then constructed the very unsatisfactory arguments about qualitative change to persuade other people that the B-relation could not hold except between terms which had changing A-characteristics. . . . Even if we reject the view that "X is earlier than Y" *means* that there is a difference in the A-characteristics of X and Y and that this difference is positive, there remains another alternative which would suffice for McTaggart's purpose. It might be suggested that the relation "earlier than" can hold only between terms which have A-characteristics; just as harmonic relations can hold only between terms which have pitch. And it might be suggested that the degree of the B-relation between two terms depends on the difference between the determinate values of their A-characteristics; just as the harmonic relations between two notes depend on the difference between the absolute pitches of the two. In fact, to use an expression of Meinong's, we might be able to see that B-relations are "founded upon" differences in the A-characteristics of the related terms.

This view seems to me to be a highly plausible one, and I know of no positive argument against it. If it were accepted, we should have to grant to McTaggart that there could not be B-relations between terms unless the terms had A-characteristics, even if we refused to admit that B-relations are definable in terms of A-characteristics and their differences. I should consider that this theory holds the field unless it can be shown that sentences which contain the words "past", "present", or "future", or their equivalents, can be translated without loss of meaning into sentences which do not contain these words or equivalents of them, but do contain the phrase "earlier than" or some equivalent of it. Now Russell and certain other philosophers have claimed that this can be done. McTaggart discusses Russell's attempt in ##313 to 318 inclusive.

A simple way of stating the theory is as follows. Take the sentence "It is now raining." A number of utterances may occur at different times, which are all alike enough in the relevant respects to count as utterances of this sentence. Now anyone who utters this sentence seriously on any occasion means to express his belief that an occurrence of rain falling in his neighborhood is simultaneous with this utterance of his. And anyone who hears and understands any such utterance will take it to mean that an occurrence of rain falling in the speaker's neighborhood is simultaneous with this utterance. Thus any utterance U of the type-sentence (to use Ramsey's phrase) "It is raining now" means "An occurrence of rain in the neighborhood of the speaker who utters U is simultaneous with this utterance." We may abbreviate this into "An occurrence of rain is spatio-temporally contiguous with the utterance U." Now both speaker and hearer actually *prehend* the utterance U, since one makes it and both hear it. So, finally, when a speaker utters the type-sentence "It is raining now", what he means is "An occurrence of rain is spatio-temporally contiguous with *this* utterance of *mine*." And what the hearer understands could be expressed by the hearer saying "An occurrence of rain is spatio-temporally contiguous with *that* utterance of *his*." Different utterances of the same type-sentence necessarily have different meanings. One will mean "An occurrence of rain is spatio-temporally contiguous with U_1." Another will mean "An occurrence of rain is spatio-temporally contiguous with U_2." If U_1 and U_2 be successive, it may well be that one expresses a true proposition and the other a false proposition, though both are utterances of the same type-sentence "It is raining now."

The theory may be summed up as follows. Any utterance of a type-sentence, which is of a certain grammatical form and contains the type-word "now" or "present" or some equivalent, is understood by speaker and hearers to mean that an event of a certain kind is *simultaneous* with *this* utterance. Any utterance of a type-sentence, which is of a certain grammatical form and contains the type-word "past" or some equivalent, is understood by speaker and hearers to mean that an event of a certain kind is *earlier than this* utterance. And the same holds, *mutatis mutandis*, for any utterance of a type-sentence which is of a certain grammatical form and contains the type-word "future" or some equivalent. Unless there were people who uttered type-sentences of these kinds nothing would be past, present, or future; though events would still be simultaneous or successive. If this be so, A-characteristics have been completely analyzed in terms of B-relations.

Can this theory be accepted? (i) In the form in which I have stated it I do not think that it can possibly be the right analysis of what a *speaker* means when he utters such a type-sentence as "It is raining now", even if it were the right analysis of what his *hearers* understand on such an occasion. For this would involve that the speaker is using the utterance to express a judgment which he is making about the utterance itself. I am very doubtful whether this is possible at all; and I am fairly certain that, when I make such an utterance, I am not making a judgment about the utterance which I am making. This difficulty does not arise about the hearers.

(ii) The objection just mentioned could be removed by a slight modification of the theory. We might say that what the speaker means by his utterance is that an occurrence of rain is simultaneous with *this*, where *this* is some particular, other than the utterance itself, which he prehends simultaneously with making the utterance. The particular in question might be one of his own experiences or some *sensum* which he is sensing. His hearers will almost certainly not prehend this particular, and therefore what they understand by the utterance cannot be exactly the same as what the speaker means to express by it. As regards the hearers, we may suppose that each interprets the utterance to mean that an occurrence of rain in the speaker's neighborhood is roughly simultaneous with certain auditory sensa which that hearer is sensing, viz., those which are manifestations to *him* of this utterance of the speaker. Let us take the theory in this amended form, and consider whether it is adequate.

(iii) The first comment to be made is this. The theory professes to give an analysis of those temporal facts which are expressed by sentences containing temporal copulas, like "is now", "was", or "will be", or temporal adjectives, like "past", "present", or "future". When we look at the proposed analysis we find that it substitutes sentences of the form "Such and such an event is simultaneous with, or is earlier than, or is later than, *this*"; where "this" is used as a logical proper name for some particular which the speaker or the hearer is prehending when he makes or hears the utterance. Now what kind of copula is the "is" in these substituted sentences? Is it a timeless copula, like the "is" in "3 is the immediate successor of 2" or in "13 is a prime number"? Or is it the temporal copula "is now"? Or is it some third kind of copula which logicians and metaphysicians have not clearly recognized and distinguished?

If it is the timeless copula, the theory has *prima facie* been successful. If it is the temporal copula "is now", the theory has certainly failed. If it is supposed to be some third kind of copula, we must await further information about it from supporters of the theory.

Now, as I pointed out in Sub-section 2.23 . . . , we do not say "The Battle of Hastings precede*s* (or *is* followed by) the Battle of Waterloo." We say "The Battle of Hastings preced*ed* (or *was* followed) by the Battle of Waterloo." Again, we do not say, on getting up in the morning, "My lunch precede*s* (or *is* followed by) a meeting of the Faculty Board of Moral Science." We say "My lunch *will* precede (or *will* be followed by) a meeting of the Faculty Board of Moral Science." Thus it seems *prima facie* that the copula in propositions which assert temporal relations between events is not the timeless copula which occurs in propositions about the qualities and relations of abstract objects like numbers. The copula seems *prima facie* to be the temporal copula "is now", "was", or "will be", as the case may be. According to the theory which we are discussing, an utterance of the type-sentence "It will rain" means "An occurrence of rain in this neighborhood is later than *this*," where "this" is used by the speaker as a proper name for a certain particular which he prehends when he makes the utterance. But no one except a philosopher doing philosophy ever does talk in this way. What we say is "An occurrence of rain in this neighborhood *will* follow (or *will* happen later than) *this*." So *prima facie* the proposed analysis has failed to analyze away the temporal copula "will". Similar remarks apply, *mutatis mutandis,* to the proposed analysis of statements of the form "My breakfast is past" or "I have had my breakfast." We are told that an utterance of such a type-sentence means "Eating my breakfast precedes *this.*" But no one ever does talk in this way in real life. Instead we say "Eating my breakfast preceded this." And so, *prima facie,* the temporal copula has not been analyzed away.

Of course it may be answered that this objection depends simply on defects in the language that we speak. It may be so. But I am more inclined to think that the obvious artificiality and awkwardness of the sentences which express temporal facts, according to this analysis of them, are a sign that we are trying and failing to force temporal facts into the mold of non-temporal facts about abstract objects such as numbers. The theory seems to presuppose that all events, past, present, and future, in some sense "coexist", and stand to each other timelessly or sempiternally in determinate relations of temporal precedence. But how are we to think of this "coexistence" of events? It seems to me that the events and their temporal relations are thought of either by analogy with *timeless* abstract objects, such as the integers in their order of magnitude, or by analogy with *simultaneous persistent* particulars, like the points on a line in spatial order from left to right. Neither of these analogies will bear thinking out; yet I suspect that the theory is made to seem intelligible and adequate to its supporters by the fact that these irrelevant analogies are always hovering about at the back of their minds.

(iv) It remains to make one more comment on the theory under discussion. It seems to me that the theory leaves altogether out of account the transitory aspect of Time. According to it, "past", "present", and "future", as used by a person at any moment, always denominate relational properties, in which the relation is "earlier than", "simultaneous with", or "later than", respectively, and the relatum is some particular which the speaker is prehending or some experience which he is having at that moment. Supposing this to be true, the transitory aspect of Time consists in the fact that the relatum is never the same on two different occasions on which these words are used.

Consider, e.g., that series of successive experiences which constitutes my mental history from the cradle to the grave. On the theory which we are discussing, there is no question of events "becoming" or "passing away". In some sense of "is", there "is" timelessly or sempiternally all that there ever has been or will be of the series. The qualitative changes that take place in the course of my experience are supposed to be completely analyzable into the fact that different terms of this series differ in quality, as different segments of a variously colored string differ in color. But this leaves out the fact that at any moment a certain short segment of the series is marked out from all the rest by the quality of presentedness; that at any two different moments the short segments thus marked out are different segments, though they may partially overlap if the two moments are near enough together; and that the relatum at any moment is, or is contained in, that short segment which has presentedness at that moment. Thus change has to be postulated in a sense not contemplated by the theory, viz., the steady movement of the quality of presentedness along the series in the direction from earlier to later. If we try to deal with this kind of change in the way in which the theory deals with the qualitative changes that take place in the course of my experience, we shall be committed to making each term in the original series a term in a second series in a second time-dimension. We shall have events of the second order, viz., the becoming presented of events of the first order. In fact we shall be landed in the endless series of time-dimensions and orders of events which I mentioned in Sub-section 1.22. . . . And this seems to me to be a most serious difficulty.

As at present advised, then, I am inclined to agree with McTaggart that A-characteristics cannot be analyzed completely in terms of B-relations, and that the notions of Time and Qualitative Change involve A-characteristics as well as B-characteristics. I am well aware how easy it is to talk nonsense about Time, and to mistake for arguments what are in fact merely verbal tangles. I think it is quite possible that

I may have done this. I have altered my mind too often on this most perplexing subject to feel any confidence that my present opinions are either correct or well-founded. But I give them for what they are worth. . . .

3.11 *Criticism of McTaggart's Main Argument.* We must consider whether this argument of McTaggart's is valid. I should suppose that every reader must have felt about it as any healthy-minded person feels about the Ontological Argument for the existence of God, viz., that it is obviously wrong somewhere, but that it may not be easy to say precisely what is wrong with it.

(i) I cannot myself see that there is any contradiction to be avoided. When it is said that pastness, presentness, and futurity are incompatible predicates, this is true only in the sense that no one term could have two of them *simultaneously* or *timelessly.* Now no term ever appears to have any of them timelessly, and no term ever appears to have any two of them simultaneously. What appears to be the case is that certain terms have them *successively.* Thus there is nothing in the temporal appearances to suggest that there is a contradiction to be avoided.

(ii) What are we to say, then, about McTaggart's alleged vicious infinite regress? In the first place we must say that, since there is no contradiction to be avoided, there is no need to start on any regress in order to avoid a contradiction. Secondly, we may well ask why McTaggart should assume that, e.g., "*M* is now present" *must* be analyzed into "There is a moment *t*, such that *M* has presentness at *t* and *t* is present." Similarly, we may ask why he should assume that, e.g., "The moment *t* has been future" *must* be analyzed into "There is a moment *t'*, such that *t* has futurity at *t'* and *t'* is past."

(*a*) In the first place, we note that McTaggart has suddenly introduced the notion of *moments,* in addition to that of *events.* No justification whatever has been given for this. It would seem to imply that the temporal copulas "is now", "has been", and "will be" presuppose some form of the Absolute Theory of Time. This is surely not obvious.

(*b*) The real motive of this analysis, and the real cause of the subsequent infinite regress, seems to me to be a certain assumption which McTaggart tacitly makes. He assumes that what is meant by a sentence with a *temporal copula* must be completely (and more accurately) expressible by a sentence or combination of sentences in which there is no temporal copula, but only *temporal predicates* and non-temporal copulas. And the regress arises because there remains at every stage a copula which, if taken as non-temporal, involves the *non-temporal* possession by a term of certain temporal predicates which could belong to it only *successively*.

Take, e.g., the general analysis of "*S* is now *P*" into "There is a moment *t*, such that *S* has *P* at *t* and *t* is present." The only motive for making this analysis is that it seems at first sight to have got rid of the temporal copula "is now". The predicate "having *P* at *t*" may be said to belong to *S* timelessly or sempiternally if it belongs to *S* at all. And we are tempted to think that the "is" in "*t* is present" is a timeless copula too. Now the source of McTaggart's regress is that, if you take the "is" in "*t* is present" to be timeless, you will have to admit that *t* is also past and future in the same timeless sense of "is". Now this is impossible, for it is obvious that *t* can have these predicates only in succession. If, to avoid this, you say that the "is" in "*t* is present" means "is now", you have not got rid of temporal copulas. Therefore, if you are committed at all costs to getting rid of them, you will not be able to rest at this stage. At every stage of the analysis you will have a copula which, if taken to be *non-temporal*, leads to a contradiction, and, if taken to be *temporal*, needs to be analyzed further in terms of temporal predicates and non-temporal copulas.

Now it seems to me that the proper interpretation of the regress is that it disproves the assumption that temporal copulas can be replaced by temporal predicates and non-temporal copulas. Since there is nothing necessary or self-evident about this assumption, the regress raises no objection to the *prima facie* appearance that events become and pass away and that they stand to each other in relations of temporal sequence and simultaneity.

(iii) It may be worth while to go into a little more detail about the question of temporal copulas and temporal predicates before leaving this topic. Let us take the sentences "It will rain", "It is now raining", and "It has rained." The utmost that can be done with the first is to analyze it into "There is (in some non-temporal sense of 'is') an event characterized non-temporally by raininess, and it is now future." The corresponding analyses of the second and third would be got by substituting "it is now present" and "it is now past", respectively, for "it is now future" in the analysis of the first. Even if this kind of analysis be accepted as correct, we have not got rid of the temporal copula "is now".

Another type of analysis would be to make "It will rain" equivalent to "There is (in some non-temporal sense of 'is') an event characterized non-temporally by raininess, and it will be present." The corresponding analyses of the second and third would be got by substituting "it is now present" and "it has been present", respectively, for "it will be present" in the analysis of the first. Here we get rid of two out of the three *A*-characteristics, but have to keep all three temporal copulas. In the previous kind of analysis we got rid of two out of the three temporal copulas, but had to keep all three *A*-characteristics. So, on neither kind of analysis, can we get rid of *all* temporal copulas; and, on both kinds of analysis, we have to introduce at least one temporal predicate in addition to temporal copulas. Now the original sentences "It will rain", "It is now raining", and "It has rained" express the facts in the most natural and simple way without introducing temporal predicates in addition to temporal copulas. So both kinds of analysis seem to be worthless. They complicate instead of simplifying; they make nothing intelligible which was not intelligible before; and they suggest false analogies with non-temporal propositions.

Quite apart from the fact that such "analyses" serve no useful purpose, it seems to me that they fail to express what we have in mind when we use such sentences as "It has rained" or "It will rain." When I utter the sentence "It has rained", I do *not* mean that, in some mysterious non-temporal sense of "is", there *is* a rainy event, which momentarily pos-

F*

sessed the quality of presentness and has now lost it and acquired instead some determinate form of the quality of pastness. What I mean is that raininess has been, and no longer is being, manifested in my neighborhood. When I utter the sentence "It will rain", I do *not* mean that, in some mysterious non-temporal sense of "is", there *is* a rainy event, which now possesses some determinate form of the quality of futurity and will in course of time lose futurity and acquire instead the quality of presentness. What I mean is that raininess will be, but is not now being, manifested in my neighborhood.

The fact is that what are called "statements about past events" are statements to the effect that certain characteristics, which constitute descriptions of possible events, have been and no longer are being manifested. What are called "statements about future events" are statements to the effect that certain characteristics, which constitute descriptions of possible events, will be but are not yet being manifested.

To sum up. I believe that McTaggart's main argument against the reality of Time is a philosophical "howler" of the same kind as the Ontological Argument for the existence of God. The fallacy of the Ontological Argument consists in treating being or existence as if it were a predicate like goodness, and in treating instantial propositions as if they were characterizing propositions. The fallacy in McTaggart's argument consists in treating absolute becoming as if it were a species of qualitative change, and in trying to replace temporal copulas by non-temporal copulas and temporal adjectives. Both these "howlers", like the Fall of Adam, have been over-ruled to good ends. In each case one can see that there is something radically wrong with the argument; and one's desire to put one's finger on the precise point of weakness stimulates one to clear up linguistic confusions which would otherwise have remained unnoticed and unresolved. I suspect that plenty of other philosophers have made the same mistake as McTaggart. But, since they did not draw such startling consequences from their confusions as these eminent men did, these errors have been allowed to rest in decent obscurity.

TIME: A TREATMENT OF SOME PUZZLES

J. N. FINDLAY

JOHN NIEMEYER FINDLAY was formerly Professor of Philosophy at the University of London (King's College) and is now Sheldon Clark Professor of Metaphysics and Moral Philosophy at Yale University. His major publications include: *Meinong's Theory of Objects and Values; Hegel: a Re-Examination; Values and Intentions; Language, Mind and Value;* and *The Discipline of the Cave.*

(This article was written in 1941. Though I still agree with its general approach, I am now inclined to attach rather more positive value and importance to the metaphysical perplexities and positions it deals with. It will be obvious that the basic ideas of this paper derive from Wittgenstein.)

The aim of this paper is to inquire into the causes of some of our persistent perplexities with regard to time and change. We do not propose to offer a solution for these difficulties, but rather to make clear how they have come to worry us. For we shall suggest that they have their origin, not in any genuine obscurity in our experience, but in our ways of thinking and talking, and we shall also suggest that the clear consciousness of this origin is the only way to cure them. It is plain that we do not, in any ordinary frame of mind, find time so hard to understand: we are in fact always competently dealing with what we may describe as 'temporal situations'. We are dealing with such situations whenever we say, without hesitation or confusion, that this lasted longer than

FROM J. N. Findlay, "Time: A Treatment of Some Puzzles," *Australasian Journal of Philosophy,* 19 (1941). Reprinted by permission of the editor and J. N. Findlay.

that, that this took place at the same time as that, that this has just happened or that that will happen soon. We have no difficulty in showing other people what we mean by such forms of statement, nor in getting them to agree that we have used them truly and appropriately. Yet all these forms of statement, and the situations to which they refer, seem capable of creating the most intense perplexity in some people: people are led to say that time is 'paradoxical', 'contradictory', 'mysterious', and to ask how certain things are 'possible' whose actuality seems obvious. Thus it has been asked how it is 'possible' for anything to reach the end of a phase of continuous change, or how it is 'possible' for that which *is* the case ever to cease being the case, or how it is 'possible' for the duration of any happening to have a length and a measure. In all such cases it seems reasonable to say that the burden of proof that there *is* a genuine problem or difficulty is on the person who feels it, and not on the person who refuses to depart from ordinary ways of speaking. And it certainly does seem odd that people who have always had to deal with changing objects and situations, and whose whole language is perfectly adapted to dealing with them, should suddenly profess to find time so very strange. If time is so odd, we may very well ask, in terms of what things more familiar and understandable shall we proceed to explain it or to throw light on its possibility? We may indeed regard it as a strange disorder that people who have spent all their days 'in time', should suddenly elect to speak as if they were casual visitors from 'eternity'. And it must be our business to cure them of this disorder through a clear awareness of its causes. There is indeed 'a short way with puzzlers' who inquire into the 'possibility' of perfectly familiar and understandable situations: we may simply point to some instance of the kind that perplexes them and say: 'That's how it is possible for so-and-so to be the case'. Thus if a man were to ask me 'How is it possible that that which *is* the case should cease to be the case?', I might simply crook my finger and say 'Now my finger is crooked', then straighten it and say 'Now it has ceased to be crooked. And that's how it's possible for that which *is* the case to cease being the case.'[1] But such an expedient, though perfectly proper in itself, and more than a man has a right to ask for in most cases, would not suffice to allay our questioner's perplexity, since he, presumably, is quite as familiar with ordinary usage as we are.

A treatment of the puzzles of time will also serve to illustrate a treatment which might be applied to many other questions and difficulties. For some people quite readily fall into a mood in which they feel that there is something mysterious and doubtful about things that they would normally regard as elementary and obvious. They are then led to ask questions which seem queer, because it is not in the least plain how one should set about answering them. Thus a man may wonder how it is possible for a number of distinct things to share in the same quality, or whether he really is the same person from year to year, or why *this* world exists rather than any other. Now in ordinary unreflective moods we should regard these questions as either unanswerable or not worth answering, but our questioner plainly wants an answer and he doesn't want an obvious answer. It is plain, in particular, that we couldn't remove our questioner's perplexity by 'appealing to experience', by pointing to anything that both he and we could observe. For he *has* all the kinds of experience that could throw light on his problem, and yet he is puzzled. It seems clear that, where the simplest and most familiar instances of something occasion profound perplexity, we cannot hope to remove such perplexity, or even to allay it, by indefinitely accumulating other instances of the same kind, some of which would be strange and others highly complex. We are accordingly brought back to our supposition that there are some questions which beset us, not because there is any-

[1] The example given and the general method indicated was suggested by Professor Moore's proof that external objects exist. He proves that there are such objects by proving that there are two human hands, the latter being proved by holding up his two hands, and saying as he makes a certain gesture with the right hand, "Here is one hand", and adding, as he makes a certain gesture with the left, "and here is another" ' (*Proof of an External World*, p. 25). Reprinted in *British Academy Proceedings*, Vol. 25 (1939).

thing genuinely problematic in our experience, but because the ways in which we speak of that experience are lacking in harmony or are otherwise unsatisfactory. We are sometimes thrown into a mood of interrogation not because we are in quest of further facts, but because we are in quest of clearer, or less discordant, or merely different ways of verbally dealing with those facts. Such moods of questioning plainly have no answers, in any ordinary sense of 'answer'; we may nevertheless hope to relieve them by becoming clearly conscious of the underlying needs that prompt them, and by deliberately adopting ways of talking that provide appeasement for those needs.

There are other reasons why there is interest in our difficulties with regard to time. These difficulties form a relatively self-contained group of puzzles, which do not seem to share their entrails with too many other philosophical problems. We can find time difficult without finding anything else difficult, but we couldn't be puzzled by matter or mind or knowledge, without being puzzled by practically everything else. Hence we can deal more cleanly with these temporal puzzles than with other issues; they provide, accordingly, a simpler paradigm of method. These puzzles are also important in that philosophical difficulties seem to flourish more readily in the temporal field than in almost any other. It would be safe to say that rapid change and the 'nothingness of the past' are things which can always be relied on spontaneously to vex a large number of unsophisticated people, and so to constitute one of the standing mysteries of our universe. We have reason, of course, to suspect such generalizations; for we know nowadays that there is no way of ascertaining the philosophical reactions of unphilosophical common sense, except by testing and questioning large numbers of people.[2] But in the absence of such testing, vague experience certainly bears witness to the generality of such puzzlement.

[2] See, e.g., Arne Ness's *Truth as conceived by those who are not professional philosophers*, Oslo, 1938. In *Skrifter utgitt av Det Norske Videnskaps—Akademi i Oslo*, II. *Hist.-Filos. Klasse*, Vol. IV.

We may now point to a circumstance which is certainly responsible for *some* of our difficulties with regard to time. This is the fact that it is possible to persuade a man, by an almost insensible process, to use certain familiar locutions in ways which become, on the one hand, steadily wider and more general, or, on the other hand, steadily narrower and stricter. This persuasive process is only one of the many processes by which an able dialectician can twist or stretch or shift or tear apart the web of words with which we overlay our world. In doing so, he relies on the fact that the boundaries of linguistic usage are seldom clear, that there are always ranges of cases in which it is simply doubtful whether a given locution is or is not applicable, and that there are, in addition, a number of deep-seated tendencies in language which facilitate linguistic shifts in certain directions. In the particular case we are now considering there are, it is plain, words and phrases whose use very readily widens: it is easy to persuade a man that they really *ought* to be used in cases in which it has never before occurred to anyone to use them. And it is also plain that there are words and phrases whose use very readily narrows, so that we are easily persuaded to say that it was 'wrong' or 'improper' to use them in cases where we previously used them without hesitation. And it is possible for the adroit dialectician, by making repeated use of a big stick called 'consistency', on the one hand, and another big stick called 'strictness', on the other hand, to persuade us to use such forms of speech so widely that they apply to everything, or so narrowly that they apply to nothing: the result in either case is to turn a serviceable mode of speaking into one that is totally unserviceable. Good examples of these dialectical processes would be arguments which led us to use the term 'know' so widely, on the one hand, that we might be said, like the monads of Leibniz, always to know everything, or so narrowly, on the other hand, that we might never be said to know anthing. There is, of course, nothing in such an exaggerated width or narrowness of reference which *necessarily* leads to paradoxes or problems. If we persuade a man to use words in new ways, we disorganize his linguistic habits for the time being, but there is no reason why he should not rapidly build up a new set of habits, which will enable him to talk of ordinary situations as plainly and as promptly as before. But the trouble is that such a sudden change of usage *may* produce a temporary disorientation, it is like a cerebral lesion from which an organism needs to recover, and in the interval before recovery sets in, and new connections take the place of the old, a man may readily become a prey to serious confusions. For even after a man has been persuaded to use certain phrases in totally new ways in certain contexts, he may still hark back to old uses in other contexts: he may even try to incorporate both uses in the same context, thus giving rise to statements and questions which cannot be interpreted in either way of speaking.

Now in regard to time it is plain that there is a strong tendency in language to use terms connected with the 'present' in an ever stricter manner, so that, if this tendency is carried to the limit, the terms in question cease to have *any* application, or, at best, a novel and artificial one. It is also plain that *some* of the problems of time are connected with this fact. We can readily be persuaded to use the present tense and the temporal adverb 'now' (as well as the imperfect past and imperfect future tenses and the words 'then', 'at that time', etc.) in stricter and stricter ways; and if we yield completely to such pressure, our normal habits of speech will be disorganized. Our use of the present tense and of the temporal adverb 'now' is not very strict in ordinary circumstances: we are prepared to say, even of happenings that last a considerable time, that they are happening *now*, e.g. we say 'The National Anthem is now being sung', 'The Derby is now being run', etc. Now the present tense and the temporal adverb 'now' *might* have been the sort of speech-form that we tended to use more and more widely, so that we might easily have been persuaded to say 'The history of England is now running its course', 'The heat death of the Universe is now taking place'. We might then have been persuaded to allow that, since a *whole* cannot be happening now, unless all its component *parts* are also happening now, John is now really signing Magna Carta, life on the earth is now really extinct, and so on. The problems that this way of speaking might occasion, would certainly be serious. The natural development of the speech-forms we are considering does not, however, lie in this direction. We tend rather, if pressed, to use the present tense and the temporal adverb 'now' more and more narrowly: thus if we had said that the National Anthem was being sung, and someone asked us 'But what are they singing *just now?*', we should not widen our reference to cover the whole evening's concert, but narrow it to apply to some line or phrase or word or note of the National Anthem. Now since our tendencies lie in *this* direction, we can readily be persuaded to give up saying that anything which takes an appreciable time is happening now. We can be bullied into admitting that this is a 'loose' and 'inaccurate' way of talking. And it is possible to force us to grant that the really strict speaker would not use these forms of speech in the case of anything but a happening which was so short that it took *no time at all.* Thus we might force a man first to admit that nothing which was *past,* nothing which was *no longer there,* could possibly be said to be happening now. We might then press him to admit the additional principle that nothing of which a *part* lay in the past could properly be said to be happening now. We might then persuade him to grant, with regard to any happening that 'takes time', that it doesn't happen 'all at once', but that it has parts which happen one after the other, and that, when any *one* of these parts *is* happening, all the *other* parts either *have* happened or *will* happen. It then becomes easy to prove that no happening which takes time can properly be said to *be* taking place, and that the only parts of it of which such a thing could ever be rightly said, would be parts that took *no time at all.*[3]

In all these arguments we are being persuaded to apply linguistic principles which are established in the case of happenings of *fairly long duration,* to happenings of very short duration; we are not obliged, but can be readily pressed, to be 'consistent' in this manner since there are no clear lines between the long and the short. But the result of yielding to

[3] The typical historical case of this argument is Augustine, *Confessions* (Book XI: 19, 20) [pp. 41–42 of this volume—Ed.].

this pressure is to turn a serviceable way of talking into one that has no use. For it is obvious that all the happenings that we can point to (in any ordinary sense of 'point to') take time, and that pointing itself takes time, so that if the only happenings of which we may say 'This is happening now' are happenings which take no time, there are no happenings which we can point to, of which we may say 'This is happening now'. Now this does not, of course, imply that a clear and useful meaning cannot be given to phrases and sentences which mention happenings that take no time: it is plain, in fact, that very clear and useful meanings *have* been given to them by a long succession of mathematicians and philosophers. But it is also plain that these new forms of diction may, at first, merely serve to disorganize existing speech-habits, and that, while this lasts, we may fail to give any clear or serviceable meaning to 'happenings which take no time'; we may tend to talk of them as if they were happenings we could point to, in the same sense in which we can point to happenings which *do* take time, and we may further credit them unthinkingly with many of the properties of happenings which *do* take time. Such ways of talking, it is plain, must lead to many quite unanswerable questions.

After this preliminary consideration of *one* source of our temporal difficulties, we may turn to Augustine's problem in the eleventh book of the *Confessions*. This we may phrase as follows: 'How can we say of anything that it lasts a long time or a short time? How can a time have length? And how can that length be measured?'[4] What was it, we may ask, that Augustine found so difficult in the length and measure of time? We may perhaps distinguish three aspects of his bewilderment, which might be grounds for anyone's bewilderment. He found it difficult, in the first place (we may suppose), to see how happenings which take *no* time could ever be 'added up' to make the happenings which *do* take time.[5] This difficulty is not peculiar to our thought of time, but

[4] The interest in Augustine as a case of philosophical puzzlement is due to Wittgenstein.

[5] Augustine: 'The present hath no space. Where then is the time which we may call long?' See above.

applies to space as well. It seems absurd to say that an accumulation of events, the duration of each of which is zero, should have, together, a duration that is more than zero. The matter might be put more strongly. We are inclined to say that, if the duration of events were reduced to zero, 'there would be nothing left of them', they would 'just be nothing', and we obviously could not hope to make something out of an accumulation of nothings.[6] We may regard this as one side of the Augustinian problem. A second slightly different side consists in the fact that the stages of any happening that takes time are never there *together*. Now it seems absurd to say of a number of things which are never together, but always apart, that they can ever *amount* to anything, or form a *whole* of any kind: it would be as if one were to try to build a house with bricks that repelled each other, so that each one moved away when the next one was brought up to it. At such a rate, it would seem, one could build no house and no interval of time.[7] But Augustine's problem has a third side which seems to have worried him particularly: that if we measure an interval of time, we must be measuring something of which a vanishing section only has reality: all the other sections of it, which give it breadth and bulk, are either *not yet there* or *not there any longer*. Now it is hard to grasp how we can measure something which is no longer there, which is 'past and gone', of which we are tempted to say that it is 'simply nothing'. And it is also hard to grasp how we can measure something which is not yet there, which is merely expected, which we are likewise tempted to describe as 'nothing'. It would be like trying to measure a building of which all but the tiniest fragment had been blasted by a bomb, or existed merely in a builder's blue-print. In such a situation we should have no building to measure, and it seems

[6] Augustine: 'If time present . . . only cometh into existence because it passeth into time past, how can we say that either this is, whose cause of being is that it shall not be' (XI, 15) [p. 40 of this volume—Ed.].

[7] Augustine: 'Therefore neither is the year now current present; and if not present *as a whole* (our italics) then is not the year present.' See above.

we should be in the same position with regard to lengths of time.[8]

We shall now briefly point to some ways—there are an indefinite number of such ways—in which we might avoid these Augustinian perplexities. We might, first of all, evade the whole argument by which we have been bludgeoned into saying that there are some events that take no time, and that only these are ever truly present. We might refuse to say, of certain happenings which are very short, that any of their parts lie in the past or future; we do not normally, in fact, make use of the past and future tenses in speaking of the parts of very short events contemporary with our utterance. Alternatively we might say that some sufficiently short events can be 'present as wholes', though most of their parts are past or future; this too agrees with ordinary usage, for we say that many fairly long events *are* happening, though we should talk in the past or future tense of some of their remoter parts. Or again we might deny—as Whitehead in his doctrine of epochal durations has denied—that certain very brief events come into being *part by part*.[9] There is, in fact, no plain empirical meaning to be given to the supposition that all events come into being part by part, since there must necessarily be a limit to the division of events by human judgements or instruments. Or again we might choose to follow certain other trends of language, and to say, of certain very brief events, that they 'took no time at all', thereby excluding from the start the whole issue of divisibility into successive parts.[10]

[8] Augustine: 'In what space then do we measure time passing? In the future, whence it passeth through? But what is not yet we measure not. Or in the present by which it passes? But no space we do not measure. Or in the past to which it passes? But neither do we measure that, which now is not' (XI, 27) [p. 45 of this volume—Ed.].

[9] 'Accordingly we must not proceed to conceive time as another form of extensiveness. Time is sheer succession of epochal durations. . . . The epochal duration is not realized *via* its *successive* divisible parts, but is given *with* its parts' (*Science and the Modern World*, p. 158).

[10] *How* brief the happenings must be, of which we say any of these things, is of course a matter for arbitrary decision.

It does not, in fact, matter, in all this choice of diction, *what* we say, provided only that we truly please ourselves: the facts are there, we can see and show them, and it is for us to talk of them in ways which will neither perplex nor embarrass us. It is desirable, in our choice of words, that we should be consistent, but it is not desirable that we should make a fetish of consistency. Consistency in language is most necessary if it means that we shall not, in a given context, fall victims to linguistic conflicts, that we shall not try to say something, while striving at the same time to unsay it.[11] Consistency is also very desirable if it means that we shall be guided by the analogies of things in what we say in *different* contexts; in the absence of *some* degree of such consistency, all language would be arbitrary and communication impossible. But consistency is wholly undesirable if it becomes a bogey, if it makes us say something in one context merely because we have said it in some other, more or less analogous context, and if it then leads us on to say further things which bewilder and confuse us. For the analogies of things are varied and conflicting, and it is impossible, without disrupting human language, to do justice to them all.

So far we have pursued a line which shakes the dialectic on which the Augustinian problem is founded. By so doing we avoid giving a sense to the phrase 'events which take no time', and are not obliged to say that these alone are truly present. Suppose however we are moved by this dialectic, or by some consideration of scientific convenience, to admit this talk of 'momentary presents', how then shall we proceed to deal with the various aspects of the Augustinian problem? As regards the first aspect, the building of a whole which has size out of parts which have *no* size, we may simply point out that it mixes up the familiar sense in which a pile of money is built up out of coins, with the new sense in which a happening which takes time may be built up out of happenings which take no time. Because one couldn't amass a fortune out of zero contributions, one tends to think one couldn't

---

[11] Unless, indeed, a linguistic conflict is deliberately used to express some personal reaction to reality, as has been done by some philosophers.

make a measurable duration out of parts with no duration. But the situations are quite different; no one has witnessed a lapse of time being built up out of instants, as he can witness a pile of money being built up out of coins, nor can the former be imagined as the latter is imagined.[12] Hence if we wish to speak of 'happenings which take no time', we are quite free to fix what may be said of them, and this means that we may simply rule that events which take time *are* made up of events which take no time. And once misleading pictures are avoided, we shall find no problem in this. We may in the same way dispose of the difficulties which spring from the tendency to say that an event which took no time would 'just be nothing'. Either we must restrain this inclination—to which we are not in duty bound to yield—or be prepared to say that certain parts of real temporal wholes are simply nothing, and that mere nothing can at times have definite properties. This way of talking would no doubt do violence to our habits, and abound in dangerous suggestions, but we should not, with a little practice, find it difficult.

The second aspect of the Augustinian problem involves a similar confusion. Because it would be absurd to say of certain wholes—houses, mountains or libraries, for instance—that they existed and were measurable, although their parts were never together, we think it would be absurd to say the same thing of happenings. But the fact that we shouldn't say that *some* of the things we call parts could constitute the things we call their wholes, unless they were present together, does not oblige us to say this in the case of *other* things we also call parts and wholes. For the sense in which the parts were parts, and the wholes wholes, and the former made up the latter, might be ruled to be different in the two sets of cases: we might say we were dealing with two totally different *sorts* of parts and wholes. And we do in fact rule so; for we regard it as nonsense to say of an event that takes time, that its parts are present together. And we recognize the difference between the two sets of cases by talking of *coexistent* parts

[12] Though a sense might be invented in which we could be said to witness or imagine the former.

in the one set of cases, and of successive parts in the other: the successive parts of a whole are, in fact, just those parts of it that *don't* need to be together. But if we feel ourselves unconquerably opposed to calling something a whole whose parts are not together, we may simply rule that some things may have magnitude although they are not wholes. And other similar expedients will meet other possible difficulties.

As regards the third difficulty of Augustine, how we manage to measure something which is in part past, we may again suggest a number of alternatives. We might, in the first place, reject the analogy between the measurement of a coexistent whole like a house, which isn't there to be measured if any parts of it lie in the past, and the measurement of a successive whole like a happening, which *must* have parts in the past. Or we might follow certain other trends of language, and say that we have succession *in the present*, and that certain happenings which are not too long are able to be present as wholes and so to be measured directly. Other longer happenings might then be measured by means of the briefer and directly measurable happenings which entered into their remembered history. Or if it is the 'nothingness of the past' that troubles us, we must remember that we are not compelled to say that the past is nothing: we may, if we like, credit it with existence or subsistence or any other suitable status. For we are only worried by the 'nothingness of the past' because we think it will stop us from finding out any facts about the past, just as the nothingness of a bachelor's children stops us from asking for their ages or appearance. But there are so many clear and agreed ways of establishing what has happened in the immediate or remoter past, that it would be nonsense to put past events in the position of a bachelor's children. So that if we wish to say that they exist or subsist, there is no good reason why we should not do so. But if the 'existence' of the past is going to suggest to us that we could by some device revive or revisit the past, as we could revive a drowned man or revisit Palermo, then it is perhaps better to go on saying that the past is nothing, allowing meanwhile that there may be measurable wholes which have certain parts that are nothing.

The puzzles of Augustine lead on very naturally to the problems of Zeno, or rather to a certain very general difficulty which seems to be involved in every one of Zeno's paradoxes. This is our difficulty in seeing how anything can happen, if *before* it happens something else must happen, and *before* that happens something else must happen, and so on indefinitely. If we make time continuous and infinitely divisible, we also feel obliged to say that before any happening is completed, an infinity of prior happenings must have been completed, and this seems to mean that *no* happening can ever be completed. We seem to be in the plight of a runner in a torch-race, who wants to hand on his torch to another runner A, but is told by A that he will only take it from B, who tells him he will only take it from C, who tells him he will only take it from D, and so on indefinitely. Or in the plight of a man who wants to interview a Cabinet Minister, and who is informed by the Minister that he must first discuss his business with the Under-Secretary, who informs him he must first discuss it with the Chief Clerk, etc., etc. Our runner obviously will never get rid of his torch, and our harassed petitioner will obviously never see his Minister, and it looks as if all happenings involve the same hopeless difficulty. The difficulty we are presenting is, of course, not identical with any one of Zeno's historical puzzles: in all of these the difficulties of duration are complicated by the introduction of change and motion. But it is plain that all these puzzles could be so restated as to deal with happenings without regard to whether those happenings were changes or persistent states, and without regard to whether they involved motion or not. A plum continuing to hang on a tree for a certain period affords, less dramatically, the same species of philosophical perplexity as an arrow in its flight. Moreover, when we strip Zeno's problem of its spatial and other wrappings, its significance becomes clearer. For it is not, essentially, a problem of space or quantity, but solely one of time: it is only because all motion is *successive*, because an infinity of positions must be passed *before* any subsequent position, that the possibility of such motion seems so utterly ruled out. If the infinite stages of a motion could be there all at once,

as the parts of a piece of space are, we should feel no problem in their infinite number. It is therefore foolish to
imagine that we can meet Zeno's puzzles by the modern
theory of the continuum or by the facts of infinite convergent
numerical series.[13] And the problem assumes its most vexing
form if we allow that ordinary happenings have ultimate
parts that take no time. For of such parts it seems most
natural to say that none can be next to any other,[14] and once
this is said it is hard to understand how any ultimate part
can ever pass away or be replaced by any other. For before
such a part can be replaced by any other similar part, it must
first have been replaced by an infinity of other similar parts.
Our admission seems to leave us with a world immobilized
and paralyzed, in which every object and process, like the
arrow of Zeno, stands still in the instant, for the simple reason that it has no way of passing on to other instants.

As before, we may deal with our difficulties in several different ways. We might, in the first place, deny that very
short happenings are divisible as fairly long ones are divisible:
the divisibility of *all* happenings is in any case without a
definite meaning. This is the line followed by Professor
Whitehead, who makes time flow in indivisible drops, and
says that it is 'sheer succession of epochal durations'.[15] But,
far less drastically, we might give to all this talk of instants
and of infinite divisibility a sense consistent with the obvious
facts of our experience, that things happen and that phases
are outlived, that the world is not immobilized, and that we
seldom have to cast about for ways of passing on to novel
stages. For the infinite happenings that must first occur before a given thing can happen, are not like ordinary happenings we can see and show, of which it would be absurd
to say that an infinite number ever were completed. They
are happenings of a new sort to which a meaning must be
arbitrarily given. And since *we* have to give a meaning to

[13] This point is clearly brought out by Whitehead. See *Process
and Reality*, p. 95.
[14] Unless we choose to say that there is a finite number of ultimate parts in any happening, or other queerer things.
[15] *Science and the Modern World*, quoted above.

these happenings, it is for us to see that they mean nothing which conflicts with our established ways of saying things. And once we strip them of pictorial vividness, we also strip them of their puzzling character. Our problem also vanishes when we note that even to be 'desperately immobilized', to 'cast about in vain for means to pass to other stages', would both, if they were anything, be states that lasted and took time. Our problem therefore takes for granted the very thing it finds so difficult.

We turn, in conclusion, from these Augustinian and Zenonian difficulties, to a different set of temporal puzzles, quite unconnected with our tendency to use the present tense in more exact and narrow ways. We shall consider briefly the very general wonderment which professes to find something 'unintelligible' or 'contradictory' in time and change. 'How is it possible', we sometimes like to ask, 'for all the solid objects and people around us to melt away into the past, and for a new order of objects and persons to emerge mysteriously from the future?' This kind of wonderment is most strongly stirred by processes of *rapid change:* we wonder at things which have no constant quality for any length of time however short, at things which only reach a state to leave it, and so forth. A similar perplexity besets us in regard to 'truths' or 'facts': we wonder how what *is* the case can ever cease to be the case, or how what was false *then* can come to be true *now*, and so on. This week the peaches in our garden are not ripe; next week we find them ripe; the following week they are no longer ripe, but rotten: in certain frames of mind we find this difficult. Our difficulty with regard to change may also be expressed in terms of 'happenings' and their 'properties' of 'pastness', 'presentness' and 'futurity', the form in which this problem was propounded by McTaggart. We wonder how it comes about that happenings which are at first remotely future, should steadily become more nearly future, how in the end they manage to be present, and how from being present they become past, and how they go on, ever afterwards, becoming more and more remotely past. McTaggart has shown plainly that we cannot solve this problem (if it is a problem) by bringing in the 'different times' at which events are present, past and future, since these themselves (whatever we may mean by them) have also to be present, past and future, and so involve the very difficulty they are called in to remove.

Now it is hard to see, if we remain in any ordinary, unreflective state of mind, what is the problem that is being raised by those who say they can't see how what *is* the case at one time, is not the case at other times, or that they can't see how a happening that is future can ever come to be a happening that is past. As we observed at the beginning of this paper, it should be possible to remove such difficulties by pointing to some ordinary happening around us, a man diving, for instance, and saying, as it happened, 'Now he's not yet diving', 'Now he's diving', 'Now he is no longer diving', or other similar phrases. And if a man were really puzzled by our usage in such situations, it would not take him very long to master it. We do not ordinarily have difficulty in knowing what to say of happenings as they pass, nor any tendency both to say and not to say the same thing in a given context, a kind of inconsistency that is seldom desirable. Occasionally, where change is rapid, we may find ourselves at a loss to say whether something is or is not yellow, or whether it is or was yellow: we may also have a tendency to say that it is both or neither. But all this only means we lack a settled and satisfactory way of talking about very swiftly changing things. But in the case of changes which are less rapid, we find ourselves quite free from conflict or confusion. *Before* an event occurs we say, if we have evidence that it is not yet happening, that it hasn't yet happened, but that it will happen, while if it *is* happening we say that it is now happening, that it hasn't ceased happening and that it isn't about to happen, and *after* it has happened we say that it has happened, that it is no longer happening and that it is not going to happen. Stated in words these semantic rules might seem circular, but taught in connection with a concrete situation they are wholly clear. And our conventions with regard to tenses are so well worked out that we have practically the

materials in them for a formal calculus.[16] Where all is so de-
sirably definite, what room is there for puzzles or perplexities?

To give an answer to this question, we must point to a
certain aspiration which all our language to some extent ful-
fils, and which we are at times inclined to follow to unreasonable lengths. We desire to have in our language only those
kinds of statement that are *not* dependent, as regards their
truth or falsity, on any circumstance in which the statement
happens to be made. We do not wish a statement which we
call 'correct' and 'justified by fact' when made by one person, to be incorrect when made by another person, and to
have to be superseded by some other statement. In the same
way we do not wish a statement which we call 'correct'
when made in one place, to be incorrect when made in another place, and to have to be superseded by some other
statement. And there are occasions when we feel the same
sort of thing about the *time* at which a statement is made:
if we are right in saying something at a certain time, then,
we sometimes feel, we must be right in saying the same thing
at all other times. This means that we object, in certain
frames of mind, even to the easy, systematic changes of tense
which statements have to undergo when they are transmitted
from period to period. We might express our general aspiration by saying that we wish our statements to be independent
of 'extraneous circumstances' in regard to their truth or falsity: 'the facts' must settle whether what we say is true, and
nothing else must come into consideration. But such a way
of talking would be gravely question-begging, for it depends
on the sort of language we are speaking whether a circumstance is or is not extraneous. If we spoke a language in
which the statements permitted in one place differed systematically from the statements permitted in another place, then

[16] The calculus of tenses should have been included in the modern development of modal logics. It includes such obvious propositions as that

x present = (x present) present;

x future = (x future) present = (x present) future;

also such comparatively recondite propositions as that

(x). (x past) future; i.e. all events, past, present and future,
will be past.

it wouldn't, in that language, be an extraneous circumstance, as regards the truth or falsity of a statement, whether that statement was made here or there. And those who used the language would protest quite legitimately that 'something was left out' by other languages which ignored all local circumstances of utterance. But the point is that we do *in part* say things which may be passed from man to man, or place to place, or time to time, without a change in their truth-value, and we look at things from *this* angle when we say that time, place and speaker are extraneous circumstances, and require our statements to ignore them.

Now the urge behind these austerities seems simply to be the urge towards more adequate communication, which is the fundamental impulse underlying language. We are prepared to sacrifice local and personal colour, or period flavour, in order that our statements may be handed on unaltered to other persons who are differently situated, or to ourselves in other situations. But it is not *this* sacrifice which gives rise to our perplexities: if we always spoke rigorously in the third person of everyone, ourselves included, if we avoided the adverbs 'here' and 'there', if we purged our language of tenses, and talked exclusively in terms of dates and tenseless participles, we should never be involved in difficulties. And for the purposes of science it is perhaps desirable that we should always talk in this manner. But our difficulty arises because we try to talk in this way but are also uneasy in doing so; we feel that something worth-while has been omitted, and try to combine our old way of talking with our new one. Thus McTaggart first offers us an order of events in which there are no differences of past, present and future, but only differences of earlier and later, in which every happening always stays the sort of happening it is, and always occupies the same position in the time-series: he then slides back into another way of talking in which events are present, past and future, and always *change* in these modalities. And his attempt to combine these ways of talking results in the unanswerable question: how can a single happening have the incompatible properties of being past and present and future? Whereas if we talk in the ordinary way we never have to say these things at once, and if we talk in an artificial, tenseless manner the question can't arise, since the modalities in question can't be mentioned. It is as if a man tried to retain the use of personal pronouns, such as 'I', 'you', 'he', etc., in a language in which everything that could truly be said by one man could truly be said by every other man, and were then led to ask: 'How can one and the same person be I and you and he?' And once we see the source of such perplexities, we should be easily rid of them.

SPATIALISING TIME

J. J. C. SMART

J. J. C. SMART is Hughes Professor of Philosophy at the University of Adelaide, Australia. He is the author of *An Outline of Utilitarian Ethics* and *Philosophy and Scientific Realism*.

In his article on 'How Specious is the Specious Present?' (*Mind*, January 1954, pp. 26–48) Mr. C. W. K. Mundle says that the doctrine of the specious present cannot be disposed of on *a priori* grounds, unless it can be shown that any attempt to think of temporal characteristics by means of spatial models is a logical misdemeanour. He then (pp. 34–36) considers a warning against 'spatialising time' which I gave in an article 'The River of Time', (*Mind*, October 1949). However, as I shall presently show, there are two quite different senses in which one might plausibly be said to be spatialising time. In one of these senses it is admittedly a reprehensible thing to do. In the other of these senses it is a thoroughly laudable thing to do. Mr. Mundle's arguments against me in effect assume that I was opposing spatialising time in this second sense, and this is a misunderstanding. I should add that Mr. Mundle cannot be blamed for so misunderstanding me: I expressed myself very badly indeed. But as the point at issue is of cardinal importance for a philosophical understanding of temporal concepts I hope I may be allowed to reopen the question.

Consider first of all two systems of solid geometry: (1) three-dimensional solid geometry, and (2) four-dimensional solid geometry. In both systems of geometry we talk of

FROM J. J. C. Smart, "Spatialising Time," *Mind*, 64 (1955). Reprinted by permission of the editor and J. J. C. Smart.

'solids'. Now I think it will be sufficiently well understood what I mean if I say that in three-dimensional solid geometry 'solid' has a three-dimensional logic and that in four-dimensional geometry it has a four-dimensional logic. Notice, furthermore, that in both systems of geometry 'solid' is a timeless concept. For example in three-dimensional or four-dimensional geometry alike the concepts of change, alteration, or staying the same, do not arise. Thus if we talked of a pyramid changing into a cube we should be moving outside the bounds of solid geometry.

If the above terminology is accepted, what are we to say of the logic of 'solid' in ordinary language? A cricket ball is a solid. But has 'cricket ball' a three-dimensional or a four-dimensional logic? The answer is that it has neither. 'Cricket ball' has not a pure three-dimensional logic. For in the case of 'cricket ball' the concepts of change, alteration, and staying the same do enter in. A cricket ball has a history. A cricket ball can begin by being spherical and become ellipsoidal. But nor does 'cricket ball' have a pure four-dimensional logic. Suppose our four-dimensional geometry is interpreted as a geometry of space-time. (As in the Minkowski representation.) Then time now does enter in, but not the terminology of change or staying the same. Let 'cricket ball$_4$' be the expression which in our four-dimensional representation refers to the cricket ball through its entire history. Then it makes no sense to talk of the cricket ball$_4$ changing or staying the same. For the cricket ball$_4$ to change we should need a second time dimension, a fifth dimension, for its changing (or not changing) to be in. What we express in our ordinary language representation by saying that the spherical cricket ball becomes ellipsoidal we express in our four-dimensional representation by saying that the three-dimensional cross-section for $t = t_1$ is spherical and that the three-dimensional cross-section for $t = t_2$ is ellipsoidal. In both these last two uses of 'is' the 'is' must of course be timeless. In our four-dimensional representation we talk about the same facts as in our ordinary language representation, but the form of representation is different. Incidentally this shows that in the *Tractatus* Wittgenstein was wrong in holding that there is only one possible form of representation for a given class of facts. What we can achieve with a four-dimensional logic ordinary language achieves by using words like 'cricket ball' with neither a three-dimensional logic nor a four-dimensional logic but with a hybrid between the two. That is, it uses 'cricket ball' with a three-dimensional logic modified by the use of concepts like 'change', 'alteration', 'staying the same'. This gives us the traditional concept of 'substance'. For many purposes the four-dimensional logic is better. The most notable example is the Minkowski world in physics. Woodger uses the four-dimensional logic in most of his writings. Quine advocates it tellingly in *Mind*, 1953, p. 442.

Corresponding to the two uses of 'solid' (in ordinary language a 'solid' can change, in geometry it neither changes nor stays the same) there are two uses of the word 'space'. In one sense space is something that endures, and could be said to change or not to change. For example, it makes sense to say that space is roughly Euclidean today but won't be so tomorrow. Again we can say that a part of space continues, or does not continue, to be unoccupied. In another use of the word 'space', and this is the mathematical one, space is a timeless entity. It is in this sense that we use the word 'space' when we talk of the space-time of the Minkowski representation as a four-dimensional space. Within the Minkowski representation we must not talk of our four-dimensional entities changing or not changing. This sort of mistake is often made in expositions of relativity. We often read of light signals being transmitted from one point of Minkowski space to another. This is liable to lead to metaphysical error, such as that of consciousness crawling up world-lines, but it is not at all difficult to see how the matter could be put aseptically, and I doubt if the error in exposition leads to errors in physics. Mr. Mundle makes a similar error on page 40 of his article when he tentatively talks of sensa as four-dimensional entities, and yet thinks it proper to consider whether they can linger and fade.

There are thus two senses of the word 'space': (1) that in which space is something that endures through time, and in which 'space' has something of the logic of 'thing' or 'sub-

G

stance'; (2) that in which we use the word in geometry, where we talk of two-, three-, four-, or n-dimensional space, or in which we refer to the space-time of the Minkowski world as 'a space'. In the first sense of 'space' the terminology of change or alteration does enter in, and it is in this sense of the word 'space' that we must not 'spatialise time', that is, think of time as an extended something along which we can move. For this to be so it would have to endure through a hyper-time. There is no objection whatever to spatialising time in the second sense, that is to thinking of space-time as a four-dimensional space in the geometrical sense of the word 'space'. What we must be careful to avoid, however, is mixing our terminologies, and talking of enduring, changing, and not changing, in the context of our four-dimensional representation. Now Mundle's arguments in favour of spatialising time are all in fact arguments in favour of spatialising time in this latter sense. My warning in my original paper was, however, only meant to be a warning against thinking of time as space in the first sense of this word, that is as a something that endures. (Like a river or a sea.)

In my original article there was this passage (quoted by Mundle): 'Now if we think of events as changing, namely, in respect of pastness, presentness and futurity, we think of them as substances changing in a certain way. But if we substantialise events, we must, to preserve some semblance of consistency, spatialise time.' This is to think of time as something in which events are, just as substances are in space. This is to take 'space' in the first, non-geometrical sense, the sense in which space endures, changes, etc. It is in *this* sense of 'spatialise time', and in this sense alone, that we must not spatialise time. My original suggestion was that we come to think of the passage of time by thinking of events as substances changing with respect to the queer properties of pastness, presentness and futurity. I now think that this diagnosis of the cause of our time-myth is probably incorrect. For etymologically the word 'past' is itself tainted with the myth of passage. Compare Latin 'praeteritus' French 'passé' and the Chinese 'kwoh liao', where 'kwoh' is an almost exact translation of the English 'to pass'. Greek, however, seems to be largely free of the 'passage' metaphor. It is also possible that there may be languages whose word for 'past' is derived from the past participle of the verb 'to be'. But whether or not my diagnosis of the causes of the myth of passage was correct is not a matter of prime importance. Other plausible diagnoses are imaginable. In any case I doubt whether it is the business of a philosopher to make such diagnoses: what is important is to be clear about the logic of the concepts in question, and to recognise a myth for a myth, whatever its origin.

THE OPEN FUTURE

INTRODUCTION

It will be recalled that the *A*-Theory held temporal becoming to be an objective property of events and claimed that because of this the past and future differ ontologically, the future being open and the past closed. Since past events have become present they have already won their ontological diplomas, unlike future events, which still exist in a limbo of mere possibility. Our ordinary concept of time contains this view, as witnessed by such gems as "Don't cry over spilt milk" and "What has been done cannot be undone." This common-sense distinction between the open future and the closed past can best be clarified by reference to certain logical asymmetries in our ordinary ways of talking about the past and the future: it is meaningful to speak of causing, deciding, and deliberating about a future, but not a past event; while, on the other hand, it makes sense to speak of having a trace (such as a memory or a photograph) of a past, but not a future event.

With these intimately related asymmetries, no doubt, in mind, certain *A*-Theorists have argued that there are further, more ontologically revealing, asymmetries between the past and future, namely: (i) all statements about the past are either true or false now while some statements about the future are neither true nor false now; and (ii) statements about the future must be general in logical form while statements about the past can be singular. (To say that a statement is singular means that its subject term identifies a particular individual.) These two purported logical asymmetries in our ways of speaking about the past and the future are independent of each other; one can, for example, deny (i) by holding that all statements about the future are either true or false, and, without inconsistency, deny that any statement about the future can be singular. Because a statement is general in logical form, for example, "Someone will be born tomorrow," does not debar it from being true or false now, and conversely a singular statement, such as "Joe Smith will die fifty years from now in a plane crash," might be neither true nor false now.

The B-Theory's assessment of these logical asymmetries would be as follows. There are no logical asymmetries between *past* and *future* because events are not intrinsically past and future, but only earlier than (past at) and later than (future at) some other chosen event(s). At best, certain of the above logical asymmetries can serve as criteria for distinguishing between earlier and later events relative to some chosen event. In other words, none of these criteria enables us to pick out some event as uniquely present, and therefore other events as past and future; since it is true of any time that only events later than (future at) that time could be deliberated about, etc., and that only events earlier than (past at) that time could be remembered, etc.

The B-Theory, however, cannot accept the two logical asymmetries outlined above—namely, that some statements about the future are neither true nor false, and that no statements about the future can be singular—even when they are demoted to the status of mere criteria for distinguishing between an earlier and a later time. The B-Theory cannot accept them because it countenances no ontological distinctions between events occurring at different times. All events comprising history are equally real and determinate, and can be completely described by timelessly true or false B-statements. By a parity of reasoning, it should also be true that all individuals, regardless of when they exist, are equally real and determinate, and therefore should be identifiable through the use of suitable referring expressions, such as proper names and definite descriptions.

We shall now discuss the mooted logical asymmetries (i) and (ii).

(i) Aristotle, in the selection from Chapter 9 of *On Inter-*

pretation, defends the belief in future contingents, that is, events that have not yet happened and are causally undetermined. A prediction about such an event, such as a sea battle tomorrow, is neither true nor false now, even though the logical disjunction formed from this prediction and its contradictory is true *as a whole.* For example, the disjunction "Either there will be a sea battle tomorrow or there will not be a sea battle tomorrow" is true as a whole, even although neither of its disjuncts is true now. If one of the two disjuncts was definitely true or false now that would entail fatalism— that nothing we do can make any difference in regard to the sea battle happening or not happening. Aristotle, according to some interpretations, felt compelled to deny the universal application of the law of the excluded middle, which requires that every proposition be true or false. He seemed to hold a three-valued logic: a proposition can be said to be "true," "false," or "neither true nor false"; and moreover, a proposition, such as a prediction about a future contingent, can change in its truth-value from being neither true nor false to being true (or to being false).

This conception of Aristotle's position has been closely followed by certain medieval logicians and in more recent times by Jan Lukasiewicz and A. N. Prior. The problem of future contingents has inspired the development of various systems of modal logic and of many-valued (especially three-valued) logics. The selection by Nicholas Rescher is an exposition of the historical situation and an attempt to elucidate the logic of future contingency by the formal machinery of modern chronological logic or "tensed logic." Rescher follows certain Arabic logicians in holding that Aristotle contended, not that propositions about future contingents are neither true nor false, but that they are not necessarily (definitely) true or necessarily false. According to this interpretation, Aristotle is not denying the universal applicability of the law of the excluded middle, but is making only a modal distinction between propositions about the future and those about the past (and present). Rescher argues that it is consistent to hold at one and the same time (a) that all propositions about the future are either true or false, and (b) that there are future contingencies, that is, genuine alternatives as to the future course of events, alternatives not to be foreclosed on the basis of deterministic or fatalistic considerations. On such a view, propositions do not change their truth-value over time, but only change modally with respect to the determinateness or inevitability of their assumption of this truth-value.

Richard Taylor, in his selection on "Fatalism," argues that logical determinism, the doctrine that every proposition about the future is either true or false (what will be will be), does indeed entail fatalism, which is the doctrine that it is never the case that it is both within our power to perform some action and also within our power to forego performing that action. The nerve of his argument, which is too complex to be discussed in detail here, is that the truth (or falsity) of statements about the future is relevant to determining what it is now within our power to do. From this it is easy to show that the universal application of the law of the excluded middle to statements about the future does rob us of our present freedom of choice and action. His argument, which has already provoked a rash of answers, is (hopefully) fallacious; but whatever fallacy it commits is not an obvious one. To answer his argument one must clarify the whole area of human action, which is as difficult to do as it is important.

R. D. Bradley's article is a criticism of the Aristotelian position, when interpreted as a defense of the three-valued logic, from the side of the B-Theory. In accordance with the B-Theory, he claims that all events are equally determinate and admit of description by timelessly true (or false) B-statements. A-statements are ambiguous and need to be rendered by B-statements. Since B-statements are timelessly true or false, their truth-value does not admit of temporal distinctions: it is nonsensical to say of such a statement that it is true *now* or *will be* true. Bradley, following W. V. Quine, charges Aristotle and certain of his followers with committing a logical howler in thinking that the logical disjunction, "Either there will be a sea battle tomorrow or there will not be a sea battle tomorrow," could be true even although neither one of its disjuncts is true. He claims that this disjunction is a truth-functional proposition which is true if and only if one of its disjuncts is true. The main brunt of Bradley's criticisms aims to show that Aristotle and his followers, such as Lukasiewicz and Prior, were wrong in thinking that logical determinism entails fatalism. Because future events are determinate, and therefore describable, does not entail even that they are causally determined. Aristotle's paradox comes from not distinguishing between the harmless tautology that what will happen will happen and the fatalistic doctrine that what will happen will happen of necessity, which entails that our choices and efforts are of no avail. Logical determinism does not entail coercive determinism. Because it is either true or false that we shall perform certain actions in the future does not entail that we are forced or compelled to do these things—that it is not now within our power both to do these things and also to desist from doing them.

It is interesting to note that no one is a fatalist about the past. No one has ever felt the need to deny the universal applicability of the law of the excluded middle to statements about the past so as to allow for human freedom. We believe that there are future, but not past, possibilities subject to our choice. The reason for this is found in the aforementioned logical asymmetries between the past and future which concern human action: we can bring about (cause), deliberate, plan, intend, and choose in regard to future events, but not past ones. In the selection on "Bringing About the Past," Michael Dummett argues that if certain unusual things were to happen it would be reasonable to speak of a present occurrence bringing about a past effect. If there were such backward causation, then agents could perform intentional actions for the purpose of bringing about past occurrences, and we could deliberate, plan, and choose in respect to the past as well as the future. If we were to allow causes to be posterior to their effects, then a Richard Taylor might think it necessary to deny the universal applicability of the law of the excluded middle to statements about the past, as well as those about the future, so as to avoid fatalism.

Numerous objections have been raised against the possi-

G*

bility of a cause being later than its effect. The really interesting and helpful objections are those that show the logical interrelations between the impossibility of a present event bearing past effects and the other logical asymmetries between past and future, such that giving up the former conceptual truth requires giving up the latter conceptual truths as well. The strategy is to show that an alteration in our ordinary concept of causality so as to allow for backward causation will cause absurdities to break out in certain neighboring concepts, such as intention and memory, with which the concept of causality has logical liaisons. Once again, this is very difficult to do.

(ii) The second logical asymmetry between past and future —that statements about the future, unlike those about the past, must be general—is forcefully defended by Bernard Mayo in his article in this section on "The Open Future." Mayo, however, was by no means the first philosopher to take this position. Charles Sanders Peirce, for example, held that all statements about the future must be general, since they are about the merely possible. And the possible is necessarily general: no amount of general specification or description can reduce a general class of possibilities to an individual case. "It is only actuality, the force of existence, which bursts the fluidity of the general and produces a discrete unity."[1] The class of great actresses *up to the present* contains identifiable individuals, even if these persons no longer exist; however, the class of future great actresses contains no such identifiable individuals. We can characterize and describe future great actresses but we cannot name any of them since they are not yet actualities: they are *as of now* mere possibilities.

C. D. Broad, in Chapter II of *Scientific Thought*, claimed that only the present and past are real, the future being literally nothing. For this reason statements about future individuals have nothing to which they can refer. And since the future has no existence, statements about it are neither

[1] Charles Sanders Peirce, *Collected Papers*, Cambridge, Mass., 1933, Vol. IV, § 172.

true nor false, since there is no fact, positive or negative, with which they can correspond. Such statements are at best only statements-to-be.

Gilbert Ryle has also defended the position that future tensed statements can convey only general information. There are good reasons, he claims, why novelists always write in the present and past tense, but never in the future tense; for if they were to cast their narratives in the future tense, they could never generate a vivid sense of reality. They would leave it an open possibility that the events they depict would never occur and that the heroes and heroines of their tales might never exist. For the same good reason, a comedian starts his act by saying "A funny thing happened to me on my way to the studio" rather than "A funny thing will happen to me on my way home from the studio." We cannot talk about the future in singular terms because we have not yet "got" future events and objects to serve as the subject of our predications. Mayo tries to articulate in what sense we have not yet "got" future individuals and why, as a result, our predictions must be general. He does this by attempting to show that all predictions have the same logical form as the general statement "A (some) S will ϕ."

Mayo, as well as his predecessors, defends an unrestricted version of the generality-of-predictions thesis to the effect that *no* statement about the future is singular. An obvious counterexample to this unrestricted thesis is a prediction whose subject term refers to a presently existing individual, such as "Professor Carnap will fly to the moon." Mayo's reply to this counterexample is that this prediction is really about a future event in the history of Professor Carnap, and not about the presently existing Professor Carnap. But the reply is rather weak, for it is based on a confusion between what is *referred* to by the subject term of a statement and the event *reported* by this statement. "Professor Carnap will fly to the moon" does *report* a future lunar flight, but its subject term certainly *refers* to the present Professor Carnap. That this prediction does *refer* to the present Professor Carnap can be seen by noting that (a) when I make this prediction I could, if I made the effort, literally *get hold* of the subject of my prediction, and (b) when my prophecy is fulfilled by Professor Carnap flying to the moon, I could rightly be asked if this moon-flier is the same man as the one I *was* referring to at the time I made my prediction. Also, if Mayo is right, appearances to the contrary, in holding that "Professor Carnap will fly to the moon" must refer to a future individual whom we have not "got" now, then to be consistent he would have to agree that the past-tensed statement "Professor Carnap was born in 1891" refers to a past individual whom we also have not "got" now. But then the desired asymmetry between the past and the future is obliterated.

Plainly, a more plausible version of the generality-of-predictions thesis is to restrict it to predictions whose subject terms refer to future individuals, that is, individuals who do not yet exist. The asymmetry between past and future would then consist in the proposition that any future-tensed statement referring to a future individual must be general, while past-tensed statements referring to a past individual, that is, an individual who no longer exists, can be singular. In defending this limited asymmetry between the past and future, Prior held that before an individual entity exists it cannot be the subject of predicates; after it has ceased to exist, however, it can still be the subject of predicates. It is only when a thing begins to exist that there begin to be facts about it. Predictions that refer to future individuals are analogous to indefinite promises. If I make an indefinite promise to give you *a* watch, when I hand a watch over to you in fulfillment of my promise, you cannot rightly ask me if it is the watch I promised, as you could if I had made instead a definite promise to give you some specific watch. Analogously, when I make the general prediction that some baby will be born ten years from now who will be called such-and-such and do so-and-so, when my prophecy is fulfilled you cannot ask me if this is the person to whom I was referring when I made my prediction.

To defend Prior's restricted version of the generality-of-predictions thesis, it must be shown that in no ordinary sense of "identify" can we identify an individual before it begins to exist. The obvious counterexamples to Prior's thesis consist in proper names made up for individuals before they exist and uniquely individuating descriptions of future individuals, for example, the first person to be born in 1998. A B-Theorist would claim that only a social convention prevents us from holding a baptism ceremony before the existence of the individual to be named. It might be claimed that descriptions, even when uniquely individuating, do not serve to identify, as do proper names and demonstratives (e.g. "this man"); for, in many contexts, a sharp distinction is made between describing and identifying. For example, a woman who had been assaulted could be said to be able to describe her assailant but unable to identify him, in that she can neither give his name nor pick him out (demonstrative sense of identify) of a police line up. Against this, a B-Theorist might contend that definite descriptions can, on some occasions, successfully answer the question "Which one are you referring to?" Thus they should be counted, with proper names and demonstratives, as identifying expressions. Furthermore, it could be argued that since proper names require a backing of definite descriptions, then if proper names serve to identify, so do definite descriptions. In other words, when we successfully use a proper name, such as "John Smith," to refer to a particular individual, we must be able to cash this name in in terms of certain definite descriptions, such as "*The* person who was born so many years ago to these parents and now resides in Brooklyn."

What is unquestionably true is that there is more chance of failure when we attempt to refer to a future individual than when we refer to a past (present) one. This may account for our reticence to give names to future individuals and to attempt to designate them by definite descriptions. The greater epistemic risk in trying to identify a future individual is due to certain logical asymmetries between past and future which have already been mentioned. We have a more intimate knowledge of the past, since we can have traces of the past but not the future. Also, there are future, but not past, possibilities about which we can deliberate and decide. Therefore, there are certain features of the future which must be unknowable to us, since we cannot know what

we are going to do while we are in the throes of deliberating
about what to do. The hesitancy of a married couple to name
their future child is due not only to the many future contingencies, such as the always possible loss of the child, but
also because they may not yet have made up their minds
about what to do.

ON INTERPRETATION

ARISTOTLE

In the case of that which is or which has taken place, propositions, whether positive or negative, must be true or false. Again, in the case of a pair of contradictories, either when the subject is universal and the propositions are of a universal character, or when it is individual, . . . one of the two must be true and the other false; whereas when the subject is universal, but the propositions are not of a universal character, there is no such necessity.

When the subject, however, is individual, and that which is predicated of it relates to the future, the case is altered. For if all propositions whether positive or negative are either true or false, then any given predicate must either belong to the subject or not, so that if one man affirms that an event of a given character will take place and another denies it, it is plain that the statement of the one will correspond with reality and that of the other will not. For the predicate cannot both belong and not belong to the subject at one and the same time with regard to the future.

Thus, if it is true to say that a thing is white, it must necessarily be white; if the reverse proposition is true, it will of necessity not be white. Again, if it is white, the proposition stating that it is white was true; if it is not white, the proposition to the opposite effect was true. And if it is not white, the man who states that it is is making a false statement; and if the man who states that it is white is making a false statement, it follows that it is not white. It may therefore be

FROM Aristotle, *On Interpretation*, Chapter 9, sections 18ᵃ–19ᵇ, translated by E. M. Edghill, *The Works of Aristotle*, W. D. Ross, ed., Clarendon Press, Oxford, 1928. Reprinted by permission of the publishers.

argued that it is necessary that affirmations or denials must be either true or false.

Now if this be so, nothing is or takes place fortuitously, either in the present or in the future, and there are no real alternatives; everything takes place of necessity and is fixed. For either he that affirms that it will take place or he that denies this is in correspondence with fact, whereas if things did not take place of necessity, an event might just as easily not happen as happen; for the meaning of the word 'fortuitous' with regard to present or future events is that reality is so constituted that it may issue in either of two opposite directions.

Again, if a thing is white now, it was true before to say that it would be white, so that of anything that has taken place it was always true to say 'it is' or 'it will be'. But if it was always true to say that a thing is or will be, it is not possible that it should not be or not be about to be, and when a thing cannot not come to be, it is impossible that it should not come to be, and when it is impossible that it should not come to be, it must come to be. All, then, that is about to be must of necessity take place. It results from this that nothing is uncertain or fortuitous, for if it were fortuitous it would not be necessary.

Again, to say that neither the affirmation nor the denial is true, maintaining, let us say, that an event neither will take place nor will not take place, is to take up a position impossible to defend. In the first place, though facts should prove the one proposition false, the opposite would still be untrue. Secondly, if it was true to say that a thing was both white and large, both these qualities must necessarily belong to it; and if they will belong to it the next day, they must necessarily belong to it the next day. But if an event is neither to take place nor not to take place the next day, the element of chance will be eliminated. For example, it would be necessary that a sea-fight should neither take place nor fail to take place on the next day.

These awkward results and others of the same kind follow, if it is an irrefragable law that of every pair of contradictory propositions, whether they have regard to universals and are stated as universally applicable, or whether they have regard to individuals, one must be true and the other false, and that there are no real alternatives, but that all that is or takes place is the outcome of necessity. There would be no need to deliberate or to take trouble, on the supposition that if we should adopt a certain course, a certain result would follow, while, if we did not, the result would not follow. For a man may predict an event ten thousand years beforehand, and another may predict the reverse; that which was truly predicted at the moment in the past will of necessity take place in the fullness of time.

Further, it makes no difference whether people have or have not actually made the contradictory statements. For it is manifest that the circumstances are not influenced by the fact of an affirmation or denial on the part of anyone. For events will not take place or fail to take place because it was stated that they would or would not take place, nor is this any more the case if the prediction dates back ten thousand years or any other space of time. Wherefore, if through all time the nature of things was so constituted that a prediction about an event was true, then through all time it was necessary that that prediction should find fulfilment; and with regard to all events, circumstances have always been such that their occurrence is a matter of necessity. For that of which someone has said truly that it will be, cannot fail to take place; and of that which takes place, it was always true to say that it would be.

Yet this view leads to an impossible conclusion; for we see that both deliberation and action are causative with regard to the future, and that, to speak more generally, in those things which are not continuously actual there is a potentiality in either direction. Such things may either be or not be; events also therefore may either take place or not take place. There are many obvious instances of this. It is possible that this coat may be cut in half, and yet it may not be cut in half, but wear out first. In the same way, it is possible that it should not be cut in half; unless this were so, it would not be possible that it should wear out first. So it is therefore with all other events which possess this kind of potentiality.

It is therefore plain that it is not of necessity that everything is or takes place; but in some instances there are real alternatives, in which case the affirmation is no more true and no more false than the denial; while some exhibit a predisposition and general tendency in one direction or the other, and yet can issue in the opposite direction by exception.

Now that which is must needs be when it is, and that which is not must needs not be when it is not. Yet it cannot be said without qualification that all existence and non-existence is the outcome of necessity. For there is a difference between saying that that which is, when it is, must needs be, and simply saying that all that is must needs be, and similarly in the case of that which is not. In the case, also, of two contradictory propositions this holds good. Everything must either be or not be, whether in the present or in the future, but it is not always possible to distinguish and state determinately which of these alternatives must necessarily come about.

Let me illustrate. A sea-fight must either take place to-morrow or not, but it is not necessary that it should take place to-morrow, neither is it necessary that it should not take place, yet it is necessary that it either should or should not take place to-morrow. Since propositions correspond with facts, it is evident that when in future events there is a real alternative, and a potentiality in contrary directions, the corresponding affirmation and denial have the same character.

This is the case with regard to that which is not always existent or not always non-existent. One of the two propositions in such instances must be true and the other false, but we cannot say determinately that this or that is false, but must leave the alternative undecided. One may indeed be more likely to be true than the other, but it cannot be either actually true or actually false. It is therefore plain that it is not necessary that of an affirmation and a denial one should be true and the other false. For in the case of that which exists potentially, but not actually, the rule which applies to that which exists actually does not hold good. The case is rather as we have indicated.

TRUTH AND NECESSITY
IN TEMPORAL PERSPECTIVE

NICHOLAS RESCHER

NICHOLAS RESCHER is Professor of Philosophy at the University of Pittsburgh and Editor of the *American Philosophical Quarterly*. His major publications include *The Development of Arabic Logic; Galen and the Syllogism; Hypothetical Reasoning; The Logic of Commands; The Philosophy of Leibniz;* and *Distributive Justice*.

I. *Historical Considerations on Future Contingency*

Regardless of any doctrinal views of the matter, it is clear that with respect to a wide spectrum of propositions we are not in a position to say whether they are true or false. (E.g., "The President of the U.S.A. in the year 2010 will have been trained as a physician.") And this is most graphically the case in those future matters with respect to which we ourselves deliberate regarding our line of conduct. (E.g., "Smith will do A" in a context in which Smith is endeavoring to decide whether to do A or B.) In such cases, the temptation may come upon us to hold not simply that *one cannot yet say* whether the statement at issue is true or false, but to hold that the statement does not yet have any truth-value whatever. The philosophical discussions revolving about this conception of propositions about future contingents as at first not having a truth-value, but acquiring one later on, were inaugurated by Aristotle's treatise *De Interpretatione* (*On Interpretation*).

Although the points at issue may seem to involve only matters of abstract logic, this appearance is deceptive, for important philosophical doctrines are critically involved. Consider the argument

(1) All propositions have a truth-value, and these truth-values do not change over time.[1]

(2) Therefore, propositions about my actions tomorrow were already true (or false) yesterday, and consequently

(3) My deliberations and decisions today can have no influence upon my actions tomorrow.

This line of reasoning grounds the philosophical doctrine of fatalism—i.e. (3)—upon the seemingly harmless theory of time and truth represented by (1). Considerations of just this sort led Aristotle, eager to preserve a doctrine of human freedom with a meaningful role for deliberation and choice, to explore the logical issues revolving about the concepts of truth and futurity. The aim of the present essay is to follow along in his footsteps and to explore whether, and how, deterministic and fatalistic consequences can be extracted from the logical conceptions of truth and necessity when viewed from a temporal perspective.

A. *The Orthodox Interpretation of Aristotle's Discussion*

On what deserves to be called the orthodox interpretation of the matter, Aristotle's teaching in Chapter 9 of *On Interpretation* can be characterized as follows: Propositions regarding the occurrence of contingent events of the future—e.g. the proposition that there will be a sea-battle tomorrow—are to be placed into a truth-status limbo, being *neither true nor false*.

According to this interpretation, Aristotle has in mind a chronologized conception of propositions, regarding them to be classifiable as follows:

(1) Atemporal or achronological propositions. ("The sum of two and two is four.")

[1] We rule out such assertions as "It rained in London yesterday" which may be true at some times and false at others, because they involve a shifting time-indicator (today, yesterday) rather than a definite date.

(2) Omnitemporal or transtemporal propositions. ("The moon is a celestial body circling about the earth.")[2]

(3) Present-oriented propositions. ("A sea-battle *is now* taking place.")

(4) Past-oriented propositions. ("A sea-battle *has* taken place yesterday.")

(5) Future-oriented propositions. ("A sea-battle *will* take place tomorrow.")

Confining attention for the moment to (3)–(5), we note that these can be temporally limited specifications of an omni-temporal proposition. For example, the omnitemporal proposition "At any and every time whatsoever, a sea-battle either does or does not take place" of course yields the future-oriented proposition "A sea-battle either will or will not take place tomorrow." Putting such limited specifications aside as degenerate cases, and concentrating upon the future-contingent specifications of (5), our orthodox interpretation of Aristotle contends that:

    i. The "Law of Bivalence," which holds that propositions must be either true or false:

$$N(Tp \lor Fp)$$

and

    ii. The "Law of Excluded Middle," which holds that of a proposition and its contradictory one must be true and one false:

$$N[Tp \lor T(\sim p)] \ \& \ N[Fp \lor F(\sim p)]$$

are applicable only to propositions of types (1)–(4), but fail to apply to propositions of type (5) which are about genuine future contingents. (Here we use 'p', 'q', etc. as propositional variables: '$\sim p$' is the contradictory of 'p'; '$\lor$' and '$\&$' stand for disjunction and conjunction, respectively; '$\rightarrow$' and '$\leftrightarrow$' represent entailment and (strong) equivalence, respectively; 'Tp,' 'Fp,' and 'Np' abbreviate "p is true," "p is false," and "necessarily p (is true)," respectively.

Thus on this orthodox interpretation, Aristotle held that virtually all propositions bear one of the usual two truth-

[2] Actually, Aristotle did not distinguish clearly between (1) and (2); he seems to have grouped them together.

values, T (true) or F (false), but that propositions about future contingents will exhibit the oddly indeterminate truth-status "neither true nor false."

This interpretation of Aristotle is espoused by J. Lukasiewicz,[3] A. N. Prior,[4] and indeed the bulk of modern students. In late antiquity it was espoused by such authorities as Ammonius and Boethius,[5] and is indeed much older. The Stoics thought they were opposing Aristotle in teaching that all propositions, even those regarding future contingents, are either true or false; and the Epicureans thought they were supporting him in attacking the Stoic position.[6] In this context the issue was sufficiently popular to be treated at some length by Cicero in De Fato.[7]

[3] Jan Lukasiewicz, "Three-Valued Logic," *Ruch Filozoficzny,* Vol. 5 (1920). Cf. also Lukasiewicz, *Aristotle's Syllogistic,* Oxford, 1958, pp. 155–56.

[4] A. N. Prior, *Time and Modality,* Oxford, 1957; see p. 86.

[5] Ammonius (fl. 490): *Commentarius in Aristotelis De Interpretatione,* ed. Adolf Busse, in the Berlin Academy edition of the *Commentaria in Aristotelem Graeca* (Berlin, 1897). ("It is therefore evident that statements about contingent matters . . . do not at all [or: *always*] have one particular part of a pair of mutually opposed contradictories to be true. . . . For whether both are exactly alike in capacity for falsity and truth . . . or [whether] the one is by nature more probably true and the other more probably false, neither [case] indeed is such that the [retrospectively] true [alternative] is always true and the false always false . . ." [154:34–155:5].) See also Manlius Severinus Boethius (fl. 510): *Minora Commentaria in Librum Aristotelis de Interpretatione, and Majora Commentaria . . .* in J. P. Migne (ed.), *Patrologiae Cursus Completus,* Latin series, Vol. 64 (Paris, 1891). Also, *Commentarii in Librum Aristotelis "Peri Hermēneias,"* ed. C. Meiser (Leipzig, 1877, 1880). (For future contingency see especially pp. 495–518 of the Migne edition. Boethius sums up as follows: *manifestum est in futuris et contingentibus propositionibus non esse veram unam, alteram falsam* [p. 518]. Cf. W. and M. Kneale, *The Development of Logic,* Oxford, 1962, p. 190.)

[6] See B. Mates, *Stoic Logic,* University of California Publications in Philosophy, 26 (1953), 28–29.

[7] M. Tullius Cicero (fl. 65 B.C.): *De Fato.* This deals at length with Stoic and Epicurean ideas regarding the truth of statements about the former attacking and the latter defending the view that: *omne igitur, quod falsum dicitur in futuro, id fieri non potest* [§ 12].

The interpretation at issue thus merits its qualification as "orthodox" in a double sense: it was the predominant (and the only?) view of the matter among the interpreters of Aristotle in antiquity, and is also espoused by the majority of students in our own day.

B. *The Medieval Interpretation of the Key Passage*

On what I shall call the *medieval* interpretation, Aristotle's position in the discussion at issue is as follows: A future-contingent proposition is indeed either true or else false (and thus does not fall into a truth-status limbo). The principles from which Aristotle seeks to exclude future contingents are neither the Law of Bivalence nor the Law of Excluded Middle as formulated above, which might be characterized as principles of *collective necessitation*, since the N-operator remains outside the disjunctions, but rather the corresponding principles of *distributive necessitation*, since the N-operator comes to be distributed through to the elements of the disjunctions:

i. $N(Tp) \lor N(Fp)$
ii. $[N(Tp) \lor N(T(\sim p))] \& [N(Fp) \lor N(F(\sim p))]$

That Aristotle is willing to apply these principles to all but future-contingent propositions is conceded on all sides. According to the present interpretation, what he is attempting to do in the discussion at issue is not to question the universal applicability of the principles of collective necessitation, but to argue that future contingents must be excluded from the sphere of application of these principles of distributive necessitation. His doctrine is not that future contingents lack a truth-status (*true* or *false*) but that they lack a necessitation-status (*necessarily true* or *necessarily false*), or rather that they are not *determinately* true or *determinately* false, as the medievals standardly put it.

Before considering Aristotle's discussion itself, it should be remarked that in the interpretation of Chapter 9 of *On Interpretation* the greatest probative weight must be given to its concluding section (19^a 18–19^b 4) which is *the only* section of this chapter where Aristotle is directly engaged in formu-

lating *in propria persona* his own view on the controversial
matters at issue. I shall now show how, according to the
medieval conception of the matter, this text is to be interpreted.[8]

*It is thus apparent that not everything is or comes to be by
necessity, but that some things come about by chance.* (The
tone of the entire ensuing discussion is set by this introduc-
tory insistence that not everything is *necessary*.) *And here
[i.e. when things come about by chance] the affirmation is
not true rather than the negation [by necessity]: even when
one [particular] alternative may be realized for the most
part, it may still be that the other [rarer] alternative may
chance to come about instead of [the usual] alternative.* (I
take the *ex anagkés* ["by necessity"] of the preceding sentence to be still operative here, so that what is at issue in
the first sentence here is not truth, but *necessary* truth. What
is thus denied in the case of future contingents subject to
chance is not that "$T(p)$ v $T(\sim p)$" but "$N(p)$ v $N(\sim p)$".
This construction seems not only possible but indeed plausible, in view of the basic underlying contrast here between
chance is not that "$T(p)$ v $T(\sim p)$" but "$N(p)$ v $N(\sim p)$."
explicit opposition of that which happens always to that
which happens sometimes or even for the most part, supports
the view that necessity, rather than mere truth is at issue
here.)

*That which is will be necessary when once it is, that which
is not [will be necessary] when it is not.* (That is, we have
"$T(p) \to N(p)$" and "$T(\sim p) \to N(\sim p)$" for propositions
regarding the past-cum-present.) *But not everything that is
is necessary, nor is all that is not necessarily not. For it is not
at all the same that "Everything is so by necessity when once
it is" and that "Everything is so by necessity."* (It is one
thing to maintain "$T(p) \to N(p)$" for propositions regarding

[8] My (deliberately tendentious) treatment of the passage should
be compared carefully with J. L. Ackrill's translation in *Aristotle's
"Categories" and "De Interpretatione"*, Oxford, Clarendon Press,
1963. See especially Ackrill's discussion of "the two main lines of
interpretation" in his notes on pp. 138–42.

the past-cum-present, and another to maintain it unqualifiedly.) *And similarly also with that which is not.* (That is,
one can only maintain "T$(\sim p)$ $\rightarrow$ N$(\sim p)$" with the same
restriction.) *And the same account holds for contradictories.*
(That is, the applicability of "N(p) v N$(\sim p)$" must also not
be made universal, but confined to propositions regarding the
past-cum-present.) *For it is necessary that everything either
be or not be; and [it is likewise necessary that everything]
either will come to be or not.* (That is, the applicability of
"N$(p$ v $\sim p)$" can be maintained without any temporal restriction.) *But we cannot say specifically that one or
the other alternative is necessary.* (We cannot maintain
"N(p) v N$(\sim p)$" unqualifiedly.)

  *For example, it is necessary that there will either be a sea-
battle tomorrow or that there will not be one.* (That is, if
p_1 is the specific proposition asserting that a sea-battle will take
place tomorrow, then we have "N$(p_1$ v $\sim p_1)$.) *But it is neither necessary that there will be a sea-battle tomorrow, nor
[is it necessary] that there will not be one.* (We do not have
"N(p_1) v N$(\sim p_1)$.") *That it will take place or will not take
place is necessary.* (So we only have "N$(p_1$ v $\sim p_1)$.") *Since
it is with the truth of statements as with the facts they state,*
(that is, while neither "a sea-battle is occurring" nor "a sea-
battle is not occurring" must necessarily represent a true
state of affairs, "a sea-battle is either occurring or not" must
necessarily represent a true state of affairs) *it is evident that
whenever there is a contingent matter that may chance to
turn out in either of opposite ways, the contradictory alternatives must be of the same status [sc. as regards necessity, NOT as regards truth].* (As I read this, Aristotle is not
saying that, for a future-contingent p we are to regard
"T(p)" and "T$(\sim p)$" as being of the same status, but rather
that "N(p)" and "N$(\sim p)$" are of the same (truth) status—
both being false.) *This is [generally] the situation with
whatever is not at all times the case or at all times not the
case [i.e. with the contingent].* (That is, we always here have
"N$(p$ v $\sim p)$" but never "N(p) v N$(\sim p)$.") *For here it is
necessary that one or the other member of the contradictory*

alternative be true or false; (here we have "N([T(p) & F($\sim p$)] v [T($\sim p$) & F(p)]).") *but it is neither necessary that this one rather than that one [be true or false]—but only whichever chances to come about.* (That is, although we have "N([T(p) & F($\sim p$)] v [T($\sim p$) & F(p)])," we do not have "N[T(p) & F($\sim p$)] v N[T($\sim p$) & F(p)]." I regard this sentence as very powerful evidence for the view that Aristotle is not here rejecting the applicability of "N[T(p) v F(p)]" and/or "N[T(p) v T($\sim p$)]" to future contingents.) *Even if one [alternative] seems true [or false] rather than the other, that does not mean it is [necessarily] true or false.* (Again we must regard the *necessity* of the entire context to be operative at this point.)

It is thus plainly not the case with all contradictorily opposed affirmations and denials that it is necessary that one be true and the other false. (I take this to affirm the need for limiting the applicability NOT of "N[T(p) v F(p)]" but of "N[T(p)] v N[F(p)]" or else "N(p) v N($\sim p$).") *For the situation is quite different with those things that actually are, and with those things that are not actual but have a potentiality to be or not to be; as we have stated above.* (The back-reference must be understood to apply to 18ᵃ 28–34, the point being that the case of future contingents differs from that of matters past-or-present as regards (on our view) necessity, not as regards having a truth-status.)

So far as I know, the medieval interpretation of our text is first found in the eminent Arabic philosopher al-Fārābī,[9] and

[9] Abū Naṣr al-Fārābī (fl. 910): Wilhelm Kutsch and Stanley Marrow (eds.), *Alfarabi's Commentary on Aristotle's "De Interpretatione,"* Beyrouth, 1960. (*Editio princeps* [Arabic text only] of al-Fārābī's *Great Commentary on De Interpretatione.*) The commentary on DI9 is given on pages 81–101. "All the kinds of necessity (are such that) one of the two contradictories is true in such cases determinately. But the kinds of matters of possibility (are such that) one of the two contradictories is true in such cases without determination. For in (contradictories which) are equally possible without any complete determination, the true and the false alternative are (determined by) whichever happens." (Page 97, lines 9–12.)

following him was adopted by other Arabic logicians, including Averroes.[10] In the West, this interpretation is first found explicitly in Abelard (fl. 1120), whose interpretation of this text has been sketched by a modern historian as follows:

No proposition *de contingenti futuro* can be either determinately true or determinately false in the same sense, but this is not to say that no such proposition can be true or false. On the contrary, any such proposition is true if the outcome is to be true as it states, even though this is unknown to us (*"si futurum sit ut propositio dicit, etsi ignoratum nobis sit"*). What Aristotle wished to maintain in his *De Interpretatione* was that, while a proposition is necessarily true when it is true, it is not therefore necessarily true simply and always.[11]

Abelard's interpretation is doubtless not original with him, even in the Latin tradition, since it conforms strictly to the teaching on future contingence of St. Anselm.[12] In any event,

[10] Ibn Rushd (= Averroes) (fl. 1165). *Commentarium Medium* (= *Expositione*) *in Aristotelis "De Interpretatione,"* Juntine edition of *Aristotelis omnia quae extant Opera cum Averrois Cordubensis commentarii* (Venice, 1562), Vol. I, Part 1 (photoreprinted Frankfurt am Main, 1962). (Averroes' interpretation is summarized: *In materia autem possibili et contingenti, in rebus futuris, si una* [of contradictory alternatives] *est vera altera est falsa, quoniam necesse est ut reperiat alterum duorum contradictorium in futuro: sed non determinate in se* [p. 82].)

[11] W. and M. Kneale, *op. cit.,* p. 214.

[12] St. Anselm (fl. 1070). *Tractatus de concordia praesentiae, et praedestinationis, et gratiae dei cum libero arbitrio.* Migne, *Patrologiae,* Vols. 158–59. [For future contingency see especially Book I, chapter 2 ("How it is necessary for a thing to exist when God knows that it will exist and nevertheless free will remains") and chapter 3 ("The free futures are not necessary with an antecedent necessity but with a subsequent necessity"). Although Anselm does not explicitly discuss here the considerations of DI9, it appears from what he does say as very likely that his reading of this text would be the Farabian. Cf. T. F. Baeumker, "Die Lehre Anselms von Canterbury über den Willen und seine Wahlfreiheit," *Beiträge zur Geschichte der Philosophie des Mittelalters,* Vol. 10, section 6 (Münster, 1912). Also see J. Fisher, "Die Erkenntnislehre

it appears to have been adopted by most of the schoolmen.[13] And we can readily understand the appeal of this interpretation to Muslim and Christian Aristotelians who had to reconcile the Master with the theological teachings of their faith. (How could God possibly have divine foreknowledge about future-contingent matters—free human acts, for example—if future-contingent statements are neither true nor false at earlier times? We cannot say that God *knows in advance*, say at time t, that a person X will perform an act A at later time $t + t'$, if it were not true, already at t, that X is to do A at $t + t'$. One can have knowledge only of that which is true— and foreknowledge is but a special case of knowledge in this regard.)

Modern neo-scholastic Aristotelians generally adopt the medieval view. Thus Jacques Maritain holds that a future contingent proposition "is *true* or *false*" but "is neither actually and determinately true nor actually and determinately false."[14] But one of the most emphatic developments of this doctrinal line is represented by Thomas Hobbes, who held

---

Anselms von Canterbury," *ibid.*, section 3 (Münster, 1911), where we read on page 60: "Schon der einfachste Satz, so führt Anselm aus, welcher eine Wahrheit ausspricht, ist und bleibt wahr, mag man ihn in der Vergangenheit oder in die Zukunft verlegen. Es lässt sich schlechterdings nicht denken, dass er jemals nicht wahr gewesen ist, noch dass er jemals nicht wahr sein wird, also keine Zeit, wo er anfangen und aufhören könnte, wahr zu sein; er ist vielmehr wahr durch alle Vergangenheit und für alle Zukunft. Seine Wahrheit ist ewig. So verhält es sich mit jeder Wahrheit."]

[13] For the position of St. Thomas Aquinas (fl. 1265) see *In Libros "Perihermeneias" Expositio* (ed. Leon); English translation by J. T. Oesterle, Milwaukee, 1962; see Lecturae 13–15. Compare also William of Ockham, *Tractatus de Praedestinatione et de Praescientia Dei et de Futuris Contingentibus*, ed. Philotheus Boehner, *Collected Articles on Ockham*, New York, 1958, pp. 420–41. Boehner's strictures on pp. 431–32 arise from the misunderstanding inherent in his words "determinately true, as I believe," at the bottom of p. 431. I so judge on the basis of Boehner's statement (p. 432). I have not checked the text. See also p. 434, the footnote.

[14] J. Maritain, *Introduction to Logic*, Sheed & Ward, New York, 1937, p. 97. One may take "actually and determinately" here as more or less equivalent with "necessarily."

the position at its necessitarian extreme: "All propositions concerning future things, contingent or not contingent . . . are either necessarily true, or necessarily false; but we call them contingent because we do not know whether they be true or false."[15] A small group of present-day authorities have in recent years advocated this interpretation.[16]

It is easy to see how the two competing interpretations we have been considering could spring up in a setting where matters are treated in a purely verbal way without any recourse to the clarifying powers of symbolism. For consider the locution:

(1) It is necessary that p has a truth-value (i.e. is true or false).

It is not hard to see that this locution is equivocal as between two (symbolically precise) interpretations:

(2) $N(\exists \xi) \ [\xi = V(p)]$ ("It is necessary that there is a truth-value which p has")

(3) $(\exists \xi) \ N[\xi = V(p)]$ ("There is a truth-value which it is necessary that p has")

Here we take "$N(. . .)$" to mean "It is necessary that $(. . .)$," "$V(p)$" to represent the truth-value of p, and "ξ" to range over the usual truth-values T and F (true and false). The difference between (2) and (3) may on first view seem small—note that it lies only in the relative placement of the initial prefix—but it is absolutely crucial. For (2) amounts to:

(2') $N([V(p) = T] \ v \ [V(p) = F])$

which is perfectly harmless on a two-valued conception of propositional truth. On the other hand, (3) amounts to

[15] Thomas Hobbes, *De Corpore,* Ch. x, "Of Power and Act," in *The Metaphysical System of Hobbes,* M. W. Calkins, ed., Open Court, Chicago, 1905, pp. 76–80.

[16] For details see Ch. v, "An Interpretation of Aristotle's Doctrine of Future Contingency and Excluded Middle"; in N. Rescher, *Studies in the History of Arabic Logic,* Pittsburgh, 1963. The present historical account draws upon this source.

$$(3') \ N[V(p) = T] \ v \ N[V(p) = F]$$

which must be judged in a far less sympathetic light by any adherent to a doctrine of future contingency. In denying (3′) with respect to some propositions we do no more than say that its truth-value (be it true or false) is not determinably so. On the other hand in denying (2′) we take the much more drastic course of insisting that the proposition at issue does not have one of the regular truth-values (T or F) at all. The point at issue between the two competing interpretations is exactly that of whether what Aristotle had in view in the discussion at issue is the rejection of (2′) or that of (3′).

C. *A Modern Variant of the Orthodox Interpretation*

According to what we have characterized as the orthodox interpretation, Aristotle denied a truth-status to future contingents. Insisting that they are neither true nor false, he in effect denies that they have any "truth-value" whatsoever. It is thus striking—and somewhat ironic—that the eminent Polish logician Jan Lukasiewicz read into Aristotle the idea of a third neutral or indeterminate truth-value, standing alongside the traditional pair of true and false.[17] Lukasiewicz's conception of the matter has been espoused by various modern scholars, including A. N. Prior, who unhesitatingly speaks of "the third or 'neuter' truth-value of Aristotle and Lukasiewicz."[18] On this modern variant of the orthodox interpretation, then, Aristotle is to be construed as holding that future contingents have a third, neutral or indeterminate, truth-value somehow intermediate between truth and falsity, and not that they lack a truth-value altogether. This view of the matter was the base from which Lukasiewicz launched forth into the pioneering development of a highly influential system of many-valued logic, a system we must consider at some length in the ensuing section.

[17] See Lukasiewicz, "Three-Valued Logic," and "Philosophische Bemerkungen . . . ," *Comptes Rendus des Séances de la Société des Sciences et des Lettres de Varsovie*, Classe III, Vol. 23 (1930).

[18] Prior, *op. cit.*, p. 86.

II. *Logical Considerations on Future Contingency*

A. *The Three-Valued System of Lukasiewicz*

The logical structure which deserves to be called the "classical" system of three-valued logic was introduced in a paper by J. Lukasiewicz in 1920.[19] It was treated in fuller detail in 1930 in a paper by J. Lukasiewicz and A. Tarski,[20] and was axiomatized by M. Wajsberg in 1931.[21] The system is based on three truth-values: T (for *true*), F (for *false*), and I (for *intermediate* or *indeterminate*).

The connectives '$\sim$,' 'v,' '$\rightarrow$,' and '$\leftrightarrow$' for the system are defined in terms of the following matrices:

q	$\sim p$	p & q			p v q			p $\rightarrow$ q			p $\leftrightarrow$ q		
p		T	I	F	T	I	F	T	I	F	T	I	F
T	F	T	I	F	T	T	T	T	I	F	T	I	F
I	I	I	I	F	T	I	I	T	T	I	I	T	I
F	T	F	F	F	T	I	F	T	T	T	F	I	T

This tabulation is to be read in line with the following examples. If "*p*" is true (has the value T in the left-hand column) then "$\sim p$" is false (has the value F—see the corresponding entry in the "$\sim p$" column). If "*p*" has the value I then "*p* & *q*" takes the values T, I, F according as "*q*" is T, I, F, as shown in the tabulation in the "*p* & *q*" column corresponding to the *p*-takes-I row (in the left margin).

First of all, notice that when "*p*" has the values T or F, the negation (contradictory) of "*p*," i.e. "$\sim p$," has the values F

[19] Lukasiewicz, "Three-Valued Logic."

[20] J. Lukasiewicz and A. Tarski, "Untersuchungen über den Aussagenkalkül," *Comptes Rendus des Séances de la Société des Sciences et des Lettres de Varsovie*, Classe III, Vol. 23 (1930).

[21] M. Wajsberg, "Aksjomatyzacia trojwarosciowego rachunku zdan," *Comptes Rendus des Séances de la Société des Sciences et des Lettres de Varsovie*, Classe III, Vol. 24 (1931).

and T respectively, so that in these two cases '~' is defined in the same way as it is for standard two-valued logic. Correspondingly, if we cross out the row in which "p" is assigned the value I and the column in which "q" is assigned the value I in each of the other matrices we are left with the truth-tables for these connectives for two-valued logic. (For example, when either "p" or "q" takes F then "p & q" takes F; when both take F, "p v q" takes F, "$p \rightarrow q$" takes T, and "$p \leftrightarrow q$" takes T, and so on.) The only strictly new cases that arise are those in which either or both variables are indeterminate in value.

As would be expected, when "p" is indeterminate then "$\sim p$" is also indeterminate. Since "p & q" is true only when both conjuncts are true, and false only when at least one conjunct is false, we have "p & q" indeterminate only when both conjuncts are indeterminate or one conjunct is indeterminate and the other is true. Accordingly since "p v q" is true only when either disjunct is true and is false only when both disjuncts are false, "p v q" is indeterminate when both disjuncts "p" and "q" are indeterminate or one is indeterminate and the other is false. Similar explanations apply to the truth-tables for '$\rightarrow$' and '$\leftrightarrow$'.

A tautology according to these matrices may be understood, in the usual way, as a formula whose matrix takes only the value T, regardless of the values of its constituents. Since these three-valued matrices agree with the usual two-valued truth-tables only when T's and F's are involved, it is clear that every three-valued tautology (e.g. "$p \rightarrow p$") must be a two-valued tautology. The converse, however, is not the case: there are two-valued tautologies that fail to be tautologies according to these three-valued matrices. Consider "p v $\sim p$" for example. When "p" takes the value I in these three-valued matrices, this two-valued tautology takes the value I and hence fails to be a three-valued tautology.

Wajsberg established in his 1931 paper that every formula that represents a three-valued tautology according to these truth-tables can be derived (by the usual rules of *modus ponens* and substitution) from the following four axioms:

(A1) $p \rightarrow (q \rightarrow p)$

(A2) $(p \rightarrow q) \rightarrow [(q \rightarrow r) \rightarrow (p \rightarrow r)]$

(A3) $[(p \rightarrow \sim p) \rightarrow p] \rightarrow p$

(A4) $(\sim p \rightarrow \sim q) \rightarrow (q \rightarrow p)$

This solves the problem of the *systematization* of these truth-tables. The problem of their *interpretation* remains, however, and is, indeed, a serious one.

The difficulty is forcefully illustrated by considering the truth-value to be given to "p & q" when both "p" and "q" take the truth-value I. For suppose that $q = p$. Then, clearly, we want "p & q"—that is, "p & p"—to have the value I. On the other hand, suppose that $q = \sim p$. Then, surely, we want "p & $\sim p$" to have the value F, although according to the truth-tables it must again be I. Or again, consider the truth-value to be given to "p v $\sim q$" when both "p" and "q" take the truth-value I. Suppose that $q = \sim p$. Then, surely, we want "p v $\sim p$" to have the value T (and not I as the truth-tables have it). But, on the other hand, suppose that $q = p$. Then clearly we want "p v q"—that is, "p v p"—to have the value I. The point brought out by these examples is that, given the sort of interpretation we have in mind for our three-valued logic, we do not actually want it to be a strictly truth-functional system at all. Neither "p & $\sim p$" nor "q v $\sim q$" are about future-contingents even when it happens that the p's and q's that serve as their constituents are.

B. *The Infinite-Series Approach to Future Contingency in Three-Valued Logic*

Let us conceive of time as discretized into successive intervals which may be supposed to be enumerated by an index of integers (as of some arbitrary origin, either a fixed origin, or *now*).

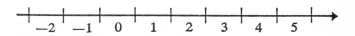

We may now class propositions—i.e. temporally definite

H

propositions (*p*-at-interval-number-X) and not temporally indefinite ones (*p*-at-*this-present*-interval)—into those which:

(1) *are always true* (bear the truth-value T in every interval),

(2) *are never true* (bear the truth-value F in every interval),

(3) *are indefinite until they become true or false* at some interval (say the i-th one), so that they are always indeterminate at every interval prior to the i-th, but true (or false) at the i-th interval and always thereafter.

A proposition of this third category—i.e. one which becomes true or false at some juncture—will concern a "future contingent" event until it acquires its (henceforth permanent) truth-status. (Note that a proposition of this type cannot be of the chronologically indefinite sort that is true on some days and false on others—e.g. "There is a sea-battle taking place *today*"—but must be chronologically definite: "There is a sea-battle on such-and-such a specific occasion.")

At any particular interval, a proposition will have exactly one of the three possible truth-values (T, F, I). Over the whole course of time, we would thus get truth-values for propositions that are of infinite series type, this series having one of the four following forms:

(1) . . . (all T's)   T   T   T   T   T (all T's) . . .
(2) . . . (all F's)   F   F   F   F   F (all F's) . . .
(3) . . . (all I's)   I   I   T   T   T (all T's) . . .
(4) . . . (all I's)   I   I   F   F   F (all F's) . . .

In cases (1) and (2) the proposition has a fixed, constant truth-value throughout history; in cases (3) and (4) the proposition remains of indefinite truth-status until it acquires a definite truth-value at some interval. In this context we immediately have the chronologized "Aristotelian" modalities (cf. Section III, A below):

necessary for case (1) (necessary = always true)
impossible for case (2) (impossible = always false)
possible for cases (1) or (3) (possible = sometimes true)
contingent for cases (3) or (4) (contingent = neither necessary nor impossible)[22]

In the case of compound propositions ($\sim p$, p v q, p & q, etc.) we would work out the serial truth-value place-by-place, using the matrices for a basic three-valued logic, such as those of Lukasiewicz treated in the preceding section.

We can now readily explicate the concept of *definite* truth (or falsity) at issue in the "medieval interpretation" of Ch. 9 of Aristotle's *De Interpretatione,* as follows:

(1) p is *indeterminate* at the t-th interval if it is then of the truth-status I, i.e. when $V_t(p) = I$; symbolically $I_t(p)$. (Here $V_t(p)$ represents the truth-value of p at the t-th interval.)

(2) p is *determinately true* at the t-th interval if it is then and ever after of the truth-status T, i.e. when $(\forall t')[(t' \geqq t) \rightarrow V_{t'}(p) = T]$; symbolically $T_t(p)$.

(3) p is *determinately false* at the t-th interval if it is then and ever after of the truth-status F, i.e. when $(\forall t')[(t' \geqq t) \rightarrow V_{t'}(p) = F]$; symbolically $F_t(p)$.

This sort of machinery shows how a precise basis can be created for the semantical theory of (temporally definite) propositions conceived of as capable of becoming true or false in the course of time after being of indeterminate truth-status prior to some particular temporal juncture.

C. *An Alternative Approach to the Logic of Future Contingency*

A variant approach to the logic of future contingency is to consider a system based on only the two standard truth-values T and F—and thus without a third, special truth-*value* I—but introducing an indeterminate truth-*status*. Let us rep-

---

[22] Note that all such propositions are, in the earlier parts of their history, of the future-contingent variety, with a (to that point) completely indeterminate truth-status.

resent this by ?, meaning, in effect: "either T or F, but either one, indeterminately." Thus a truth-status of ? excludes the possibilities "*definitely* T" and "*definitely* F,"[23] but not T or F as such.

The resulting "three-valued" system (which will not be a strictly truth-functional one) will have its matrices set up as follows:

q \ p	~p	p & q T	?	F	p v q T	?	F
T	F	T	?	F	T	T	T
?	?	?	(? or F)	F	T	(? or T)	?
F	T	F	F	F	T	?	F

Moreover, defining

$$p \Rightarrow q \text{ FOR } \sim p \vee q$$
$$p \Leftrightarrow q \text{ FOR } (p \Rightarrow q) \ \& \ (q \Rightarrow p)$$

we also obtain the matrices

q \ p	p ⇒ q T	?	F	p ⇔ q T	?	F
T	T	?	F	T	?	F
?	T	(? or T)	?	?	(? or T)	?
F	T	T	T	F	?	T

These truth-tables lend themselves to a natural interpretation in terms of a "truth-status limbo" for future contingents. But since this system is not strictly truth-functional, but only quasi-truth functional,[24] it is much harder to systematize. (For example, the truth-tables fail to bring out the tautologousness of "$p \Rightarrow p$.") The best course here is to introduce

[23] Note that ? is not actually a truth-value at all, but rather represents an essentially metalinguistic remark about the truth-status of the proposition at issue.

[24] See N. Rescher, "Quasi-Truth Functional Systems of Propositional Logic," *The Journal of Symbolic Logic,* 27 (1962), 1–10.

the conception of a quasi-tautology for any formula which always takes either T or ? for any assignment of (T, ?, F) to its variables. It is not difficult to establish that the quasi-tautologies in this sense coincide with the usual two-valued tautologies. This machinery of T = definitely true, F = definitely false, and ? = neither definitely true nor definitely false provides all the conceptions needed for a rigorous systematization of the medieval interpretation of Aristotle's doctrine of future contingency. It provides all that is required of a semantical theory of a chronologized truth concept for averting the lack of predetermination in situations of deliberation and choice within the human sphere and in the causal indeterminism of stochastic processes in nature.

III. *Time and Necessity*

A. *The Chronological Conception of Necessity in Aristotle and Diodorus*

To this point we have been concerned with a chronologized conception of truth. We shall now place this idea into the wider setting of chronologized modalities, also found in the ancients (Aristotle and the Stoics). Here the modalities are put into a chronologized or temporalized framework: that which *once was* merely possible *is now* actually true and *will henceforth* be strictly necessary. To systematize this tensed way of viewing the matter of modality, we introduce the following items of machinery:

$T_t(p)$ *for* p is *true* at time t (chronologized modality of actuality)

$N_t(p)$ *for* p is *necessary* at time t (chronologized modality of necessity)

$P_t(p)$ *for* p is *possible* at time t (chronologized modality of possibility)

On the basis of these ideas, we can consider the maneuver by Aristotle and the Stoics to reduce the modalities of necessity and possibility to the chronologized concept of truth, as follows:

ARISTOTELIAN MODALITIES

The *necessary* is that which is true at all times (past, present, and future):

$$N^a(p) \text{ FOR } (\forall t)T_t(p)$$

The *possible* is that which is true at some time:

$$P^a(p) \text{ FOR } (\exists t)T_t(p)$$

(Note that these are interrelated by the general negation-duality of necessity and possibility: $P \leftrightarrow \sim N \sim$.)

DIODOREAN MODALITIES (AS OF NOW)

The necessary is that which is true now and ever after:

$$N^d(p) \text{ FOR } (\forall t)[(t \geq n) \to T_t(p)]$$

(Here $n =$ now, i.e. the present.) The *possible* is that which is true either now or at some future time:

$$P^d(p) \text{ FOR } (\exists t)[(t \geq n) \ \& \ T_t(p)]$$

(If we assume the Law of Excluded Middle in the form $T \leftrightarrow \sim T \sim$, then these definitions are again interrelated by the general negation-duality of necessity and possibility: $P \leftrightarrow \sim N \sim$.) Note that it is impossible to make sense of the Diodorean conception of modality only if one is prepared to regard future contingent propositions as capable of being true, and thus as having a truth-value (even if not determinately so).

It should be remarked that the Aristotelian modalities are essentially timeless (i.e. without explicit reliance on any temporal parameter). On the other hand, the Diodorean modalities require an explicit temporalization—concealed in our use of the constant $n =$ now—as follows:

DIODOREAN MODALITIES (AS OF t)

That is *necessary at a certain time t* which is true then and ever after:

$$N_t^d(p) \text{ FOR } (\forall t')[(t' \geq t) \to T_{t'}(p)]$$

That is *possible at a certain time t* which is true either then or at some subsequent time:

$$P_t{}^d(p) \text{ FOR } (\exists t')[(t' \geqq t) \ \& \ T_{t'}(p)]$$

By means of this last set of definitions, the Stoic logicians were able to devise a theory of chronologically relativized necessity and possibility purely on the basis of a chronologized conception of truth.

This conception of temporal modalities as developed in antiquity was extended and developed by the Arabic logicians of the Middle Ages (especially in the tradition of Avicenna), and also played a role in the writings of the scholastic logicians.[25] After the Middle Ages, these ideas lay fallow in the main until their revival in the twentieth century.

B. *Necessity and Determinism in the Context of the "Master Argument"*

The fullest single account of the Master Argument of Diodorus Cronus to have come down to us is that of Epictetus:

The Master Argument seems to have been formulated with some such starting points as this. There is an incompatibility between the following three propositions:
(1) Everything that is past and true is necessary;
(2) The impossible does not follow (from? after?) the possible;
(3) What neither is nor will be is possible.
Seeing this incompatibility, Diodorus used the plausibility of the first two propositions to establish the thesis that nothing is possible which neither is nor will be true.[26]

The upshot of Diodorus' argument is thus to lead us to the startling conclusion that *every possibility is realized in the present and/or future.*

[25] On the historical situation see N. Rescher, *Temporal Modalities in Arabic Logic,* Supplementary Series of *Foundations of Language,* Dordrecht, 1967.
[26] *Dissertationes,* ed. Schenkl, Vol. II, Ch. 19, Frag. 1.

Let us now attempt to apply the machinery of chronological logic as set forth above to the reconstruction of this argument:

Consider to begin with the first premiss: *Everything that is past and true is* (*now*) *necessary*. The most plausible construction appears to be:

$$(1) \quad (\forall t) \{[T_t(p) \ \& \ (t < n)] \to N_n(p)\}^{27}$$

the generalized version of this premiss would be: *What is past and true is necessary thereafter,* or symbolically

$$(1a) \quad (\forall t)(\forall t')\{[T_t(p) \ \& \ (t < t')] \to N_{t'}(p)\}$$

These principles are straightforwardly in line with any theory of temporalized modalities that implements the medieval dictum: *Unumquodque, quando est, oportet esse* ("Anything, when it is, is necessary" construed here as "Anything, when *once* it is, is *henceforth* necessary").

Consider now the second premiss: *The impossible does not follow* (*from? after?*) *the possible*. We propose to follow Zeller in giving an essentially temporal reading to the verb *akolouthein* ("follow"): "The impossible does not follow *after* the possible"—that is, what is once possible does not later become impossible, but rather is possible at all later times:

$$(2) \quad (\forall t)(\forall t')\{[P_t(p) \ \& \ (t < t')] \to P_{t'}(p)\}$$

A straightforwardly equivalent version of this principle is

$$(\forall t)(\forall t')\{[\sim P_{t'}(p) \ \& \ (t < t')] \to \sim P_t(p)\}$$

In other words: *What is once impossible was never possible at a prior time*.[28] Either way, the premiss thus construed is

---

[27] Note that we must take the variables here to range over temporally definite propositions ("It rains in London on 1 January 1966") and not temporally indefinite ones ("It rains in London today"). Otherwise, leads to absurd consequences. (E.g. let t be *yesterday,* n be *today,* and p be *It is raining now*.)

[28] In this version the weakness of the thesis comes to light clearly. There is substantial plausibility to the view that the course of history closes off possibilities that were once realizable but are no

clearly the possibility-conservation principle which says: the once possible is always possible thereafter.[29]

The third premiss asserts: *What neither is nor will be is possible*. It is clear from other contexts that this is to be construed as "*Something* that neither is nor will be true is nonetheless possible." This is plausibly to be interpreted as:

(3) For some p_o: $P_n(p_o)$ & $(\forall t)[(n \leqq t) \leftrightarrow \sim T_t(p_o)]$

What the Master Argument purports to show is that (1)-(3) are mutually incompatible, so that if we accept (1) and (2) —as, according to Diodorus, we ought—then we must also accept the denial of (3), and subscribe in general to the thesis:

$$P_n(p) \to \langle\exists t)[(n \leqq t) \ \& \ T_t(p)]$$

For just exactly this is the Diodorean thesis that every (present) possibility must be realized at some present-or-future time.[30]

---

longer so. But this view, of course, stands in sharp conflict with the cyclic cosmology of the Stoics and other ancients.

[29] Note that this premiss consequences with markedly deterministic overtones. For by the duality-relationship between P and N (viz. the equivalence of N with $\sim P \sim$), (2) is equivalent with

$$(\forall t)(\forall t')\{[N_{t'}(p) \ \& \ (t < t')] \to N_t(p)\}$$

That is, the thesis: *What is necessary at a time was always necessary theretofore.*

[30] Strengthening this thesis to an equivalence

$$P_n(p) \leftrightarrow (\exists t)[(n \leqq t) \ \& \ T_t(p)]$$

we note that it is, in turn, equivalent with

$$\sim P_n(p) \leftrightarrow (\forall t)[(n \leqq t) \to \sim T_t(p)]$$

i.e. with the Diodorean dictum: *The impossible is that which neither is, nor will be true.* This, in turn, is equivalent (by uniform substitution of '$\sim p$' for 'p') with

$$\sim P_n(\sim p) \leftrightarrow (\forall t)[(n \leqq t) \to \sim T_t(\sim p)]$$

But, given the duality-relationship between P and N (viz. the equivalence of N with $\sim P \sim$), and postulating the equivalence of T with $\sim T \sim$ (see below), this principle is seen to come to

$$N(p) \leftrightarrow (\forall t)[(n \leqq t) \to T_t(p)]$$

Just this is the Diodorean dictum: *The necessary is that which is and always will be true.* Our prime source for these "Diodorean

н*

How is the incompatibility of (1)-(3) to be demonstrated? This now becomes the focal issue in our elucidation of the Master Argument. Before embarking on our proposed reconstruction, two preparatory maneuvers are in order.

Consider again premiss (1), or rather its general counterpart (1a):

$$(\forall t)\,(\forall t')\,\{[T_t(p)\ \&\ (t < t')] \to N_{t'}(p)\}$$

This is patently equivalent with

(A) $(\forall t)\,(\forall t')\,\{[\sim N_{t'}(p)\ \&\ (t < t')] \to \sim T_t(p)\}$

Making the uniform substitution of '$\sim p$' for 'p,' we obtain

(B) $(\forall t)\,(\forall t')\,\{[\sim N_{t'}(\sim p)\ \&\ (t < t')] \to \sim T_t(\sim p)\}$

Postulating the usual duality-principle relating necessity and possibility (viz. the equivalence of P with $\sim N\sim$), we obtain:

(C) $(\forall t)\,(\forall t')\,\{[P_{t'}(p)\ \&\ (t < t')] \to \sim T_t(\sim p)\}$

This completes our first maneuver.

The second maneuver is to assume the general applicability of the Law of the Excluded Middle.[31] We thus postulate the thesis that, at any given time, any given proposition is either true, or else its contradictory is true:

$$(\forall t)\,[T_t(p)\ v\ T_t(\sim p)]$$

---

dicta" is Boethius, *Commentarii in Librum Aristotelis "Peri Hermēneias,"* secunda editio, ed. Meiser, p. 234:

> Diodorus defines the possible as that which either is or will be (*quo aut est aut erit*), the impossible as that which being (now) false, will not be true (*quod cum falsum sit, non erit verum*), the necessary as that which, being (now) true, will not be false (*quod cum verum sit, non erit falsum*), the non-necessary as that which either is already or will be false (*aut jam est aut erit falsum*).

For a discussion of the passage see W. and M. Kneale, *op. cit.,* pp. 117–18.

[31] Actually, when we speak here (and below) in traditional terminology of the "Law of the Excluded Middle" we refer to what most writers (e.g. the Kneales) nowadays call the "Law of Bivalence."

In the face of this thesis, (C) at once leads to:

(D) $(\forall t)\,(\forall t')\{[P_{t'}(p)\ \&\ (t < t')] \to T_t(p)\}$

We are now in a position to present in short compass the *reductio ad absurdum* reasoning of the Master Argument. The starting point is provided by the three premisses (let us restate them):

(1a) $(\forall t)\,(\forall t')\{[T_t(p)\ \&\ (t < t')] \to N_{t'}(p)\}$
(2) $(\forall t)\,(\forall t')\{[P_t(p)\ \&\ (t < t')] \to P_{t'}(p)\}$
(3) $P_n(p_o)\ \&\ (\forall t)[(n \leqq t) \leftrightarrow \sim T_t(p_o)]$, for some p_o

The purportedly imminent contradiction is now straightforwardly derivable as follows:

(a) $P_n(p_o)$ by (3)
(b) $\sim T_{n+\epsilon}(p_o)$ by (3); letting t be $n + \epsilon$
(c) $P_{n+2\epsilon}(p_o)$ from (a) by (2); letting t be n and t' be $n + 2\epsilon$
(d) $T_{n+\epsilon}(p_o)$ from (c) by (1a) via (D). In (D) let t' be $n + 2\epsilon$ and t be $n + \epsilon$

The fact that (b) and (d) are mutual contradictories yields the sought-for absurdity.

This completes our exposition of the reconstructed Master Argument. It remains to take note of one striking feature of this reconstruction. This turns on the pivotal second premiss, which—as we remarked above[32]—leads to the consequence

$$(\forall t)\,(\forall t')\{[N_{t'}(p)\ \&\ (t < t')] \to N_t(p)\}$$

This, in effect, says that what is necessary at any time must be *necessary at all earlier times*. But consider this thesis in the context of the (plausible) premiss (1) asserting that which is true at a time is necessary at all later times. The result is the conclusion that the only truths are those which are necessary at all times: i.e. that all that is true—and indeed all that is possible—is also necessary (in the Aristotelian Megarian chronological sense of this term).

[32] See fn. 6.

Seen in this light, the materials of our reconstruction of the Master Argument are thus sufficient of themselves to lead us willy-nilly to the well-known determinism of the Megarians and Stoics, as attributed by Cicero preeminently to Diodorus himself:

> This is a view that you, Chrysippos, will not allow at all, and this is the very point about which you are specially at issue with Diodorus. He says that only what either is true or will be true is a possibility, and *whatever will be, he says must necessarily happen and whatever will not be, according to him cannot possibly happen.* You say that things which will not be are also possible—for instance it is possible for this jewel to be broken even if it never will be. . . .[33]

Our construction of the Master Argument of Diodorus Cronus is thus not only adequate to the purposes envisaged by Diodorus, but involves ingredients from which there follows, as an inexorable consequence, a deterministic position of just the sort he in fact espoused.

What juncture of the argument offers the most vulnerable spot for avoiding its deterministic conclusion? One promising possibility is its (essential) reliance on the applicability of the Law of the Excluded Middle in the context of a chronologically relativized concept of truth:

$$(\forall t) \, [T_t(p) \lor T_t(\sim p)]$$

For since p is a chronologically definite proposition of the sort X-at-t_o, the truth status of it and its contradictory at the *time-of-reference* t_o must in fact settle the matter once-for-all.[34] We obviously would not want:

[33] Cicero, *De Fato*, § 13 (tr. H. Rackham); my italics.

[34] For reasons already indicated, our reconstruction of the Master Argument departs in this regard from that of W. and M. Kneale, *op. cit.*, where it is maintained that "Diodorus' definitions of the modal notions are based on the assumption that truth-values change" (p. 121). The truth-value of the temporally indefinite statement "It rains in Athens today" will indeed change, but if this statement is made on January 1, 1966, then the truth-value of its

$$T_{t'}(\text{X-at-}t_o)$$
$$T_{t''}(\text{Not: X-at-}t_o)$$

The Law of the Excluded Middle thus, in effect, leads us—in the context of a truth-stability principle of the type "$T_t(p) \to T_{t'}(p)$"—to an acceptance of the principle

$$T_{t'}(p) \to (\forall t)\, T_t(p)$$

And this principle, given the chronologized concept of necessity operative within the context of the discussion, leads to

$$T_{t'}(p) \to (\forall t)\, N_t(p)$$

It thus appears that the most convenient exit from the sphere of necessitation within which our reconstruction of the Master Argument has unfolded is provided by the path credited to Aristotle by the "orthodox" sector of the tradition: the denial of the applicability of the Law of the Excluded Middle[35] in the context of a temporally relativized conception of truth. We would be able to maintain "$T_t(\text{X-at-}t_o)$" whenever $t \geqq t_o$, but reject both this and "$T_t(\text{Not: X-at-}t_o)$" whenever $t < t_o$, avoiding the deterministic consequences at issue and making room for a doctrine of "future contingency."[36]

C. Conceptualizing an "Open Future"

Considering a "course (sequence) of events," say $E_1 \ldots E_2 \ldots E_4$, we may view it as one among various possible (i.e. physically possible) alternatives, including also, say $E_1 \ldots E_2 \ldots E_5$ and $E_1 \ldots E_3 \ldots E_6$. We can consider all these possible courses as represented in a tree-like diagram shown on following page.

---

temporally definite propositional counterpart "It rains in Athens on January 1, 1966" will not change over time. And our interpretation takes the p's at issue to be of the second type.

[35] I have, however, argued earlier that Aristotle's basic discussion in Ch. 9 of *De Interpretatione* need not be interpreted in this manner.

[36] The present section has drawn upon the writer's paper "A Version of the 'Master Argument' of Diodorus," *Journal of Philosophy*, 63 (1966), 436–45.

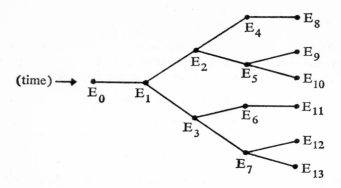

Here E_1 and E_2 and E_3 (but not E_0 or E_4 or E_6) may be called *branching events*—for obvious reasons.

Against the background of such a representation of the possible courses of events, it is plausible to introduce the idea of relative determination of one event with respect to another. This idea is presented by the definition:

> E_y is *determined with respect to* E_x if there is no possibility of a "branching off" in going from E_x to E_y; that is, if either (1) E_y lies in the past of E_x, or else (2) in tracing a path from E_x to E_y one does not encounter any branching event (including E_x itself).

Thus, for example, E_{11} is determined with respect to E_6, while E_9 is not determined with respect to E_5. (Note that the relationship of relative determination is a *partial ordering* in the mathematicians' sense of the term.) An event which lies in the past of another is always determined with respect to it—there being only one way of moving "backwards" along the tree.

If E_y is *not* determined with respect to E_x, then E_y may be said to lie in the "open future" of E_x: it is then a matter of contingent fact—in the face of the intervening of branching events—whether, once arrived at E_x, we shall ever get to E_y at all. In a world containing an event E_x with respect to which some other (possible) event E_y is not determined there will be an event (specifically E_x) which has—not a uniquely possible future, but—*different alternative* futures. And this is not an epistemological matter inherent in our knowledge or ignorance of the course of events in such a world, but an ontological matter inherent in type of causal structure governing its "course of events."

In a completely determined world, in which every event is wholly determined with respect to all others, we have an event diagram of the following sort:

$$\text{.------.------.------.------}$$
$$E_0 \quad E_1 \quad E_2 \quad E_3$$

That is, the diagram is linear. (The ordering is a complete ordering in the mathematicians' sense.) Here there are no branching events whatsoever. Correspondingly, no event has an open future.

It has been suggested (by A. N. Prior) that the conception of an open future is to be articulated with reference to the nature of time itself in contradistinction to the nature of the course of events occurring in time. Thus consider the two possible alternative courses of developments over time:

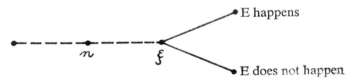

Here n = now (i.e. the present), and the future course of developments branches at ξ leading either to E or to $\sim$E, so that E is a paradigmatically "future contingent" event, a possible occurrence in the "open future." Prior suggests that we regard ξ as a *branching point in the "course of time" itself.* Thus ξ is not to be thought of as an event at all, but as a feature of the temporal channel in which the "course of events" flows (so to speak). Here, then, we are confronted by a multiplicity of alternative "possible futures" in a sense stronger than that merely of "possible future courses of events."

Against this odd view of the nature of time, it can be urged that we can always take a quite different point of view. For we can (along the lines of our previous discussion) regard ξ as a *branching event* in the "course of events" taking place in a single, unique time (course of time). Here, then, there is but a single "course of time" itself, although these may be a multiplicity of possible future courses of events within this unique time.

These two perspectives lead us to conceive rather differently of the future contingencies at issue, and point towards different semantical theories of future contingence. The difference can be brought out as follows:

On a Prior-type approach, the contingency of the future is inherent in the ontological structure of time itself. On such a view, a future contingency cannot even really be *specified*. It thus makes no sense to characterize a future contingent proposition either as true or false: it must be set apart into a truth-status limbo.

On our own view, on the other hand, the infeasibility of making definite assertions about future contingence inheres in the (epistemic) impossibility of specifying the outcome of branching events, and is thus a matter not of the nature of time itself, but of the natural laws governing the course of events in time. It is thus plausible to characterize a future contingency as true or false (albeit one cannot say which). The (temporally definite) future-contingent proposition p is, even as of n, either true or false (whatever ultimately turns out), although it does not yet (i.e. at n) possess this truth-value in a *determinate* way, but only acquires a determinate truth-value after ξ. On this view of the matter, the contingency of the future thus inheres in the causal structure of the course of events, not in the nature of time as such.

In a comparison of these two approaches, it seems clear that the advantage lies with the second theory, based on the idea of a single course of time. First, it has the advantage of simplicity. For substantial conceptual economy results from viewing alternative possible courses of events laid out in a single course of time, rather than using the idea of alternative courses of time as such. Second, it is not clear that the idea of distinct courses of time can in the final analysis be made viable. What are we to say, for example, about the temporal comparison of events placed within different courses of time. Is a temporal comparison between them to be in principle impossible? An affirmative answer here visits havoc upon our most elemental ideas of time—we are asked to think of possible events that are neither earlier, later, nor simultaneous with the present occurrences in the world about us. A negative answer, however, simply brings us to a single super-time, providing a co-ordinating framework for all the alternative courses of time with which we began. And to take this view is to fall back, however reluctantly and covertly, upon the theory of a single, unique course of time.

To return to future contingency in its Aristotelian setting, it would seem that the advantages lie on the side of the medieval interpretation which does not deny to propositions about future contingents a truth-status as such, but only denies that this truth-status is *determinate*. Good sense can be made of what is at issue here in a relatively simple and straightforward way. For we can say that a proposition p is determinately true (or false) at a given time t, with respect to a set L of presumed natural laws if it is possible, in principle, to deduce p (or $\sim p$, respectively) from the body of information consisting of

(1) the standard machinery of logic and mathematics
(2) the set of natural laws L, and
(3) a complete history of the world up to and including the time t.[37]

If, with respect to these data, we can settle the question of the truth or falsity of p, then we may say that p has a *determinate* truth-value as of the time t.

[37] This *complete history* must be "complete" only with respect to descriptive terms which are "chronologically pure" (e.g. "it is raining now") rather than "chronologically impure" ("it is now three days before a rainy day"). On the problems at issue here see N. Rescher and J. Robison, "Temporally Conditioned Descriptions," *Ratio*, 8 (1966), 46–54; and cf. R. Gale, "Pure and Impure Descriptions," *Australasian Journal of Philosophy*, 45 (1967).

The philosophical motivation of this definition is clearly set forth in an illuminating passage by C. S. Peirce:

> A certain event either will happen or it will not. There is nothing now in existence to constitute the truth of its being about to happen, or of its being not about to happen, unless it be certain circumstances to which only a law or uniformity can lend efficacy. But that law or uniformity, the nominalists say, has no real being, it is only a mental representation. If so, neither the being about to happen nor the being about not to happen has any reality at present. . . . If, however, we admit that the law has a real being, and of the mode of being of an individual, but even more real, then the future necessary consequent of a present state of things is as real and true as the present state of things itself.[38]

In the wake of this definition, all propositions regarding the present and past must be determinately true or false. Some propositions, however, will be genuinely of the future contingent type, namely those which do not have a determinate truth-value, so that it is in principle impossible to say *now* how matters "will turn out" with respect to them.

This approach does not deny a truth-value (of the standard T, F sort) to propositions—not even to future-contingent ones. For what we are proposing to do is to construe the *present* assertion of a future-oriented proposition, for example,

$$T_{today}(p\text{-tomorrow})$$

as amounting to a *future* assertion of a present-oriented proposition, viz.

$$T_{tomorrow}(p\text{-today})$$

Our semantical perspective is to let the issue of the truth or falsity of a chronological proposition hinge entirely upon *how matters turn out at the time at issue,* so that the allocation of a truth-status to future-contingents is perfectly innocuous, because it prejudges nothing. No suggestion is intended that the truth-status which a future-contingent proposition certainly *has* times prior to the time of reference can be *specified* at these earlier times without any reference to "how matters turn out."

This approach preserves intact the standard group of logical and semantical concepts that cluster about the notions of truth and falsity. At the same time, it averts consequences of a necessitarian and fatalistic kind. The truth-status of a future-contingent proposition is made to hinge upon what happens at that future time: there is no suggestion that its *having* a truth-value, and an (ultimately) knowable one, in any way fixes beforehand or predetermines what that truth-value is to be. This view of the matter as based on the "medieval interpretation" of Aristotle—it seems to us—is not only tenable in itself, but possessed of significant advantages over the alternative semantical bases of a theory of the temporal aspects of the concept of truth.

APPENDIX ON THE LOGIC OF DETERMINATION AND DETERMINISM

We have seen above how the basic premisses of the Master Argument of Diodorus entail a thoroughgoing determinism. This consequence must be avoided in any adequate semantical theory of the logic of chronological propositions. The question of the correctness of determinism must not be prejudged by the formal apparatus we construct for the treatment of the relevant issues. But this is easier said than done. The doctrine of determination and predetermination is one whose root conception is of remarkable subtlety. It tends to come upon us unawares, and its exclusion from chronological logic is an object of interest precisely because it is neither straightforward nor simple.

In an article published in *Mind*,[39] I had sought to develop the logic of temporalized determination within the framework of a general theory of the logic of chronological propositions. This logical theory of temporal "predetermination" was based upon a parametrized truth-modality T operating upon chron-

[39] "On the Logic of Chronological Propositions," *Mind*, 75 (1966), 75–95.

ological propositions, such that "$T_t(p)$" is to be read as "p is true (or is realized) at the time t," t being a numerical time-index. (T is thus the temporalized version of the assertoric modality.) To fix the logical rules for this operator, we shall specify the system S based on the following axioms:

(T0) Axioms for propositional logic
(T1) $T_t(\sim p) \leftrightarrow \sim T_t(p)$
(T2) $T_t(p \,\&\, q) \leftrightarrow [T_t(p) \,\&\, T_t(q)]$
(T3) $(\forall t)T_t(p) \to p$
(T4) $T_{t'}[(\forall t)T_t(p)] \leftrightarrow (\forall t)T_t(p)$
(T5) $T_{t'}[T_t(p)] \leftrightarrow T_t(p)$

We shall also consider the alternate system S°[40] in which (T5) is replaced by

(T5°) $T_{t'}[T_t(p)] \leftrightarrow T_{t'+t}(p)$

(The difference between (T5) and (T5°) turns on differences between two different styles of establishing temporal reference conventions.)

The chronological character of the operator T_t is made self-evident by the parameter-subscript t. On the other hand, its status as a truth operator is readily established by construing $T_t(\alpha)$ as being simply α itself, since this reduces all the axioms to overt tautologies.

Against the background of these axiomatizations of T we can now introduce the operator D of chronological determination, such that "$D_t(p)$" is to be read as "p is determined (to be true) as of the time t." To fix the logical rules for this operator, the following seemingly obvious axioms were specified:

(D0) $D_t[\sim T_{t'}(p)] \to \sim D_t[T_{t'}(p)]$,   for all t, t'
(D1) $T_t(p) \to D_{t'}[T_t(p)]$ whenever $t \leqq t'$
(D2) $D_t[T_{t'}(p)] \to T_{t'}(p)$ whenever $t < t'$
(D3) $N(p) \to D_t[T_{t'}(p)]$ for all t, t'
(D4) If 'p' is a theorem, then: $N(p)$

Here N is the achronological modality of necessity. "$N(p)$"

could be construed in the "quasi-Aristotelian" manner as "$(\forall t)(\forall t') D_t[T_{t'}(p)]$," in which case (D3) becomes superfluous, since it follows from the definition. The other axioms also all seem perfectly innocuous. (D0) and (D4) are self-explanatory. (D1) says that what is true at a certain time is determinately so thereafter. And (D2) says that what is predetermined to be true must correspondingly be true.

With this modality of temporally qualified determination in hand, we can now introduce the concept of predetermination by the definition:

$$(D^\circ) \quad D^\circ[T_t(p)] = (\exists t')([t' < t] \ \& \ D_{t'}[T_t(p)])$$

These two concepts of chronological determination D_t and of predetermination D° are intended to capture the Aristotelian idea that statements are sometimes, but not invariably determined as definitely true (e.g. *ex post facto*). What is to be avoided is a determination that is *complete* and all-embracing, and so provides a possible basis for fatalism, since if *everything*—including all our own choices and actions—is predetermined, there seems little point in our deliberations, since their outcome will always be "a foregone conclusion." Technically, this amounts to avoiding the deterministic thesis that the realization of a state of affairs is invariably such that it was predetermined. The consequence to be avoided is represented by the thesis:

$$(A) \quad T_t(p) \rightarrow D^\circ[T_t(p)]$$

It is thus an unhappy, indeed shocking development that A. N. Prior was able to demonstrate[41] that (A) is forthcoming in both the systems S and S° provided only that one adds the very plausible further rule for the operator D_t:

$$(D5) \ D_t[T_{t'}(p) \rightarrow T_{t''}(q)] \rightarrow \{D_t[T_{t'}(p)] \rightarrow D_t[T_{t''}(p)]\},$$
$$\text{for all } t, \ t', \ t''$$

The addition of this wholly unobjectionable rule (a straightforward analogue of a standard thesis of modal logic) pro-

---

[41] Professor Prior conveyed his (unpublished) findings in correspondence.

vides all that is needed to derive the catastrophic consequence (A) in both systems S and S°. (It caused me more
than a little chagrin to find that I had unwittingly followed
Diodorus and his Stoic confreres into an all-embracing determinism.)

The argument developed by Prior goes essentially as follows:

Demonstration in S
Let $t' < t$

(1)	$T_t(p) \rightarrow T_{t'}[T_t(p)]$		(T5)
(2)	" $\rightarrow D_{t'}(T_{t'}[T_t(p)])$		(D1)
(3)	" $\rightarrow D_{t'}[T_t(p)]$	(D3), (D4), (D5)[42]	
(4)	" $\rightarrow (\exists t'')[(t' < t) \& D_{t''}[T_t(p)]]$		(3)
(A)	" $\rightarrow D°[T_t(p)]$		(D°)

Demonstration in S°
Let $t'' < t' + t'' < t + t' + t''$

(1)	$T_{t'' + t' + t}(p) \rightarrow T_{t''}[T_{t' + t}(p)]$		(T5°)
(2)	" $\rightarrow D_{t''}(T_{t''}[T_{t' + t}(p)])$		(D1)
(3)	" $\rightarrow D_{t''}[T_{t'' + t' + t}(p)]$		(D5)[43]
(4)	" $\rightarrow (\exists t''')[(t'' < t'' + t' + t) \&$ $D_{t''' + t' + t}(p)]$		(3)
(A)	" $\rightarrow D°[T_{t'' + t' + t}(p)]$		(D°)

Since the "catastrophic consequence" (A) can thus be obtained in both the systems S and S°, it is clear that some
rather fundamental change—presumably in the D-axioms—
will be necessary to assert this consequence.

On first thought, it might seem that a weakening of (D1)
by excluding the case $t' = t$ might be what is needed. However, even if we restrict (D1) in this seemingly plausible
way, (A) can still be derived, as follows:

[42] (a) $N[T_{t'}[T_t(p)] \rightarrow T_t(p)]$ (D4), (T5)
    (b) $D_{t'}[T_{t'}[T_t(p)] \rightarrow T_t(p)]$ (D3)
    (c) $D_{t'}(T_{t'}[T_t(p)]) \rightarrow D_{t'}[T_t(p)]$ (D5)
[43] (a) $N[T_{t''}[T_{t' + t}(p)] \rightarrow T_{t'' + t' + t}(p)]$ (T5°), (D4)
    (b) $D_{t''}[T_{t''}[T_{t' + t}(p)] \rightarrow T_{t'' + t' + t}(p)]$ (D3)
    (c) $D_{t''}[T_{t''}[T_{t' + t}(p)] \rightarrow D_{t''}[T_{t'' + t' + t}(p)]$ (D5)

Demonstration in S
Let $t' < t'' < t$

(1) $\quad T_t(p) \to T_{t'}[T_t(p)]$ $\hfill$ (T_5)

(2) $\quad$ " $\quad \to D_{t''}(T_{t'}[T_t(p)])$ $\hfill$ (D_1)

(3) $\quad$ " $\quad \to D_{t''}[T_t(p)]$ $\hfill$ $(D_3), (D_4), (D_5)$[44]

(4) $\quad$ " $\quad \to (\exists t'')[(t'' < t) \,\&\, D_{t''}\cdot[T_t(p)]]$ $\hfill$ (3)

(A) $\quad$ " $\quad \to D^\circ[T_t(p)]$ $\hfill$ (D°)

Demonstration in S$^\circ$
Let $t' < t''$ and $t'' < t' + t$

(1) $\quad T_{t' + t}(p) \to T_{t'}[T_t(p)]$ $\hfill$ (T_5°)

(2) $\quad$ " $\quad \to D_{t''}(T_{t'}[T_t(p)]$ $\hfill$ (D_1)

(3) $\quad$ " $\quad \to D_{t''}[T_{t' + t}(p)]$ $\hfill$ $(D_3), (D_4), (D_5)$[45]

(4) $\quad$ " $\quad \to (\exists t'')[(t'' < t' + t) \,\&\,$
$\qquad\qquad\qquad D_{t''}\cdot[T_{t' + t}(p)]]$ $\hfill$ (3)

(A) $\quad$ " $\quad \to D^\circ[T_{t' + t}(p)]$ $\hfill$ (D°)

It is therefore clear that the proposed restriction upon (D_1) will not serve to avoid the unwanted deterministic thesis (A). But it is also apparent from a careful inspection of the D-axioms that they are most vulnerable at the point of (D_1). In fact our own proposal for the avoidance of (A) takes the form of a modification of (D_1), as follows:

(D_{1a}) $T_t(p) \to D_{t'}[T_t(p)]$, whenever $t \leqq t'$, provided that p does not itself take the form "$T_{t''}(q)$" for $t'' \neq n$ (n for *now*).

Given the indicated restriction—which takes the plausible step of restricting the basic variable of (D_1) to "chronologically absolute" propositions—the inference from steps (1) to (2) in all the derivations we have considered becomes invalid. For in each case this step requires a substitution for "p" in (D_1) which violates the restriction introduced in (D_{1a}).

[44] (a) $N[T_{t'}[T_t(p)] \to T_t(p)]$ $\hfill$ $(T_5), (D_3)$

$\quad$ (b) $D_{t''}(T_{t'}[T_t(p)]) \to T_t(p)]$ $\hfill$ (D_3)

$\quad$ (c) $D_{t''}(T_{t'}[T_t(p)]) \to D_{t''}[T_t(p)]$ $\hfill$ (D_5)

[45] (a) $N[T_{t'}[T_t(p)] \to T_{t' + t}(p)]$ $\hfill$ $(T_5^\circ), (D_4)$

$\quad$ (b) $D_{t''}[T_{t'}[T_t(p)] \to T_{t' + t}(p)]$ $\hfill$ (D_3)

$\quad$ (c) $D_{t''}(T_{t'}[T_t(p)]) \to D_{t''}[T_{t' + t}(p)]$ $\hfill$ (3)

Alternatively, we could restrict (D1) as follows:

(D1b) $T_t(p) \rightarrow D_{t'}[T_t(p)]$,   whenever $t \leq t'$, provided that p does not take the form "$T_{t''}(q)$" for $t'' < t$.

This (even more intuitive) restriction invalidates the move from (1) to (2) in all of the S-demonstrations; though not in the last S^*-demonstration. One could thus also avert the fatalistic consequence (A) by restricting oneself to the system S, and accepting (D1) only in the modified form (D1b).

In any case, the discussion of this Appendix will have served the purpose of illustrating the fact that the adequate treatment of the concepts of determination and predetermination in the framework of a rigorous logical system of chronological logic is by no means trivial, but is indeed a rather subtle matter. The devising of a set of rules of chronological logic capable of establishing—in a precise and rigorous way— a judicious line between occasional and pervasive determination is by no means as simple as one might expect it to be on first thought.[46]

[46] In writing this paper I have profited from Professor R. M. Gale's helpful comments on a draft version. I am also grateful to Anne (Mrs. Michael) Pelon for her help in checking some of the formal arguments.

FATALISM

RICHARD TAYLOR

RICHARD TAYLOR has taught at Brown University and Colum-
bia University and is now Professor of Philosophy at the University of Rochester. His major works are *Metaphysics* and
Action and Purpose.

A fatalist—if there is any such—thinks he cannot do anything about the future. He thinks it is not up to him what is
going to happen next year, tomorrow, or the very next moment. He thinks that even his own behavior is not in the least
within his power, any more than the motions of the heavenly
bodies, the events of remote history, or the political developments in China. It would, accordingly, be pointless for him
to deliberate about what he is going to do, for a man de-
liberates only about such things as he believes are within his
power to do and to forego, or to affect by his doings and
foregoings.

A fatalist, in short, thinks of the future in the manner in
which we all think of the past. For we do all believe that it is
not up to us what happened last year, yesterday, or even a
moment ago, that these things are not within our power, any
more than are the motions of the heavens, the events of remote history or of China. And we are not, in fact, ever
tempted to deliberate about what we have done and left undone. At best we can speculate about these things, rejoice
over them or repent, draw conclusions from such evidence as
we have, or perhaps—if we are not fatalists about the future

FROM Richard Taylor, *Metaphysics,* Prentice-Hall, 1963. Printed
also as "Fatalism" in *Philosophical Review,* 71 (1964). Richard
Taylor. *Metaphysics.* © 1963. Reprinted by permission of Prentice-
Hall, Inc., Englewood Cliffs, N.J.

—extract lessons and precepts to apply henceforth. As for what has in fact happened, we must simply take it as given; the possibilities for action, if there are any, do not lie there. We may, indeed, say that some of those past things *were* once within our power, while they were still future—but this expresses our attitude toward the future, not the past.

There are various ways in which a man might get to thinking in this fatalistic way about the future, but they would be most likely to result from ideas derived from theology or physics. Thus, if God is really all-knowing and all-powerful, then, one might suppose, perhaps he has already arranged for everything to happen just as it is going to happen, and there is nothing left for you or me to do about it. Or, without bringing God into the picture, one might suppose that everything happens in accordance with invariable laws, that whatever happens in the world at any future time is the only thing that can then happen, given that certain other things were happening just before, and that these, in turn, are the only things that can happen at that time, given the total state of the world just before then, and so on, so that again, there is nothing left for us to do about it. True, what we do in the meantime will be a factor in determining how some things finally turn out—but these things that we are *going* to do will perhaps be only the causal consequences of what will be going on just before we do them, and so on back to a not distant point at which it seems obvious that we have nothing to do with what happens then. Many philosophers, particularly in the seventeenth and eighteenth centuries, have found this line of thought quite compelling.

I want to show that certain presuppositions made almost universally in contemporary philosophy yield a proof that fatalism is true, without any recourse to theology or physics. If, to be sure, it is assumed that there is an omniscient god, then that assumption can be worked into the argument so as to convey the reasoning more easily to the unphilosophical imagination, but this assumption would add nothing to the force of the argument, and will therefore be omitted here. And similarly, certain views about natural laws could be appended to the argument, perhaps for similar purposes, but they, too, would add nothing to its validity, and will therefore be ignored.

Presuppositions. The only presuppositions we shall need are the six following.

First, we presuppose that any proposition whatever is either true or, if not true, then false. This is simply the standard interpretation, *tertium non datur,* of the law of excluded middle, usually symbolized $(p \lor -p)$, which is generally admitted to be a necessary truth.

Second, we presuppose that, if any state of affairs is sufficient for, though logically unrelated to, the occurrence of some further condition at the same or any other time, then the former cannot occur without the latter occurring also. This is simply the standard manner in which the concept of *sufficiency* is explicated. Another and perhaps better way of saying the same thing is that, if one state of affairs *ensures* without logically entailing the occurrence of another, then the former cannot occur without the latter occurring. Ingestion of cyanide, for instance, *ensures* death under certain familiar circumstances, though the two states of affairs are not logically related.

Third, we presuppose that, if the occurrence of any condition is necessary for, but logically unrelated to, the occurrence of some other condition at the same or any other time, then the latter cannot occur without the former occurring also. This is simply the standard manner in which the concept of a *necessary condition* is explicated. Another and perhaps better way of saying the same thing is that, if one state of affairs is *essential* for another, then the latter cannot occur without it. Oxygen, for instance, is *essential* to (though it does not by itself ensure) the maintenance of human life—though it is not logically impossible that we should live without it.

Fourth, we presuppose that, if one condition or set of conditions is sufficient for (ensures) another, then that other is necessary (essential) for it, and conversely, if one condition or set of conditions is necessary (essential) for another, then that other is sufficient for (ensures) it. This is but a logical consequence of the second and third presuppositions.

Fifth, we presuppose that no agent can perform any given

act if there is lacking, at the same or any other time, some condition necessary for the occurrence of that act. This follows, simply from the idea of anything being essential for the accomplishment of something else. I cannot, for example, live without oxygen, or swim five miles without ever having been in water, or read a given page of print without having learned Russian, or win a certain election without having been nominated, and so on.

And *sixth*, we presuppose that time is not by itself "efficacious"; that is, that the mere passage of time does not augment or diminish the capacities of anything and, in particular, that it does not enhance or decrease an agent's powers or abilities. This means that if any substance or agent gains or loses powers or abilities over the course of time—such as, for instance, the power of a substance to corrode, or a man to do thirty push-ups, and so on—then such gain or loss is always the result of something other than the mere passage of time.

With these presuppositions before us, we now consider two situations in turn, the relations involved in each of them being identical except for certain temporal ones.

The first situation. We imagine that I am about to open my morning newspaper to glance over the headlines. We assume, further, that conditions are such that only if there was a naval battle yesterday does the newspaper carry a certain kind (shape) of headline—i.e., that such a battle is essential for this kind of headline—whereas if it carries a certain different sort (shape) of headline, this will ensure that there was no such battle. Now, then, I am about to perform one or the other of two acts, namely, one of seeing a headline of the first kind, or one of seeing a headline of the second kind. Call these alternative acts S and S' respectively. And call the propositions, "A naval battle occurred yesterday" and "No naval battle occurred yesterday," P and P' respectively. We can assert, then, that if I perform act S, then my doing such will ensure that there was a naval battle yesterday (i.e., that P is true), whereas if I perform S', then my doing that will ensure that no such battle occurred (or, that P' is true).

With reference to this situation, then, let us now ask

whether it is up to me which sort of headline I shall read as I open the newspaper; that is, let us see whether the following proposition is true:

(A) It is within my power to do S, and it is also within my power to do S'.

It seems quite obvious that this is not true. For if both these acts were equally within my power, that is, if it were up to me which one to do, then it would also be up to me whether or not a naval battle has taken place, giving me a power over the past which I plainly do not possess. It will be well, however, to express this point in the form of a proof, as follows:

1. If P is true, then it is not within my power to do S' (for in case P is true, then there is, or was, lacking a condition essential for my doing S', the condition, namely, of there being no naval battle yesterday).

2. But if P' is true, then it is not within my power to do S (for a similar reason).

3. But either P is true, or P' is true.

∴.4. Either it is not within my power to do S, or it is not within my power to do S';

and (A) is accordingly false. A common-sense way of expressing this is to say that what sort of headline I see depends, among other things, on whether a naval battle took place yesterday, and that, in turn, is not up to me.

Now this conclusion is perfectly in accordance with common sense, for we all are, as noted, fatalists with respect to the past. No one considers past events as being within his power to control; we simply have to take them as they have happened and make the best of them. It is significant to note, however, that, in the hypothetical sense in which statements of human power or ability are usually formulated, one *does* have power over the past. For we can surely assert that, *if* I do S, this will ensure that a naval battle occurred yesterday, whereas *if*, alternatively, I do S', this will equally ensure the nonoccurrence of such a battle, since these acts are, in terms of our example, quite sufficient for the truth of P and P' respectively. Or we can equally say that I can ensure the occurrence of such a battle yesterday simply by doing S and that I can ensure its nonoccurrence simply by doing S'. Indeed, if I should ask *how* I can go about ensuring that no naval battle occurred yesterday, perfectly straightforward instructions can be given, namely, the instruction to do S' and by all means to avoid doing S. But of course the hitch is that I cannot do S' *unless* P' is true, the occurrence of the battle in question rendering me quite powerless to do it.

The second situation. Let us now imagine that I am a naval commander, about to issue my order of the day to the fleet. We assume, further, that, within the totality of other conditions prevailing, my issuing of a certain kind of order will ensure that a naval battle will occur tomorrow, whereas if I issue another kind of order, this will ensure that no naval battle occurs. Now, then, I am about to perform one or the other of these two acts, namely, one of issuing an order of the first sort or one of the second sort. Call these alternative acts O and O' respectively. And call the two propositions, "A naval battle will occur tomorrow" and "No naval battle will occur tomorrow," Q and Q' respectively. We can assert, then, that, if I do act O, then my doing such will ensure that there will be a naval battle, whereas if I do O', my doing that will ensure that no naval battle will occur.

With reference to this situation, then, let us now ask whether it is up to me which sort of order I issue; that is, let us see whether the following proposition is true:

(B) It is within my power to do O, and it is also within my power to do O'.

Anyone, except a fatalist, would be inclined to say that, in the situation we have envisaged, this proposition might well be true, that is, that both acts are quite within my power (granting that I cannot do both at once). For in the circumstances we assume to prevail, it is, one would think, up to me as the commander whether the naval battle occurs or not; it depends only on what kind of order I issue, given all the other conditions as they are, and what kind of order is issued is something quite within my power. It is precisely the denial that such propositions are ever true that would render one a fatalist.

But we have, unfortunately, the same formal argument to

show that (B) is false that we had for proving the falsity of
(A), namely:

1′. If Q is true, then it is not within my power to do O'
(for in case Q is true, then there is, or will be, lacking
a condition essential for my doing O', the condition,
namely, of there being no naval battle tomorrow).

2′. But if Q' is true, then it is not within my power to do
O (for a similar reason).

3′. But either Q is true, or Q' is true.

∴.4′. Either it is not within my power to do O, or it is not
within my power to do O';

and (B) is accordingly false. Another way of expressing this
is to say that what sort of order I issue depends, among other
things, on whether a naval battle takes place tomorrow—for
in this situation a naval battle tomorrow is (by our fourth
presupposition) a necessary condition of my doing O, whereas
no naval battle tomorrow is equally essential for my doing O'.

Considerations of time. Here it might be tempting, at first,
to say that *time* makes a difference, and that no condition can
be necessary for any other *before* that condition exists. But
this escape is closed by both our fifth and sixth presuppositions. Surely if some condition, at *any* given time, whether
past, present, or future, is necessary for the occurrence of
something else, and that condition does not in fact exist *at
the time it is needed,* then nothing we do can be of any avail
in bringing about that occurrence for which it is necessary.
To deny this would be equivalent to saying that I can do
something now which is, together with other conditions prevailing, sufficient for, or which ensures, the occurrence of
something else in the future, *without* getting that future
occurrence as a result. This is absurd in itself and contrary
to our second presupposition. And if one should suggest, in
spite of all this, that a state of affairs that exists *not yet* cannot, just because of this temporal removal, be a necessary
condition of *anything* existing prior to it, this would be logically equivalent to saying that no present state of affairs can
ensure another subsequent to it. We could with equal justice
say that a state of affairs, such as yesterday's naval battle,
which exists *no longer,* cannot be a necessary condition of

anything existing subsequently, there being the same temporal interval here; and this would be arbitrary and false. All that is needed, to restrict the powers that I imagine myself to have to do this or that, is that some condition essential to my doing it *does* not, *did* not, or *will* not occur.

Nor can we wriggle out of fatalism by representing this sort of situation as one in which there is a simple loss of ability or power resulting from the passage of time. For according to our sixth presupposition, the mere passage of time does not enhance or diminish the powers or abilities of anything. We cannot, therefore, say that I have the power to do O' until, say, tomorrow's naval battle occurs, or the power to do O until tomorrow arrives and we find no naval battle occurring, and so on. What restricts the range of my power to do this thing or that is not the mere *temporal* relations between my acts and certain other states of affairs, but the very existence of those states of affairs themselves; and according to our first presupposition, the fact of tomorrow's containing, or lacking, a naval battle, as the case may be, is no less a fact than yesterday's containing or lacking one. If, at any time, I lack the power to perform a certain act, then it can only be the result of something, other than the passage of time, that has happened, is happening, or will happen. The fact that there *is going* to be a naval battle tomorrow is quite enough to render me unable to do O', just as the fact that there *has been* a naval battle yesterday renders me unable to do S', the nonoccurrence of those conditions being essential, respectively, for my doing those things.

Causation. Again, it does no good here to appeal to any particular analyses of causation, or to the fact, if it is one, that causes only "work" forwards and not backwards, for our problem has been formulated without any reference to causation. It may be, for all we know, that causal relations have an unalterable direction (which is an unclear claim in itself), but it is very certain that the relations of necessity and sufficiency between events or states of affairs have not, and it is in terms of these that our data have been described.

The law of excluded middle. There is, of course, one other way to avoid fatalism, and that is to deny one of the premises used to refute (*B*). The first two, hypothetical, premises cannot be denied, however, without our having to reject all but the first, and perhaps the last, of our original six presuppositions, and none of these seems the least doubtful. And the third premise—that either *Q* is true, or *Q'* is true—can be denied only by rejecting the first of our six presuppositions, that is, by rejecting the standard interpretation, *tertium non datur,* of what is called the law of excluded middle.

This last escape has, however, been attempted, and it apparently involves no absurdity. Aristotle, according to an interpretation that is sometimes rendered of his *De Interpretatione,* rejected it. According to this view, the disjunction (*Q* v *Q'*) or, equivalently, (*Q* v −*Q*), which is an instance of the law in question, is a necessary truth. Neither of its disjuncts, however—i.e., neither *Q*, nor *Q'*—is a necessary truth nor, indeed, even a truth, but is instead a mere "possibility," or "contingency" (whatever that may mean). And there is, it would seem, no obvious absurdity in supposing that two propositions, neither of them true and neither of them false, but each "possible," might nevertheless combine into a disjunction which is a necessary truth—for that disjunction might, as this one plainly does, exhaust the possibilities.

Indeed, by assuming the truth of (*B*)—i.e., the statement that it is within my power to do *O* and it is also within my power to do *O'*—and substituting this as our third premise, a formal argument can be rendered to prove that a disjunction of contradictories might disjoin propositions which are neither true nor false. Thus:

1″. If *Q* is true, then it is not within my power to do *O'*.
2″. But if *Q'* is true, then it is not within my power to do *O*.
3″. But it is within my power to do *O*, and it is also within my power to do *O'*.
∴4″. *Q'* is not true, and *Q* is not true;

and to this we can add that, since *Q* and *Q'* are logical contradictories, such that if either is false then the other is true, then *Q* is not false, and *Q'* is not false—i.e., that neither of them is true and neither of them false.

There seems to be no good argument against this line of

I

thought which does not presuppose the very thing at issue, that is, which does not presuppose, not just the truth of a disjunction of contradictories, which is here preserved, but one special interpretation of the law thus expressed, namely, that no third value, like "possible," can ever be assigned to any proposition. And that particular interpretation can, perhaps, be regarded as a more or less arbitrary restriction.

We would not, furthermore, be obliged by this line of thought to reject the traditional interpretation of the so-called law of contradiction, which can be expressed by saying that, concerning any proposition, not both it and its contradictory can be true—which is clearly consistent with what is here suggested.

Nor need we suppose that, from a sense of neatness and consistency, we ought to apply the same considerations to our first situation and to proposition (A)—that, if we so interpret the law in question as to avoid fatalism with respect to the future, then we ought to retain the same interpretation as it applies to things past. The difference here is that we have not the slightest inclination to suppose that it is at all within our power what happened in the past, or that propositions like (A) in situations such as we have described are ever true, whereas we do, if we are not fatalists, believe that it is sometimes within our power what happens in the future, that is, that propositions like (B) are sometimes true. And it was only from the desire to preserve the truth of (B), but not (A), and thus avoid fatalism, that the *tertium non datur* was doubted, using (B) as a premise.

Temporal efficacy. It now becomes apparent, however, that if we seek to avoid fatalism by this device, then we shall have to reject not only our first but also our sixth presupposition; for on this view time will by itself have the power to render true or false certain propositions which were hitherto neither, and this is an "efficacy" of sorts. In fact, it is doubtful whether one can in any way avoid fatalism with respect to the future while conceding that things past are, by virtue of their pastness alone, no longer within our power without also conceding an efficacy to time; for *any* such view will entail that future possibilities, at one time within our power to realize or not, cease to be such *merely* as a result of the passage of time—which is precisely what our sixth presupposition denies. Indeed, this is probably the whole point in casting doubt upon the law of excluded middle in the first place, namely, to call attention to the status of some future things as mere possibilities, thus denying both their complete factuality and their complete lack of it. If so, then our first and sixth presuppositions are inseparably linked, standing or falling together.

The assertion of fatalism. Of course one other possibility remains, and that is to assert, out of a respect for the law of excluded middle and a preference for viewing things under the aspect of eternity, that fatalism is indeed a true doctrine, that propositions such as (*B*) are, like (*A*), never true in such situations as we have described, and that the difference in our *attitudes* toward things future and past, which leads us to call some of the former but none of the latter "possibilities," results entirely from epistemological and psychological considerations—such as, that we happen to *know* more about what the past contains than about what is contained in the future, that our memory extends to past experiences rather than future ones, and so on. Apart from subjective feelings of our power to control things, there seem to be no good philosophical reasons against this opinion, and very strong ones in its favor.

MUST THE FUTURE BE WHAT
IT IS GOING TO BE?

R. D. BRADLEY

RAYMOND D. BRADLEY is Professor of Philosophy at the University of Auckland, New Zealand.

Although logical determinism, correctly understood, simply asserts some logical truisms about past, present, and future events and states of affairs, it has often been confused with a very different view, *viz.* fatalism, and so has been made to share, undeservedly, the disrepute of the latter. Let us see how this has come about.

If we use the symbols x and F as variables whose values respectively are the logical subjects and logical predicates of propositions, we may say that logical determinism simply asserts of every proposition that:

(1) Fx entails Fx (law of identity);

(2) 'Fx and not-Fx' is logically impossible (law of non-contradiction); and

(3) either Fx or not-Fx must be true (law of excluded middle). That is to say, for any x and any F, if F can significantly be predicated of x, Fx must be either true or false; if Fx is true, then not only must what Fx asserts be the case, but it is logically impossible that it should *not* be the case (since otherwise Fx would not be true); and if Fx is false, then not only must what Fx asserts not be the case, but it is logically impossible that it *should* be the case (since otherwise Fx would not be false). Thus, according to logical determinism, everything is determined or rather *determinate* in

FROM "Must the Future Be What It Is Going to Be?" *Mind,* 68 (1959). Reprinted by permission of the editor and R. D. Bradley.

the sense that it is what it is and logically cannot be otherwise. And this holds of past and future states of affairs as well as present ones. The past was what it was and could not have been different; it is as though its record is indelible, for if an event occurred in the past there is nothing that anyone (even God) can do to erase the fact that it has occurred or to bring it about that it has not occurred. In this sense, the past is closed; it cannot be tampered with or altered by any means whatever. In the same sense the future too is closed. For it is a logically necessary truth that what will be will be; if an event is to occur, there is nothing and no-one that can conceivably bring it about that it will not occur; even God is impotent in the face of logical necessity. You cannot make the future other than it will be any more than you can make the past other than it was.

What disturbs many people about this is that, despite its apparently unquestionable logical credentials, logical determinism seems to deny some obvious and important truths. Certainly, on the one hand, it *looks* like a tautology to say, for example, that what is to be will be, but on the other hand, this apparent tautology seems to imply that all activity is fruitless, that there is, for instance, no point in obtaining medical advice and attention even when dangerously ill since, if the patient is going to recover he might as well dispense with the doctor's services, and if he is not going to recover no amount of skill or attention on the doctor's part will make any difference. There are, of course, some religious sects whose adherents strenuously oppose medical aid when they and their children are ill on grounds rather like these, *e.g.* "God knows best" and "God's will be done", but most of us regard this sort of attitude as wrongheaded and perhaps, in cases where it leads to serious ill-health or death, even criminally reprehensible. That is, we deny that all effort and activity is pointless and hence are committed to denying whatever statement or statements fatalism is implied by. The argument is that if logical determinism implies fatalism and logical determinism is necessarily true, then fatalism must be true; but we all agree that fatalism is false, therefore it must be false either that logical determinism is necessarily true or that logical determinism entails fatalism. We want to know which.

To put it a little differently, we are faced with the following inconsistent triad:

(1) Logical determinism is true;
(2) Fatalism is false;
(3) Logical determinism entails fatalism.

We accept (2) but must reject either (1) or (3) since each of them, in conjunction with (2), implies the contradictory of the other. The issue at stake is whether belief in logical determinism is warranted. Thus, on the one hand, determinists accept (1) and (2) and so conclude that (3) is false; that is, they believe both that logical determinism is true and that fatalism is false, but recognise that they can do so if and only if logical determinism does not entail fatalism. On the other hand, however, many libertarians accept (3) and (2) and so conclude that (1) is false; that is, they use the supposed fatalist implications of logical determinism in order to discredit logical determinism. The question to be decided, then, is this: "Does logical determinism involve fatalist conclusions?"

I propose to examine, first, the consequences of, and secondly, the purported reasons for the affirmative answer to this question.

I

Some libertarians think that logical determinism *is* fatalistic and this, I believe, is what leads them to deny that the law of excluded middle is applicable to statements about future events and states of affairs, and thereby to deny also that the laws of identity and non-contradiction apply to them either. Their argument, as we have seen, takes the form: "(3) and (2), therefore not (1)." This form of libertarianism holds that future events are logically contingent since neither they, nor statements about them, are subject to the above-mentioned logical laws. They are contingent, not in the sense in which to say that the future is 'contingent' is merely to say euphemistically that we are ignorant about the future, but rather in the sense of *real* contingency, *i.e.* of being in themselves indeterminate. Of such events it cannot be said either that they will or will not occur, nor can it be said that statements about them are either true or false. As Aristotle put it: "when in future events there is a real alternative, and a potentiality in contrary directions, the corresponding affirmation and denial have the same character",[1] *i.e.* statements about them are only potentially true or false but are actually neither.

Clearly, this involves the rejection of ordinary two-valued logic according to which every proposition must, by definition, be either true or false; or rather, it involves the *restriction* of the area of application of two-valued logic and hence also of the laws of excluded middle, non-contradiction and identity. That is to say, only those statements which are about present and past states of affairs can be said to be either true or false since they alone refer to determinate facts the knowledge of which enables us to assess their truth-values; when we purport to be talking about the future our presumptive statements can be neither true nor false since, unless we accept fatalism, we cannot allow that the future contains any determinate facts to which they can refer and by reference to which their truth-values can be ascertained. Strictly speaking, of course, it is improper, on this view, to talk about either "statements in the future tense" or "propositions about the future" for, according to present-day usage, a sentence which does not assert or deny that something determinate is the case is not a statement any more than a sentence which is neither true nor false can express a proposition. However, there is an established precedent for using these terms rather more loosely, *i.e.* in such a way that it is *not* self-contradictory to speak of statements or propositions which are neither true nor false. Aristotle, for instance, spoke in this sort of way when this so-called 'problem of present truth and future contingents' was first discussed.[2] Similarly, proponents of three-valued logic talk about 'propositions' (about contingent future events) which have neither the

[1] *De Interpretatione,* ch. 9 (19ª 33 [p. 182 of this volume]).
[2] *De Interpretatione,* ch. 9.

determinate value '1' (true), nor the determinate value '0' (false), but the indeterminate value '½' (neuter or possible).

The interesting thing is that quite a few philosophers have actually resorted to three-valued logic principally as a means of escape from the kind of logical fatalism to which they think the law of excluded middle and ordinary two-valued logic commits us. This is clearly recognised by Prior who recently suggested that the oddity of some of the features of three-valued logic largely disappears if we "relate the system to the problem which it was originally designed for handling —the problem of 'future contingents'".[3] Again, according to Waismann, the argument from fear of fatalism was "actually propounded by Lukasiewicz in favour of a three-valued logic with 'possible' as a third truth-value alongside 'true' and 'false'".[4] Apparently, then, the confusion of logical determinism with logical fatalism has generated not only the doctrine of real counter-logical contingency but at least some three-valued logics.

It would be wrong, however, to think that everyone who claims to have renounced the law of excluded middle or adopted a system of three-valued logic is a logical libertarian, for on at least some interpretations of what it means to say that a proposition is 'true' or 'false' this certainly does not follow. For instance, Professor C. D. Broad is able to remain largely uncommitted on the determinism *versus* libertarianism issue despite the fact that he has argued that propositions which profess to be about the future are not literally true or false since they "do not refer to any fact . . . at the time when they are made",[5] even although "it is possible for any-one who understands their meaning to see what kind of fact *will* eventually make them true or false as the case may be".[6] Again, anyone who held that a proposition could be said to be true if and only if it is capable of immediate or direct

[3] "Three-Valued Logic and Future Contingents," *Philosophical Quarterly*, 3 (1953), 322.
[4] "How I See Philosophy," *Contemporary British Philosophy*, third series, p. 456.
[5] *Scientific Thought*, p. 73.
[6] *Ibid.*, p. 77.

verification would have to say that the law of excluded middle did not apply to propositions about the future, but he would not, or need not, say this in a sense which is inconsistent with the thesis of logical determinism. In such cases it is important to distinguish between saying that future states of affairs are indeterminate with respect to our knowledge and saying that they are indeterminate in themselves, or again between saying that propositions about the future are not *known* to be true or *known* to be false and saying that they are in fact neither true nor false. So long as the future is indeterminate only in a relative or epistemic sense these assertions are quite consistent with logical determinism. Similarly, there is no inconsistency between the principle of excluded middle as it is usually understood and three-valued logics so long as the terms 'true' and 'false' as they occur in the latter are given interpretations different from those that we ordinarily give them.

Lukasiewicz is far from being the only philosopher to suppose that the laws of excluded middle, identity and non-contradiction, when applied to the future, carry with them fatalist consequences. Other examples, too, may readily be cited. Aristotle for instance, concludes his discussion of the problem of future contingents by observing: "It is therefore plain that it is not necessary that of an affirmation and a denial one should be true and the other false. For, in the case of that which exists potentially but not actually, the rule which applies to that which exists actually does not hold good."[7] This, he argued, followed from the fact that the contrary supposition that it is an "irrefragable law that of every pair of contradictory propositions . . . one must be true and the other false" leads to the "impossible conclusion" that there could be "no real alternatives", that everything that is or takes place would be the "outcome of necessity",[8] and that there would therefore be "no need to deliberate or take trouble".[9] True, Aristotle thought that he could at the same

[7] (19^b 1 [p. 182 of this volume—Ed.]).
[8] (18^b 26 [p. 181 of this volume—Ed.]).
[9] (18^b 32 [p. 181 of this volume—Ed.]).

1*

time safeguard the law of excluded middle by allowing that the entire disjunction "Either there will be a sea-battle tomorrow or there will not" is necessarily true although neither of its component propositions, "There will be a sea-battle tomorrow" and "There will not be a sea-battle tomorrow", is either true or false, but here he was obviously mistaken. As Professor D. C. Williams comments: "This is a downright contradiction, not to be saved by the traditional apology that S or *not*-S can be 'indeterminately' true while neither S nor *not*-S is 'determinately' true."[10] Or, to put it in another way: the disjunction 'Either p or not-p' is a truth-function which is true if and only if one of its components, 'p' or 'not-p', is true. A recent example is Professor A. N. Prior who, according to his pupil, R. J. Butler,[11] reasons thus:

"Belief in free-will is warranted;
  Belief in free-will entails the adoption of a logic admitting propositions neither true nor false;
  Therefore, the adoption of a logic admitting propositions neither true nor false is warranted."

Even determinists have sometimes failed to distinguish between logical determinism and fatalism and so have incautiously renounced the former because of the latter. Thus, Nowell-Smith has written about "logical determinism or fatalism, according to which we cannot help doing what we do since things are what they are and our actions will be what they will be", and observed: "I shall forbear to comment on this brand of determinism, since I doubt whether anyone is now seriously deceived by it."[12] Similarly Waismann uses the expressions "logical determinism", "fatalism", and "logical predestination" as if they all meant exactly the same.[13] Now certainly fatalism, *viz.* the view that "we cannot help doing what we do", is, as Nowell-Smith correctly says, one of the

[10] "Professor Linsky on Aristotle," *Philosophical Review*, 63 (1954), 253.
[11] "Aristotle's Sea Fight and Three-valued Logic," *Philosophical Review*, 6 (1955), 272.
[12] "Determinists and Libertarians," *Mind*, 63 (1954), 331.
[13] "How I See Philosophy," p. 323.

"bogeys that go under the name of 'determinism'"[14] and needs therefore to be exorcised, but logical determinism, *viz.* the claim that "things are what they are and our actions will be what they will be", is not: rather is it presupposed by all determinists—whether they realise it or not.

II

We have seen what are the consequences of thinking that, on pain of fatalism, we must deny that statements about the future can be either true or false and so deny also that the future will be what it will be and not otherwise, but what are the *reasons* for this? That is to say, what are the sources of the belief that logical determinism implies fatalism? The answer, I suggest, is that people who believe this are misled by certain confusions about the expressions "it is true now" and "it cannot possibly be otherwise".

"It is true now." The confusion about present truth arises in this way: logical determinists assert not only that every proposition is either true or false, but also that it is true or false, as the case may be, "once and for all"; or in other words, that if a proposition is true it is *always* true and that if it is false it is *always* false. Perhaps it is this expression "always true" which is the original source of the trouble since it seems reasonable to infer that if it makes sense to say that something is always the case it must also make sense to say that it is the case *now* or *at present*, and this in turn seems to some people to carry implications of logical doom or fate. Thus, in the eyes of the logical libertarians, the thesis of logical determinism is destroyed by the following *reductio ad absurdum:*

If it is the case that for any proposition 'p', 'p' must be either true or false, and that " 'p' is true" implies that the state of affairs p was, is, or will be the case, while " 'p' is false" implies that not-p was, is, or will be the case, then if 'pf' is a proposition about the future, 'pf' must be either true or false and the assertion " 'pf' is true" implies that

[14] *Loc. cit.*

pf will be the case while the assertion "'pf' is false" implies that not-pf will be the case. Now, this means that something which *now* is the case (the truth or falsity of 'pf') logically requires something that is *not yet* the case (either the state of affairs pf or the state of affairs not-pf); hence, either pf or not-pf is logically doomed to occur or not to occur no matter what anyone might do to bring about the contrary. But since this is ridiculous, it follows (by denial of the consequent) that it cannot be the case that every proposition is either true or false.

The argument is formally valid but the conclusion will be true only if the following three suppositions are also true:

(1) that it strictly *makes sense* to talk about statements being true or false "now" or "already",

(2) that whenever we say that a statement about the future is true or false we mean that it is true or false now, and

(3) that if statements about the future were at present true or false, the future would be unalterable by anything that anyone did since, as Prior puts it, "what is the case already has passed out of the realm of alternative possibilities into the realm of what cannot be altered".[15]

I propose to show that each of these is false. Of course, since both (3) and (2) themselves presuppose (1) it would suffice to show that (1) is false, but, as there is something to be learnt from a complete diagnosis, we shall consider all three.

(1) The first supposition betrays a confusion of thought about what is meant by saying that if a statement is true it is 'always true'. Determinists *do* say this but they do not say what the logical libertarians think this implies, *viz*. that it makes strict sense to talk about the truth-value of a particular proposition or statement at a particular time so that, for instance, propositions about the future can significantly be said to be true, or false, at present. The point is that the inference

[15] "Three-Valued Logic and Future Contingents," p. 323.

from "true always" to "true now" is illegitimate since the former means "true at *any* time" while the latter is ordinarily taken to mean "true at *this* time but not at some other time"—which is very different. To put it another way: the "now" in the expression "true now" either is to be understood here, as elsewhere, as allowing the possibility that whatever is said to be the case "now" might not be so at some other time, in which case to say that a true proposition (which is true always) is "true now" is to assert a contradiction; or else its use in this expression is both redundant (if it is true at all it need not be said that it is true now) and seriously misleading (the mere fact that it *is* said suggests that something significant is being added to the claim that it is true, *viz.* that at some other time it might not be true). According to logical determinism, then, there is no answer to the question, "Is it true or false *now* that so-and-so was, is, or will be the case?" since the truth-values of propositions do not admit of temporal distinctions. This is what is meant by "the timelessness of truth" and, for that matter, of falsity too; that is, it just does not make sense to ask at what particular time a statement is true or false.

Logical libertarians might reply, however, that on this point ordinary usage is on their side. They would remind us that in actual fact we commonly do speak as if the truth or falsity of our statements could alter with the passage of time, *e.g.* when we say such things as, "Yes, admittedly it was true in those days that five pounds a week was considered a good wage, but it isn't now", or again, "What you are saying about the stability of the Canadian economy may be true now but it won't be in a few years' time". The objection seems to gain further weight still from Prior's contention that "ancient and medieval usage was generally such that logicians could speak (as Aristotle did speak) of 'Socrates is sitting down' as a 'proposition' which is 'true at those times at which he *is* sitting down and false at those times at which he is not".[16] But we may grant all this without conceding the point at issue, for the libertarian's time-dependent truth-

16 *Ibid.,* p. 322.

values are significantly different from those of ordinary usage, past as well as present, in at least two respects.

In the first place, the so-called 'statements' of which these varying truth-values are predicated are not the same: although it certainly is the case that the truth-values of *grammatical* statements or declarative sentences can be said to vary from time to time, and even from place to place and speaker to speaker—consider, for example, the declarative sentences "It rained yesterday" (said on different days), "We are not far from the sea" (said in different places), and "I am twenty-six years old" (said by different persons)—this does not settle the question at issue which is not whether *grammatical* statements, *i.e.* indicative sentences, have varying truth-values, but whether *logical* statements or *propositions* do. The relevant difference between them is that, on the one hand, a 'statement' (in the grammarian's sense of the word) does not always specify, or specifies only incompletely, the precise state of affairs to which it refers, *i.e.* it contains words and phrases (*e.g.* "yesterday", "we", and "I" in the above examples) whose reference is vague, ambiguous or otherwise indeterminate, so that it admits of being used in different spatial and temporal contexts and by different speakers with consequently varying truth-values, whereas, on the other hand, a proposition or statement in logical form has had these deficiencies remedied by the replacement of vague expressions by precise ones, and further by the use of spatial and temporal indicators specifying the context of utterance, so that its reference is determinate and its truth-value accordingly fixed and unvarying. Thus, as Quine observes: "logical analysis is facilitated by requiring . . . that each statement be true once and for all and false once and for all, independently of time. This can be effected by rendering verbs tenseless and then resorting to explicit chronological descriptions when need arises for distinctions of time."[17] He illustrates this point when, in his discussion of the (grammatical) statement 'There was at least one woman among the survivors', he writes: "The way to render Mr. Straw-

---

[17] *Elementary Logic,* p. 6.

son's example is '(∃x) (x [is] a woman. x was among the survivors)', with tenseless '[is]' and, as always, '∃'. The 'was' here involves reference presumably to some time or occasions implicit in the missing context; if we suppose it given by some constant 'D' (*e.g.* 'The sinking of the Lusitania'), then the whole amounts to '(∃x [is] a woman. x [is] among the survivors of D)', tenseless throughout."[18] Clearly the admitted instability of truth-values in ordinary usage, where the 'statements' of which truth and falsity are predicated are merely sentences in the indicative mood, does nothing to refute the contention that it does not strictly make sense to admit temporal distinctions and variations in the truth-values of propositions, *i.e.* statements in logical form. Indeed, to take a simpler example, as soon as the indicative sentence (about the future), "I shall be Prime Minister of this country in twenty years' time", is supplemented in such a way as to make it quite clear just what logical statement or proposition it is meant in a particular context to express, *e.g.* "Robert Hawke of Masson St., Canberra, is [tenseless] Prime Minister of Australia in 1977", we no longer wish to say that its truth-value can vary with the person, place, or time of utterance, but rather that it must be either true *once and for all* or false *once and for all*—or at any rate, no-one but a logical libertarian still wants to say this.

This brings us to the second point of difference. Not only does ordinary usage fail to corroborate the logical libertarian thesis that temporal distinctions can significantly be predicated of the truth-values of statements *in logical form*, but the temporal variations that it does recognise in the truth-values of *indicative sentences* are very different from those which the logical libertarian urges upon us. Thus, consider the crucial case of an assertion about the future, *e.g.* (to borrow from Quine),[19] "The Nazis will annex Bohemia" as uttered before 1939. According to ordinary usage, this assertion was true before 1939 but is now false. But according to the logical libertarian view neither this assertion nor the proposition which it expresses, *viz.* "The Nazis annex [tense-

18 "Mr. Strawson on Logical Theory," *Mind,* 62 (1953), 442.
19 *Elementary Logic,* p. 6.

less] Bohemia after 9th May 1939", is either true or false before 9th May 1939, although it *becomes* true on that date and remains so thereafter.

Further difficulties in the view that it makes sense to talk about propositions being "true now" but "undecided" at some time in the past are brought out by Waismann. There are some philosophers, he tells us, who seem to suppose "that a statement referring to an event in the future is at present undecided, neither true nor false, but that when the event happens the proposition enters into a sort of new state, that of being true. But how are we to figure the change from 'undecided' to 'true'? Is it sudden or gradual? At what moment does the statement 'It will rain tomorrow' begin to be true? When the first drop falls to the ground? And supposing that it will not rain, when will the statement begin to be false? Just at the end of the day, at 12 p.m. sharp? Supposing that the event *has* happened, that the statement *is* true, will it remain so for ever and ever? If so, in what way? Does it remain uninterruptedly true, at every moment of day and night? . . . We wouldn't know how to answer these questions; this is due not to any particular ignorance or stupidity on our part but to the fact that something has gone wrong with the way the words 'true' and 'false' are applied here."[20] The fact is, he concludes, that "the clause 'it is true that—' does not allow of inserting a date. To say of a proposition like 'Diamond is pure carbon' that it is true on Christmas Eve would be just as poor a joke as to say that it is true in Paris and not in Timbuctoo."[21]

(2) The second supposition can be dismissed summarily by observing that since, as has just been shown, it does not make sense to admit temporal distinctions and variations in the truth-value of *any* propositions, it cannot make sense to admit them concerning propositions about the future. Thus, it should be clear from what has already been said that when we say that a proposition about the future is true we do not mean to say that it is true 'now' in any sense which

[20] "How I See Philosophy," p. 455.
[21] *Ibid.*, p. 456.

implies that perhaps it was not or will not be true at some
other time: rather do we mean that, if it is true, it is true
now and always, and similarly that, if it is false, it is false
now and always. This fact reacts both to the benefit of logical
determinists and to the detriment of their opponents, the
logical libertarians, inasmuch as it not only helps to clear the
logical determinist of the *reductio ad absurdum* which the
logical libertarian presses against him but also, in so doing,
deprives the latter of the argument on which much of the
plausibility of his own view rested. Thus, if the logical determinist, when he says that all propositions, including those
about the future, are either true or false, is not committed
to saying that they are *now* either true or false, it no longer
sounds so plausible either to say that he is committed to a
fated future, or to reason on the basis of this (*i.e.* by denial
of the consequent) that since fatalism is unacceptable such
propositions must have some *other* truth-value, *i.e.* be neither true nor false but indeterminate.

(3) The third supposition, which involves the unwarranted
inference from present truth about the future to a logically
doomed future, takes several forms each of which needs to
be examined and rejected in turn.

(*a*) For a start, consider the inference in the form in
which Prior states it, *viz.* "what is the case already . . . cannot be altered". Even if we were to allow the propriety of
talking in this sort of way about propositions being 'true now'
—and we do not—there would be two further objections to
make. In the first place, that which "is the case already", in
Prior's argument, is simply the *truth* of 'pf', *i.e.* of some
proposition about a future state of affairs, *not* that state of
affairs itself. To assert the latter would be to assert a contradiction for if a state of affairs is "already the case" it cannot be a *future* state of affairs. It should be noted that there
is no corresponding tendency to argue that the truth of an
assertion about a past state of affairs implies that that state of
affairs "is the case at present", which would also be a contradiction. The truth of a proposition about the future implies, not that something *is* the case, but that something *will*
be the case, just as the truth of a proposition about the past

implies, not that something in the past exists *now* but that something in the past *did* exist—in the past. Secondly, the expression "cannot be altered" troubles us only because, as it is used here, it is, as it were, swimming out of depth. We know of course, what it is like to change or alter things contemporaneous with our efforts and activities, and even what it is like to alter our plans for the future, but what would it be like to alter the future itself? In a strict sense, what the future holds for us cannot be altered for it would then not be part of the future. But does this mean that the future is fated and that it owes nothing to our efforts and activities? We do not think that the past was fated because it cannot be altered. Why, then, should we think this of the future? Certainly, the future cannot be changed from what it is to be (isn't this a tautology?), but equally certainly it *can* be altered from what it *might* otherwise have been *if* we had not taken the actions that we did. The notion of 'altering' bedevils the real issue which is not whether the future will be what it is to be but rather whether *what* it is to be owes anything to our present or future efforts and activities —and on this question the logical relationship between a true proposition and what it is true about has no bearing.

(*b*) The fact that something which "is the case already", *viz.* the truth of some assertion about the future, necessitates something which is not yet the case, *viz.* the future state of affairs about which the assertion is made, is sometimes taken to mean that so-called present truths are the *causes* of what they truly assert about the future, and this latter is thought to involve fatalism. Of course, this form of the supposition would not even arise if it were not for the initial muddle about "present truth", but even apart from this it must be rejected on two other grounds. The first is that it assimilates logical necessity to causal necessity. It may be natural, but it is nonetheless wrong, to think that whenever something present necessitates something future the necessitation is causal. Thus, in the case in question, what is supposed to be 'present' is not an event, which *is* the sort of thing that can be a cause, but the truth of a proposition, which is *not*. No doubt it makes sense to say that someone's *assertion* (which is an event) about the future is the cause of the future event which it is true about, *e.g.* a prediction about the effects of making that prediction, but this does not affect the point at issue. The relationship between so-called "present truths" and what they are true about is that of logical necessity not causal necessity; that is to say, it would be a contradiction, not just a factual error, to say that the one was not "followed" by the other, and this, of course, simply confirms the fact that the relationship between truths and what they assert to be true is a non-temporal one. The second mistake is to assimilate causal necessity to fatalism. It should suffice to observe that there is a vast difference, indeed an inconsistency, between saying that the future will be what it will be solely because of what the present is (causal determinism), and saying that *what* the future will be owes nothing to what our actions at present are (fatalism).

(*c*) There is a further argument still which pretends to derive the fatalist conclusion from the supposition that statements about the future can be true at present. It proceeds in two stages: it is contended, first that propositions about the future could not be either true or false unless the future states of affairs which they are about were causally determined by antecedent states of affairs, and secondly that to say that the future is caused is to say that it is fated. But the inference fails at both stages; the second because, as I have just said and therefore need not repeat at length, it erroneously assimilates causation to fatalism, and the first because it confuses causal determination with logical determinateness. Now to say that the future is logically determinate, *i.e.* that it will be what it is going to be, is not to say anything about whether it is also causally determined, *i.e.* whether it will be what it is going to be *because* of what happens before it. It may be but it may not be so determined. The inference from 'x is causally determined' to 'x is logically determinate' is a legitimate one but the reverse is not. Thus when we say that statements about the future are either true or false we are saying only that the future is logically determinate and this, by itself, does not warrant the further inference, on which the above argument depends, that it is causally determined.

It might be suggested, however, that we could never know that any given statement about the future was true or false unless the future were causally related to the present, *i.e.* unless there were causal laws, a knowledge of which along with a knowledge of initial conditions would enable us to make correct predictions about the future. But this, of course, is quite beside the point, for the issue is not whether propositions about the future can be known to be true or known to be false but whether they can *be* true or *be* false. Moreover, predictive inference proceeding by way of our knowledge of causal laws, is not the only logically qualified candidate for the job of telling us what the future will be, for although the empirical evidence for the occurrence of precognition may be, as it undoubtedly is, still very weak, there are no fatal objections to it on purely logical grounds. Now all that is required for precognition to be possible is that the future which is to be precognised should be logically determinate—not that it should be causally determined. Thus, it is not hard to conceive of a world in which all events occurred purely at random, or without causes, and in which a being with the power of precognition could at any moment foretell what was to happen next: indeed, according to some theologians, this is what our own world is like, except, perhaps, that God, the precognising being, is not usually regarded as being in the world but rather as transcending it. Now the mere fact that such non-inferential knowledge of the future is logically possible means that we can conceivably know whether our statements about it are true or false even although it is not causally related to the present. That is to say, all that precognition demands is that there should be a determinate, not a causally determined, future to be precognised.

"*It cannot possibly be otherwise.*" It seems that many philosophical confusions arise from the failure to distinguish between the multiple senses of the correlative terms 'necessary' and 'impossible'. One of these confusions is that of thinking that if it is logically necessary that the future should be what it is going to be, *i.e.* that it is logically impossible for it not to be what it is going to be, there can be no point in doing anything since whatever we do must have happened anyway, and whatever we do not do could not have happened even if we had tried to make it happen. In other words, the supposition that the future cannot possibly be otherwise seems to imply that the future is fated and that all our efforts are doomed to frustration.

Now I suggest that we need only remind ourselves of the distinction between logical necessity and impossibility, on the one hand, and coercive necessity and impossibility, on the other hand, in order to see that this inference is completely unwarranted. What follows from the fact that a proposition about the future, *e.g.* "E will occur at tf", is true is simply that E *will* occur at tf, not that E will occur at tf in spite of anything that we may do to prevent it. Thus, if E-at-tf is something that I am going to do, then it follows only that I *will* do E at tf, not that I shall be *forced* to do it irrespective of what else I want and try to do. Certainly, whatever we are going to do must (logically) be going to happen—otherwise it could not be said that we are going to do it—but it is seriously misleading to say that it must happen "anyway", *i.e.* as if what is going to happen owes nothing at all to my efforts and activities. No doubt there will be some events in the future whose occurrence will owe nothing whatever to my efforts to bring them about just as there will be some whose occurrence will thwart my efforts to prevent them, but this is no more surprising or ominous than is the fact that in the past there have been events which I did not produce and events which I could not prevent. There is no more reason for saying that the future is fated because it will be what it will be than there is for saying that the past is fated because it was what it was or the present because it is what it is. We do not say the latter, so why should we say the former? It is clear that the sense in which things "cannot possibly be otherwise" because they are what they are is very different from the sense in which they "cannot possibly be otherwise" because other things *compel* them to be what they are: in the former sense *nothing* can possibly be otherwise, while in the latter sense at least *some* things obviously can. It is further important to realise that the future, of which it is asserted that it is logically necessary that it should be what it is going to be and logically impossible that it should be anything other than it is going to be, includes whatever I am going to do and the consequences of what I am going to do. This means that the same logical necessity which requires that the future should be what it will be, also requires that such efforts as I might then make should have the effects that they are going to have; that is to say, it does not make my activities futile since it extends its logical guarantee to all events— my actions and their consequences, if they have any, included. Similarly, if it is logically impossible for the future to be different from what it will be, it is also logically impossible for the causal efficacy of my future actions to be other than it is going to be: if they are to be frustrated (and this often happens without our thinking that they are *doomed* to be frustrated) then certainly it is logically impossible that they should not be frustrated, but equally if they are to be effective it is logically impossible that they should not be effective. The answer to the factual question which *will* be the case, *i.e.* whether my activities will make any difference to the future or whether they will not, obviously cannot be deduced from the logical truism that both they and the future will be what they will be whichever is the case.

Thus the final and decisive argument in defence of logical determinism against the bogey of fatalism is that you cannot derive fatalism from a mere tautology or set of tautologies. Fatalism pretends to give us definite and indeed quite startling information about the world we live in—information which, if it were true, would enable us to distinguish this world from other possible worlds: it asserts that in our world the present is causally discontinuous with the future and so concludes that our actions are completely futile since nothing we do can influence the future. But logical determinism, since it asserts no more than a set of tautologies, tells us *nothing*—that is, it tells us nothing that would enable us to distinguish this world from any other simply because it tells us what this world *and* every other possible world *must* be like, *viz.* that its future (if it has one) will be what it will be and logically cannot be otherwise. Whereas fatalism makes a factual assertion that this or that is the case, logical determinism asserts only the logical truism that *whatever* is the case is the case, and there clearly can be no passage from the latter to the former. As soon as we understand this, fatalism loses its terror, logical determinism stands vindicated, and the case for logical libertarianism collapses for want of an argument.

BRINGING ABOUT THE PAST

MICHAEL DUMMETT

MICHAEL DUMMETT is a Reader in Mathematics at All Souls College, Oxford.

I observe first that there is a genuine sense in which the causal relation has a temporal direction: it is associated with the direction earlier-to-later rather than with the reverse. I shall not pause here to achieve a precise formulation of the sense in which this association holds; I think such a formulation can be given without too much difficulty, but it is not to my present purpose to do this. What I do want to assert is the following: so far as I can see, this association of causality with a particular temporal direction is not merely a matter of the way we speak of causes, but has a genuine basis in the way things happen. There is indeed an asymmetry in respect of past and future in the way in which we describe events when we are considering them as standing in causal relations to one another; but I am maintaining that this reflects an objective asymmetry in nature. I think that this asymmetry would reveal itself to us even if we were not *agents* but mere *observers*. It is indeed true, I believe, that our concept of cause is bound up with our concept of intentional action: if an event is properly said to cause the occurrence of a subsequent or simultaneous event, I think it necessarily follows that, if we can find any way of bringing about the former event (in particular, if it is itself a voluntary human action), then it must make sense to speak of bringing it about *in order* that the subsequent event should occur. Moreover, I be-

FROM Michael Dummett, "Bringing About the Past," *Philosophical Review*, 73 (1964). Reprinted by permission of the editor and Michael Dummett.

lieve that this connection between something's being a cause and the possibility of using it in order to bring about its effect plays an essential role in the fundamental account of how we ever come to accept causal laws: that is, that we could arrive at any causal beliefs only by beginning with those in which the cause is a voluntary action of ours. Nevertheless, I am inclined to think that we could have some kind of concept of cause, although one differing from that we now have, even if we were mere observers and not agents at all—a kind of intelligent tree. And I also think that even in this case the asymmetry of cause with respect to temporal direction would reveal itself to us.

To see this, imagine ourselves observing events in a world just like the actual one, except that the order of events is reversed. There are indeed enormous difficulties in describing such a world if we attempt to include human beings in it, or any other kind of creature to whom can be ascribed intention and purpose (there would also be a problem about memory). But, so far as I can see, there is no difficulty whatever if we include in this world only plants and inanimate objects. If we imagine ourselves as intelligent trees observing such a world and communicating with one another, but unable to intervene in the course of events, it is clear that we should have great difficulty in arriving at causal explanations that accounted for events in terms of the processes which had *led up to* them. The sapling grows gradually smaller, finally reducing itself to an apple pip; then an apple is gradually constituted around the pip from ingredients found in the soil; at a certain moment the apple rolls along the ground, gradually gaining momentum, bounces a few times, and then suddenly takes off vertically and attaches itself with a snap to the bough of an apple tree. Viewed from the standpoint of gross observation, this process contains many totally unpredictable elements: we cannot, for example, explain, by reference to the conditions obtaining at the moment when the apple started rolling, why it started rolling at that moment or in that direction. Rather, we should have to substitute a system of explanations of events in terms of the processes that led back to them from some subsequent moment.

If through some extraordinary chance we, in this world, could consider events from the standpoint of the microscopic, the unpredictability would disappear theoretically ("in principle") although not in practice; but we should be left—so long as we continued to try to give causal explanations on the basis of what leads up to an event—with inexplicable coincidences. "In principle" we could, by observing the movements of the molecules of the soil, predict that at a certain moment they were going to move in such a way as to combine to give a slight impetus to the apple, and that this impetus would be progressively reinforced by other molecules along a certain path, so as to cause the apple to accelerate in such a way that it would end up attached to the apple tree. But not only could we not make such predictions in practice: the fact that the "random" movements of the molecules should happen to work out in such a way that all along the path the molecules always happened to be moving in the same direction at just the moment that the apple reached that point, and, above all, that these movements always worked in such a way as to leave the apple attached to an *apple* tree and not to any other tree or any other object— these facts would cry out for explanation, and we should be unable to provide it.

I should say, then, that, so far as the concept of cause possessed by mere observers rather than agents is concerned, the following two theses hold: (i) the world is such as to make appropriate a notion of causality associated with the earlier-to-later temporal direction rather than its reverse; (ii) we can conceive of a world in which a notion of causality associated with the opposite direction would have been more appropriate and, so long as we consider ourselves as mere observers of such a world, there is no particular conceptual difficulty about the conception of such a backwards causation. There are, of course, regions of which we are mere observers, in which we cannot intervene: the heavens, for example. Since Newton, we have learned to apply the same causal laws to events in this realm; but in earlier times it was usually assumed that a quite different system of laws must operate there. It *could* have turned out that this was right; and then it could also have turned out that the system of laws we needed to explain events involving the celestial bodies required a notion of causality associated with the temporal direction from later to earlier.

When, however, we consider ourselves as agents, and consider causal laws governing events in which we can intervene, the notion of backwards causality seems to generate absurdities. If an event *C* is considered as the cause of a preceding event *D,* then it would be open to us to bring about *C* in order that the event *D* should have occurred. But the conception of doing something in order that something else should have happened appears to be intrinsically absurd: it apparently follows that backwards causation must also be absurd in any realm in which we can operate as agents.

We can affect the future by our actions: so why can we not by our actions affect the past? The answer that springs to mind is this: you cannot *change* the past; if a thing has happened, it has happened, and you cannot make it not to have happened. This is, I am told, the attitude of orthodox Jewish theologians to retrospective prayer. It is blasphemous to pray that something should *have* happened, for, although there are no limits to God's power, He cannot do what is logically impossible; it is logically impossible to alter the past, so to utter a retrospective prayer is to mock God by asking Him to perform a logical impossibility. Now I think it is helpful to think about this example, because it is the only instance of behavior, on the part of ordinary people whose mental processes we can understand, designed to affect the past and coming quite naturally to us. If one does not think of this case, the idea of doing something in order that something else should previously have happened may seem sheer raving insanity. But suppose I hear on the radio that a ship has gone down in the Atlantic two hours previously, and that there were a few survivors: my son was on that ship, and I at once utter a prayer that he should have been among the survivors, that he should not have drowned; this is the most natural thing in the world. Still, there are things which it is very natural to say which make no sense; there are actions which can naturally be performed with intentions which *could* not be fulfilled. Are the Jewish theologians right in stigmatizing my prayer as blasphemous?

They characterize my prayer as a request that, if my son has drowned, God should make him not have drowned. But why should they view it as asking anything more self-contradictory than a prayer for the future? If, before the ship set sail, I had prayed that my son should make a safe crossing, I should not have been praying that, if my son was going to drown, God should have made him not be going to drown. Here we stumble on a well-known awkwardness of language. There is a use of the future tense to express present tendencies: English newspapers sometimes print announcements of the form "The marriage that was arranged between X and Y will not now take place." If someone did not understand the use of the future tense to express present tendencies, he might be amazed by this "now"; he might say, "Of course it *will* not take place *now:* either it *is* taking place *now*, or it *will* take place *later*." The presence of the "now" indicates a use of the future tense according to which, if anyone had said earlier, "They are going to get married," he would have been right, even though their marriage never subsequently occurred. If, on the other hand, someone had offered a bet which he expressed by saying, "I bet they will not be married on that date," this "will" would normally be understood as expressing the *genuine* future tense, the future tense so used that what happens on the future date is the decisive test for truth or falsity, irrespective of how things looked at the time of making the bet, or at any intervening time. The future tense that I was using, and that will be used throughout this paper, is intended to be understood as this genuine future tense.

With this explanation, I will repeat: when, before the ship sails, I pray that my son will make the crossing safely, I am not praying that God should perform the logically impossible feat of making what will happen not happen (that is, not be-going-to happen); I am simply praying that it will not happen. To put it another way: I am not asking God that He should now make what is going to happen not be going to happen; I am asking that He *will* at a future time make something not to happen at that time. And similarly with my retrospective prayer. Assuming that I am not asking for a miracle—asking that if my son has died, he should now be brought to life again—I do not have to be asking for a logical impossibility. I am not asking God that, even if my son has drowned, He should *now* make him not to have drowned; I am asking that, at the time of the disaster, He should then have made my son not to drown at that time. The former interpretation would indeed be required if the list of survivors had been read out over the radio, my son's name had not been on it, and I had not envisaged the possibility of a mistake on the part of the news service: but in my ignorance of whether he was drowned or not, my prayer will bear another interpretation.

But this still involves my trying to affect the past. On this second interpretation, I am trying by my prayer *now* to bring it about that God made something not to happen: and is not this absurd? In this particular case, I can provide a rationale for my action—that is why I picked this example —but the question can be raised whether it is not a bad example, on the ground that it is the only kind for which a rationale *could* be given. The rationale is this. When I pray for the future, my prayer makes sense because I know that, at the time about which I am praying, God will remember my prayer, and may then grant it. But God knows everything, both what has happened and what is going to happen. So my retrospective prayer makes sense, too, because at the time about which I am praying, God knew that I was going to make this prayer, and may then have granted it. So it seems relevant to ask whether foreknowledge of this kind can meaningfully be attributed only to God, in which case the example will be of a quite special kind, from which it would be illegitimate to generalize, or whether it could be attributed to human beings, in which case our example will not be of purely theological interest.

I have heard three opinions expressed on this point. The first, held by Russell and Ayer, is that foreknowledge is simply the mirror image of memory, to be explained in just the same words as memory save that "future" replaces "past," and so forth, and as such is conceptually unproblematic: we do not have the faculty but we perfectly well might. The second is a view held by a school of Dominican theologians. It is that God's knowledge of the future should be compared rather to a man's knowledge of what is going to happen, when this lies in his intention to make it happen. For example, God knows that I am going to pray that my son may not have drowned because He is going to make me pray so. This leads to the theologically and philosophically disagreeable conclusion that everything that happens is directly effected by God, and that human freedom is therefore confined to wholly interior movements of the will. This is the view adopted by Wittgenstein in the *Tractatus,* and there expressed by the statement, "The world is independent of my will." On this view, God's foreknowledge is knowledge of a type that human beings do have; it would, however, be difficult to construct a nontheological example of an action intelligibly designed to affect the past by exploiting this alleged parallelism. The third view is one of which it is difficult to make a clear sense. It is that foreknowledge is something that can be meaningfully ascribed only to God (or perhaps also to those He directly inspires, the prophets; but again perhaps these would be regarded not as themselves possessing this knowledge, but only as the instruments of its expression). The ground for saying this is that the future is not something of which we could, but merely do not happen to, have knowledge; it is not, as it were, *there* to be known. Statements about the future are, indeed, either-true-or-false; but they do not yet have a particular one of these two truth values. They have present truth-or-falsity, but they do not have present truth or present falsity, and so they *cannot* be known: there is not really anything to be known. The nontheological part of this view seems to me to rest on a philosophical confusion; the theological part I cannot interpret, since it appears to involve ascribing to God the performance of a logical impossibility.

We saw that retrospective prayer does not involve asking God to perform the logically impossible feat of changing the past, any more than prayer for the future involves asking

Him to change the future in the sense in which that is logically impossible. We saw also that we could provide a rationale for retrospective prayer, a rationale which depended on a belief in God's foreknowledge. This led us to ask if foreknowledge was something which a man could have. If so, then a similar rationale could be provided for actions designed to affect the past, when they consisted in my doing something in order that someone should have known that I was going to do it, and should have been influenced by this knowledge. This inquiry, however, I shall not pursue any further. I turn instead to more general considerations: to consider other arguments designed to show an intrinsic absurdity in the procedure of attempting to affect the past—of doing something in order that something else should have happened. In the present connection I remark only that if there is an intrinsic absurdity in *every* procedure of this kind, then it follows indirectly that there is also an absurdity in the conception of foreknowledge, human or divine.

Suppose someone were to say to me, "Either your son has drowned or he has not. If he has drowned, then certainly your prayer will not (cannot) be answered. If he has not drowned, your prayer is superfluous. So in either case your prayer is pointless: it cannot make any *difference* to whether he has drowned or not." This argument may well appear quite persuasive, until we observe that it is the exact analogue of the standard argument for fatalism. I here characterize fatalism as the view that there is an intrinsic absurdity in doing something in order that something else should subsequently happen; that any such action—that is, any action done with a further purpose—is necessarily pointless. The standard form of the fatalist argument was very popular in London during the bombing. The siren sounds, and I set off for the air-raid shelter in order to avoid being killed by a bomb. The fatalist argues, "Either you are going to be killed by a bomb or you are not going to be. If you are, then any precautions you take will be ineffective. If you are not, all precautions you take are superfluous. Therefore it is pointless to take precautions." This belief was extended even to particular bombs. If a bomb was going to kill me, then it "had

my number on it," and there was no point in my attempting
to take precautions against being killed by *that* bomb; if it did
not have my number on it, then of course precautions were
pointless too. I shall take it for granted that no one wants to
accept this argument as cogent. But the argument is formally
quite parallel to the argument supposed to show that it is
pointless to attempt to affect the past; only the tenses are
different. Someone may say, "But it is just the difference in
tense that makes the difference between the two arguments.
Your son has either *already* been drowned or else *already*
been saved; whereas you haven't *yet* been killed in the raid,
and you haven't *yet* come through it." But this is just to reiter-
ate that the one argument is about the past and the other
about the future: we want to know what, if anything, there
is *in* this fact which makes the one valid, the other invalid.
The best way of asking this question is to ask, "What refutation is there of the fatalist argument, to which a quite parallel
refutation of the argument to show that we cannot affect the
past could not be constructed?"

Let us consider the fatalist argument in detail. It opens
with a tautology, "Either you are going to be killed in this
raid or you are not." As is well known, some philosophers
have attempted to escape the fatalist conclusion by faulting
the argument at this first step, by denying that two-valued
logic applies to statements about future contingents. Although
this matter is worth investigating in detail, I have no time to
go into it here, so I will put the main point very briefly.
Those who deny that statements about future contingents
need be either true or false are under the necessity to explain the meaning of those statements in some way; they
usually attempt to do so by saying something like this: that
such a statement is not true or false now, but *becomes* true
or false at the time to which it refers. But if this is said, then
the fatalist argument can be reconstructed by replacing the
opening tautology by the assertion, "Either the statement 'You
will be killed in this raid' is going to become true, or it is
going to become false." The only way in which it can be consistently maintained not only that the law of excluded middle does not hold for statements about the future, but that

there is no other logically necessary statement which will serve the same purpose of getting the fatalist argument off the ground, is to deny that there is, or could be, what I called a "genuine" future tense at all: to maintain that the only intelligible use of the future tense is to express present tendencies. I think that most people would be prepared to reject this as unacceptable, and here, for lack of space, I shall simply assume that it is. (In fact, it is not quite easy to refute someone who consistently adopts this position; of course, it is always much easier to make out that something is not meaningful than to make out that it is.) Thus, without more ado, I shall set aside the suggestion that the flaw in the fatalist argument lies in the very first step.

The next two steps stand or fall together. They are: "If you are going to be killed in this raid, you will be killed whatever precautions you take" and "If you are not going to be killed in this raid, you will not be killed whatever precautions you neglect." These are both of the form, "If p, then if q then p"; for example, "If you *are* going to be killed, then you will be killed even if you take precautions." They are clearly correct on many interpretations of "if"; and I do not propose to waste time by inquiring whether they are correct on "the" interpretation of "if" proper to well-instructed users of the English language. The next two lines are as follows: "Hence, if you are going to be killed in the raid, any precautions you take will be ineffective" and "Hence, if you are not going to be killed in the raid, any precautions you take will have been superfluous." The first of these is indisputable. The second gives an appearance of sophistry. The fatalist argues from "If you are not going to be killed, then you won't be killed even if you have taken no precautions" to "If you are not going to be killed, then any precautions you take will have been superfluous"; that is, granted the truth of the statement "You will not be killed even if you take no precautions," you will have no motive to take precautions; or, to put it another way, if you would not be killed even if you took no precautions, then any precautions you take cannot be considered as being effective in bringing about your survival—that is, as effecting it. This employs a well-known principle. St. Thomas, for instance, says it is a condition for ignorance to be an excuse for having done wrong that, if the person had not suffered from the ignorance, he would not have committed the wrongful act in question. But we want to object that it may be just the precautions that I am going to take which save me from being killed; so it cannot follow from the mere fact that I am not going to be killed that I should not have been going to be killed even if I had not been going to take precautions. Here it really does seem to be a matter of the way in which "if" is understood; but, as I have said, I do not wish to call into question the legitimacy of a use of "if" according to which "(Even) if you do not take precautions, you will not be killed" follows from "You will not be killed." It is, however, clear that, on any use of "if" on which this inference is valid, it is possible that both of the statements "If you do not take precautions, you will be killed" and "If you do not take precautions, you will not be killed" should be true. It indeed follows from the truth of these two statements together that their common antecedent is false; that is, that I am in fact going to take precautions. (It may be held that on a, or even the, use of "if" in English, these two statements cannot both be true; or again, it may be held that they can both be true only when a stronger consequence follows, namely, that not only am I as a matter of fact going to take precautions, but that I could not fail to take them, that it was not in my power to refrain from taking them. But, as I have said, it is not my purpose here to inquire whether there are such uses of "if" or whether, if so, they are important or typical uses.) Now let us say that it is correct to say of certain precautions that they are capable of being effective in preventing my death in the raid if the two conditional statements are true that, if I take them, I shall not be killed in the raid, and that, if I do not take them, I shall be killed in the raid. Then, since, as we have seen, the truth of these two statements is quite compatible with the truth of the statement that, if I do not take precautions, I shall not be killed, the truth of this latter statement cannot be a ground for saying that my taking precautions will not be effective in preventing my death.

Thus, briefly, my method of rebutting the fatalist is to allow him to infer from "You will not be killed" to "If you do not take precautions, you will not be killed"; but to point out that, on any sense of "if" on which this inference is valid, it is impermissible to pass from "If you do not take precautions, you will not be killed" to "Your taking precautions will not be effective in preventing your death." For this to be permissible, the truth of "If you do not take precautions, you will not be killed" would have to be incompatible with that of "If you do not take precautions, you will be killed"; but, on the sense of "if" on which the first step was justified, these would not be incompatible. I prefer to put the matter this way than to make out that there is a sense of "if" on which these two are indeed incompatible, but on which the first step is unjustified, because it is notoriously difficult to elucidate such a sense of "if."

Having arrived at a formulation of the fallacy of the fatalist argument, let us now consider whether the parallel argument to demonstrate the absurdity of attempting to bring about the past is fallacious in the same way. I will abandon the theological example in favor of a magical one. Suppose we come across a tribe who have the following custom. Every second year the young men of the tribe are sent, as part of their initiation ritual, on a lion hunt: they have to prove their manhood. They travel for two days, hunt lions for two days, and spend two days on the return journey; observers go with them, and report to the chief upon their return whether the young men acquitted themselves with bravery or not. The people of the tribe believe that various ceremonies, carried out by the chief, influence the weather, the crops, and so forth. I do not want these ceremonies to be thought of as religious rites, intended to dispose the gods favorably towards them, but simply as performed on the basis of a wholly mistaken system of causal beliefs. While the young men are away from the village the chief performs ceremonies—dances, let us say—intended to cause the young men to act bravely. We notice that he continues to perform these dances for the whole six days that the party is away, that is to say, for two days during which the events that the dancing is supposed to influence have already taken place. Now there is generally thought to be a *special* absurdity in the idea of affecting the past, much greater than the absurdity of believing that the performance of a dance can influence the behavior of a man two days' journey away; so we ought to be able to persuade the chief of the absurdity of his continuing to dance after the first four days without questioning his general system of causal beliefs. How are we going to do it?

Since the absurdity in question is alleged to be a *logical* absurdity, it must be capable of being seen to be absurd however things turn out; so I am entitled to suppose that things go as badly for us, who are trying to persuade the chief of this absurdity, as they can do; we ought still to be able to persuade him. We first point out to him that he would not think of continuing to perform the dances after the hunting party has returned; he agrees to that, but replies that that is because at that time he *knows* whether the young men have been brave or not, so there is no longer any point in trying to bring it about that they have been. It is irrelevant, he says, that during the last two days of the dancing they have already either been brave or cowardly: there is still a point in his trying to make them have been brave, because he does not yet know which they have been. We then say that it can be only the first four days of the dancing which could possibly affect the young men's performance; but he replies that experience is against that. There was for several years a chief who thought as we did, and danced for the first four days only; the results were disastrous. On two other occasions, he himself fell ill after four days of dancing and was unable to continue, and again, when the hunting party returned, it proved that the young men had behaved ignobly.

The brief digression into fatalism was occasioned by our noticing that the standard argument against attempting to affect the past was a precise analogue of the standard fatalist argument against attempting to affect the future. Having diagnosed the fallacy in the fatalist argument, my announced intention was to discover whether there was not a similar fallacy in the standard argument against affecting the past. And it indeed appears to me that there is. We say to the chief, "Why go on dancing now? Either the young men have already been brave, or they have already been cowardly. If they have been brave, then they have been brave whether you dance or not. If they have been cowardly, then they have been cowardly whether you dance or not. If they have been brave, then your dancing now will not be effective in making them have been brave, since they have been brave even if you do not dance. And if they have not been brave, then your dancing will certainly not be effective. Thus your continuing to dance will in the one case be superfluous, and in the other fruitless: in neither case is there any point in your continuing to dance." The chief can reply in exactly the way in which we replied to the fatalist. He can say, "If they have been brave, then indeed there is a sense in which it will be true to say that, even if I do not dance, they will have been brave; but this is not incompatible with its also being true to say that, if I do not dance, they will not have been brave. Now what saying that my continuing to dance is effective in causing them to have been brave amounts to is that it is true both that, if I go on dancing, they have been brave, and that, if I do not dance, they have not been brave. I have excellent empirical grounds for believing both these two statements to be true; and neither is incompatible with the truth of the statement that if I do not dance, they have been brave, although, indeed, I have no reason for believing *that* statement. Hence, you have not shown that, from the mere hypothesis that they have been brave, it follows that the dancing I am going to do will not be effective in making them have been brave; on the contrary, it may well be that, although they have been brave, they have been brave just *because* I am going to go on dancing; that, if I were not going to go on dancing, they would not have been brave." This reply sounds sophistical; but it cannot be sophistical if our answer to the fatalist was correct, because it is the exact analogue of that answer.

We now try the following argument: "Your *knowledge* of whether the young men have been brave or not may affect whether you *think* there is any point in performing the dances; but it cannot really make any difference to the *effect* the dances have on what has happened. If the dances are capable of bringing it about that the young men have acted bravely, then they ought to be able to do that even after you have learned that the young men have *not* acted bravely. But that is absurd, for that would mean that the dances can change the past. But if the dances cannot have any effect after you have learned whether the young men have been brave or not, they cannot have any effect before, either; for the mere state of your knowledge cannot make any difference to their efficacy." Now since the causal beliefs of this tribe are so different from our own, I could imagine that the chief might simply deny this: he might say that what had an effect on the young men's behavior was not merely the performance of the dances by the chief as such, but rather their performance by the chief when in a state of ignorance as to the outcome of the hunt. And if he says this, I think there is really no way of dissuading him, short of attacking his whole system of causal beliefs. But I will not allow him to say this, because it would make his causal beliefs so different in kind from ours that there would be no moral to draw for our own case. Before going on to consider his reaction to this argument, however, let us first pause to review the situation.

Suppose, then, that he agrees to our suggestion: agrees, that is, that it is his dancing as such that he wants to consider as bringing about the young men's bravery, and not his dancing in ignorance of whether they were brave. If this is his belief, then we may reasonably challenge him to try dancing on some occasion when the hunting party has returned and the observers have reported that the young men have *not* been brave. Here at last we appear to have hit on something which has no parallel in the case of affecting the future. If someone believes that a certain kind of action is effective in bringing about a subsequent event, I may challenge him to try it out in all possible circumstances: but I cannot demand that he try it out on some occasion when the event is *not* going to take place, since he cannot identify any such occasion independently of his intention to perform the action. Our knowledge of the future is of two kinds: prediction based on causal laws and knowledge in intention. If I think I can predict the nonoccurrence of an event, then I cannot consistently also believe that I can do anything to bring it about; that is, I cannot have good grounds for believing, of any action, both that it is in my power to do it, and that it is a condition of the event's occurring. On the other hand, I cannot be asked to perform the action on some occasion when I believe that the event will not take place, when this knowledge lies in my intention to prevent it taking place; for as soon as I accede to the request, I thereby abandon my intention. It would, indeed, be different if we had foreknowledge: someone who thought, like Russell and Ayer, that it is a merely contingent fact that we have memory but not foreknowledge would conclude that the difference I have pointed to does not reveal a genuine asymmetry between past and future, but merely reflects this contingent fact.

If the chief accepts the challenge, and dances when he knows that the young men have not been brave, it seems that he must concede that his dancing does not *ensure* their bravery. There is one other possibility favorable to us. Suppose that he accepts the challenge, but when he comes to try to dance, he unaccountably cannot do so: his limbs simply will not respond. Then we may say, "It is not your dancing (after the event) which causes them to have been brave, but rather their bravery which makes possible your dancing: your dancing is not, as you thought, an action which it is in your power to do or not to do as you choose. So you ought not to say that you dance in the last two days in order to make them have been brave, but that you try to see whether you can dance, in order to find out whether they have been brave."

It may seem that this is conclusive; for are not these the only two possibilities? Either he does dance, in which case the dancing is proved not to be a sufficient condition of the previous bravery; or he does not, in which case the bravery must be thought a causal condition of the dancing rather than vice versa. But in fact the situation is not quite so simple.

For one thing, it is not justifiable to demand that the chief should either consider his dancing to be a sufficient condition of the young men's bravery, or regard it as wholly unconnected. It is enough, in order to provide him with a motive for performing the dances, that he should have grounds to believe that there is a significant positive correlation between his dancing and previous brave actions on the part of the young men; so the occurrence of a certain proportion of occasions on which the dancing is performed, although the young men were not brave, is not a sufficient basis to condemn him as irrational if he continues to dance during the last two days. Secondly, while his being afflicted with an otherwise totally inexplicable inability to dance may strongly suggest that the cowardice of the young men renders him unable to dance, and that therefore dancing is not an action which it is in his power to perform as he chooses, any failure to dance that is explicable without reference to the outcome of the hunt has much less tendency to suggest this. Let us suppose that we issue our challenge, and he accepts it. On the first occasion when the observers return and report cowardly behavior on the part of the young men, he performs his dance. This weakens his belief in the efficacy of the dancing, but does not disturb him unduly; there have been occasions before when the dancing has not worked, and he simply classes this as one of them. On the second occasion when the experiment can be tried, he agrees to attempt it, but, a few hours before the experiment is due to be carried out, he learns that a neighboring tribe is marching to attack his, so the experiment has to be abandoned; on the third occasion, he is bitten by a snake, and so is incapacitated for dancing. Someone might wish to say, "The cowardice of the young men caused those events to happen and so prevent the chief from dancing," but such a description is far from mandatory: the chief may simply say that these events were accidental, and in no way *brought about* by the cowardice of the young men. It is true that if the chief is willing to attempt the experiment a large number of times, and events of this kind repeatedly occur, it will no longer appear reasonable to dismiss them as a series of coincidences. If accidents which prevent his dancing occur on occasions when the young men are known to have been cowardly with much greater frequency than, say, in a control group of dancing attempts, when the young men are known to have been brave, or when it is not known how they behaved, then this frequency becomes something that must itself be explained, even though each particular such event already has its explanation.

Suppose now, however, that the following occurs. We ask the chief to perform the dances on some occasion when the hunting party has returned and the observers have reported that the young men have not acquitted themselves with bravery. He does so, and we claim another weakening of his belief that the dancing is correlated with preceding bravery. But later it turns out that, for some reason or other, the observers were lying (say they had been bribed by someone): so after all this is not a counterexample to the law. So we have a third possible outcome. The situation now is this. We challenge the chief to perform the dances whenever he knows that the young men have not been brave, and he accepts the challenge. There are three kinds of outcome: (i) he simply performs the dances; (ii) he is prevented from performing the dances by some occurrence which has a quite natural explanation totally independent of the behavior of the young men; and (iii) he performs the dances, but subsequently discovers that this was not really an occasion on which the young men had not been brave. We may imagine that he carries out the experiment repeatedly, and that the outcome always falls into one of these three classes; and that outcomes of class (i) are sufficiently infrequent not to destroy his belief that there is a significant correlation between the dancing and the young men's bravery, and outcomes of class (ii) sufficiently infrequent not to make him say that the young men's cowardice renders him incapable of performing the dances. Thus our experiment has failed.

On the other hand, it has not left everything as before. I have exploited the fact that it is frequently possible to discover that one had been mistaken in some belief about the past. I will not here raise the question whether it is *always* possible to discover this, or whether there are beliefs about the past about which we can be *certain* in the sense that nothing could happen to show the belief to have been mistaken. Now before we challenged the chief to perform this series of experiments, his situation was as follows. He was prepared to perform the dancing in order to bring it about that the young men had been brave, but only when he had no information about whether they had been brave or not. The rationale of his doing so was simply this: experience shows that there is a positive correlation between the dancing and the young men's bravery; hence the fact that the dances are being performed makes it more probable that the young men have been brave. But the dancing is something that is in my power to do if I choose: experience does not lead me to recognize it as a possibility that I should try to perform the dances and fail. Hence it is in my power to do something, the doing of which will make it more probable that the young men have been brave: I have therefore every motive to do it. Once he had information, provided by the observers, about the behavior of the young men, then, under the old dispensation, his attitude changed: he no longer had a motive to perform the dances. We do not have to assume that he was unaware of the possibility that the observers were lying or had made a mistake. It may just have been that he reckoned the probability that they were telling the truth as so high that the performance of the dances after they had made their report would make no significant difference to the probability that the young men had been brave. If they reported the young men as having been brave, there was so little chance of their being wrong that it was not worth while to attempt to diminish this chance by performing the dances; if they reported that the young men had been cowardly, then even the performance of the dances would still leave it overwhelmingly probable that they *had* been cowardly. That is to say, until the series of experiments was performed, the chief was prepared to discount completely the probability conferred by his dancing on the proposition that the young men had been brave in the face of a source of information as to the truth of this proposition of the kind we ordinarily rely upon in deciding the truth or falsity of statements about the past. And the reason for this attitude is very clear: for the proposition that there was a positive correlation between the dancing and the previous bravery of the young men could have been established in the first place only by relying on our ordinary sources of information as to whether the young men had been brave or not.

But if we are to suppose that the series of experiments works out in such a way as not to force the chief either to abandon his belief that there is such a positive correlation or that the dancing is something which it is in his power to do when he chooses, we must suppose that it fairly frequently happens that the observers are subsequently proved to have been making false statements. And I think it is clear that in the process the attitude of the chief to the relative degree of probability conferred on the statement that the young men have been brave by (i) the reports of the observers and (ii) his performance of the dances will alter. Since it so frequently happens that, when he performs the dances *after* having received an adverse report from the observers, the observers prove to have been misreporting, he will cease to think it pointless to perform the dances after having received such an adverse report: he will thus cease to think that he can decide whether to trust the reports of the observers independently of whether he is going to perform the dances or not. In fact, it seems likely that he will come to think of the performance of the dances as itself a ground for distrusting, or even for denying outright, the adverse reports of the observers, even in the absence of any *other* reason (such as the discovery of their having been bribed, or the reports of some other witness) for believing them not to be telling the truth.

The chief began with two beliefs: (i) that there was a positive correlation between his dancing and the previous brave behavior of the young men; and (ii) that the dancing was something in his power to do as he chose. We are tempted to think of these two beliefs as incompatible, and I described people attempting to devise a series of experiments to convince the chief of this. I tried to show, however, that these experiments could turn out in such a way as to allow the chief to maintain both beliefs. But in the process a third belief, which we naturally take for granted, has had to be abandoned in order to hang onto the first two: the belief, namely, that it is possible for me to find out what has happened (whether the young men have been brave or not) independently of my intentions. The chief no longer thinks that there is any evidence as to whether the young men had been brave or not, the strength of which is unaffected by whether he intends subsequently to perform the dances. And now it appears that there really is a form of incompatibility among these *three* beliefs, in the sense that it is always possible to carry out a series of actions which will necessarily lead to the abandonment of at least one of them. Here there is an exact parallel with the case of affecting the future. We *never* combine the beliefs (i) that an action A is positively correlated with the subsequent occurrence of an event B; (ii) that the action A is in my power to perform or not as I choose; and (iii) that I can know whether B is going to take place or not independently of my intention to perform or not to perform the action A. The difference between past and future lies in this: that we think that, of any past event, it is in principle possible for me to know whether or not it took place independently of my present intentions; whereas, for many types of future event, we should admit that we are never going to be in a position to have such knowledge independently of our intentions. (If we had foreknowledge, this might be different.) If we insist on hanging onto this belief, for all types of past event, then we cannot combine the two beliefs that are required to make sense of doing something in order that some event should have previously taken place; but I do not know any reason why, if things were to turn out differently from the way they do now, we *could* not reasonably abandon the first of these beliefs rather than either of the other two.

My conclusion therefore is this. If anyone were to claim, of some type of action A, (i) that experience gave grounds for holding the performance of A as increasing the probability of the previous occurrence of a type of event E; and (ii) that experience gave no grounds for regarding A as an action which it was ever not in his power to perform—that is, for entertaining the possibility of his trying to perform it and failing—then we could either force him to abandon one or other of these beliefs, or else to abandon the belief (iii) that it was ever possible for him to have knowledge, independent of his intention to perform A or not, of whether an event E had occurred. Now doubtless most normal human beings would rather abandon either (i) or (ii) than (iii), because we have the prejudice that (iii) must hold good for every type of event: but if someone were, in a particular case, more ready to give up (iii) than (i) or (ii), I cannot see any argument we could use to dissuade him. And so long as he was not dissuaded, he could sensibly speak of performing A in order that E should have occurred. Of course, he could adopt an intermediate position. It is not really necessary, for him to be able to speak of doing A in order that E should have occurred, that he deny all possibility of his trying and failing to perform A. All that is necessary is that he should not regard his being informed, by ordinary means, of the nonoccurrence of E as making it more probable that if he tries to perform A, he will fail: for, once he does so regard it, we can claim that he should regard the occurrence of E as making possible the performance of A, in which case his trying to perform A is not a case of trying to bring it about that E has happened, but of finding out whether E has happened. (Much will here depend on whether there is an ordinary causal explanation for the occurrence of E or not.) Now he need not really deny that learning, in the ordinary way, that E has not occurred makes it at all more probable that, if he tries to perform A, he will fail. He may concede that it makes it to some extent more probable, while at the same time maintaining that, even when he has grounds for thinking that E has not occurred, his intention to perform A still makes it more probable than it would otherwise be that E has in fact occurred. The attitude of such a man seems paradoxical and unnatural to us, but I cannot see any rational considerations which would force him out of this position. At least, if there are any, it would be interesting to know what they are: I think that none of the considerations I have mentioned in this paper could serve this purpose.

My theological example thus proves to have been a bad— that is, untypical—example in a way we did not suspect at the time, for it will never lead to a discounting of our ordinary methods of finding out about the past. I may pray that the announcer has made a mistake in not including my son's name on the list of survivors; but once I am convinced that no mistake has been made, I will not go on praying for him to have survived. I should regard this kind of prayer as something to which it was possible to have recourse only when an ordinary doubt about what had happened could be entertained. But just because this example is untypical in this way, it involves no tampering with our ordinary conceptual apparatus at all: this is why it is such a natural thing to do. On my view, then, orthodox Jewish theology is mistaken on this point.

I do not know whether it could be held that part of what people have meant when they have said "You cannot change the past" is that, for every type of event, it is in principle possible to know whether or not it has happened, independently of one's own intentions. If so, this is not the mere tautology it appears to be, but it does indeed single out what it is that makes us think it impossible to bring about the past.

THE OPEN FUTURE

BERNARD MAYO is a former editor of *Analysis* and a Reader in
Moral Philosophy at the University of Birmingham, England.
His major publications include *The Logic of Personality* and
Ethics and the Moral Life.

I

How should we characterise the difference between
future-tensed statements and present- and past-tensed ones?
Or is there no difference except the commonplace ones (1)
that the events described stand in different temporal relations
with the event which is the utterance of the sentence in
question (2) that the kinds of evidence available are generally different and have different degrees of reliability?

But if these are the only differences there are, why is there
always something rather uncanny about doctrines that emphatically assimilate future to past: precognition, reversed
causation, fatalism and the like?

On this last point, it may be enough to show (as Ayer
does in *The Problem of Knowledge*) that discomfort about
these doctrines rests on misunderstandings. Fatalism, for instance, appears to deny the obvious fact that, while we cannot in the least choose what the past shall have been, we can
to a considerable extent choose what the future shall be.
Yet the fatalist maxim "What will be, will be", and even the
stronger version "What will be, must be", and "What now
is, must needs have been", are all tautologies and therefore

FROM Bernard Mayo, "The Open Future," *Mind*, 71 (1962).
© Thomas Nelson and Sons Ltd., 1962. Reprinted by permission
of the editor and Bernard Mayo.

cannot even tell us anything of interest, let alone anything uncanny. The "must" in these maxims is the "must" of logical necessity: if something is going to happen, then it necessarily follows that it is going to happen; if it is now happening, then it necessarily follows that it was going to happen and will have happened; if it did happen, it necessarily follows that it had been going to happen and has happened. In so far, it is perfectly true that we can no more change the future than we can change the past; we cannot choose that the future be different from what in fact it will be, any more than we can choose that the past be different from what in fact it was. But—and here Fatalism goes wrong—we can choose that the future be different from what it will be *if we do not choose*.

Similarly we *were* able to choose that the past be different from what it would have been *if* we had not chosen. But this similarity is not the complementarity required to substantiate the thesis that "in logic" the past is just as much, or as little, "open" as the future. For while it is the case that we can here and now choose that the future be different from what it will be if we do not choose, it is not the case that we can here and now choose that the past be different from what it would have been if we had not chosen, either now or at any other time. Ayer is, indeed, forced to admit that there is, after all, a sense in which the future is open and the past is closed: namely that, "whereas our present actions can have no effect upon the past, they can have an effect upon the future" (p. 170).

As a means of characterising the difference between past and future, however, this is open to the *prima facie* objection that it is the inefficacy of our present actions on the past which depends on the pastness of the past, and not the other way round. One may easily insist that the difference between future-tensed statements and past-tensed ones is that one sort refers to the future and the other sort to the past, and that this difference remains to be explained. Ayer's final answer, indeed, is not in terms of cause and effect; he holds that the only relevant difference is a difference in the extent of our knowledge. We know very little about the future, but we know rather more about the past. But this is only a difference of degree: the commonplace distinction (2). It cannot be made at all precise, since there are large local variations in the relative degrees of our knowledge (some future events are better known than some past ones); and there is the suspicion that the cart is before the horse again, that it is the futurity of the future that curtails our knowledge.

Why do Ayer and others look to agent-centred criteria—to questions about what *we* can do or know? Is there an *a priori* reason why Nature should not be consulted? It seems that there is. For it is easy to agree that no events are, as such, past, present or future; these are relational predicates and the other term of the relation is the event constituted by the utterance of a sentence or the occurrence of a thought. But sentences and thoughts require speakers and thinkers; therefore no elucidation of time-concepts is possible without reference to persons.

"But this is a mistake . . ." It is perfectly conceivable that natural processes should exhibit characteristic non-symmetries, so that, given a certain phase of such a process occurring at t_n, then phases occurring between t_n and t_{n+x} showed a characteristic difference from those occurring between t_n and t_{n-x}, irrespective of the presence of any sentient being, whether as agent or observer. (Knowing and doing might themselves be regarded as sub-classes of just such a class of processes.) All that would be required would be for these multiple non-symmetries to be capable of alignment in the same one dimension, and this would give us a time-order indicator.

An interesting example of a philosopher who looks in this fashion to the nature of things is Professor J. J. C. Smart, who wrote an article revealingly entitled "The Temporal Asymmetry of the World"[1] in which he maintained that the disparity between past and future depends on the existence of what he called *traces*. A trace is a changed state of affairs initiated by a specific occurrence which can be inferred very reliably from it; but while we can nearly always infer the *initiating* event of such a state, we can very seldom infer

[1] *Analysis,* 14 (1953), 79.

the *terminating* event. Footprints on the sand are very reliable evidence that someone has been walking on it; but the virgin sand is no evidence at all that someone *will* walk on it. This appeal to traces is very plausible; here we do seem to have an unambiguously past-pointing arrow, and there does seem to be no correlative future-pointing one; it is only in a very feeble and metaphorical way that coming events cast their shadows before. Yet we do speak of *signs;* and I am afraid that this appeal to traces is only another case of the commonplace distinction (2)—different degrees of reliability. There are signs which are more reliable than traces, even if this is exceptional. A counter-example to Smart's footprints would be a broken rail in front of an express train, where we can infer the future derailment with much greater certainty than we can infer the antecedents of the break.

Among those who look for differences in the nature of things, we must of course count the physicists who claim to find irreversible processes in the physical world which are time's arrow. We are told, for instance, that if we measure the temperatures of a pair of bodies isolated from external sources of energy and if we find that on occasion A their temperatures are nearly equal, while on another occasion B the warmer one is warmer and the cooler one is cooler, then the second occasion B is necessarily earlier than the first A, because according to the laws of thermodynamics such a system will always tend towards, and not away from, thermal equilibrium. On this it seems enough to say that, even if the physicists have identified an irreversible process, it can only be regarded as correlated with, and not as defining, the time-direction; it does not seem self-contradictory to suppose that thermal energy should tend to become more and more unequally distributed in an isolated system; that the process might be reversed at any time, with no more drastic consequences than the breakdown of a physical law.

It does look as if we shall have to find the difference in ourselves after all, and not in the world. The notion of cause and effect is promising at first sight as a time-direction indicator, for it does seem as certain as anything can be that cause always precedes effect, and exceptionally preposterous to suggest that an effect might precede its cause. Yet it is not easy to see why, especially if we adopt an orthodox view about causation, namely that a cause is a sufficient condition for the occurrence of the event in question, and perhaps a necessary condition as well. For sufficient and necessary conditions are strictly neutral with respect to time. If A is a sufficient condition for B, then B is a necessary condition for A; for whenever we can say "If A occurs, then B occurs" we can also assert its logical equivalent "If B does not occur, then A does not occur". Similarly, if A is a necessary condition for B, then B is a sufficient condition for A. It is no use saying that A must be both a sufficient condition for B, *and earlier,* if it is to cause B; for this begs the question.

I am inclined to think that a good deal could be done with a more primitive notion than that of cause and effect, namely the notion of means and end. Cause and effect is observer's language; means and end is participator's language; and if we must in the end rely on agent-centred criteria, then the notion of means and end is the most promising, since it is much more deeply embedded in action than is the more theoretical notion of cause and effect, which was one of Ayer's candidates (let alone his other candidate, the still more theoretical notion of knowing). But I expect difficulties in the way of disentangling the notions of cause and effect, and of means and end, from each other, and also further objections of the cart-before-the-horse type—that what we are able to think of as means, or as ends, is already determined for us by the pastness or futurity of the events in question. Similar difficulties might attend yet another promising line of enquiry which would start from the difference between sense-experience, on the one hand, and such experiences as wishing, hoping and fearing, on the other. This enquiry would rely heavily on the non-indicative uses of language, especially on the optative and the imperative moods of verbs. It is still a worthwhile exercise, however, to try to reach the limit of what can be done within the province of the indicative mood: and this is what I shall do. My route will take us over some logical territory, from which we shall emerge more or less where we started—at the concept of a particular speaker in a particular situation—but somewhat richer, I hope, for the journey.

II

A block of stone, so Michelangelo is said to have said, already contains the statue that is going to be carved out of it. It also, of course, contains an infinite number of statues that are not going to be carved out of it. This is true in a whimsical but not outrageous sense. But the corresponding backward-pointing statement does seem to be outrageous. The existing statue was contained by the block out of which it was carved; but can we say, even whimsically, that it was also contained by an infinite number of blocks out of which it was not carved? Actual blocks, it seems, can contain possible statues, but can possible blocks contain actual statues? It does look as if the actualisation of potentiality is a one-way process; the possible can become the actual, but the actual cannot become the (merely) possible. Possibilities that are open can be closed, those that are closed can sometimes be reopened, but possibilities that have been closed in the special way of being realised cannot be reopened. We might try saying, then, that the future just is the region of the merely possible.

But surely it will not do to say simply that the future is the region of the possible. It will be objected that the past and present also contain possibilities; for we certainly do have a use for the expression "It is possible that" followed by either past- or present-tensed verbs. As an example of a present-tense uncertainty: it is possible that a rocket is now on its way to the moon. As an example of a historical uncertainty: it is possible that the Dark Lady of the Sonnets was Mary Fitton, or that she was Elizabeth Vernon, or somebody else. And it is no use our saying "Well, it is certain that a rocket either is on its way to the moon or it isn't, only we don't know which", or that the Dark Lady was certainly either Mary Fitton or some other woman, only we don't know which—because exactly the same can be said of a future-located possibility: it is certain that there either will or won't be a sea-battle tomorrow, only we don't know which.

What can—indeed must—be said is this. Past- and present-located possibilities are actualised possibilities and, therefore, irrevocably closed; future-located ones are not. Of the two possibilities about the rocket, one of them is not merely possible, but actual; and similarly with the two possible women who might have been the Dark Lady.

But does this say anything? Is the jargon of possibility and actuality any more than a verbal expedient; does it really come to any more than that some possible happenings *have* happened, and some other, equally possible and otherwise indistinguishable happenings have *not yet* happened?

I think it does. But to show this I shall need to translate the somewhat archaic language of possibility and actuality into something less intractable. I shall suggest that the difference between speaking of a possibility as such, and speaking of a possibility as actualised, is just the difference between enunciating or formulating or entertaining a proposition, and asserting that proposition as true. In the case of the moon rocket, I can enunciate both the proposition that the rocket is on its way to the moon, and the proposition that it is not; I can assert as true the (merely logical) proposition that either it is on its way or it isn't; I cannot (though somebody else perhaps can) assert one of the propositions as true. In the case of the statue, the sculptor just about to start work can assert as true the proposition that this is an unchiselled block of marble ("actual block"); he cannot assert as true any proposition about a statue made out of this block, but he can, or at least could in principle, enunciate a proposition containing a specification for a statue, such as a three-dimensional equation or a list of co-ordinates ("possible statue"). When at last he is in a position to assert as true a proposition stating that this statue is of such and such dimensions, possibility has become actuality. Now is this process irreversible, so that it could be used as a time-criterion? Before we can answer this question, we must distinguish at least four possible ways of interpreting the question.

(1) Is there a permanent logical asymmetry between propositions of a certain kind, that can only be enunciated but not asserted, and those of another kind which can be asserted as true? Obviously not. Propositions do not bear the marks of their own assertibility.

(2) Is there a necessary correlation (in something less than a logical sense) between the kind of processes exemplified by the sculptor's activities, and the process of coming to be in a position to assert a proposition which formerly could only be entertained? To see that the answer to this, too, is No, we have only to imagine an eccentric sculptor whose speciality is the reconstruction of blocks of stone by encasing existing statues with concrete. In his case, the assertibility of the two propositions, about the statue and about the stone, is reversed.

(3) Is there a necessary correlation between statements about the present and past, on the one hand, with propositions that are assertible, and between statements about the future, on the other hand, with propositions that are not assertible? Again, clearly not, since we do claim that some propositions about events in the future relative to the time of assertion, *can* be asserted, and not merely entertained.

(4) Is there a necessary correlation between the two kinds of statement (past and present, and future) and two *types* of proposition, or two *ways* of asserting a proposition? The answer to this is Yes.

To elaborate this, I shall start with something rather crude, which will get me as far as the thesis which Ryle adopts in the essay "It Was to Be" (*Dilemmas*); but I shall not stop there, because Ryle's position, though correct in essentials, is highly vulnerable. He has selected examples which favour his analysis while ignoring others which seem to defy it, and which opponents such as Ayer[2] have been quick to seize on. In fact the critical cases are not intractable; but this remains to be shown.

[2] In an (unpublished) address to the Muirhead Society, 1957.

III

As a crude beginning, then, consider the two sentences:

> (S1) The cat is drinking milk
> (S2) A cat is drinking milk

Each of these sentences formulates a proposition which can, of course, be asserted as true. The important difference is that (S1), if it is asserted at all, is necessarily being used to describe an actual particular situation: this is the force of the demonstrative "the". (S2), if it is asserted, is not necessarily used to describe any particular situation. There must be, of course, if it is to be true, some actual situation such as (S1) would correctly describe; but this is just what (S2) says, and no more: just that there is, somewhere or other, an instance of cat-drinking-milk; that the descriptive expression "cat drinking milk" is satisfied.

Often and typically we use different modes of assertion for (S1) and (S2), and not just a change of article. We use the ordinary subject-predicate form as in (S1) *when we are able to pinpoint one of the actors* in a particular situation; we use the existential expression "There is . . ." when we wish to say that some type of situation is exemplified, as in (S2).

The proposal now is: All future-tensed statements are of type (S2) and none are of type (S1), whereas present- and past-tensed statements may be of either type. We can say indifferently, "William invaded England in 1066" or "There was an invasion of England by William in 1066": the difference is largely a matter of style and emphasis. But typically, past- and present-tensed statements are of type (S1). We usually are in a position to pinpoint the actual participators in historical and contemporary dramas. We are never in a position to pinpoint the actors in future dramas.

This last point will be challenged. Surely it just is not true that we are never in a position to pinpoint the actors in future dramas. This is the objection made by Ayer, who clearly thought it was a knock-out blow, against Ryle's thesis in "It Was to Be". Ryle discusses statements like "This accident could have been prevented" and points out that such a statement involves a sort of contradiction. For if the accident *had* been prevented, there would never have been *this accident* at all; neither I nor anyone could, logically, have prevented *it;* for *it* was an accident that was not prevented, and the fact that it was not prevented is already contained in the reference to *this* accident. What this points to is that words like *this* and *that,* personal pronouns and the whole apparatus of singular propositions—our pinpointing equipment—are out of place in talking about what can be prevented or promoted, and in general about the future. "Roughly," says Ryle, "statements in the future tense cannot convey singular, but only general propositions, where statements in the present and past tense can convey both. More strictly, a statement to the effect that something will exist or happen is, *in so far,* a general statement".[3]

Not that Ryle is the only sinner. Prior, in *Time and Modality,* admits that "it is very difficult to deny that a statement like 'Professor Carnap will fly to the moon' is about Professor Carnap", yet he *does* deny it, holding (for reasons which I shall not discuss) that what does not yet exist cannot properly be named—and what cannot be named cannot be talked about.[4] Half a century earlier C. S. Peirce made very similar remarks: "We cannot assign proper names to each . . . of the possible or probable theatrical stars of the immediate future . . . the individual actors to which our discourse now relates become largely merged into general varieties"; "there is an approach to want of identity in the individuals of the collections of persons who are to commit suicide in the year 1899".[5]

We can understand Ayer's impatience with all this. Surely Prior's statement about Professor Carnap flying to the moon really is about Professor Carnap and the moon, both of which are here to be referred to, genuine individuals, yet also named as actors in a future drama? Surely it is flying in the face of common sense to insist that a singular future-tensed

[3] *Dilemmas,* p. 27.
[4] A. N. Prior, *Time and Modality,* p. 33.
[5] Quoted by Prior, *op. cit.,* pp. 113–14.

statement isn't really singular at all, isn't really about its ostensible subject?

These objections may look less overwhelming if we consider another case. You may make plans for your child before he is born, or even conceived. You may even give him a name, and put his name down for a public school. Is there anything outrageous about saying "Johnny will go to Rugby" before Johnny is born, or even conceived? Not outrageous— just a somewhat reckless assumption that it will be a boy. Less odd still, when he is conceived but unborn. Less odd still, when he is born but still in nappies. And so on. But there is no line to be drawn. At no stage do you reach the privileged position of being able to speak of a particular— until you have ceased to talk about the future.

IV

The only way of breaking the deadlock as between the Ryle-Prior-Peirce thesis (hence RPP) and its opponents is to return to logic and say something more about types of propositions (singular, general) and modes of asserting them. I shall choose ordinary simple subject-predicate propositions ("Socrates is wise", "Plato speaks"), not, however, for the sake of simplicity, but because these are the very cases that constitute a stumbling-block to the RPP. Nearly all logical systems take singular propositions as elementary, and if no singular propositions can be about the future, as the RPP holds, then either logic has not succeeded in formalising statements about the future, or else such statements are somewhat more complex than they appear to be. I shall choose the second alternative.

In a proposition like "Socrates is wise" or "Plato speaks", we have two elements, a subject term and a predicate term. Neither of these can stand alone, if we are trying to say something that is true or false; they are strictly complementary; but neither of them logically requires any particular complement; we can say a lot of things about Socrates other than that he is wise, and we can say of other men than Socrates that they are wise. A predicate term, in general, can be attached to a number of different subject terms, and a subject term can have a number of different predicate terms attached to it. This is represented by what is usually called a propositional function but which I prefer to call a propositional schema:

$$\phi x \quad \ldots \ldots \ldots \quad (1)$$

Conventionally the predicate is written first. "x", with other letters from the end of the English alphabet, is a subject-term variable or individual variable; all that "variable" means is that where "x" stands in the schema you are to think of a blank space into which some subject term, such as "Socrates", must be entered if you want to make up a sentence. Similarly "ϕ", with other letters from the end of the Greek alphabet, is a predicate variable, which means another blank space to be filled up with a predicative expression, like "is wise" or "speaks", if you want to complete your sentence.

Imagine both spaces in (1) filled by some appropriate expressions, such as "Socrates is wise". To show that a space has been filled by an appropriate expression, we use letters from the beginning of the English and Greek alphabets:

$$\theta c \quad \ldots \ldots \ldots \quad (2)$$

This stands for an ordinary sentence which expresses a proposition which is true or false (the empty schema, ϕx, is not true or false).

Now suppose we have filled only one of the blanks:

$$\theta x \quad \ldots \ldots \ldots \quad (3)$$
$$\phi c \quad \ldots \ldots \ldots \quad (4)$$

These formulae represent incomplete sentences; (3) says, for example, "—— is wise", (4) says "Socrates ——". Partly blank sentences, as opposed to totally blank ones, invite us to supply the missing part; (3) invites the question "Is there anybody who is wise, and if so who?" while (4) asks "Is there something that characterises Socrates, and if so what?" (4) will be ignored in what follows.

Now the question which the formula (3) invites falls into two parts; we answer the first part if we say, "Yes, there is someone who is wise", but not the second part; to answer this we have to add, "namely, Socrates" or "namely, Socrates, Plato, Aristotle . . ." if there is more than one wise man. If the answer to the first part is "No, there is no one who is wise", then the second question is shown not to arise. The two answers to the first part, affirmative and negative, are symbolised thus:

$$\exists x(\theta x) \ . \ . \ . \ . \ . \ . \ . \ (5)$$
$$\sim\exists x(\theta x) \ . \ . \ . \ . \ . \ . \ . \ (6)$$

(5) is to be read as "There is a value of x such that θx is true"; more informally, "It is possible to fill the blank space in the schema '— is wise' in such a way as to get a sentence which expresses a true statement"; more colloquially, "There is a wise man", or "Someone is wise" or "A man is wise" (compare "A cat is drinking milk").

The important feature to notice here is that (5) *is a complete sentence,* and expresses a proposition which is true or false, even though it contains variables, or blank spaces, and two blank spaces at that; whereas (3) which contained only one blank space was a mere schema and not a sentence at all. The logicians say that this is because (5) contains only bound variables, whereas (3) contains a free variable; but for our purposes it is enough to notice that (5), since it contains no singular terms, must be a general statement. When we proceed to answer the second part of the question, "namely, who?" by saying "namely, Socrates", we do introduce a singular term. But this singular term *is not a subject term* and the sentence remains essentially general:

$$\exists x(\theta x. \ x = c) \ . \ . \ . \ . \ . \ (7)$$

This is to be read, say, "There is a wise man, namely, Socrates". In certain contexts, the sentence "Socrates is wise" (which is normally of type θc (2)) could be used to express what (7) expresses: namely, when it is the answer to the question "Who, if anyone, is wise?" This ambiguity—that "Socrates is wise" may be either of type (2) or of type (7)— will be important in the sequel.

V

So far we have not introduced tenses. It is a natural assumption that in a singular statement the time-reference is carried by the predicate-term, since temporal relations are predicable like any other relations. If we have θc, say "Plato speaks", we might try to represent "Plato spoke", "Plato is speaking", and "Plato will speak", by $\theta^{-n}c$, $\theta^{o}c$, $\theta^{+n}c$, where the superscripts indicate a temporally qualified predicate. But what is the temporal datum-line to which the superscripts relate? Obviously the utterance of the sentence in question; but this introduces a difficulty, since part of the meaning of a proposition is now being given by the context in which it is uttered. We must needs accept this complication, since statements about the future are statements about the future as determined by the time of stating. And we cannot avoid it by making the temporally qualified predicates relate to some standard event other than the utterance of the sentence, for example by using ordinary dates such as $\theta^{399\ \text{B.C.}}c$, since this would merely be a statement about a time, not necessarily about a past or future time.

It is important to distinguish between the logical structure of propositions, and the conditions or contexts of asserting them which is an extra-logical consideration. The simple existential (5), since it does not refer to any particular event, does not refer to anything past, present or future, and can be asserted independently of the time-location of any event or events which happen to verify it. The simple singular (2) can be asserted of past and present events, but *cannot be asserted of future events* according to the RPP. This, if true, would constitute a time-order criterion; we should be in a position to say that those statements which we were unable to assert as singular propositions, but only as general propositions, were statements about the future; all other statements are about the present and past. The direction of time would be determined by the progressive accumulation of singular statements becoming available to match statements which hitherto had been only general. In the case of the sculptor, as the work proceeds (either in the orthodox or in the eccentric fashion) singular statements become available for assertion as the counterparts of general statements; a statement about the dimensions of a statue becomes available for assertion, and is (if things go according to plan) the counterpart of a general statement such as a list of co-ordinates.

The RPP is disputed. But perhaps its opponents have failed to observe the fact on which all the above hinges: that from the occurrence of a singular term in a sentence it does not follow that that sentence expresses a singular proposition. We have seen how the apparently singular proposition "Socrates is wise" can be a general proposition of type (7), if it occurs as the answer to the question "Who, if anyone, is wise?" Similarly, we have to see that an apparently singular proposition about the future, such as "Professor Carnap will fly to the moon", may well be a general proposition in disguise. It could be the answer to a question "Will anyone fly to the moon, and if so who?" More formally, "There is a value of x such that 'x flies to the moon' and 'x is Professor Carnap' are both true".

What are the reasons for insisting on this move? Simply the difficulty which Ryle notices: the difficulty of seeing how we can talk about "what we have not got" (to use his own calculatedly crude expression): more precisely, the difficulty of seeing how the conditions for assertibility can be satisfied. For a subject-predicate sentence to have a meaning, to express a proposition which can be true or false, it is necessary that it should contain a subject term. For such a proposition to be *asserted*, a further condition must be satisfied: the subject term, which purports to name some particular thing, must actually name some particular thing: it must be given a reference. The difficulty of giving a reference to singular terms occurring in future-tensed statements is not obvious in the case of the "Professor Carnap" example, just because we have indeed got Professor Carnap; and opponents of the RPP trade on just such examples as this. But it remains to be pointed out that, although we have "got" the present Professor Carnap, we have not "got" the future Professor Carnap, which is what the sentence is supposed to be about. The difficulty of giving a reference is certainly still there, however impatient we may be at the pedantic discrimination between two Professor Carnaps—what's the difference? But the difficulty is obvious, and the discrimination surely not pedantic, in the strictly analogous case of our imaginary unborn son who is going to go to Rugby. What my statement purports to refer to either doesn't exist at all, or exists in some pre- or post-natal stage of growth; it certainly is not the future schoolboy, whom I have not "got". The sentence cannot refer at all and must, therefore, if asserted at all be asserted as a general statement, as the RPP holds. When you say "My son will be at Rugby" what you are saying is that there will be some individual who satisfies both the descriptive expressions "being my son" and "being at Rugby" (and, if you like, "being named Johnny"). But just so, when you say "Professor Carnap will fly to the moon", what you are saying is that there will be some individual who satisfies both the descriptive expressions "flying to the moon" and "being identical with Professor Carnap"—where "being identical with" conceals no logical tricks but merely refers to ordinary personal continuity. There is no difference in principle between the case of our future moon-traveller being closely similar to, though more aged than, the present distinguished professor, and the case of the future Rugby schoolboy being more aged than, though *not* closely similar to, a present-day infant. In neither case have we "got", as Ryle would say, the actual subject of our discourse.

Certainly Ryle's talk of what we have and have not "got" is provocatively slipshod and demands refinement. We might well want to say that there is quite a lot of the present that we have not "got" either, and even more of the past, perhaps the whole of it. I can only roughly hint at possible ways of meeting that challenge. All statements in the past or present tense can in principle be tied down to sense-experience; they contain referring expressions as well as descriptive ones, or where they do not—where type (S2) statements occur—they occur in a framework of discourse which does typically contain referring expressions, type (S1). Such referring expressions always carry with them a context of sensation. I shall not go into the question whether sensations must be distinguished from memory—whether all experience is memory, or whether there is a specious present as distinct from memory; whatever the answer to this, it seems undeniable that the phenomenal present shades off into the phenomenal past in contrast with the sharp break between present and future. There is no phenomenal future.

But where sense-experience leaves off, wishes, hopes and fears remain. I have already hinted that this is the best place to look for an unambiguous pointer. It is no use crying over spilt milk; but unspilled milk is a proper thing to cry for or against. Prayers, incantations and imprecations, however irrational they may be, are at least not irrational in the special sense in which lamentation is (and perhaps remorse). Or to put it in a more linguistic vein: the indicative mood does indeed span all three temporal regions, but its proper home is in the present and the past, and its resources are stretched to the limit when it enters the region proper to the imperative and optative moods.

HUMAN TIME

INTRODUCTION

In this section we shall explore the question: What aspects of time are a result of the existence of human beings who perceive and talk about time? We are concerned with finding out what features of our concept of time have only an anthropomorphic significance. This large question will be broken up into three smaller ones: (1) What distinction is there between the perceptual present and the real or physical present? (2) Is temporal becoming subjective? and (3) To what extent does the grammatical structure of our language determine our way of conceiving time?

(1) Is the span of what we are perceptually acquainted with punctal, durationless, or does it encompass a finite duration? The usual reply is that the present of perceptual awareness has a finite width, not being confined to a mathematical instant of time. According to C. D. Broad, in a given instant we see (hear, etc.) some finite event or succession of events, such as the movement of the second hand of a watch or the successive beats of a drum, which covers a period of time between some moment in the past and the instant at which our perceptual act occurs. The apprehended content displays a continuous shift in its degree of presentedness or liveliness, from a maximum degree of presentedness at the instant of our perceptual act to a minimum degree of this quality at the past instant at which the span of the perceptual present ends. Were it not for the fortunate fact that in a single perception we apprehend successive events, such as the notes of a melody, we could have no idea of succession; for a mere succession of perceptions is not a perception of succession.

According to some versions of the perceptual or psychological present, such as those of James, Husserl, and Heidegger, the span of our immediate awareness encompasses a small part of the future as well as the past. James spoke of the perceptual present as being saddleback. For Husserl, we not only have retentions of the past through a type of immediate or primary memory, i.e., memory in which what is remembered has not passed out of conscious awareness, but also protensions of the future through anticipation. This doctrine of the phenomenology of time consciousness is given a sympathetic exposition in the article by William Barrett on "The Flow of Time."

The perceptual present, be it that of the Broad or James variety, is often referred to as the "specious present." The term "specious" is used to indicate that an invidious distinction is being made between the perceptual present and the *real* or *true* present, which is supposed to be punctal. There are two reasons for assigning the perceptual present to the lowly status of a mere appearance. First, there is the purely conceptual consideration, eloquently put forth in the selection in Section I from Augustine's *Confessions*, that if the present were to have a finite duration it could be subdivided into an earlier and later portion, but earlier and later portions of time cannot, without contradiction, be copresent. Second, many philosophers look to physics for a description of the real or objective world; and since the events postulated by modern physics are punctal, it is claimed that the real or objective present must also be punctal. Some philosophers, among whom are James, Bergson, and Whitehead, place the shoe on the other foot. Using the deliverances of our perceptual experiences as decisive in determining the nature of reality, and claiming that the theoretical concepts of physics must be constructible out of this gross experience (e.g. Whitehead's method of extensive abstraction for defining instants and points), they would charge the present of physical theory with speciousness.[1]

[1] Whitehead's method of extensive abstraction defines mathematical points and instants in terms of a set of finite volumes and intervals, respectively. On analogy with a set of Chinese boxes, a mathematical point is defined as the set of all volumes that enclose

The perceptual present has been called not only specious but also suspicious. According to J. D. Mabbott, in his contribution to this section, Broad's doctrine of the specious present harbors serious conceptual muddles; for although the span of the specious present is said to be finite, the perceptual act that grasps this content is itself said to be punctal. How, it is asked, can a perceptual act be durationless? Another set of difficulties concerns the notion of varying degrees of presentedness or liveliness that characterize the different parts of the specious present. If, upon hearing the final note of a melody, I were also perceptually aware of the preceding notes, though not in as vivid a manner, would I not then be hearing a chord the notes of which differ in volume? No doubt, Husserl's use of the idea of immediate or primary memory is an attempt to meet this difficulty. Furthermore, all the evidence for determining the length of the specious present is purely behavioral; it is based, for example, on our ability to play back rhythmic sequences that we have just heard. Suppose that I were a skilled musician, and as a result could play back a rhythmic sequence of ten minutes: would this show that when I heard the final beat I were in some sense also hearing all the previous beats?

(2) The question of the subjectivity of temporal becoming has already been touched on in Section II "The Static Versus the Dynamic Temporal." Further, it was pointed out in the section on "The Open Future" that if temporal becoming were to be subjective then the various logical asymmetries between past and future would be reduced to the status of criteria for distinguishing between earlier and later times. Here it is crucial to realize that there are two radically different kinds of arguments that *B*-Theorists have used to show the subjectivity of temporal becoming. One kind of argument is a priori, since it is based on a conceptual analysis of the ordinary concept of an *A*-determination. In this argument the claim of the *B*-Theory's Linguistic and Psychology Reductions is that the very *meaning* of "present (past, fu-

the point: and a mathematical instant of time is defined as the set of all temporal intervals that enclose the instant.

ture)" is such that an essential reference is made to a linguistic or mental event. *B*-Theorists, however, sometimes appeal to the discoveries of modern science to support their claim about the subjectivity of temporal becoming, thereby giving *empirical* arguments. Adolf Grünbaum's attempt to show the mind-dependency of becoming in his article in this section is of the latter sort.

The a priori arguments are based on an *analysis* of the meaning of an *A*-determination. Two such analyses have been put forth, one the token-reflexive analysis, which aims to demonstrate the linguocentricity of *A*-determinations, and the other the egocentric-particular analysis, which is directed toward showing the mind-dependency of *A*-determinations.

According to the token-reflexive analysis, which occurs in the first step of the Linguistic Reduction,[2] *A*-statements are self-referring or token-reflexive. Thus, the statement "The chair is now (was, will be) red," is analyzed into "The chair's being red is (tenselessly) simultaneous with (earlier than, later than) this token," in which "this token" refers to the occurrence of the entire sentence token within which the token of the phrase "this token" occurs. Every time "this token" is used it refers to a different sentence token, namely the one within which it occurs. The philosophical significance of the token-reflexive analysis of *A*-statements is that it brings out the linguocentricity and therefore the subjectivity of *A*-determinations. This analysis, according to Smart, brings out the reference to a human utterance implicit in the use of words like "past," "present," and "future": it shows that these notions, unlike "earlier" and "later," are without cosmic significance.[3]

There seems to me to be a telling objection to the token-reflexive analysis. *That the chair is now red* could not possibly mean the same thing as *that the chair's being red is*

[2] See pp. 71 ff of this volume. The token-reflexive analysis was first given by Hans Reichenbach in *Elements of Symbolic Logic,* Macmillan, New York, 1947, pp. 284–87.

[3] J. J. C. Smart, " 'Tensed Statements': A Comment," *Philosophical Quarterly,* 12 (1962), 264. A similar account is given by Smart in his *Philosophy and Scientific Realism,* London, 1963, p. 134.

(*tenselessly*) *simultaneous with this token* because the latter statement entails that there exists a token, while the former statement does not. Statements that have different entailment relations cannot have the same meaning. "The chair is now red, even though no token occurs" is not contradictory, as is "The chair's being red is (tenselessly) simultaneous with this token, even though no token occurs." The former statement is false, but it is contingently false: it could be true. What is peculiar about it is that it is made through the use of a sentence that makes a false statement every time it is used, and yet the statement that it makes is not necessarily false. We might call such sentences "pragmatically self-falsifying," a famous example of which is "I do not exist." Our *ordinary* concept of an A-determination does not contain any reference to a language-user or a linguistic token, and for this reason there is no contradiction in conceiving of a world devoid of language-users in which events become present one after the other, even though unspoken of at the time or at any time.

The egocentric-particular analysis, which is Russell's creation, claims that an A-statement, such as "The chair is now (was, will be) red," can be analyzed into "The chair's being red is (tenselessly) simultaneous with (earlier than, later than) this," in which "this" is a "logically proper name" for a sense-datum experienced by the speaker at the time he makes his utterance. Since a sense-datum is a mental event, i.e., an event which in principle cannot be experienced by anyone other than the person who experiences it, it follows that an A-determination contains a reference to a mental event (and therefore consciousness).

One difficulty with the egocentric-particular analysis is that it renders communication impossible. Only the speaker can know the referent of "this," since it denotes a sense-datum private to the speaker. Therefore, the hearer cannot know what event the chair's being red is simultaneous with (earlier than, later than). Any analysis of language that entails the impossibility of communication is an absurdity. An even more basic objection to this analysis, which parallels that made to the token-reflexive analysis, is that the *ordinary* concept of an A-determination does not involve a reference to a mental event, for there is no contradiction in saying that an event is now present although no mental event occurs. No absurdity is attached to conceiving a world devoid of minds in which events nevertheless undergo temporal becoming.[4]

In summary of the a priori arguments, it seems to me that both the token-reflexive and egocentric-particular analyses misconstrue the logic or meaning of ordinary temporal discourse, which, I have claimed, commits us to a realistic view of A-determinations and temporal becoming. Whether or not this common-sense realism is naïve, in that it cannot be squared with the *empirical* findings of modern science, is completely irrelevant to what is ordinarily *meant* by A-determinations.

Plainly a more promising approach to showing the subjectivity of A-determinations is to give *empirical* arguments based on the findings of science. Often the theory of relativity is appealed to, as it is in the following quotations from Weyl and Eddington:

> The objective world simply *is*, it does not happen. Only to the gaze of my consciousness crawling upward along the life (world-) line of my body does a section of this world come to life as a fleeting image.[5]

> Events do not happen; they are just there, and we come across them. 'The formality of taking place' is merely the indication that the observer has on his voyage of exploration passed into the absolute future of the event in question; and it has no important significance.[6]

If taken literally, these representations of temporal becoming are absurd, since the concepts of crawling and voyaging re-

---

[4] We might alter the egocentric-particular analysis so that "this" need not denote a mental event. But then this analysis does nothing to show that A-determinations are in any way mind-dependent.

[5] H. Weyl, *Philosophy of Mathematics and Natural Science*, Princeton, N.J., 1949, p. 116.

[6] A. Eddington, *Space, Time and Gravitation*, Cambridge, 1920, p. 51.

quire a change of spatial position over an interval of time; herein it is a time-interval that is being crawled and voyaged along over an interval of time. These representations, however, are only metaphors, which, when translated into literal language, amount to saying that physical events have A-determinations only because they bear B-relations to mental events, a physical event being present, for example, when the mind "comes across it," i.e., when it is simultaneous with a perception of it. What Grünbaum adds to the Psychological Reduction of previous B-Theorists, such as Russell, Braithwaite, and Ducasse, is the further requirement that the mental events in question be ones of which the experient is self-consciously aware. A physical event is present only if it is either the object of a perception of which the perceiver is self-consciously aware or simultaneous with such a perception.

The crucial question is the following: Exactly what features of relativity theory, or any physical theory for that matter, require us to deny that A-determinations are objective properties of events? Must we do so because of the *empirical* fact that signals, such as light rays, have a finite velocity, and, as a result, there is a relativity of simultaneity between spatially separated events and even a relativity in regard to the order of precedence between events which are not causally connected? If this is the reason given, then, if, as is logically possible, signals were to have an infinite velocity, A-determinations would be objective. Adolf Grünbaum, however, does not appeal to the relativity of simultaneity in arguing for the mind-dependency of A-determinations. His argument is that if A-determinations are objective, non-mind-dependent features of the world, then physics should take cognizance of them. But relativity theory (as well as other physical theories) makes no allowance for the A-determinations of events, representing only space-time separations between events. Grünbaum feels that the entire common-sense framework, with its commitment to the objectivity of secondary qualities (colors, sounds, etc.) as well as temporal becoming, has been rendered untenable by science since the time of Galileo, and should be replaced by a more scientifically respectable conceptual system for philosophical purposes. His analysis of A-determinations attempts, in part, to do just this.

There are several questions that an A-Theorist might raise about Grünbaum's argument. First, is it true that physicists take no note of A-determinations? In their efforts to discover and verify laws and theories, they make ample use of A-determinations. The reply to this might be that A-determinations, though of significance in the *pragmatic* dimensions of physics, do not enter into the *semantic* content of physical laws and theories. Second, why must every non-mind-dependent property of events be taken note of by physics conceived in this rather narrow manner as a set of laws and theories? Might not temporal becoming be *sui generis* and not capable of any further explanation in terms of something more basic? Third, how can temporal becoming be intrinsic to mental events but not to the physical events (such as events in the brain) with which these mental events are correlated and upon which they are, for a naturalist, causally dependent? Grünbaum tries to show that there is no absurdity in temporal becoming's being intrinsic only to mental events of a certain sort.

Barrett's article in this section is the antithesis of Grünbaum's, not only in that Barrett denies that temporal becoming is mind-dependent, but even more in that he widely differs from Grünbaum in his philosophical method. Crudely put, Grünbaum's basic assumption is that the objective world —reality—is as our most advanced physical theories tell us it is. Barrett, on the other hand, using the phenomenological method of Husserl and Heidegger, believes that reality is what reveals itself in our everyday experiences of the world. Accordingly, he attacks those who hold that reality ought to be understood in terms of the abstract theoretical concepts of science. Specifically, he attacks Weyl, to whose views Grünbaum closely adheres, for claiming that we must shatter the common belief in the objectivity of temporal becoming. Barrett holds that Weyl's view is a "violent inversion of the abstract and concrete" in which we lose sight of the "life-world" (the *lebenswelt* of Husserl). The flow of time, which is Barrett's expression for temporal becoming, is not only an irreducible feature of everything we experience but of our consciousness as well. Temporal becoming is not an object of discovery—a thing in the world—but an ontological presupposition for there to be a world or consciousness at all. It is interesting to note that the conclusion Barrett reaches through the use of the phenomenological method is in general agreement with that reached by certain A-Theorists through the method of linguistic or conceptual analysis. According to the latter philosophers, A-determinations are logically presupposed by the basic concepts in terms of which we think and talk about the world.

(3) If we are going to argue, as these A-Theorists do, that A-determinations are ultimate features of reality because they are presupposed by the basic concepts by means of which we think and talk about the world, the question of other possible ways of thinking and talking immediately presents itself. The very exciting and suggestive article by Benjamin Whorf defends the thesis of "linguistic relativism," which posits that the language used by a person determines the way in which he experiences and conceives of the world. More specifically, it is the grammatical structure of a particular language that determines the way in which a native speaker conceptually carves up the world into various kinds of facts. Each language contains its own implicit metaphysic. Whorf's thesis is relevant to our question concerning the anthropocentricity of A-determinations because it suggests that the grammar of the language one speaks determines whether one takes A-determinations to be objective facts. Indo-European languages, with their tensed verbs and temporal adjectives of "past," "present," and "future," lead a native speaker to conceive of past, present, and future as objective features of events. However, Whorf tells us, there are languages such as Hopi that contain no tensed verbs, no temporal adjectives, nor any other device that refers to A-determinations. Rather the Hopi conceives of time in a Bergsonian manner, as dynamic process not admitting of distinction between past, present, and future.

L*

Whorf's hypothesis raises many basic questions, for which there are no easy answers. First, is it legitimate to infer from the vocabulary and grammar of a language how a speaker of this language perceives and conceives reality? Do we not, at least in part, have non-linguistic behavioral criteria for ascribing a certain conceptual capacity to a person?[7] Second, even if it were true that perceptual and conceptual capacities were molded by our language, what significance would this have for metaphysics? If, for example, the language of some tribe contained no words for physical objects, would this show that physical objects are not part of the furniture of the world? Or, would it just show that this is a very primitive tribe? Third, does it follow that because a language, such as Hopi, contains no tensed verbs or specific words for past, present, and future, it cannot be used to make A-determinations? This question warrants some further exploration, since it will help to clarify the nature of A-statements, and thus the nature of A-determinations.

It is true that Indo-European languages make A-determinations through the grammatical device of tensed verbs. But why should this particular grammatical device for conveying such temporal information be sacrosanct? Eskimo[8] and many American Indian languages seem to be able to express the pastness, presentness, or futurity of a reported event or state of affairs by altering the end of a substantive. In certain African languages, like Mende and Hausa, pronouns are inflected, rather than verbs or nouns, for the purpose of making A-determinations. "The chief went" would be translated by words meaning "Chief he-past go." The latter sentence translated into Mende or Hausa obeys the same rules of use as the English sentence "The chief went," in that both can be used to make a true statement only if uttered or in-

---

[7] As Max Black has said, if the Hopis really can get by without making any reference to past, present, and future we would like to know their secret. See his fine review of Whorf's *Selected Papers,* "Linguistic Relativity: the Views of Benjamin Lee Whorf," *Philosophical Review,* 58 (1959).

[8] See Otto Jespersen, *The Philosophy of Grammar,* George Allen & Unwin, London, 1935, p. 283.

scribed later than the chief's leaving. These sentences are subject to the same temporal restrictions in their use for making true statements. It will be recalled from the Introduction to Section II that sentences used for making *B*-statements had no temporal restrictions placed upon them: if they could be used at one time to make a true statement they could be used at any other time so as to make a true statement.

Just as two chessmen that differ in size, shape, and material can both play the role of the king in a chess game in virtue of being used in accordance with the same rules of use (i.e. the rules that specify the way in which the king is to be positioned and moved in chess) so too can two sentences of radically different grammatical structure both play the role of expressing *A*-determinations in virtue of being subject to the same temporal restrictions in their use for making true and false statements. To think that *A*-determinations can be expressed only by tensed verbs is analogous to thinking that a king in chess must be made of ivory.

OUR DIRECT EXPERIENCE OF TIME

J. D. MABBOTT

J. D. MABBOTT was a Fellow of St. John's College at Oxford University and became President of the College in 1963. His major publications include *The State and the Citizen* and *Introduction to Ethics.*

I

The problem I discuss in this paper is that of our direct awareness of the passage of events as distinct from our awareness through memory.

The problem arises in the epistemological classics in the form of various answers to the question 'Has an idea duration?' Locke says 'There is a train of ideas which constantly succeed one another in the understanding' (*Essay*, II, xiv, p. 3), and further 'The distance between the appearance of any two ideas in the mind is what we call *duration*' (*ibid.*). There is thus, he adds, 'no perception of duration but by considering the train of ideas that take their turns in our understandings' (*ibid.*, p. 4). It would seem from these and similar statements that we cannot find the characteristic called 'duration' in a single idea. If so, ideas must be instantaneous. But Locke, as usual, contradicts himself. He says 'The mind cannot fix long on one invariable idea' (*ibid.*, p. 13). Here it seems that an idea can endure for a limited but not a long period. Or again 'Every part of duration is duration too . . . capable . . . of division *in infinitum* . . . a small part of duration may be called a moment and is the

FROM J. D. Mabbott, "Our Direct Experience of Time," *Mind*, 60 (1951). Reprinted by permission of the editor and J. D. Mabbott.

time of one idea in our mind' (*Essay*, II, xv, p. 9). On this view we can find duration in a single idea.

Hume appears to accept the first of Locke's mutually contradictory propositions. He says 'Time as it exists must be composed of indivisible moments' (*Treatise*, Book I, Part II, ch. ii; ed. Selby Bigge, Oxford, 1896, p. 31), and again 'The idea of duration is always derived from a succession of changeable objects' (*ibid.*, ch. iii, p. 37). But if he had applied to time the same kind of analysis that he applied to space he would have found himself left with Locke's second alternative. For the spatial elements into which a perceived colour-expanse must be analysed are coloured points; and by a 'coloured point' Hume makes it clear that he does not mean a mathematical point having position but no magnitude, for such mathematical points can neither exist nor be perceived. He means a very small area, the area in fact of a *minimum visible* (*Treatise*, Book I, Part II, chs. iii and iv; especially p. 42). By similar reasoning he should have concluded that a mathematical instant, having date but no duration, could not exist or be perceived; and that our direct experience of a sound must be analysed into brief sounds, each of them the shortest sound which still remains audible, each having duration.

Reid drove home the second answer. 'There must be duration in every single interval or element of which the whole duration is composed. Nothing indeed is more certain than that every elementary part of duration must have duration' (*Essays on the Intellectual Powers*, Book III, ch. v; ed. A. D. Woozley, p. 209), and again 'we assign to sense not an indivisible point of time but that small portion of time which we call the present, which has a beginning, a middle and an end' (*ibid.*, p. 208).

The problem re-emerged in recent epistemology. 'Ideas' vanish. 'Sense-data' reign in their stead. The question now becomes 'How long does a sense-datum last?' If sense-data are to be the elements into which our direct experience of physical objects (perhaps all our experience of physical objects) is to be analysed, Reid's argument would seem to hold. They must last for *some* time, however brief. Russell referred to them as 'lasting only for a very short time' (*Philosophy of Logical Atomism*, II, p. 325).

But there is obviously a difficulty in sorting out these brief particulars from the temporally continuous experience in which they are embedded. Let us recall again the parallel problem concerning space. It has been made clear (by Price, for example) that what is directly given to sight is not a sense-datum but a sense-field. Sense-data are items in sense-fields; they are distinguished from one another or from the rest of the sense-field by content (in the case of sight, by colour). Now this process of discrimination seems to be to some extent arbitrary and in some cases impossible. When I see a tomato I have a sense-datum which is red and circular and bulgy. But suppose my tomato has a green spot on it. Shall I say I have one sense-datum (red-with-a-green-spot) or two sense-data (a green one completely surrounded by a ring-shaped red one)? It does not matter which I say. Now suppose you are looking at a curtain of shot silk so close to you that it occupies your whole field of view. It is clear that you see colours, in the plural. But it would be impossible to say how many sense-data (distinguished by colour) this sense-field contains. However all this may be, sense-data are distinguished by their content, and Russell and Broad and Price will have no truck with Hume's *minima visibilia*.

Now translate this into terms of time. I lie awake in the dark for half an hour listening to the swishing of the rain. After fifteen minutes the swishing is drowned by the monotone shriek of an owl, lasting three seconds. Shall I say I had one swishing sense-datum half an hour long, interrupted at half-time by a shrieky sense-datum? Or shall I say I had three sense-data: swishy, shrieky, swishy? It does not seem to matter. But suppose the interruption was not an owl but the ululating Air Raid Danger Signal. Now I ask whether I have heard one note or many; and, if many, how many sense-data, distinguishable by content, the siren noise included. No answer is possible. Nevertheless again, despite these difficulties, it might be reasonable to hold that the only way in which a temporally continuous experience can be broken up into elements is by content—*i.e.* by qualitative differences between the elements. This is implied by a remark of Ayer's. 'A sense content occurs in each of a series of successive sense-fields, each sense-field differing in content from its predecessor. . . . For if there were no difference at all in content there would not be two sense-fields' (*Proceedings of the Aristotelian Society*, xxxiv, p. 54). This means that a sense-field retaining its content unaltered for two minutes would be a single sense-field; what alone differentiates one sense-field from a later one is its content. On this view the duration of any sense-field and therefore of any sense-datum is a purely empirical matter. There is no reason in principle why a sense-datum should not endure for three minutes or three hours. Brief life is here their portion, only because we are busy people or because we are bored with monotony.

There is, however, quite a different kind of answer to the question how long a sense-datum can last. Price says 'It is highly probable that every sense-datum has a finite duration and certain that most have. On the other hand, it is also certain that the duration is at the best very small, probably never more than a few seconds (it will depend on our span of attention which is notoriously never great)' (*Perception*, p. 115). Broad agrees. 'A sensible event has a finite duration which may be roughly defined as the time during which it is sensed, as distinct from being remembered . . . what can be sensed at any moment stretches a little way back behind that moment' (*Scientific Thought*, p. 348). Broad explicitly and Price implicitly are referring here to the psychological doctrine of the 'Specious Present'. This is not surprising for (of all philosophers who have tackled systematically the problems of perception) these two have shown a pre-eminent knowledge of and interest in psychology. It must be noted that, when Price says 'our span of attention is notoriously never great', he does not mean that we cannot attend to any one subject for long because of fatigue or boredom. He means that the stretch of time which can be apprehended at a given moment by an attentive act of apprehension is not great. This is clear in the last sentence quoted from Broad.

Now philosophers have generally tended to believe that the psychologists have shown experimentally that our direct apprehension of time is restricted to a certain short duration and that they have determined the normal length of this duration by measurement. It is usually given as 0.75 second. The *locus classicus* in English for all this is in William James. He says 'We are constantly aware of a certain duration —the specious present—varying from a few seconds to probably not more than a minute, and this duration (with its content perceived as having one part earlier and another part later) is the original intuition of time' (*Principles of Psychology*, Vol. I, p. 642). On this view it is of course impossible that a sense-datum should last two minutes. If I hear a continuous homogeneous sound lasting two minutes, I must be having a series of exactly similar successive sense-data, each of them x seconds long (whatever the length of the specious present is experimentally found to be).

What was the experimental evidence on which the duration of the specious present was first determined? Wundt (1874) and some of his colleagues tried to determine the maximum group of sounds which could be 'remembered as a whole and identified without error'. (I think the truth is that they discovered the group could be identified without error, and inferred that it was therefore remembered as a whole and must accordingly have been heard as a whole.) The maximum duration of such a group was found by Wundt to be six seconds, by Dietze (1885) to be thirty-six seconds. About the same time another group of Wundt's followers tried to discover the time interval which could be estimated with the greatest accuracy. This was found by Kollert (1882) to be 0.75 second and by Mehner (1885) to be 0.71 second. Shorter intervals than these were regularly overestimated, longer intervals regularly underestimated. Estel (1884) and Mehner even found a periodicity by which such 'indifference points' (or maximum accuracy intervals) recurred at regular intervals; according to Estel at multiples of 0.75 second (1.50 seconds, 2.25 seconds, etc.). This led to the general acceptance of 0.75 second as the unit of temporal experience. It does not seem to have troubled people at that time that the two sets of experiments reached such very different results. (We have seen how both are covered by James when he says the specious present 'varies from a few seconds to probably not more than a minute'.)

The second set of experiments, however, which gave the result 0.75 second, has been carefully repeated with negative results. L. F. Stevens (*Mind,* O.S., xi, 1886) failed to find any such periodicity as Estel and Mehner hàd noted, and he commented that indifference points varied greatly from subject to subject, though the average for those he tested was about 0.6 second. Woodrow (*Journal of Experimental Psychology,* 1930, 1934) showed conclusively that there is nothing absolute about the indifference point. Individual variations were too large for an average to be taken as having any general significance. So we are left with the first set of experiments (the recognition without error of sound groups) which gave a specious present of six or thirty-six seconds.

The notion of the specious present is full of difficulties, and Professor Broad has rendered one of his signal services to the philosophy of science in clarifying it. He gives two presentations of it: in *Scientific Thought* (pp. 348 ff.) and in *An Examination of McTaggart's Philosophy* (Part II, Vol. I, pp. 281 ff.). I do not see how any improvement on his analysis is possible, so I shall summarize it briefly with the aid of his diagram.[1] The upper horizontal line represents successive acts of apprehension (A, B, C . . .) following each other in the direction of the arrow. The lower horizontal line represents contents of awareness; sounds, colour-patches, etc. A point on the lower line vertically below a point on the upper line is simultaneous with it.

Broad's first point (and the one on which most of the difficulties hinge) is that the definition of the specious present requires the conception of a momentary act of awareness. Let such an act occur at A. Now the doctrine holds that this act A will be aware *of* an event which lasts from V to X (a sound or other datum). This stretch VX is the specious

[1] Adapted from *Scientific Thought,* p. 349. With the kind permission of the author and his publishers, Messrs. Kegan Paul, Trench, Trubner & Co.

present of act A. It ends at a moment simultaneous with A but includes a short stretch which is past when A is present. A later act of awareness B would be aware of the content WY, and one at C aware of XZ. Now there cannot be momentary acts of awareness just as there cannot be momentary sense-data. Broad raises this difficulty and deals with it with characteristic ingenuity. Let us assume the specious present of an act is six seconds long. If B occurs three seconds after A the specious presents of A and B will overlap (VX overlapping WY). Now A and B cannot represent acts of awareness (since they would be momentary) but AB can. This would be an act of awareness lasting three seconds.

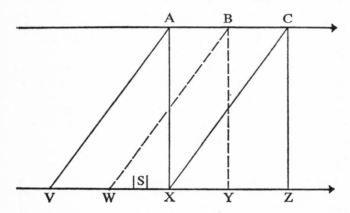

What would be its specious present? What event could this act apprehend as a whole? One is tempted to say 'the event VY'. The answer is 'the event WX'. For the stretch VW cannot be given to act AB as a whole, because at all moments after A it has vanished into the past and is accessible only to memory. And the stretch XY cannot be given to AB as a whole because at all moments before B it is still in the future and therefore not accessible to inspection at all. Now suppose there is an act of awareness lasting six seconds, from A to C. What will be the specious present of that act? What content can be given to it as a whole? The answer is *nil*. For at moment A nothing after X can be experienced because it has not happened yet and at moment C nothing before X can be directly experienced because it has all vanished into the past. Thus we conclude (still supposing that the specious present is six seconds in length) that the specious present of an act of awareness varies inversely with the duration of the act. As the duration of the act approximates to zero the duration of its specious present approximates to six seconds. As the act approaches six seconds its specious present approximates to zero. All acts of six seconds or more have no specious present. Then, using the Method of Extensive Abstraction, we can define 'the specious present' as the set of all specious presents of actual acts of awareness. They will 'converge' to six seconds. This seems to me a most effective piece of analysis. If the Wundt doctrine does not mean this, I cannot see what it could mean; though no doubt Wundt and his followers had no idea of what was involved.

Broad seems to accept the doctrine, thus explained, as giving an accurate description of our direct experience of time. The effect on me is the exact reverse. It drives me to conclude that the doctrine of the specious present is untenable and sheds no light on our normal apprehension of temporal events.

II

Broad himself draws from his own analysis some corollaries which would have surprised the previous holders of the doctrine. To begin with, he rejects James's 'saddleback' description. 'The present is a saddleback on which we sit perched and from which we look in two directions into time' (*op. cit.*, p. 609). This means that at moment A we apprehend a short stretch of the past and a short stretch of the future. Broad thinks we cannot be directly aware of any future event; in this agreeing with E. R. Clay who originated the term 'specious present'. Clay says 'The present to which the datum refers is really part of the past' ('The Alternative', p. 167, quoted by James, p. 609). Broad also draws attention to a second corollary of his view, though he does not emphasize its paradoxical character. Every actual act of apprehension must have some finite duration. But then no act of apprehension can apprehend any event simultaneous with it. For example, in the diagram, the act which lasts from A to B apprehends as a whole the content WX which has finished occurring at the moment AB begins. As Broad puts it 'The prehended content is completely past at the moment at which it first begins to be prehended' (*Examination of McTaggart*, II, i, p. 288). Thus, if my dentist hurts me, he has always stopped hurting me before I begin to feel the hurt. And this has nothing to do with the time taken by nerve transmission; it is a direct corollary of the specious present theory. Broad thought it an inacceptable paradox of James's saddleback theory that it involved apprehension of the future. I think it an almost equally unacceptable paradox of Broad's theory that it denies all direct awareness of the present. A third and the most important corollary Broad draws from his analysis is that the specious present cannot be, as James said it was, 'the unit of composition of our perception'. In summing up his view (*op. cit.*, p. 642) James says 'This duration (with its content perceived as having one part earlier and another part later) is the original intuition of time. Longer times are conceived by adding shorter times by dividing portions of this vaguely bounded unit.' Here then is our unit of psychological time; a long experience consists of a number of these units added together. But the diagram shows that this will not do. VX is the specious present of act A and is one unit. The next unit is XZ which is the specious present of act C (six seconds later). If then the *content* of our experience is to be analysed into specious presents as units (each say six seconds long) then our acts of apprehension must take place at intervals of six seconds, intervals during which no apprehension occurs. There could for example be no act of apprehension at B. If, however, there are stretches of continuous awareness ABC then specious presents must overlap each other (VX, WY, XZ) and therefore cannot be the units of which the content of awareness is composed and into which it can be analysed.

If we are to take the doctrine as true and if Broad's analysis is accepted, we must say that a direct experience of a sound lasting say three seconds will be the awareness of an infinite set of overlapping specious presents. Broad accepts this. He says 'No specious present has an immediate successor'. 'The series of specious presents must be compact.' 'Between any two specious presents there will always be an infinite number of others' (*Examination of McTaggart*, II, i, p. 285). I find 'between' an unsatisfactory word to describe the relation between overlapping specious presents—for example 'WY is between VX and XZ'—but it is clear enough what Broad means. I find it hard to believe that this is a description of our experience; but I find it completely convincing that anyone who accepted this doctrine of the specious present should have to describe our experience in this way.

In particular I find the overlapping character puzzling. Take a simple case. Suppose there is a brief sound marked on the diagram as S, I shall experience it at moment A as part of the specious present VX. Three seconds later at moment B I shall experience it again as part of the specious present WY. Every brief sound I hear I shall hear not once but repeatedly. Nothing in my direct experience confirms this repetition. If it occurred it would obviously make listening to music or to continuous sentences a matter of the greatest complexity and difficulty.

It is possible, however, to take all this talk of infinite sets and series as an intellectual construction meant to represent, but inevitably falsifying, the continuous character of our experience. To say that our experienced content *consists of* a compact series of overlapping specious presents results from saying that an act of awareness consists of a compact series of instantaneous acts of awareness. But there are no such acts. Our acts of awareness are continuous within their limits and this mathematical analysis of continuity as a compact series of dimensionless points corresponds to nothing in the psychological facts except the continuity. The specious present doctrine might now be restated, with the help of the diagram, thus. Suppose a searchlight mounted on the upper line and shining downwards on the lower line, with a

constant span of illumination equal to VX. If you could stop
the searchlight at moment A (which you can't) it would
illuminate VX. As it moves along the top line X begins to
be illuminated at moment A and ceases to be illuminated at
moment B. So my objection that I find no repetitions in my
experience can be met. When a searchlight moves over a
landscape it does not illuminate one object *repeatedly;* it
illuminates it *continuously.*

What is wrong with this simile? The answer is that it
makes the source of illumination punctiform. As we have
seen this would represent a momentary act of apprehension;
but these cannot occur. If it is said that the movement of a
punctiform source from A to B is again just a mathematical
fiction representing the continuity of the act of awareness
AB, that again will not do. For it would mean that the content of (= area illuminated by) act AB would be VY
whereas (as we have seen) the content apprehended on
Broad's view is WX.

In the exposition of the doctrine in previous sections I have
followed *Scientific Thought.* In the treatment of the corollaries, I have followed *An Examination of McTaggart* in
which they are given much more fully and clearly. The exposition in the later work is more fully developed but I do
not find the additions make the theory clearer. *Scientific
Thought* lays much more emphasis on the way in which the
theory depends on momentary acts of apprehension, as I
think it does. The *Examination* seems to substitute for the
distinction between act of apprehension and content apprehended a distinction between 'occurring' and 'being prehended' which conceals the problem. It also adds a characteristic of contents which Broad calls 'presentedness' which
pervades a specious present, is at its maximum at the part of
the specious present most nearly simultaneous with the act of
apprehension, and tails off towards zero towards the past. (In
my searchlight simile, it is as if the specious present VX had
its maximum illumination at X and the degree of illumination diminished leftwards until at V it merges into total
darkness.) 'Presentedness' seems to be Broad's name for the
characteristic Hume called 'force and vivacity'. But if we are

to try to talk this language we shall find 'presentedness' a very odd characteristic. It is (presumably) conferred on the specious present by the act of apprehension (which occurs only after the content has ceased to exist). Moreover there are puzzles about the degree of this characteristic. While the searchlight source remains punctiform the picture of diminution from a maximum (at X) to a minimum (at V) makes sense. But, for any concrete act of awareness, puzzles arise. Take the act AB, whose specious present is WX. Now with what intensity (degree of presentedness) is WX illuminated (presented)? Presumably X is more brightly illuminated than W. But, at moment A, W was illuminated at half strength and, at moment B, at zero strength. At moment A, X is illuminated at full strength, at moment B, at half strength. When the specious present WX is apprehended *as a whole* by the act AB with what degree of presentedness is it endowed? (This is also another way of showing that the searchlight simile will not work.) So I do not find the later presentation in the *Examination* helpful in making the doctrine easier to understand or to accept. My impression is that when Broad wrote *Scientific Thought* he was satisfied that the specious present theory as worked out by him provided an adequate analysis of the temporal character of direct experience. But in the *Examination,* while he still thinks there is something in the doctrine, he seems less certain of its adequacy as providing such a complete analysis.

III

I now return to the psychological evidence on which the doctrine was founded, in order to raise a number of difficulties about it which are not dealt with by Broad. The aim was to discover the unit of temporal experience. So far as the experiments discovered anything, they found what was the maximum duration of a set of sounds which could be recognized without error. But we must not suppose that we are always apprehending data of the maximum duration. James sometimes seems to remember this—for instance when he refers, in the passage quoted above, to experiences which vary from a few seconds to not more than a minute. But on other occasions he seems to take the maximum as the norm. 'The specious present has a vaguely vanishing backward and forward fringe but its nucleus is probably the dozen or so seconds which have just elasped' (*Principles of Psychology*, I, p. 613). Why should not *minima* be taken as the units, as Hume would have implied? (*Minima* vary a good deal with the kind of apparatus used, but results as low as 0.002 second for hearing and 0.04 second for sight have been recorded.)

Secondly, the maxima will vary from individual to individual and with practice and with fatigue. What general conclusions about normal experience and its units can be based on the fact that Jones when fresh and in practice can recognize a group of sounds six (or thirty-six) seconds long?

Thirdly, the experiments rest on one sense only, hearing. It is clear that similar experiments could be performed for sight or touch (with light flashes or taps on the skin). But we have seen that the *minimum* for sound is one-twentieth of the minimum for sight. It seems likely that maxima for different senses would vary as widely.

Fourthly, it is possible to be using two senses at once (at a ballet performance). But then I shall be simultaneously apprehending specious presents of different lengths. And what then is *the* unit? Broad would have a particular difficulty here. For he says 'The special sense-fields of the various senses [sc. of a single subject] form part of a single general sense-field so far as temporal characteristics are concerned. Now *it* is of finite duration' (*Scientific Thought*, p. 360). But *what* duration, if two of the senses which contribute to its content have different specious presents?

Finally, the psychological evidence was based on hearing and was simply rhythmic. It included no variation in pitch. It was inferred that the group of sounds had been heard as a whole because it was recognized without error and without any analytic or symbolic aids, such as counting. But suppose pitch is added to rhythm; then you get a tune, instead of African drums. Now what is the longest tune which can be recognized without error? I should be surprised if the answer was as low as a minute (except for those with no musical ear at all). And I should not be surprised if a trained musician could run that figure up to five minutes or ten. Mozart said he could imagine a complete musical work in his mind. 'Nor do I hear in my imagination the parts successively; I hear them as it were all together' (Holmes, *Life of Mozart*, p. 317). If this is true it seems likely that he could have recognized without error an item half an hour long.

These points all seem to arise directly from the experimental evidence and to require no special analysis. They all tend to show that this evidence should not have been taken as leading to any general conclusions about the units of normal time experience.

There is a further point which arises if Broad's analysis is accepted. It will be remembered that he defined a specious present in terms of a momentary act of awareness and then got rid of the momentary act by the method of extensive abstraction. But this involved the admission that any *actual* specious present—being the datum of an act which endures a finite time, would be less than the 'defined' specious present. For example if the specious present as defined—*i.e.* for a momentary act—is six seconds, the specious present of an act of awareness lasting three seconds will be three seconds, that of an act lasting six seconds or more will be *nil*. My problem is this. It is clear that the empirical evidence was not based on momentary acts of awareness (for there are none). It is equally clear that no attempt was made to measure the duration of the acts of awareness, as well as measuring the duration of the sound groups apprehended. Yet without such additional measurement no definite results could be attained. But how could the duration of the act of attention have been measured? Suppose I listen to a drum-tap group and then listen to a second drum-tap group and identify it without error as having the same number of taps as the first. The question is this. How long did the act of awareness take which apprehended either group? Surely the most natural answer is that the act took as long as the group. But if the group is a maximum, we then have a contradiction; for the specious present of an act as long as the maximum is *nil*.

IV

It is interesting and, I think, significant that psychologists, ever since the original work of Wundt and his followers have tended to neglect the specious present. Woodrow's experiments which refuted the indifference point theory are the only ones of which I know in this field since 1890. Was this due to the fact that the notion had not been so clarified as to be a possible basis for future experiment? Or was it perhaps that the notion cannot be so clarified?

The only psychologist who has given consecutive and serious attention to the subject appears to be E. G. Boring. (*The Physical Dimensions of Consciousness* [1933], pp. 127 ff. *Temporal Perception and Operationism* [*American Journal of Psychology*, 48 (1936), p. 591]. *Sensation and Perception in the History of Experimental Psychology*, pp. 575 ff. I owe these references to Mr. B. A. Farrell.) I was interested to find how considerably Boring agreed with the conclusions I had already reached. In the first of these works Boring accepted the doctrine of the specious present and tried to make sense of it. But he makes two points. First, he is doubtful whether the specious present should be described as immediately or directly given since it involves an integration or principle of organization (the *rhythm* in the experiments of Wundt and Dietze) which can 'pick unities out of the continuous stream of time'. Secondly, he notices the difficulty of the 'act of apprehension'. 'If a duration is immediately observed, *when* do you observe it? . . . It is a foolish question. Observation is a process. It is not instantaneous and therefore cannot be confined to a single moment. . . . In the case under consideration, the observation in a way begins with the duration in question and it ends a little way after it, when the integration has fulfilled itself observationally. . . . It is just as true to say the observation is the end phase of the integration and therefore comes after it. In either case it is a process' (*op. cit.*, p. 137). In the article in the *American Journal of Psychology*, Boring develops his attack on 'immediacy', and links the specious present with this attack. Finally, in his later book (which includes a full account of the work on the specious present and a bibliography) he completely gives up the specious present doctrine. He points out that the doctrine was the outcome of the analytic method current in Wundt's time. 'What these men in Wundt's laboratory were hoping to find was a psychological unit of time. . . . Munsterberg was nearer the truth in 1889. He said that it was futile to look for fixed units of mental duration' (*op. cit.*, p. 580). Boring thinks this whole approach was mistaken. 'In modern positivistic psychology the problem has disappeared' (*op. cit.*, p. 577).

v

What are we to conclude? Our experience of temporal process is continuous (except during periods of total unconsciousness). Any sub-divisions within it can be made only in terms of content. Such sub-division is always to some extent arbitrary and sometimes impossible. (Arbitrary in the case of a *glissando* on the piano—a two-second *glissando* noise or thirty-seven brief noises; impossible in the case of a *glissando* on the violin—one noise or many, and if many how many?) But what then of the empirical evidence on which the specious present originally rested? We need not deny that groups of sounds can be recognized and identified without error. But this seems to be just a piece of empirical information which throws no light at all on the normal and invariable characteristics of our experience of time. In just the same way, the experiments on *minima* give us empirical information about certain time experiences. But we should not go on to conclude that they have any bearing on our normal experience—for example that my awareness of a sound consists of a series of sounds each 0.002 second long.

The specious present theory was right in holding that it is impossible to be aware of an event with no duration at all. But Reid had insisted on this long before Wundt's time. Any attempt to discover the duration of the unit-events which make up the temporal process of normal experience is doomed to failure.

The recognition of sound groups is a particular case of 'gestalt' apprehension. The experimentalists found that a group of sixteen sounds was more easily recognized if it were given in a pattern of four fours or eight pairs than if given evenly or in random sub-groups. Gestalt psychologists themselves do not appear to have emphasized the gestalt character as defining the units of our experience of time. An example of such a definition is, however, given by M. A. Tinker (*Psychology*, edited by Boring, Langfeld and Weld, 1935, p. 247). 'The conscious present is the length of time than an integrated whole—a musical phrase or a joke—takes; it is the duration of any series of events that depends on its temporal completeness for its proper psychological functioning.' This goes further than Tinker supposes. A Bach fugue depends on its temporal completeness for its proper psychological functioning and it may last fifteen minutes. So does one of the démodé short stories of O. Henry with the point in the tail. And there are longer jokes still—for example George Orwell's *Animal Farm*. Koffka himself deals with the units of time-perception in chapter xv of the *Principles of Gestalt Psychology*. He says 'The present or the unit for time perception is determined by homogeneity of stimulation'. This, I take it, is the physiological equivalent of my view that qualitative differences of content alone determine subdivisions within our continuous experience. But Koffka also gives examples to show how the past determines the present, for example how the perceived character of a note depends on its setting in a phrase or tune. Here the isolated note cannot be taken as the unit.

VI

To sum up. I have been arguing that the whole conception of units of temporal experience is mistaken; that this conception provided the stimulus for the experiments on which the specious present theory was founded; that the work on the specious present theory (while providing interesting empirical data about certain gestalt time experiences) does not justify any conclusions about time experience in general; and that the specious present doctrine as described and defended by psychologists and as rationalized and clarified by Broad is an untenable hypothesis. These conclusions are of course mainly negative. I have a further negative conclusion which I add more tentatively. This paper is called 'Our Direct Experience of Time'. In the course of my analysis of the specious present theory I have become (as Boring did for very different reasons) steadily more dubious about the word 'direct'. Owl cries and swishings of rain might be said to be directly experienced. But then follow gestalt cases where the unity depends on a form or pattern, which might be repeated in different keys and still recognized without any awareness of the change of key. Or they might be repeated in a different medium altogether, buzzes instead of taps, and recognized again. Then there were musical phrases and tunes; and then again there are jokes. All the time we are moving further from the notion of direct or immediate experience, if this means absence of organization, of structure, of intelligible relations. Immediate experience, pure sensation, here as elsewhere seems to be not a ubiquitous datum, not a necessary ingredient, not a basic constituent of our experience, to be revealed there by careful analysis. It seems to be more like a limiting case to which experience sometimes approximates, but into which it would be dangerous to import those discriminable time factors discoverable in developed experience. But these more tentative conclusions go beyond the intentions of the present paper, which is meant primarily to show that the specious present is 'specious' in a sense not intended by its supporters.

THE STATUS OF TEMPORAL BECOMING

ADOLF GRÜNBAUM

ADOLF GRÜNBAUM is Andrew Mellon Professor of Philosophy at the University of Pittsburgh and President of the Philosophy of Science Association (1965–68). He is the author of *Philosophical Problems of Space and Time* and of *Modern Science and Zeno's Paradoxes.*

1. *The Issue of the Mind-Dependence of Becoming*

In the common-sense view of the world, it is of the very essence of time that events occur now, or are past or future. Furthermore, events are held to change with respect to belonging to the future or the present. Our commonplace use of tenses codifies our experience that any particular present is superseded by another whose event-content thereby "comes into being." It is this occurring *now* or coming into being of previously future events and their subsequent belonging to the past which is called "becoming." But the past and the future can be characterized as respectively before and after the present. Hence I shall center my account of becoming on the status of the present or now as an attribute of events which is encountered in *perceptual* awareness.

Granted that becoming is a prominent feature of our temporal awareness, I ask: *Must* becoming therefore also be a feature of the temporal order of physical events *independently* of our awareness of them, as the common-sense view supposes it to be? And if not, is there anything within physical theory per se to warrant this common-sense conclusion?

It is apparent that the becoming of physical events in our temporal awareness does not itself guarantee that becoming has a mind-independent physical status. Common-sense color attributes, for example, surely *appear* to be properties of physical objects independently of our awareness of them and are held to be such by common sense. And yet scientific theory tells us that they are mind-dependent qualities the way that sweet and sour are. Of course, if physical theory claims that, contrary to common sense, becoming is not a feature of the temporal order of physical events with respect to earlier and later, then a more comprehensive scientific and philosophical theory must take suitable cognizance of becoming as a conspicuous characteristic of our temporal awareness of both physical and mental events.

In this article, I aim to clarify the status of temporal becoming by dealing with each of the questions posed above. Clearly, an account of becoming that provides answers to these questions is *not* an *analysis* of what the common-sense man actually *means* when he says that a physical event belongs to the present, past, or future; instead, such an account is concerned with how these ascriptions ought to be construed within the framework of a theory which supplants the scientifically untutored view of common sense. That the common-sense view is indeed scientifically untutored is evident from the fact that *at a time t,* both of the following physical events qualify as occurring "now" or "belonging to the present" according to that view: (i) a stellar explosion that occurred several million years before time *t* but is first seen on earth at time *t,* (ii) a lightning flash originating only a fraction of a second before *t* and observed at time *t.* If it be objected that present-day common-sense beliefs have begun to allow for the finitude of the speed of light, then I reply that they err at least to the extent of associating absolute simultaneity with the now.

The temporal relations of earlier (before) and later (after) can obtain between two physical events independently of the transient now and independently of any mind. On the other hand, the classification of events into past, present and future, which is inherent to becoming, requires reference to the transient now as well as to the relations of earlier and later. Hence the issue of the mind-dependence of becoming turns on the status of the transient now. And to assert in this context that becoming is mind-dependent is *not* to assert that the obtaining of the relation of temporal precedence among physical events is mind-dependent.

That being understood, I can state my thesis as follows: Becoming is mind-dependent because it is not an attribute of physical events per se but requires the occurrence of states of *conceptualized awareness*. These states of awareness register the occurrence of physical and mental events as sustaining certain apparent time relations to the states of awareness. The doctrine that becoming is mind-dependent has been misnamed "the theory of the block universe." I shall therefore wish to dissociate the thesis both from serious misunderstandings of its critics and from the very misleading suggestions of the metaphors used by some of its exponents. Besides stating my positive reasons for asserting the mind-dependence of becoming, I shall defend my thesis against the major objections that have been raised against it.

2. *The Distinction between Temporal Becoming and the Anisotropy of Time*

In order to treat these various issues without risking serious confusions, we must make a sharp distinction between two questions: (i) Do physical events *become* independently of any conceptualized awareness of their occurrence, and (ii) Are there any kinds of physical or biological processes which are *irreversible* on the strength of the laws of nature and/or of *de facto* prevailing boundary conditions? I shall first state how these two questions have come to be identified with each other and will then explain why to do so is indeed an error of consequence. The second, which pertains to irreversibility, is often formulated by asking whether the time of physics and biology has an "arrow." Then the existence of an arrow is misleadingly spoken of as though it constituted a "one-way forward flow of time"—the same metaphor used for becoming, on the strength of its being conceived as the forward "movement" of the present. And this misidentification is used to buttress the false belief that an affirmative answer to the question about irreversibility entails an affirmative answer to the question about becoming. To see why I claim that there is indeed a weighty misidentification here, let us first specify what is involved logically when we inquire into the existence of kinds of processes in nature which are irreversible.

If the system of world lines, each of which represents the career of a physical object, is to exhibit a one-dimensional temporal order, relations of simultaneity between spatially separated events are required to define world states. For our purposes, it will suffice to use the simultaneity criterion of some one local inertial frame of the special theory of relativity instead of resorting to the cosmic time of some cosmological model.

Assume now that the events belonging to *each* world line are invariantly ordered by a *betweenness* relation having the following formal property of the spatial betweenness of the points on a Euclidean straight line: of any three elements, only one can be between the other two. This betweenness of the events is clearly temporal rather than spatial, since it *invariantly* relates the events belonging to each individual world line while no such spatial betweenness obtains invariantly.[1] So long as the temporal betweenness of the world lines is formally Euclidean in the specified sense, any two events on one of them or any two world states can serve to define two time senses which are *ordinally* opposite to each other with respect to the assumed temporal betweenness relations.[2] And the members of the simultaneity-classes of events constituting one of these two opposite senses can then bear lower real number co-ordinates while those of the other sense can bear the higher co-ordinates. It is immaterial at this stage which is assigned the higher real numbers. All we

[1] For example, consider the events in the careers of human beings or of animals who return to a spatially fixed terrestrial habitat every so often. These events occur at space points on the earth which certainly do *not* exhibit the betweenness of the points on a Euclidean straight line.

[2] For details, cf. A. Grünbaum, *Philosophical Problems of Space and Time*, New York, 1963, pp. 214–16. Hereafter this work will be cited as *PPST*.

require is that the real number co-ordinatization reflect the temporal betweenness relations among the events as follows: events that are temporally between two given events E and E' must bear real number co-ordinates that are numerically between the time co-ordinates of E and E'. Employing some one-time co-ordinatization meeting this minimal requirement, we can use the locutions "initial state," "final state," "before" and "after" on the basis of the magnitudes of the real number co-ordinates, entirely without prejudice as to whether there are irreversible kinds of processes.[3] By an "irreversible process" (à la Planck) we understand a process such that no counterprocess is capable of restoring the original *kind* of state of the system at another time. Note that the temporal vocabulary used in this definition of what is meant by an irreversible kind of process does *not* assume tacitly that there *are* irreversible processes: as used here, the terms "original state," "restore," and "counterprocess" presuppose only the co-ordinatization based on the assumed betweenness.

It has been charged that one is guilty of an illicit spatialization of time if one speaks of temporal betweenness while still leaving it open whether there are irreversible kinds of processes. But this charge overlooks the fact that the *formal* property of the betweenness on the Euclidean line which I invoked is abstract and, as such, neither spatial nor temporal. And the meaningful attribution of this formal property to the betweenness relation among the events belonging to each world line without any assumption of irreversibility is therefore *not* any kind of illicit spatialization of time. It would be no more absurd to say that since temporal betweenness does have this abstract property, the ascription of the latter to the

[3] This non-committal character of the term "initial state" seems to have been recognized by O. Costa de Beauregard in one part of his paper entitled "Irreversibility Problems," *Proceedings of the 1964 International Congress for Logic, Methodology and Philosophy of Science*, North-Holland Publishing Co., Amsterdam, 1965, p. 327. But when discussing my criticism of Reichenbach's account of irreversibility (*PPST*, pp. 261–63), Beauregard (*op. cit.*, p. 331) overlooks the fact that my criticism invokes initial states in only the non-committal sense set forth above.

betweenness among the points on a line of space is a temporalization of space.[4]

Thus the assumption that the events belonging to each world line are invariantly ordered by an abstractly Euclidean relation of temporal betweenness does not entail the existence of irreversible kinds of processes, but allows every kind of process to be reversible. If there are irreversible processes, then the two ordinally opposite time senses are indeed *further* distinguished structurally as follows: there are certain kinds of sequences of states of systems specified in the order of increasing time co-ordinates such that these same kinds of sequences do *not* likewise exist in the order of decreasing time co-ordinates. Or, equivalently, the existence of irreversible processes *structurally* distinguishes the two opposite time senses as follows: there are certain kinds of sequences of states of systems specified in the order of *decreasing* time co-ordinates such that these same kinds of sequences do *not* likewise obtain in the order of increasing time co-ordinates. Accordingly, if there are irreversible kinds of processes, then time is *anisotropic*.[5] When physicists say with Eddington that time has an "arrow," it is this anisotropy to which they are

[4] Thus, it is erroneous to maintain, as M. Capek does (*The Philosophical Impact of Contemporary Physics*, Princeton, N.J., 1961, p. 349, also pp. 347 and 355) that the distinction between temporal betweenness and irreversibility is "fallacious" in virtue of being "based on the superficial and deceptive analogy of 'the course of time' with a geometrical line" (*ibid.*, p. 349). If Capek's condemnation of this distinction were correct, the following fundamental question of theoretical physics could not even be intelligibly and legitimately asked: Are the *prima facie* irreversible processes known to us indeed irreversible, and, if so, on the strength of what laws and/or boundary conditions are they so? For this question is predicated on the very distinction which Capek rejects as "fallacious."

By the same token, Capek errs (*ibid.*, p. 355) in saying that when Reichenbach characterizes entropically counterdirected epochs as "succeeding each other," then irreversibility "creeps in" along with the asymmetrical relations of before and after.

[5] For a discussion of the various kinds of irreversible processes which make for the anisotropy of time and furnish specified criteria for the relations of temporal precedence and succession, see Beauregard, *op. cit.*, p. 327, and Grünbaum, *PPST*, ch. 8.

referring metaphorically. Specifically, the spatial opposition between the head and the tail of the arrow represents the structural anisotropy of time.

Note that we were able to characterize a process as irreversible and time as anisotropic without any explicit or tacit reliance on the transient now or on tenses of past, present, and future.[6] By the same token, we are able to assert metaphorically that time has an "arrow" without any covert or outright reference to events as occurring *now*, happening at present, or coming into being. Nonetheless, the anisotropy of time symbolized by the arrow has been falsely equated in the literature with the transiency of the now or becoming of events via the following steps of reasoning: (1) the becoming of events is described by the kinematic metaphor "the flow of time" and is conceived as a *shifting* of the now which *singles out the future direction of time* as the sense of its "advance"; (2) although the physicist's arrow does not involve the transient now, his assertion that there is an arrow of time is taken to be equivalent to the claim that there is a *flow* of time in the direction of the future; this is done by attending to the head of the arrow *to the neglect of its tail* and identifying the former with the direction of "advance" of the now.

[6] Some have questioned the possibility of stating what specific physical events do occur in point of fact at particular clock times without covert appeal to the transient now. In their view, any physical description will employ a time co-ordinatization, and any such co-ordinatization must ostensively invoke the now to designate at least one state as, say, the origin of the time co-ordinates. But I do not see a genuine difficulty here, for two reasons. First, it is not clear that the designation of the birth of Jesus, for example, as the origin of time co-ordinates tacitly makes logically indispensable use of the now or of tenses. And secondly, in some cosmological models of the universe, an origin of time co-ordinates can clearly be designated non-ostensively: in the "big bang" model, the big bang itself can be designated uniquely and *non*-ostensively as the one state having no temporal predecessor. For a defense of the view that the specification of dates involves essential logical use of indexical signs like "now," cf. R. Gale, "Indexical Signs, Egocentric Particulars, and Token-Reflexive Words," to appear in *The Encyclopedia of Philosophy*, 1967. Gale's article also contains further references to some of the literature on this issue.

The physicist's assertion that time has an "arrow" discerningly codifies the empirical fact that the two ordinally opposite time senses are *structurally different* in specified respects. But in thus codifying this empirical fact, the physicist does *not* invoke the transient now to single out one of the two time senses as more significant than the other. By contrast, the claim that the present or now shifts in the direction of the future does invoke the transient now to single out one of the two time senses and—as we are about to see—is a mere truism like "all bachelors are males." For the terms "shift" or "flow" are used in their literal kinematic senses in such a way that the *spatial* direction of a shift or flow is specified by the locations of the shifting object at later times. Hence when we speak metaphorically of the now as "shifting" temporally in a particular *temporal* direction, it is then simply a matter of definition that the now shifts or advances in the direction of the future. For this declaration tells us no more than that the nows corresponding to later times are later than those corresponding to earlier ones, which is just as uninformative as the truism that the earlier nows precede the later ones.[7]

It is now apparent that to assert the existence of irreversible processes in the sense of physical theory by means of the metaphor of the arrow does not entail at all that there is a

[7] The claim that the now advances in the direction of the future is a truism as regards both the correspondence between nows and physically later clock times and their correspondence with psychologically (introspectively) later contents of awareness. What is *not* a truism, however, is that the *introspectively* later nows are *temporally correlated* with states of our physical environment that are later as per criteria furnished by irreversible physical processes. This latter correlation depends for its obtaining on the laws governing the physical and neural processes necessary for the *mental* accumulation of memories and for the registry of information *in awareness*. (For an account of some of the relevant laws, see Grünbaum, *PPST*, ch. 9, parts A and B.) Having exhibited the afore-mentioned truisms as such and having noted the role of the empirical laws just mentioned, I believe I have answered Beauregard's complaint (*op. cit.*, p. 337) that "stressing that the arrows of entropy and information increase are parallel to each other is *not* proving that the flow of subjectivistic time has to follow the arrows!"

mind-independent becoming of physical events as such. Hence those wishing to assert that becoming is independent of mind cannot base this claim on the anisotropy of physical time.

As it is only a tautology, the kinematic metaphor of time flowing in the direction of the future does not itself render any empirical fact about the time of our experience. But the role played by the present in becoming is a feature of the experienced world codified by common-sense time in the following informative sense: to each of a great diversity of events ordered with respect to earlier and later by physical clocks, there corresponds a particular experience of the event as occurring *now*. Hence we shall say that our experience exhibits a *diversity of "now-contents"* of awareness which are temporally ordered with respect to each of the relations earlier and later. Thus, it is a significant feature of the experienced world codified by common-sense time that there is a sheer diversity of nows, and in that sheer diversity the role of the future is no greater than that of the past. In this *directionally neutral* sense, therefore, it is informative to say that there is a *transiency* of the now or a coming-into-being of different events. And, of course, in the context of the respective relations of earlier and later, this flux of the present makes for events being past and future.

In order to deal with the issue of the mind-dependence of becoming, I wish to forestall misunderstandings that can arise from the use of the terms "become" and "come into being" in senses which are *tenseless*. These senses do *not* involve being present or occurring now as understood in tensed discourse, and I must emphasize strongly that my thesis of the mind-dependence of becoming pertains only to the *tensed* variety of becoming. Examples of tenseless uses of the terms "come into being," "become," and "now" are the following: (1) A child *comes into being* as a legal entity the moment it is conceived biologically. What is meant by this false assertion is that for legal purposes, the career of a child *begins* (tenselessly) at the moment at which the ovum is (tenselessly) fertilized. (2) If gunpowder is suitably ignited at any particular time t, an explosion comes into being at that time *t.* The species of coming into being meant here involves a common-sense event which is here asserted to *occur tenselessly at time t.* (3) When heated to a suitable temperature, a piece of iron becomes red. Clearly, this sentence asserts that after a piece of iron is (tenselessly) suitably heated, it is (tenselessly) red for an unspecified time interval. (4) In Minkowski's two-dimensional spatial representation of the space-time of special relativity, the event shown by the origin-point is called the "Here-NOW," and correlatively certain event classes in the diagram are respectively called "Absolute PAST" and "Absolute FUTURE"; but Minkowski's "Here-NOW" denotes an arbitrarily chosen event of reference which can be chosen *once and for all* and continues to qualify as "now" at various times independently of when the diagram is used. Hence there is no transiency of the now in the relativistic scheme depicted by Minkowski, and his absolute past and absolute future are simply absolutely earlier and absolutely later than the arbitrarily chosen fixed reference event called "Here-NOW."[8] Accordingly, we must be mindful that there are tenseless senses of the words "becoming" and "now."

But conversely we must realize that some important *seemingly* tenseless uses of the terms "to exist," "to occur," "to be actual," and "to have being or reality" are in fact laden with the present tense. Specifically, all of these terms are often used in the sense of to occur NOW. And by tacitly making the *nowness* of an event a necessary condition for its occurrence, existence, or reality, philosophers have argued fallaciously as follows: They first assert that the universe can be held to exist only to the extent that there are present events; then they invoke the correct premise that the existence of the physical universe is not mind-dependent and conclude from the first assertion that being present, occurring now, or becoming is *independent* of mind or awareness. Thus, Thomas Hobbes wrote: "The present only has a being in nature; things

[8] A very illuminating account of the logical relations of Minkowski's language to tensed discourse is given by W. Sellars in "Time and the World Order," *Minnesota Studies in the Philosophy of Science,* Vol. III, ed. by H. Feigl and G. Maxwell, Minneapolis, 1962, p. 571.

past have a being in the memory only, but things to come have no being at all, the future being but a fiction of the mind. . . ."[9] When declaring here that only present events or present memories of past events "have being," Hobbes *appears* to be appealing to a sense of "to have being" or of "to exist" which is *logically independent* of the concept of existing-NOW. But his claim depends for its plausibility on the invocation of *present* occurrence as a necessary condition for having being or existing. Once this fact is recognized, his claim that "the present only has a being in nature" is seen to be the mere tautology that "only what exists now does indeed exist now." And by his covert appeal to the irresistible conviction carried by this triviality, he makes plausible the utterly unfounded conclusion that nature can be held to exist only to the extent that there are *present* events and *present* memories of past events. Clearly the fact that an event does not occur now does not justify the conclusion that it does not occur at some time or other.

3. *The Mind-Dependence of Becoming*

Once cognizant of these logical pitfalls, we can turn to the following important question: if a physical event occurs *now* (at present, in the present), what attribute or relation of its occurrence can warrantedly be held to qualify it as such.

In asking this question, we are being mindful of the following fact: if at a given clock time t_0 it is true to say of a particular event E that it is occurring now or happening at present, then this claim could not also be truly made at all other clock times $t \neq t_0$. And hence we must distinguish the tensed assertion of *present* occurrence from the tenseless assertion that the event E occurs at the time t_0: namely, the latter tenseless assertion, if true at all, can truly be made at all times t other than t_0 no less than at the time t_0. By the same token we must guard against identifying the tensed assertion that the event E happens at present from the tenseless assertion that the event E occurs or "is present" at time t_0. And similarly for the distinction between the tensed senses of being past or being future, on the one hand, and

[9] Quoted from G. J. Whitrow, *The Natural Philosophy of Time*, London, 1961, pp. 129–30.

the tenseless senses of being past *at time* t_0 or being future at time t_0, on the other. Thus our question is: what *over and above its otherwise tenseless occurrence at a certain clock time t*, in fact at a time t, characterizes a physical event as *now* or as belonging to the present? It will be well remembered from Section 1 why my construal of this question does *not* call for an analysis of the common-sense meaning of "now" or of "belonging to the present" but for a critical assessment of the status which common sense attributes to the present.[10] Given this construal of the question, my reply to it is: what qualifies a physical event at a time t as belonging to the present or as now is not some physical attribute of the event or some relation it sustains to other purely physical events; instead what so qualifies the event is that at the time t at least one human or other *mind-possessing* organism M is conceptually aware of experiencing the event at that time.[11] But what is the content of M's conceptual awareness at time t that he is experiencing a certain event *at that time*? M's experience of the event at time t is coupled with a state of *knowing* that he has that experience at all. And that awareness does not, in general, comprise information concerning the date and numerical clock time of the occurrence of the event. In other words, M experiences

[10] For a searching treatment of the ramifications of the contrast pertinent here, see W. Sellars, "Philosophy and the Scientific Image of Man," *Frontiers of Science and Philosophy*, edited by Robert G. Colodny (Pittsburgh: University of Pittsburgh Press, 1962), pp. 35-78.

[11] It will be noted that I speak here of the dependence of nowness on an organism M which is mind-possessing in the sense of having conceptualized or judgmental awareness, as contrasted with mere sentiency. Since biological organisms other than man (e.g., extra-terrestrial ones) may be mind-possessing in this sense, it would be unwarrantedly restrictive to speak of the mind-dependence of nowness as its "anthropocentricity." Indeed, it might be that conceptualized awareness turns out not to require a *biochemical* substratum but can also inhere in a suitably complex "hardware" computer. That a physical substratum of some kind is required would seem to be abundantly supported by the known dependence of the content and very existence of consciousness in man or the adequate functioning on the human body.

M*

the event at t and is aware at t of having that certain experience *simultaneously* with an awareness of the fact of having it at all. For example, if I just hear a noise at a time t, then the noise does not qualify at t as *now* unless at t I am judgmentally aware of the fact of my hearing it at all and of the temporal coincidence of the hearing with that awareness.[12] If the event at the time t is itself a mental event (e.g. a pain), then there is no distinction between the event and our experience of it. With this understanding, I claim that what confers nowness at a time t on either a physical or a mental event is that the *experience* of the event satisfies the specified requirements. And by satisfying these requirements, the *experience* of a physical event qualifies at the time t as occurring *now*. Moreover, the mere fact that the experience of a physical event qualifies as now at a time t allows that in point of physical fact the physical event itself occurred millions of years before t, as in the case of now seeing an

[12] The distinction pertinent here between the mere hearing of something and judgmental awareness that it is being heard is well stated by R. Chisholm as follows:

We may say of a man simply that he observes a cat on the roof. Or we may say of him that he observes *that* a cat is on the roof. In the second case, the verb "observe" takes a "that"-clause, a propositional clause as its grammatical object. We may distinguish, therefore, between a "propositional" and a "nonpropositional" use of the term "observe," and we may make an analogous distinction for "perceive," "see," "hear," and "feel."

If we take the verb "observe" propositionally, saying of the man that he observes that a cat is on the roof, or that he observes a cat to be on the roof, then we may also say of him that he *knows* that a cat is on the roof; for in the propositional sense of "observe," observation may be said to imply knowledge. But if we take the verb nonpropositionally, saying of the man only that he observes a cat which is on the roof, then what we say will not imply that he knows that there is a cat on the roof. For a man may be said to observe a cat, to see a cat, or hear a cat, in the nonpropositional sense of these terms, without his knowing that a cat is what it is that he is observing, or seeing, or hearing. "It wasn't until the following day that I found out that what I saw was only a cat." [R. M. Chisholm, *Theory of Knowledge* (Englewood Cliffs, New Jersey: Prentice-Hall, Inc., 1966), p. 10.] I am indebted to Richard Gale for this reference.

explosion of a star millions of light years away. Hence the perceptual ascription of presentness to a physical event at a time *t* does *not* warrant the conclusion that the clock time of the event is *t* or some *particular* time before *t*.

Note several crucial commentaries on this characterization of the now:

(1) My characterization of *present* happening or occurring *now* is intended to *deny* that belonging to the present is a physical attribute of a physical event E which is *independent* of any judgmental awareness of the occurrence of E. But I am *not* offering a *definition* of the adverbial attribute now, which belongs to the conceptual framework of tensed discourse, in terms of attributes and relations drawn from the tenseless (Minkowskian) framework of temporal discourse familiar from physics. Thus, my characterization is *non-viciously circular*. And I am very much less concerned with the adequacy of the specifics of my characterization than with its thesis of mind-dependence. For example, my characterization may need some revision, if an awareness cannot have its own simultaneity relation as an intentional object.

(2) It makes nowness (and thereby pastness and futurity) depend on the existence of conceptualized awareness that an experience is being had and points out the insufficiency of the mere having of the experience. If I at time *t* express such conceptualized awareness in a linguistic utterance, then the quasi-simultaneity of the experience with that utterance can serve to qualify the experienced event as occurring now.[13]

[13]The judgmental awareness which I claim to be essential to an event's qualifying as now may, of course, be expressed by a linguistic utterance, but it clearly need not be so expressed. I therefore consider an account of nowness which is *confined* to utterances as inadequate. Such an overly restrictive account is given in J. J. C. Smart's otherwise illuminating defense of the anthropocentricity of tense [*Philosophy and Scientific Realism* (London: Routledge & Kegan Paul, 1963), Chapter vii]. But this undue restrictiveness is quite inessential to his thesis of the anthropocentricity of nowness. And the non-restrictive treatment which I am advocating in its stead would obviate his having to rest his case on (i) *denying* that "this utterance" can be analyzed as "the utterance which is *now*" and (2) insisting that "now" must be elucidated in terms of "this utterance" [*ibid.*, pp. 139-140].

(3) *In the first instance,* only an experience (i.e. a mental event) can ever qualify as occurring now, and moreover a mental event (e.g. a pain) must meet the specified awareness requirements in order to qualify. A *physical* event like an explosion can qualify as now at some time t only *derivatively* in one of the following two ways: (a) someone's *experience* of the physical event does so qualify, or (b) if unperceived, the physical event must be simultaneous with another physical event that does so qualify in the derivative sense indicated under (a). For the sake of brevity, I shall refer to this complex state of affairs by saying that independently of being perceived, physical events themselves qualify at no time as occurring now and hence as such do not become.

(4) My characterization of the now is narrow enough to exclude past and future events since they do not satisfy its simultaneity requirement. It is to be understood here that the *reliving* of an event, however vivid it may be, is *not* to be misleadingly called an "experience" of the event.

My claim that nowness is mind-dependent does not assert at all that the nowness of an event is arbitrary. On the contrary, it follows from my account that it is not at all arbitrary what event or events qualify as being *now* at any given time t. To this extent, my account accords with common sense. But I repudiate much of what common sense conceives to be the status of the now. Thus, when I wonder in thought (which I *may* convey by means of an interrogative verbal utterance) whether it is 3 P.M. Eastern Standard Time now, I am asking myself the following: Is the particular percept of which I am now aware when asking this question a member of the simultaneity class of events which qualify as occurring at 3 P.M. EST on this particular day? And when I wonder in thought about what is happening now, I am asking the question: What events of which I am not aware are simultaneous with the particular now-percept of which I *am* aware upon asking this question?

That the nowness attribute of an occurrence when ascribed non-arbitrarily to an event is inherently mind-dependent seems to me to emerge from a consideration of the kind of information which the judgment "It is 3 P.M. EST now" can be warrantedly held to convey. Clearly such a judgment is informative, unlike the judgment "All bachelors are males." But if the word "now" in the informative temporal judgment does not designate a particular content of conceptualized awareness or the linguistic utterance which renders it at the time, then there would seem to be nothing left for it to designate other than either the events already identified as occurring at 3 P.M. EST or those identified as occurring at some other time. In the former case, the initially informative temporal judgment "It is 3 P.M. EST now" turns into the utter triviality that the events of 3 P.M. EST occur at 3 P.M. EST! And in the latter case, the initially informative judgment, if false in point of fact, becomes self-contradictory.

What of the retort to this objection that, independently of being perceived, physical events themselves possess an unanalyzable property of presentness (i.e. nowness) over and above merely occurring at certain clock times? I find this retort wholly unavailing for several reasons. (1) It must construe the assertion "It is 3 P.M. EST now" as claiming *nontrivially* that when the clock strikes 3 P.M. on the day in question, this clock event and all the events simultaneous with it intrinsically have the unanalyzable property of nowness or presentness. But I am totally at a loss to see that anything non-trivial can possibly be asserted by the claim that at 3 P.M. nowness (presentness) inheres in the events of 3 P.M. For all I am able to discern here is that the events of 3 P.M. are indeed those of 3 P.M. on the day in question! (2) It seems to me of decisive significance that no cognizance is taken of nowness (in the sense associated with becoming) in any of the extant theories of physics. If nowness were a fundamental property of physical events themselves, then it would be very strange indeed that it could go unrecognized in all extant physical theories *without detriment to their explanatory success.* And I hold with Reichenbach[14] that "if there is Becoming [independently of awareness] the physicist must know it." (3) As we shall have occasion to note near the end of § 4, the thesis that nowness is *not* mind-dependent poses a serious perplexity pointed out by J. J. C.

[14] H. Reichenbach, *The Direction of Time*, Berkeley, 1956, p. 16.

Smart, and its defenders have not even been able to hint how they might resolve that perplexity without utterly trivializing the thesis.

The claim that an event can be now (present) only upon being experienced accords fully, of course, with the common-sense view that there is no more than one time at which a particular event is present and that this time cannot be chosen arbitrarily. But if an event is ever experienced at all in such a way that there is simultaneous awareness of the fact of that experience, then there exists a time at which the event does qualify as being now.

The relation of the conception of becoming espoused here to that of common sense may be likened to the relation of relativity physics to Newtonian physics. My account of now-ness as mind-dependent disavows rather than vindicates the common-sense view of its status. Similarly, relativity physics entails the falsity of the results of its predecessor. Though Newtonian physics cannot be reduced to relativity physics (in the technical sense of reducing one theory to another), the latter enables us to see why the former works as well as it does in the domain of low velocities: relativity theory shows (via a comparison of the Lorentz and Galilean transformations) that the observational results of the Newtonian theory in that domain are sufficiently correct numerically for some practical purposes. In an analogous manner, my account of nowness enables us to see why the common-sense concept of becoming can function as it does in serving the practical needs of daily life.

A *now-content* of awareness can comprise awareness that one event is later than or succeeds another, as in the following examples: (1) When I perceive the "tick-tock" of a clock, the "tick" is not yet part of my past when I hear the "tock."[15] As William James and Hans Driesch have noted, melody awareness is another such case of quasi-instantaneous aware-ness of succession.[16] (2) Memory states are ingredients in now-contents when we have awareness of other events as be-

[15] P. Fraisse, *The Psychology of Time*, tr. by J. Leith, Eyre & Spottiswoode, London, 1964, p. 73.

[16] Grünbaum, *PPST*, p. 325.

ing earlier than the event of our awareness of them. (3) A now-content can comprise an envisionment of an event as being later than its ideational anticipation.

4. Critique of Objections to the Mind-Dependence of Becoming

Before dealing with some interesting objections to the thesis of the mind-dependence of becoming, I wish to dispose of some of the caricatures of that thesis, under the misnomer of "the theory of the block universe," with which the literature has been rife. The worst of these is the allegation that the thesis asserts the timelessness of the universe and espouses, in M. Capek's words, the "preposterous view . . . that . . . time is merely a huge and chronic hallucination of the human mind."[17] Even the most misleading of the spatial metaphors that have been used by the defenders of the mind-dependence thesis do not warrant the inference that the thesis denies the objectivity of the so-called "time-like separations" of events known from the theory of relativity. To assert that nowness and thereby pastness and futurity are mind-dependent is surely *not* to assert that the earlier-later relations between the events of a world line are mind-dependent, let alone hallucinatory.

The mind-dependence thesis does deny that physical events themselves happen in the tensed sense of coming into being apart from anyone's awareness of them. But the thesis clearly avows that physical events do happen independently of any mind in the tenseless sense of merely occurring at certain clock times in the context of objective relations of earlier and later. Thus it is a travesty to equate the objective *becominglessness* of physical events asserted by the thesis with a claim of *timelessness*. In this way the thesis of mind-dependence is misrepresented as entailing that all events happen simultaneously or form a *"totum simul."*[18] But it is

[17] Capek, *op. cit.*, p. 337.

[18] On the basis of such a misunderstanding, Capek incorrectly charges the thesis with a "spatialization of time" in which "successive moments already *coexist*" (*op. cit.*, pp. 160–63) and in which "the universe with its whole history is conceived as a single huge and timeless bloc, given at once" (p. 163). See also p. 355.

an egregious blunder to think that if the time of physics lacks *passage* in the sense of there not being a transient now, then physical events cannot be temporally separated and must all be simultaneous.

A typical example of such a misconstrual of Weyl's and Einstein's denial of physical passage is the supposition that they claimed "that the world is like a film strip: the photographs *are already there* [my italics] and are merely being exhibited to us."[19] When photographs of a film strip "are already there," they exist *simultaneously*. But it is wrong to identify Weyl's denial of physical becoming with the pseudo-image of the "block universe" and then to charge his denial with entailing the absurdity that all events are simultaneous. Thus Whitrow says erroneously: "the theory of 'the block universe' . . . implies that past (and future) events coexist with those that are present."[20] We shall see in § 5 that a corresponding error vitiates the allegation that determinism entails the absurd contemporaneity of all events. And it simply begs the question to declare in this context that *"the passage of time . . . is the very essence of the concept."*[21] For the undeniable fact that passage in the sense of transiency of the now is integral to the common-sense concept of time may show only that, in this respect, this concept is anthropocentric.

The becomingless physical world of the Minkowski representation is viewed *sub specie aeternitatis* in that representation in the sense that the relativistic account of time represented by it makes no reference to the particular times of anyone's *now*-perspectives. And, as J. J. C. Smart observed, "the tenseless way of talking does not therefore imply that physical things or events are eternal in the way in which the number 7 is."[22] We must therefore reject Whitrow's odd claim that according to the relativistic conception of Minkowski, "external events *permanently* [my italics] exist and we merely come across them."[23] According to Minkowski's con-

[19] Whitrow, *op. cit.*, p. 228. For a criticism of another such misconstruction, see Grünbaum, *PPST*, pp. 327–28.

[20] Whitrow, *op. cit.*, p. 88.

[21] *Ibid.*, pp. 227–28.

[22] Smart, *op. cit.*, p. 139.

[23] Whitrow, *op. cit.*, p. 88, n. 2.

ception, an event qualifies as a *becomingless* occurrence by occurring in a network of relations of earlier and later and thus can be said to occur "at a certain time *t*." Hence to assert tenselessly that an event exists (occurs) is to claim that there is a time or clock reading *t* with which it coincides. But surely this assertion does not entail the absurdity that the event exists (occurs) at *all* clock times or "permanently." To occur tenselessly at some time *t* is not at all the same as to exist "permanently."

Whitrow himself acknowledges Minkowski's earlier-later relations when he says correctly that "the relativistic picture of the world recognizes only a difference between earlier and later and not between past, present, and future."[24] But he goes on to query: "if no events *happen*, except our observations, we might well ask—why are the latter exceptional?"[25] I reply first of all: But Minkowski asserts that events happen tenselessly in the sense of occurring at certain clock times. And as for the exceptional status of the events which we register in observational awareness, I make the following obvious but only partial retort: being registered in awareness, these events are *eo ipso* exceptional.

I say that this retort is only partial because behind Whitrow's question there lurks a more fundamental query, a query that must be answered by those of us who claim with Russell that "past, present and future arise from time-relations of subject and object, while earlier and later arise from time-relations of object and object."[26] The query is: Whence the becoming in the case of mental events that become and are causally dependent on physical events, given that physical events themselves do not become independently of being perceived but occur tenselessly? More specifically, the question is: if our *experiences* of (extra- and/or intradermal) physical events are causally dependent upon these events, how is it that the former *mental* events can properly qualify

[24] *Ibid.*, p. 293.
[25] *Ibid.*, p. 88, n. 2.
[26] B. Russell, "On the Experience of Time," *Monist*, 25 (1915), 212.

as being "now," whereas the eliciting physical events *themselves* do not so qualify, and yet both kinds of events are (severally and collectively) alike related by quasi-serial relations of earlier and later?[27]

But, as I see it, this question does not point to evidence refuting the mind-dependence of becoming. Instead, its force is to demand the recognition (a) that the complex mental states of judgmental awareness as such have distinctive features of their own and (b) that the articulation of these features as part of a theoretical account of "the place of mind in nature" acknowledge *what may be peculiar to the time of awareness*. That the existence of features peculiar to the time of awareness does not pose perplexities militating against the mind-dependence of becoming seems to me to emerge from the following three counter questions, which I now address to critics:

(1) Why is the mind-dependence of becoming more perplexing than the mind-dependence of common-sense color attributes? That is, why is the former more puzzling than that physical events such as the reflection of certain kinds of photons from a surface causally induce mental events such as seeing blue, which are qualitatively fundamentally different in some respects? In asking this question, I am *not* assuming that nowness is a *sensory quality* like red or sweet, but only that nowness and sensory qualities alike depend on awareness.

(2) Likewise assuming the causal dependence of mental on physical events, why is the mind-dependence of becoming more puzzling than the fact that the raw-feel components of mental events, such as a particular event of seeing green, are not members of the *spatial* order of physical events?[28] Yet mental events and the raw-feel ingredient in them are

[27] The need to deal with this question has been pointed out independently by Donald C. Williams and Richard Gale.

[28] Mental events, as distinct from the neurophysiological counterpart states which they require for their occurrence, are *not* in our heads in the way in which, say, a bio-chemical event in the cortex or medulla oblongata is.

part of a time system that comprises physical events as well.[29]

(3) Mental events must differ from physical ones in some respect qua being mental, as illustrated by their not being members of the same system of spatial order. Why then should it be puzzling that on the strength of the *distinctive* nature of conceptualized awareness and self-awareness, mental events differ further from physical ones with respect to becoming, while both kinds of events sustain temporal relations of simultaneity and precedence?

What is the reasoning underlying the critics' belief that their question has the capability of pointing to the refutation of the mind-dependence of becoming? Their reasoning seems to me reminiscent of Descartes' misinvocation of the principle that there must be nothing more in the effect than is in the cause apropos of one of his arguments for the existence of God: the more perfect, he argued, cannot proceed from the less perfect as its efficient and total cause. The more perfect, i.e., temporal relations involving becoming, critics argue, cannot proceed from the less perfect, i.e., becomingless physical time, as its efficient cause. By contrast, I reason that nowness (and thereby pastness and futurity) are features of events *as experienced* conceptually, *not* because becoming is likewise a feature of the physical events which causally elicit our awareness of them, but because these elicited states are indeed specified states of *awareness*. Once we recognize the role of awareness here, then the diversity and order of the events of which we have awareness in the form of now-contents give rise to the transiency of the now as explained in § 3 above—if due caution is exercised, as I emphasized there, that this transiency not be construed tautologically.

In asserting the mind-dependence of becoming, I fully allow that the kind of neurophysiological brain state underlying our mere awareness of an event as simply occurring now differs in specifiable ways from the kinds underlying ticktock or melody-awareness, memory-awareness, anticipation-

[29] Thus a conscious state of elation induced in me by the receipt of good news from a telephone call C_1 could be *temporally between* the physical chain C_1 and another such chain C_2 consisting of my telephonic transmission of the good news to someone else.

awareness, and dream-free sleep. But I cannot see why the states of awareness that make for becoming must have physical event-counterparts that isomorphically become in their own right. Hence I believe I have coped with Whitrow's question as to why only perceived events become. Indeed, it seems to me that the thesis of mind-dependence is altogether free from an important perplexity which besets the opposing claim that physical events are inherently past, present, and future. This perplexity was stated by Smart as follows: "If past, present, and future were real properties of events [i.e. properties possessed by physical events independently of being perceived], then it would require [non-trivial] explanation that an event which becomes present [i.e. qualifies as occurring *now*] in 1965 becomes present [now] at that date and not at some other (and this would have to be an explanation over and above the explanation of why an event of this sort occurred in 1965)."[30] It would, of course, be a complete trivialization of the thesis of the mind-*in*dependence of becoming to reply that *by definition* an event occurring at a certain clock time *t* has the unanalyzable attribute of nowness at time *t*.

Thus to the question "Whence the becoming in the case of mental events that become and are causally dependent on physical events that do not themselves become?", I reply: "Becoming can characterize mental events qua their being both bits of *awareness* and sustaining relations of temporal order."

The awareness which each of several human percipients has of a given physical event can be such that all of them are alike prompted to give the same tensed description of the external event. Thus, suppose that the effects of a given physical event are simultaneously registered in the awareness of several percipients such that they each perceive the event as occurring at essentially the time of their first awareness of it. Then they may each think at that time that the event be-

[30] Smart, *op. cit.*, p. 135.

longs to the present. The parity of access to events issuing in this sort of intersubjectivity of tense has prompted the common-sense belief that the nowness of a physical event is an intrinsic, albeit transient attribute of the event. But this kind of intersubjectivity does not discredit the mind-dependence of becoming; instead, it serves to show that the becoming present of an event, though mind-dependent no less than a pain, need not be private as a pain is. Some specific person's particular pain is private in the sense that this person has privileged access to its raw-feel component.[31] The mind-dependence of becoming is no more refuted by such intersubjectivity as obtains in regard to tense than the mind-dependence of common-sense color attributes is in the least disproven by agreement among several percipients as to the color of some chair.

5. Becoming and the Conflict Between Determinism and Indeterminism

If the doctrine of mind-dependence of becoming is correct, a very important consequence follows, which seems to have been previously overlooked: since the nowness of events is generated by our conceptualized awareness of them, their *nowness is made possible by processes sufficiently macro-deterministic (causal) to assure the requisitely high correlation between the occurrence of an event and someone's being made suitably aware of it.* In short, insofar as there is a transient present, it is made possible—as is empirical knowledge generally—by the existence of the requisite degree of macro-determinism in the physical world. And clearly, therefore, the transiency of the present can obtain in a completely deterministic physical universe, be it relativistic or Newtonian.

The theory of relativity has repudiated the uniqueness of the simultaneity slices within the class of physical events which the Newtonian theory had affirmed. Hence Einstein's

[31] I am indebted to Dr. Richard Gale for pointing out to me that since the term "psychological" is usefully reserved for mind-dependent attributes which are private, as specified, it would be quite misleading to assert the mind-dependence of tense by saying that tense is "psychological." In order to allow for the required kind of intersubjectivity, I have therefore simply used the term "mind-dependent."

theory certainly precludes the conception of "the present" that some defenders of the objectivity of becoming have linked to the Newtonian theory. But it must be pointed out that the doctrine of the mind-dependence of becoming, being entirely compatible with the Newtonian theory as well, does not depend for its validity on the espousal of Einstein's.

Our conclusion that there can be a transient now in a completely deterministic physical universe is altogether at variance with the contention of a number of distinguished thinkers that the indeterminacy of the laws of physics is a both necessary and sufficient condition for becoming. And therefore I now turn to the examination of their contention.

According to such noted writers as A. S. Eddington, H. Bergson, H. Reichenbach, H. Bondi, and G. J. Whitrow, it is a distinctive feature of an *indeterministic* universe, as contrasted with a deterministic one, that physical events belong to the present, occur *now*, or come into being over and above merely becoming present in awareness. Examining the arguments of Reichenbach and Bondi, I now wish to show the following: insofar as events do become, the indeterminacy of physical laws is neither sufficient nor necessary for conferring nowness on the occurrences of events. And thus my analysis of their arguments will uphold my previous conclusion that far from depending on the indeterminacy of the laws of physics, becoming requires a considerable degree of macro-determinism and can obtain in a completely deterministic world. I shall go on to point out that not only the becoming of nature's events but the temporal order of earlier and later among physical events depends on the at least quasi-deterministic character of the macrocosm. And it will then become apparent in what way the charge that a deterministic universe must be completely *timeless* rests on a serious misconstrual of determinism.

Reichenbach contends that "When we speak about the progress of time [from earlier to later] . . . , we intend to make a synthetic [i.e. factual] assertion which refers both to an immediate experience and to physical reality."[32] Further,

[32] H. Reichenbach, *The Philosophy of Space and Time*, tr. by M. Reichenbach and J. Freund, Dover Publications, New York, 1958, pp. 138–39.

he claims that this assertion about events coming *into* being independently of mind—as distinct from merely occurring tenselessly at a certain clock time—can be justified in regard to physical reality on the basis of indeterministic quantum mechanics by the following argument:[33] In classical deterministic physics, both the past and the future were determined in relation to the present by one-to-one functions even though they differed in that there could be direct observational records of the past and only predictive inferences concerning the future. On the other hand, while the results of past measurements on a quantum mechanical system are *determined* in relation to the present by the present records of these measurements, a present measurement of one of two conjugate quantities does *not* uniquely determine in any way the result of a *future* measurement of the other conjugate quantity. Hence, Reichenbach concludes that

The concept of "becoming" acquires significance in physics: the present, which separates the future from the past, is the moment at which that which was undetermined becomes determined, and "becoming" has the same meaning as "becoming determined.". . .

. . . it is with respect to "now" that the past is determined and that the future is not.

I join Hugo Bergmann[34] in rejecting this argument for the following reasons. In the indeterministic quantum world, the relations between the sets of measurable values of the state variables characterizing a physical system at different times are, in principle, *not* the one-to-one relations linking the states of classically behaving closed systems. But I can assert correctly in 1966 that this holds for a given state of a physical system and its absolute future quite independently of whether that state occurs at midnight on December 31, 1800, or at noon on March 1, 1984. Nay, if we consider *any one* of the temporally successive regions of space-time, we can veridically assert the following at *any* time: the events

[33] H. Reichenbach, "Les Fondements Logiques de la Mécanique des Quanta," *Annales de l'Institut Poincaré*, 13 (1953), 154–57.

[34] Cf. H. Bergmann, *Der Kampf um das Kausalgesetz in der jüngsten Physik*, Braunschweig, 1929, pp. 27–28.

belonging to that particular region's absolute past could be (more or less) uniquely specified in records which are a part of that region, whereas its particular absolute future is thence unpredictable in quantum mechanics. Accordingly, *every* event, be it Plato's birth or a birth taking place in A.D. 2000, *at all times* constitutes a divide in Reichenbach's sense between its own recordable past and its unpredictable future, *thereby satisfying Reichenbach's definition of the "present" or "now" at any and all times!* And if Reichenbach were to reply that the indeterminacies of the events of the year of Plato's birth have already been transformed into a determinacy, whereas those of A.D. 2000 have not, then the rejoinder would be: this tensed conjunction holds for any state between sometime in 428 B.C. and A.D. 2000 that qualifies as now during that interval on grounds other than Reichenbach's asymmetry of determinedness; but the second conjunct of this conjunction does not hold for any state after A.D. 2000 which qualifies as now after that date. Accordingly, contrary to Reichenbach, the now of conceptualized awareness must be invoked tacitly at time *t*, if the instant *t* is to be non-trivially and non-arbitrarily singled out as present or now by Reichenbach's criterion, i.e., if the instant *t* is to be uniquely singled out at time *t* as being "now" in virtue of being the threshold of the transition from indeterminacy to determinacy.

Turning to Bondi, we find him writing:

> . . . the flow of time has no significance in the logically fixed pattern demanded by deterministic theory, time being a mere co-ordinate. In a theory with indeterminacy, however, the passage of time transforms statistical expectations into real events.[35]

If Bondi intended this statement to assert that the indeterminacy makes for our human inability to know in advance of their actual occurrence what particular kinds of events will in fact materialize, then, of course, there can be no objection.

[35] H. Bondi, "Relativity and Indeterminacy," *Nature*, 169 (1952), 660.

For in an indeterministic world, the attributes of specified kinds of events are indeed not uniquely fixed by the properties of earlier events and are therefore correspondingly unpredictable. But I take him to affirm beyond this the following traditional philosophical doctrine: in an indeterministic world, events come *into* being by becoming present with time, whereas in a deterministic world the status of events is one of merely occurring tenselessly at certain times. My objections to his appeal to the transformation of statistical expectations into real events by the passage of time fall into several groups as follows.

(1) Let us ask: What is the character and import of the difference between a micro-physically indeterministic and a deterministic physical world in regard to the attributes of future events? The difference concerns only the type of functional connection linking the attributes of future events to those of present or past events. Thus, *in relation to the states existing at other times,* an indeterministic universe allows alternatives as to the attributes of an event that occurs at some given time, whereas a deterministic universe provides no corresponding latitude. But this difference does *not* enable micro-physical indeterminism—as contrasted with determinism—to make for a difference in the *occurrence-status* of future events by enabling them to come *into* being. Hence in an indeterministic world, physical events no more *become* real (i.e. present) and are no more precipitated into existence, as it were, than in a deterministic one. In either a deterministic or an indeterministic universe, events can be held to come into being or to become "actual" by becoming *present in (our) awareness;* but becoming actual in virtue of thus occurring *now* no more makes for a mind-independent coming into existence in an indeterministic world than it does in a deterministic one.

(2) Nor does indeterminacy as contrasted with determinacy make for any difference whatever at any time in regard to the *intrinsic attribute-specificity* of the future events themselves, i.e., to their being (tenselessly) what they are.

For in either kind of universe, it is a fact of logic that what will be, will be, no less than what is present or past is indeed present or past![36] The result of a future quantum mechanical measurement may not be definite prior to its occurrence in relation to earlier states, and thus our prior knowledge of it correspondingly cannot be definite. But a quantum mechanical event has a tenseless occurrence status at a certain time which is fully compatible with its intrinsic attribute-definiteness just as a measurement made in a deterministic world does. Contrary to a widespread view, this statement holds also for those events that are constituted by energy states of quantum mechanical systems, since energy *can* be measured in an arbitrarily short time in that theory.[37] In an indeterministic world, there is a lack of attribute-specificity of events *in relation to events at other times*. But this relational lack of attribute-specificity cannot alter the fact of logic that an event is intrinsically attribute-specific in the sense of tenselessly being what it is at a certain clock time t.[38]

[36] I am indebted to Professor Wilfrid Sellars for having made clarifying remarks to me in 1956 which relate to this point. And Costa de Beauregard has reminded me of the pertinent Spanish dictum "Qué será, será."

[37] Y. Aharonov and D. Bohm have noted that time does not appear in Schrödinger's equation as an operator but only as a parameter and have pointed out the following: (1) The time of an energy state is a dynamical variable belonging to the measuring apparatus and therefore *commutes* with the energy of the observed system; (2) hence the energy state and the time at which it exists do *not* reciprocally limit each other's well-defined status in the manner of the non-commuting conjugate quantities of the Heisenberg Uncertainty Relations; (3) analysis of illustrations of energy measurement (e.g. by collision) which seemed to indicate the contrary shows that the experimental arrangements involved in these examples did not exhaust the measuring possibilities countenanced by the theory. Cf. their two papers on "Time in the Quantum Theory and the Uncertainty Relation for Time and Energy," *Physical Review*, 122 (1961), 1649, and *Physical Review*, 134 (1964), B1417. I am indebted to Professor A. Janis for this reference.

[38] A helpful account of the difference relevant here between being *determinate* (i.e. intrinsically attribute-specific) and being *determined* (in the relational sense of causally necessitated or informationally ascertained) is given by Donald C. Williams in *Prin-*

It is therefore a mistake of far-reaching consequence to suppose that unless and until an event of an indeterministic world belongs to the present or past, the event must be *intrinsically* attribute-indefinite. This error is illustrated by Capek's statement that in the case of an event "it is only its presentness [i.e. nowness] which creates its specificity . . . by eliminating all other possible features incompatible with it."[39] Like Bondi, Capek overlooks that it is only with respect to some now or other that an event can be future at all to begin with, and that the lack of attribute-specificity or "ambiguity" of a future event is not intrinsic but relative to the events of the prior now-perspectives.[40] In an indeterministic world, an event is intrinsically attribute-determinate by being (tenselessly) what it is (tenselessly), regardless of whether the time of its occurrence be now (the present) or not. What makes for the coming into being of a future event at a later time t is *not* that its attributes are indeterministic with respect to prior times but only that it is registered in the now-content of awareness at the subsequent time t.

(3) Two quite different things also seem to be confused when it is inferred that in an indeterministic quantum world the future events distinctively come into being with the passage of time over- and above merely occurring and becoming present to awareness, whereas in a deterministic universe they do not come into being. These two things are: (i) the epistemic precipitation of the *de facto* event-properties of future events out of the wider matrix of the possible properties allowed in advance by the quantum-

ciples of Empirical Realism, Charles C. Thomas, Springfield, Ill., 1966, pp. 274 ff [pp. 98–116 of this volume—Ed.].

[39] Capek, *op. cit.,* p. 340.

[40] Capek writes further: "As long as the ambiguity of the future is a mere appearance due to the limitation of our knowledge, the temporal character of the world remains necessarily illusory" and "the principle of indeterminacy . . . means the *reinstatement of becoming in the physical world*" (*ibid.,* p. 334). But granted that the indeterminacy of quantum theory is ontological rather than merely epistemological, this indeterminacy is nonetheless relational and hence unavailing as a basis for Capek's conclusion.

mechanical probabilities, a precipitation or becoming definite which is constituted by our getting to *know* these *de facto* properties at the later times; and (ii) a mind-independent coming into being over and above merely occurring and becoming present to awareness at the later time. The *epistemic* precipitation is indeed effected by the passage of time through the transformation of a merely statistical expectation into a definite piece of available information. But this does *not* show that in an indeterministic world, there obtains any kind of becoming present ("real") with the passage of time that does not also obtain in a deterministic one. And in either kind of world, becoming, as distinct from mere occurrence at a clock time, requires conceptualized awareness.

We see then that the physical events of the indeterministic quantum world as such do not come into being any more than do those of the classical deterministic world, but that both alike occur tenselessly. And my earlier contention that the transient now is mind-dependent and irrelevant to physical events as such therefore stands.

Proponents of indeterminism as a physical basis of objective becoming have charged that a deterministic world is timeless. Thus, Capek writes:

> . . . the future in the deterministic framework . . . becomes something *actually* existing, a sort of disguised and hidden present which remains hidden only from our limited knowledge, just as distant regions of space are hidden from our sight. "Future" is merely a label given by us to the unknown part of the *present* reality, which exists in the same degree as scenery hidden from our eyes. As this hidden portion of the present is *contemporary* with the portion accessible to us, the temporal relation between the present and the future is eliminated; the future loses its status of "futurity" because instead of succeeding the present it *coexists* with it.[41]

41 Capek, *op. cit.*, pp. 334–35; cf. also p. 164.

In the same vein, G. J. Whitrow declares:

There is indeed a profound connection between the reality of time and the existence of an incalculable element in the universe. Strict causality would mean that the consequences pre-exist in the premises. But, if the future history of the universe pre-exists logically in the present, why is it not already present? If, for the strict determinist, the future is merely "the hidden present," whence comes the illusion of temporal succession?[42]

But I submit that there is a clear and vast difference between the relation of one-to-one functional connection between two temporally separated states, on the one hand, and the relation of temporal coexistence or simultaneity on the other. How, one must ask, does the fact that a future state is uniquely specified by a present state detract in the least from its being later and entail that it paradoxically exists at present? Is it not plain that Capek trades on an ambiguous use of the terms "*actually* existing" and "*coexists*" to confuse the time sequential relation of being *determined* by the present with the simultaneity relation of contemporaneity with the present? In this way, he fallaciously saddles determinism with entailing that future events exist now just because they are determined by the state which exists now. When he tells us that according to determinism's view of the future, "we are already dead without realizing it now,"[43] he makes fallacious use of the correct premise that according to determinism, the present state uniquely specifies at what later time any one of us shall be dead. For he refers to the determinedness of our subsequent deaths misleadingly as our "already" being dead and thence concludes that determinism entails the absurdity that we are dead *now!* Without this ambiguous construal of the term "already," no absurdity is deducible.

When Whitrow asks us why, given determinism, the future is not already present even though it "pre-exists logically in

42 Whitrow, *op. cit.*, p. 295.
43 Capek, *op. cit.*, p. 165.

the present," the reply is: precisely because existing at the present time is radically different in the relevant temporal respect from what he calls "logical pre-existence in the present." Whitrow ignores the fact that states hardly need to be simultaneous just because they are related by one-to-one functions. And he is able to claim that determinism entails the illusoriness of temporal succession (i.e. of the earlier-later relations) only because he uses the term "hidden present" just as ambiguously as Capek uses the term "coexists." But, more fundamentally, we have learned from the theory of relativity that events sustain *time-like* separations to one another *because* of their *causal* connectibility or deterministic relatedness, not despite that deterministic relatedness. And nothing in the relativistic account of the temporal order depends on the existence of an indeterministic micro-physical substratum. Indeed, in the absence of the causality assumed in the theory in the form of causal (signal) connectibility, it is altogether unclear how the system of relations between events would possess the kind of *structure* that we call the "time" of physics.[44]

In this article, I have given reasons for denying that nowness and temporal becoming are entitled to a place within physical theory, be it deterministic or indeterministic. This denial will turn out to be essential to my philosophical and mathematical examination of Zeno's paradoxes of motion, which appears in the next section of this book.

[44] Accordingly, we must qualify the following statement by J. J. C. Smart: "We can now see also that the view of the world as a space-time manifold no more implies determinism than it does the fatalistic view that the future 'is already laid up.' It is compatible both with determinism and with indeterminism, i.e. both with the view that earlier time slices of the universe are determinately related by laws of nature to later time slices and with the view that they are not so related" (*op. cit.*, pp. 141–42). This statement needs an important qualification, since it would not hold if "indeterminism" here meant a macro-indeterminism such that macroscopic causal chains would not exist.

THE FLOW OF TIME

WILLIAM BARRETT

WILLIAM BARRETT is Professor of Philosophy at New York University. He is the author of *What Is Existentialism?* and *Irrational Man.*

1. Discussions of time, among modern philosophers, have tended to become polarized around two radically different kinds of temporality. The distinction has been expressed variously as that between clock time and real duration (Bergson); between *actual* becoming as the radically discontinuous emergence of events and the continuum of time as mere mathematical *possibility* (Whitehead); between primordial temporality and the "vulgar" understanding of time (Heidegger). There is also the common distinction between cosmic and human time; or, in its most crude formulation, between psychological and physical time (where the meaning of "psychological" is rarely specified with any precision).

The conceptions behind these varying terminologies are, of course, very different one from another. Yet there seems to be a common theme running through all the variations; and that theme is a dualism, either already established in fact or incipient in tendency. I shall argue here that any radical bifurcation between the two "times" is unnecessary; that in most cases the two are aspects of a unitary phenomenon; and that, finally, the main points of the ordinary and traditional understanding have to be preserved alongside whatever novel and subtle insights the contemporary analyses have validly brought forward.

2. For purposes of length I shall restrict myself mainly to the position of Heidegger, which, though one of the most

original of contemporary views on this ancient subject, is not generally understood by American philosophers. The questions I raise, therefore, whether successful as criticism or not, may at least perform the service of bringing this rather difficult view of time more clearly into the light.

Heidegger's fundamental conception developed in *Being and Time* (1927) is that time is basically given as a temporal spread or field, and not as a sequence of disjunct Now's. Not a present Now, then another present Now, and another, etc. etc., but the whole spread—and an indefinitely finite spread at that—of future-present-past (where the hyphenization of these three terms is intended to signify the holding together of future-present-past as a unifying synthesis).

The elemental accessibility of time in this sense is so plain that everybody seems to disregard it, as indeed most philosophers before Heidegger seem to have done; and it is therefore worth dwelling on for a moment. Let us take an example from our everyday pre-reflective consciousness: I enter a room, my study, not reflecting on this or any other philosophical matter; at the doorway there spreads before me, immediately, without any construction or inference, the familiar space in which are the table, chairs, windows, and the rest. But just as immediately, though we are much less used to taking account of it, there is a spread of time toward the future as I look across the room from the threshold. I could not perceive that object there as a chair unless I were given now that future region of time in which I will be able to cross the room, touch the chair as solid, sit down in it. The Now as I am crossing the threshold is in this case less primordial, less an original datum (and indeed it may not be given at all as a datum unless I pronounce the word "Now" as I pass through the door) than the spread toward futurity that both constitutes and grounds my present perception. And this spread toward the future likewise takes into itself the spread backward into the past with all its already established familiarities with the structure of the room and the objects in it. Hence the unifying hyphenization of future-present-past, with the future taking the lead as the actively unifying tense.

This basic temporality fits into Heidegger's general interpretation of human existence as *Ek-sistenz*, literally the standing beyond oneself. Experience is never a subcutaneous process from which we infer an external world. A world is given, immediately and directly, in experience, and therefore, we are immediately beyond ourselves within that world. Our experience does not occur at a point-instant in metric space and time; rather, it always takes in some expanse or region of what is. Accordingly, Heidegger calls this basic temporality "ek-static" temporality, for in experiencing the present we already stand beyond it. If for momentary clarification we permit ourselves an analogy that would be ultimately distorting, we can think of a point marked on a line, noting that we can perceive the point only by perceiving the whole line. In this sense, we may also speak of ecstatic temporality as horizontal temporality: viz. it stretches immediately along the whole horizontal line. But, of course, time is not space, and the horizontal stretch of temporality has the unique feature of the co-presence of the three tenses: future-present-past.

This view of time was already implicit in Kant's *Critique of Pure Reason*, although Kant was not able to bring it clearly to light. Heidegger, in fact, claims that he is really reading his view out of Kant's first edition of the *Critique*, though the consequences of this position were such that Kant, largely through the influence of his writings on morals, later recoiled from them. If we put the interpretations advanced by Heidegger in the first of his two books on Kant (*Kant and the Problem of Metaphysics*, 1929) alongside the views expressed two years earlier in *Being and Time*, then the whole position becomes at once more compelling and more radical. Kantian scholars may complain that Heidegger stretches Kant a bit in order to find his own ideas latent in Kant's work; but from a philosophical rather than a doxographical point of view, Heidegger's use of the Kantian apparatus and analysis is justified by the significance of his conclusions. And it may be remarked by the way that the

Kantian experts are beginning to find Heidegger's interpretation much less eccentric than it first may have appeared to them, and that time does indeed stand, in a quite extraordinary fashion, at the center of Kant's thought in the first *Critique*. Kant had emphasized the continuity of consciousness—in anticipation, preserving, repeating—as the indispensable ground for the mind's forming any concepts whatsoever. Hence, time is the necessary condition for there being any human meanings at all. A concept, any concept, as Kant understands it, is a synthesis of actual and *possible* intuitions (for present purposes, we may read this last as perceptions). As such, it always stands in the service of possible experience, and consequently is, in its very nature, an opening into the future. To return to our previous very ordinary example: my concept of chair (as I apprehend that chair across the room) is a synthesis of past experience and of possible future experience, such as, for example, the experience of feeling its supporting solidity if I were to cross the room and sit in it. Hence the concept of chair stretches forward into the future.

The future, then, is that realm of the open out of which man temporalizes—that is, establishes himself meaningfully within time. This statement may sound very dramatic, and in some contexts it surely is, but we have to guard here against some very common misunderstandings.

First of all, this view does not refer merely to our struggles, heroic or unheroic as the case may be, toward some future goal that will be the crown and meaning of our lives. This intrinsic connection of meaning and futurity applies to the driest and most formal items that can come before our attention. Take the formula:

$$KCpAqErsKsNp$$

For the ordinary person this is a meaningless jumble of letters that perhaps got on the page because a child was playing with a typewriter. To the logician, however, it has meaning as a way of *going toward* other possible formulae, such as:

$$KsNp$$

come back again, even though the brave little engine will move back again to the same position. The *then* that is gone is part of the past that—in one fundamental sense at least— will never be again.

We can record these elemental facts without immediately passing into the dialectical subtleties attendant upon dividing time. The facts are what they are whatever the dialectical puzzles engendered when we try to reason about them. Our own entanglements when we try to think or talk about a reality cannot become an argument for making that reality disappear. St. Augustine, for example, in his magnificent discourse upon time, makes the divisibility of time almost an argument for its disappearance. Today is present, he intones, yesterday is no longer, and tomorrow is not yet. We make these apparently simple statements, and they seem to be unquestionably true. Then we ask, What part of today is present?, and we have to record that part of it is no longer and part is not yet. And so for the present hour too, part of it has already gone and part has not yet come. It begins to look then as if the present—which had been alleged alone to be real— would turn into an indivisible and unreal, because unexperienced, knife-edge between the past and the future, both of which are non-existent. No wonder St. Augustine had to pray to God for illumination that would deliver him from this intellectual snarl!

It is possible to go astray on such minutiae. We lose, as it were, the gross macroscopic feature of a phenomenon by squinting only at the microscopic details. Phenomenology (as the systematic description of what is given in experience) can look at details as minute as you please; but it must not thereby lose its grasp of the large bulk phenomena that are overwhelmingly given in experience. Accordingly, any phenomenological description of time must record as a basic datum (before encumbering it with all the minute riddles, of which there are, God knows, enough) that the present is now, the past no longer, and the future not yet. The present year (as I write) is 1966, and 1965 is certainly past. And we do sometimes have to say to an unhistorical contemporary that this, after all, is now the 20th century, not the 19th or

the 13th or whatever. The present thus can be of quite varying length depending upon the purposes of one's discourse,
or the interest that now engages us. It is a mistake to think
that the specious present gives us the ultimately real present.
In the first place, as we have already said, the specious present is specified by a fairly complex apparatus in a psychology
laboratory, and is therefore, a high-level abstraction and not
a basic datum. Even where such tiny flickerings of consciousness may occur, they may flow by relatively unnoticed within
a larger structuring present that is indeed much more the
controlling present before my mind. An hour of concentrated
thought may be the size of my present while the small variations of consciousness that may embroider it are scarcely
noted and not at all remembered. A piece of music, heard as
a whole, is much more the real present of experience than
the single notes that occur within its structuring presence.

But if the present is relative in the length that engages our
interest, and thus can be a century, a year, or an hour, there
is nevertheless another sense in which it is given as *absolute*.
This Now, which I may bring before my mind by striking
the table, is experienced as a Now-for-the-world. The word
"absolute" may be distressing for those whose minds have
become cluttered with the facile popularizations of relativity
physics. If it were only the popularizers who were at fault,
their confusions would not much matter; but eminent scientists as well, on holiday from their strict calling, are still
pleased to ride roughshod over direct experience. "The first
step in explaining relativity theory," writes Hermann Weyl,
"must always consist in shattering the dogmatic belief in the
temporal terms past, present, future." And he prefaces this
statement with the remark: "The scientist must thrust through
the fog of abstract words to reach the concrete rock of reality." There could hardly be a more violent inversion of the
abstract and the concrete than here, or a more flagrant example of the fallacy of misplaced concreteness. So long as
such mental habits persist in our culture, we are in danger,
as Husserl prophesied just before his death, of losing the life-
world altogether. In some (and notice that it is some and not
all) parts of physics, equations that express abstract functional

relations can move freely back and forth between the future and the past, so that a past event in one frame of reference can become a future event in another frame. But in the flow of time within the life-world the present moves irretrievably into the past. When I say, here and now, perhaps striking the table for emphasis, "Now in Tokyo," I do intend now in Tokyo even though news from there may not arrive until that now has vanished irretrievably. And similarly, "Now on Sirius," does intend Now on Sirius, though news from there will not arrive for 8.7 years, and even though three years from now (the now which will have vanished irretrievably) I might learn that Sirius had ceased to exist 5.7 years before I put these words down here and now. The Now is thus given as a Now for the world, and consequently as a now for all objects within the world. In this sense, time is given to us as *cosmic* time, certainly not as a so-called "human" distinct from a so-called "cosmic" time. On the other hand, it is to be distinguished from cosmological time, if this latter adjective be taken to derive its meanings from the abstract cosmology of the astrophysicist.

But at this point we are almost certain to be asked: What is it that flows when we speak of the flow of time? Language here can easily mislead us. When we talk about the flow of a river, water can be identified as the fluid substance that is flowing. We can scoop out a glassful and hold it still. But time is nothing apart from its flow. We might put it somewhat paradoxically by saying that it is its own flow. Then the phrase of our title would be more properly written with hyphens as the flow-of-time in order to indicate the unique and unitary reality with which we are dealing.

Yet such phrases are not enough, and—refractory though language may be here—it is possible to say more about the nature of this flow. Consider again that fundamental conclusion of Kant, which Heidegger's interpretation had brought out so prominently: that without the flow of consciousness, as persisting identity with itself, there would be no consciousness at all. A mind absolutely enclosed and changeless within its own completeness, like the One of Plotinus, would be a pure object, and not a consciousness at all. The flow of consciousness, then, as this persisting identity, is a condition for anything like a world to be given at all. It is thus also the condition for perceiving any particular changes and movements within the world.

We have here arrived at a position from which we can discern the fundamental issue at stake in Plotinus' famous quarrel with Aristotle on the question of time. Aristotle had defined time as the measure of movement with regard to earlier and later. As an illustration of this meaning, consider a body moving at uniform velocity over a straight path. In half the time, we say, it will cover half the distance. We thus seem to measure movement by time. Plotinus protested that we are in fact measuring movement against movement. Thus when we say that a body moves so far in a certain time, we are measuring it against some regular movement (of the sun or the uniform drip of a water clock) that we have already agreed upon. The movement of the measuring instrument is thus intended to measure time, and not the other way around, as Aristotle had it. But Plotinus has also a larger objection in mind. The Aristotelian conception attributes movement to a particular substance, and time in turn is taken as an attribute of movement, namely as a certain proportionate relation of that moment to some standard uniform movement. Time is thus taken as a particular phenomenon located *within* the world. But for Plotinus time is a cosmic reality within which we count off the movement of any individual thing. But at this point his analysis faltered, and he passed over into mythology, describing this cosmic flow of time as the development and becoming of the World Soul.

Kant permits us to take the first step toward rescuing Plotinus' insight from its mythical expression. According to Kant, as we have here interpreted him, the flow of time (as the persisting flow of consciousness) is a condition that a world can be given at all. Hence, time is not an isolated fact within the world, connected with this or that individual moving substance (as in Aristotle), but a phenomenon that is strictly co-ordinate with the world as such.

But a second step must be taken beyond Kant with the aid of Husserl and his doctrine of the intentional nature of consciousness. Kant left the flow of consciousness as a rather self-contained fact. But if, as Husserl maintained, consciousness is essentially intentional—i.e. intends or refers beyond itself—then a scrutiny of the flow of consciousness must lead us beyond consciousness. Consciousness does not disclose itself as a container with changing contents, nor as a channel through which anything is flowing. When we seek to look inside consciousness, we are always looking through it and beyond it into the world and beings within the world. The flow *of* consciousness is always a flow *for* consciousness. It reveals itself to be a flow of the world and of objects within the world.

But world here is not to be understood as a merely ontic fact (in the sense of "ontic" previously distinguished). It is not the mere aggregate of all the objects and beings that are. Rather, it is the concrete structuring totality *within which* all the *things* of experience are found. It itself, however, remains a non-thing, an ontological structure within which the ontic things are found. Consequently, what we here call the flow-of-the-world differs from what Bergson calls *durée* and Whitehead variously calls "passage" or "process." Both these philosophers leave becoming only with the status of an *object*, the ceaselessly seething surd at the heart of things, a vast and overpowering but nevertheless merely ontic fact. An ontological structure, on the other hand, is always a condition of understanding or meaning. The flow of time, as we intend it, is ontological; and therefore we take it as one and inseparable from the "ecstatic" temporality described by Heidegger as the open-*ing* toward the disclosing and revealing horizon of the future. The flow of the world, then, is the ceaseless widening or shrinking, opening or shifting, disclosing and revealing of horizons and regions, as well as of objects within those regions. Process is presence—that is, the revealing opening of the world toward futurity. But presence is also presen*cing*—the becoming and remaining accessible within our horizon or of vanishing from that horizon. Presence and process are thus one and inseparable.

I am within this flow of time, but it is also within me. Both of these statements are true in a way, but both are inaccurate.

The words "within" and "without"—like "outside" or "inside" —do not apply to this basic flow. Time as flow-of-the-world is neither "psychological" nor "physical." The meaning of both these adjectives can be established only within a context that already presupposes the basic flow of time. In the same way, this flow of time, as directly given in experience, transcends the distinction between subjective and objective. That distinction too can only be established within a context that presupposes the flow of time as given.

Sartre speaks of transcendental consciousness, emptied of an ego, as a pure and impersonal spontaneity of becoming. This view resembles what we have been trying to describe as the flow of time. However, since Sartre has already emptied the transcendental consciousness of an ego-subject as well as of so-called "contents," it seems misleading to retain the word "consciousness" at all. For Sartre, consciousness is nothing but intentionality and the pure flow of intentionalities. But intentionality is possible only within the world. I can point to that chair across the room only because it is in my world. Thus it would be better if Sartre spoke not of the flow of consciousness but of the flow of the world, within which alone anything like intentionality can become possible. We would agree with him too that this flow of Being-Becoming is indeed a spontaneity, at least in the sense that we cannot go behind it and derive it from anything else. Physical changes, for example, that might be alleged to cause changes in our consciousness would themselves have to be apprehended within this basic flow of time. But to call it a *pure* spontaneity may invite us to be overcome by vertigo, as Sartre himself often seems to be, at the lavish and unpredictable possibilities of Becoming. Hence, it is not at all surprising that he should go on from celebrating it as "pure" to rebuking it as a "monstrous" spontaneity. After all, time does flow forward in great part along fairly routine roads as well as into the occasional abyss of the unpredicted or unpredictable.

If the words "within" and "without," as suggesting the subjective-objective distinction, are misleading, there is one sense in which we can properly say we are within the flow of time: namely, in the sense that we are in something when we cannot get out of it—i.e. escape it. Indeed, if Kant is right, we cannot even *understand* what it would mean to be out of time. Consequently, time, as this flowing sequence, is not merely a human instrument that Heidegger permits to the authentic man in order to regulate his projects. He may use it, but he is also caught in it. Nor is it, on the other hand, encountered only when we are cowering in abject inauthenticity and letting time flow by us. If it were, then a great deal of the world's great literature lamenting the passage of time, youth, and possibility would merely be the cry of the undifferentiated man of the crowd. We do in fact encounter time as passage in some of the most authentic of our experiences. Suppose we are able to spend a few days with someone we love, after which we have to say good-by and depart. If we merely sat wringing our hands at the passage of time, we would be feckless, irresolute, and inauthentic indeed. But even while we resolutely make best use of our time, the shadow hovers in the background and the moment of departure constantly approaches. Shakespeare has put it well:

> Like as the waves make towards the pebbled shore,
> So do our minutes hasten to their end

Hardly the voice of inauthentic experience!

Heidegger's view of time as the opening into futurity, and therefore into possibility, brings forward what might be called a "positive" side of time. In doing so, he has redeemed time from the denigration that the tradition, most notably in Platonism, has passed upon time as a kind of metaphysical slag at the bottom of existence which we must purge off in order to arrive at the Idea, the essence, the timeless. The view which Heidegger has so laboriously extricated from Kant, on the other hand, points out that all our understanding must be within the perspectives of time. Time is thus elevated into the realm of the understanding. Nevertheless, we must not forget that the oldest myth about time (too old to be due to the misconceptions of philosophers) is of Kronos devouring his children. Putting both positive and negative together, we might say: the being of Kronos is to engender ceaselessly the children whom he must devour. As Samuel Beckett has put

it, time is the double-headed monster of salvation and dam-
nation.

6. We have here attempted to advance beyond a position
of Heidegger, while yet remaining fundamentally within the
circle of his thinking.[1] We have in fact used Heidegger
against Heidegger. Following a certain principle of Kant as
to the essential temporality of consciousness (for which, in
fact, we leaned heavily on Heidegger's own interpretation of
Kant), we attempted to follow this principle to its source and
discover time not "buried in the depths of the human mind,"
as Kant put it, but as the flow of the world which the intentional nature of consciousness requires. This view of time as
primordial flow does not, it seems to me, contradict the view
of it as ecstatic-horizontal temporality, but rather completes
this latter and frees it from any semblance of a subjective
idealism. (And it is the case that many of Heidegger's readers have been led into this misinterpretation of *Being and
Time*.) When a thinker lays hold of a new insight, he is apt
to emphasize it at the expense of the traditional view that
had either ignored it or pushed it into the background. It is
only natural that Heidegger too should have done this.

Nevertheless, the traditional view that the present alone is
actual and therefore real, the past non-existent, and the future a mere possible that is not yet, has henceforth to be
maintained with considerably more qualification and subtlety
in the light of the Heideggerian temporality. But it is also the
case, I believe, that the traditional view of time as flow can
shed light on some of the crucial points in Heidegger's

[1] Perhaps the whole of this paper is no more than an elucidation
of one brief sentence from *Being and Time: Die Welt weltet*
('The world worlds'). This sentence has been cited by some
philosophic readers as another instance of Heidegger's high-
handed tactics with language. But perhaps he could not have
chosen, or coined, a verb to express more powerfully the fact that
the world is not static but perpetually flows in upon us, presses
upon us. In the light of this sentence, then, and such has been the
contention of this paper, he should have given a different account
of how the concept of time as flowing sequence arises in experience.

Section V

ZENO'S PARADOXES OF MOTION

INTRODUCTION

Because of their extreme subtlety and profundity, there is little of value that can be said in a short space about Zeno's four paradoxes of motion.[1] Accordingly, this introduction will be limited to brief comments upon the selections and will end by considering the relevance that the problems they discuss have to the main question of the previous sections—the objectivity of temporal becoming.

Zeno's paradoxes of motion have been refuted by philosophers for 2400 years. What gives them their perennial life, what enables them to survive constant refutation and, like the famous Hollywood monsters, to return again (or to reappear as their sons) is that they can be deployed in so many different ways—as paradoxes for the mathematician, metaphysician, and physicist. No one answer will satisfy all these different persons, nor will it always satisfy one and the same person at different moments of his life.

For the mathematician, Zeno's paradoxes of motion, along with his paradox of plurality, raise problems that concern the logical foundations of the calculus. Both the dichotomy and the Achilles paradoxes involve the traversal of an infinite convergent series of distances.[2] Zeno reasoned that since this series of distances contained an infinite number of distances,

[1] Whether the arguments of the historical Zeno really were so profound and subtle is subject to debate; but if Zeno is not the father of the problems discussed in this section he is certainly, to borrow Wesley Salmon's phrase, their grandfather. See Salmon's excellent introduction to his anthology, *Zeno's Paradoxes*, New York, 1967.

[2] For an account of the dichotomy paradox see pp. 422 ff of the Grünbaum selection below.

each of a finite value, that the sum of the series must be infinite; and therefore it could not be traversed in a finite time. It was not until the early part of the nineteenth century, in the work of Cauchy, that an adequate definition of the sum of such a series was given; and that sum, it was shown, has a finite value. Great progress was made by Dedekind, Weierstrass, and Cantor in the latter half of the nineteenth century in arithmetizing the calculus and thereby eliminating certain anomalies concerning infinitesimals, the "movement" of a function and its ability to "reach" its limit. Such difficulties were removed by conceiving of the limit as a number and the values of the function as numbers also, thus banishing from the calculus the temporal notions of a function "moving" and "reaching" its limit.[3]

Precisely because mathematics has banished all reference to motion and time, it alone is not sufficient to answer Zeno's paradoxes, which are concerned with *physical* space, time, and motion. Merely showing that the mathematical doctrine of continuity is logically consistent is not enough; one must also show that the mathematical theory can be applied to physical space, time, and motion. It is at this point that several twentieth-century metaphysicians, among them Bergson, James, and Whitehead, join in the discussion. While not calling into question the logical consistency of the mathematical theory of continuity, they have agreed with Zeno's dichotomy and Achilles paradoxes that *if* time is mathematically continuous, then indeed a person cannot traverse any finite spatial interval and that the faster runner cannot overtake the slower. With the possible exception of Bergson, they have preferred to adopt a discrete, rather than a continuous, time; and then to take their chances in answering Zeno's other two paradoxes of motion—the arrow and the stadium—both of which are directed against a discrete time.[4] Let us first look at Bergson's position.

[3] For a thorough account of this see C. B. Boyer, *The Concepts of the Calculus,* New York, 1949.

[4] In a discrete time each event has an immediate predecessor and successor, while in a continuous time there is no immediate predecessor or successor for any given event. Between any two

On the surface it appears wrong to classify Bergson with those who hold to a discrete time, for Bergson repeatedly says that time is "continuous." By "continuous," however, he does not mean mathematically continuous, but rather incapable of a distinction between earlier and later parts. Yet because Bergson denies that temporal becoming—the *durée*— is mathematically continuous, it by no means follows that he holds it to be discrete, i.e. that what becomes present or happens is an indivisible event of finite duration, each event having an immediate successor. I do not believe that Bergson meant to assert the absurd view that time as a whole is continuous in his sense, in which case it would not be possible to discriminate between earlier and later events,[5] for he says in *Creative Evolution:*

> All movement is articulated inwardly. It is either an indivisible bound (which may occupy, nevertheless, a very long duration) *or a series of indivisible bounds.* (My italics)

The italicized disjunct makes it quite clear that a movement, in Bergson's view, can contain a sequence of earlier and later events. In the case of Achilles' movement, each of his steps forms an indivisible bound: his track coach might have told him, as track coaches often do, to run his race with the tortoise one step at a time, and would have consoled him by pointing out that after a *finite* number of such steps he would have overtaken the tortoise.

One of the main themes of Bergson's philosophy is our intellect's inability to grasp the true nature of time, as well as other ultimate features of reality. Our intellect operates in a

---

events in continuous time there is another event, in fact, a super-denumerable number of them. Not only metaphysicians but also ordinary language philosophers practicing therapeutic analysis have felt it necessary to take time to be discrete. See Findlay's discussion of the "droplet theory of time" on pp. 157 ff of this volume.

[5] This might be dubbed the Blob Theory of Time. If no distinction can be made between earlier and later events then, by the strangest turn of the philosophical wheel, Bergson, who is supposed to be the great champion of temporality, would be espousing an Eleatic view of the unreality of time.

"cinematographical" manner, to use Bergson's famous phrase,[6] in which a movement is represented as a series of static states, just as a motion picture is made up of a number of frames each picturing a different static state of an object. It will be recalled[7] that tenet (4) of the B-Theory is based on the cinematographical technique; for it analyzes change in terms of successive states of a single object which differ qualitatively or quantitatively. This concept of change, when applied to the case of movement, has been aptly dubbed the "at-at" theory, since it analyzes the movement of a thing in terms of its being *at* a different place *at* one time than it is *at at* a later time. As we shall see, Bergson wants to replace the "at-at" theory of movement with a "from-to" view.

For Bergson, the only true way in which to grasp the nature of time and motion is to introspect the temporal becoming or flow of our own consciousness. Bergson contrasts metaphysical or absolute knowledge with relative knowledge: the former involves an act of *intuition* in which we directly experience something without the use of any concepts (or symbols) or empathically identify with that thing, while the latter involves comparing one object with another.[8] For example, relative knowledge of a movement involves noting a difference in the spatial relation between two objects at different times: metaphysical knowledge of the same movement involves putting ourselves inside one of the objects and experiencing its movement internally, as we experience the movement of one of our limbs. Bergson wants us to intuit the "from-to" aspect of movement, how Achilles gets *from* one place *to* another.

There is some similarity between Bergson's intuitive man-

---

[6] Russell reports somewhere that the one and only time he went to see a motion picture was prompted by his desire to understand what Bergson meant by this phrase. Judging by the severity of his criticisms of Bergson, it would appear that his sacrifice was in vain.

[7] See p. 70 of this volume.

[8] For a fuller treatment of the distinction between metaphysical and relative knowledge see Bergson's *Introduction to Metaphysics*, tr. by T. E. Hulme, New York, 1912.

ner of gaining metaphysical knowledge and the phenomenological method of Husserl and the Existentialists. In both
cases it is assumed that the ultimate features of reality are
those which are directly revealed to us in our pre-analytic
experiences. We must let reality directly reveal itself; any
superposition of concepts or symbols upon a revealing experience will distort the nature of reality. One of the major
themes in Bergson's philosophy is that all language and concepts—all the tools by means of which our intellect operates
—viciously distort the true nature of the given, or reality.
Grünbaum would take issue with Bergson's reliance on intuition for much the same reason that he would argue with
Barrett's reliance on the phenomenological method for determining what reality is, countering that the nature of reality
or the objective world is best determined by reference to our
most advanced and sophisticated scientific theories.

It was pointed out that someone who holds time to be discrete must still answer Zeno's arrow and stadium arguments,
which assume a discrete time. Bergson's manner of meeting
the arrow paradox, for example, is to deny the "at-at" theory
of movement upon which it is based.[9] The arrow paradox
falsely reduces the flight of the arrow to a sequence of static
positions along the path of its flight. Bergson seems to take
the entire flight of the arrow to be a single indivisible event:
this assumes a lot, since arrows can't tell us what their movements feel like to them. The arrow is not at a given place at
a given time; for there is no way in which the flight of the
arrow can be generated out of a sequence of immobilities,
even if there be an infinite number of such immobile states.

Numerous objections have been raised to Bergson's philosophy. (a) His distinction between absolute (metaphysical) and relative knowledge of movement commits him to a

[9] One way of stating the paradox of the arrow is as follows. At
every instant of time the arrow occupies a space equal to itself,
and therefore is at rest. But since the arrow is always (at all
times) at rest it cannot move. For a discussion of the stadium
paradox see Russell, *The Principles of Mathematics*, Cambridge,
1903, p. 352. The stadium paradox also assumes an "at-at" theory
of movement, so that Bergson's reply would apply to it also.

theory of absolute motion, difficult to maintain in the light of relativity theory. (b) His claim that a motion or change cannot be composed of immobilities—an object being *at* different places *at* different times—commits the fallacy of composition, similar to the claim that a friendship must be composed of friendships rather than people, to use Russell's example.[10] (c) His charge that symbols must distort the reality they symbolize amounts to nothing more than the trivial fact that symbols are qualitatively different from their referents: the word "amorous," for example, is not itself warm and passionate. One does not say that a physicist's vector diagram of a motion is a vicious distortion of reality because it does not get up and run around the room. His symbolism is not intended to "generate" or "produce" a motion, but rather to give a conceptual representation of movement that will be fruitful in helping us to systematize, explain, and predict a vast array of empirical phenomena. Grünbaum might add that the physicist's way of doing this is far superior to the intuitive or common-sense manner of understanding movement, and therefore the latter should be replaced by the former. (d) It is often felt that Bergson's view of the discreteness or atomicity of becoming, along with James's and Whitehead's, is paradoxical; it asserts that an event of finite duration occurs as a whole and admits of no distinction between earlier and later parts. Whitehead has tried to meet this difficulty by claiming that there is a becoming of continuity but not a continuity of becoming.[11] He agrees with Bergson that temporal becoming is atomic: what becomes present is a finite chunk of reality. An event is *internally* indivisible, as Bergson claimed; but, Whitehead goes on to add, *externally* it is infinitely divisible since it is caught up in a web of spatio-temporal relations with other events. Many have found Whitehead's view as difficult to understand as Bergson's.

In the stimulating article by James Thomson on "Tasks

[10] See Russell's *History of Western Philosophy*, New York, 1945, p. 833.

[11] A. N. Whitehead, *Process and Reality*, New York, 1929, p. 53.

and Super-tasks" we find a reformulation of Zeno's dichotomy and Achilles paradoxes. The question has now become whether it is logically possible for a person or a machine to perform in a finite time an infinite number of tasks, such as switching a light on and off an infinite number of times in a minute or counting all the digits in the decimal expansion of *pi* in a minute. Thomson refers to such tasks as "super-tasks." He argues that there is something absurd about the accomplishment of a supertask; but we find Grünbaum arguing convincingly that certain kinds of supertasks are logically possible. He carefully distinguishes between several different kinds, and shows that in certain cases there are dynamic absurdities, e.g., the expenditure of an infinite amount of energy in the case of his staccato runner (see pp. 462 ff), but no kinematic absurdity, such as the traversal of an infinite space in a finite time.[12]

Grünbaum's diagnosis of the seductive allurement of Zeno's dichotomy and Achilles paradoxes, along with the arguments against the logical possibility of performing a supertask, is as follows. Bergson, James, and Whitehead are correct in their intuitive or phenomenological accounts of our common-sense experience of temporal becoming: it is atomic or discrete, for there is a minimum duration, based on the span of our specious present, to any event of which we are aware. But we err when we attempt to understand the continuous time of modern physics in terms of our ordinary temporal experiences. Our attempt to visualize or intuit the continuity of time is not metrically faithful, since the events of which we

[12] Gregory Vlastos, in his fine article "Zeno's Race Course," *Journal of the History of Philosophy*, 4 (1966), argues that there is a crucial disanalogy between Achilles' supertask in traversing an infinite number of converging spatial intervals and the super-tasks performed by various kinds of "infinity machines," such as the Thomson lamp and Black's Beta machine. (See pp. 464 and 465 for a discussion of these machines.) The disanalogy consists in the fact that the machines are finite discrete state systems while Achilles' movement is not. Thus, even if there were a contradiction involved in one of the infinity machines completing its supertask, it would not show that Achilles' successful completion of his supertask is contradictory.

are aware have a lower minimum duration while the infinitely many sub-runs which make up a single finite run have no minimum duration. Whitehead's claim that time cannot pass if it is continuous, since then there would be no *next* instant of time, is an example of the unwarranted incursion of common-sense notions into physics.

What plainly emerges from Grünbaum's very carefully worked out paper, which, in my opinion, is the finest work ever done on Zeno's paradoxes, is that there is no way in which we can picture or intuit a continuous time. Any attempt to reduce it to common-sense notions will result in absurdities. But there is no reason why we should be able to picture or experience the continuity of time if we are to adopt, as it seems we must, a physical theory which employs the mathematical theory of the continuity of space and time. A continuous time is made up of a superdenumerable number of punctal events: although we cannot experience a punctal event, and for this reason cannot give a co-ordinating definition of this theoretical notion, we can give a co-ordinating definition of a continuous *duration* by reference to an observable process, such as a movement.[13] It is an overly narrow empiricism which demands that every theoretical concept of a physical theory be directly linked with observables through co-ordinating definitions. All that is required is that a sufficient number of the theoretical concepts of a theory be so linked, the remaining theoretical terms receiving their meaning because of their relation to them.

In closing, we shall consider what relevance the problem of the continuity of time has to the problem of the objectivity of temporal becoming, which figured prominently in sections II, III, and IV of this volume.

It might be held that if time really is continuous, then

[13] A co-ordinating definition of a term supplies an empirical referent for it, and thereby enables it to be given a physical interpretation. Hans Reichenbach, in *The Philosophy of Space and Time* (tr. by M. Reichenbach and J. Freund, Dover Publications, New York, 1958) introduces the concept of a co-ordinating definition.

temporal becoming is not objective. One might argue that both the discreteness of time and the objectivity of temporal becoming are included in the common-sense concept of time, and that, therefore, if you discard one of these beliefs you must also discard the other. For example, if science establishes the continuity of time, then we must give up our common-sense belief in the objectivity of temporal becoming. But that by no means follows. For certainly it would not be advanced—by an exactly parallel argument—that since the belief in the objectivity of B-relations is also part of the common-sense concept of time, it too must be jettisoned if we accept a continuous time. All that follows from the proposition that time is discrete is the hypothetical proposition that temporal becoming if it exists, must be continuous. Further, the same reasons that can be advanced to show that there are no Zenoian absurdities in a continuous B-Series of events can be utilized to establish that there are no absurdities in a continuous temporal becoming.

Many A-Theorists who have argued for the objectivity of temporal becoming have also held time to be discrete. But their adherence to the former doctrine does not logically commit them to accepting the latter as well. Broad, in his *Examination of McTaggart's Philosophy*, held that temporal becoming is both objective and mathematically continuous: what becomes present in the strict sense is a punctal event which has no immediate predecessor or successor.[14] Broad did go on, using Whitehead's method of extensive abstraction, to try to construct these punctal events out of experience.[15] There may be insuperable difficulties inherent in any such attempt to define a punctal event in terms of events of finite duration—which is the only sort of event we can

[14] Broad's doctrine of the specious present (see his contribution to this volume) is not inconsistent with this view, since the temporally extended content of a single specious present is apprehended by a *punctal* act of perception: these punctal acts of perception themselves form a dense series and undergo temporal becoming.

[15] This section in Broad's *Examination of McTaggart's Philosophy* has been deleted in Section II of this volume.

experience.[16] But there is no reason why an A-Theorist must be shackled with what we have previously termed an overly narrow empiricism. There is nothing in the A-Theory which claims or entails that every concept must be capable of being directly connected with, or constructed out of, the contents of our experience.

Another reason that might be given for the claim that temporal continuity is not consistent with the objectivity of temporal becoming is that an essential part of the meaning of the ordinary concept of temporal becoming involves the discreteness of time, so that it would be a contradiction in terms to speak of a continuous temporal becoming. But certainly no one would want to advance the exactly parallel argument that since an essential part of the ordinary meaning of "earlier than" is that time is discrete (each event having an immediate predecessor), it is meaningless to speak of a punctal event as being earlier than another punctal event in a continuous time. If it is true that our ordinary concept of time involves the discreteness of time, though it is by no means clear that it does, then to speak meaningfully of temporal becoming as continuous, we must drop that feature of our ordinary concept of time. We can, however, retain all the remaining features of this ordinary concept, e.g., that the present is objective, just as, analogously, we retain all the features of the ordinary concept of *earlier than* when we speak of punctal events ordered by the relation of *earlier than* in a continuous time, except that it is no longer required that each event have an immediate predecessor.[17]

[16] These difficulties are too technical to be taken up here. See A. Grünbaum, "Whitehead's Method of Extensive Abstraction," *The British Journal for the Philosophy of Science*, 4 (1954).

[17] It hardly needs to be said that if time is discrete nothing follows about the objectivity (subjectivity) of temporal becoming. Another question that might be thought relevant to the problem of the objectivity of temporal becoming, but is not, is whether events or things are the basic or fundamental entities (substances in the philosophical sense). There is no inconsistency in an A-Theorist holding to an event ontology, as many of them do.

FORM AND BECOMING

HENRI BERGSON

HENRI BERGSON (1859–1941) was professor at the Collège de France in Paris. His major works include *Time and Free Will, Introduction to Metaphysics, Creative Evolution,* and *The Two Sources of Morality and Religion.*

Now, if we try to characterize more precisely our natural attitude towards Becoming, this is what we find. Becoming is infinitely varied. That which goes from yellow to green is not like that which goes from green to blue: they are different *qualitative* movements. That which goes from flower to fruit is not like that which goes from larva to nymph and from nymph to perfect insect: they are different *evolutionary* movements. The action of eating or of drinking is not like the action of fighting: they are different *extensive* movements. And these three kinds of movement themselves —qualitative, evolutionary, extensive—differ profoundly. The trick of our perception, like that of our intelligence, like that of our language, consists in extracting from these profoundly different becomings the single representation of becoming *in general,* undefined becoming, a mere abstraction which by itself says nothing and of which, indeed, it is very rarely that we think. To this idea, always the same, and always obscure or unconscious, we then join, in each particular case, one or several clear images that represent *states* and which serve to distinguish all becomings from each other. It is this composition of a specified and definite state with change general and undefined that we substitute for the specific change. An

FROM Henri Bergson, *Creative Evolution,* translated by Arthur Mitchell, Macmillan, London, 1911, Chapter IV, and Henry Holt, New York, 1911, Chapter IV. Reprinted by permission of the publishers.

o*

infinite multiplicity of becomings variously colored, so to speak, passes before our eyes: we manage so that we see only differences of color, that is to say, differences of state, beneath which there is supposed to flow, hidden from our view, a becoming always and everywhere the same, invariably colorless.

Suppose we wish to portray on a screen a living picture, such as the marching past of a regiment. There is one way in which it might first occur to us to do it. That would be to cut out jointed figures representing the soldiers, to give to each of them the movement of marching, a movement varying from individual to individual although common to the human species, and to throw the whole on the screen. We should need to spend on this little game an enormous amount of work, and even then we should obtain but a very poor result: how could it, at its best, reproduce the suppleness and variety of life? Now, there is another way of proceeding, more easy and at the same time more effective. It is to take a series of snapshots of the passing regiment and to throw these instantaneous views on the screen, so that they replace each other very rapidly. This is what the cinematograph does. With photographs, each of which represents the regiment in a fixed attitude, it reconstitutes the mobility of the regiment marching. It is true that if we had to do with photographs alone, however much we might look at them, we should never see them animated: with immobility set beside immobility, even endlessly, we could never make movement. In order that the pictures may be animated, there must be movement somewhere. The movement does indeed exist here; it is in the apparatus. It is because the film of the cinematograph unrolls, bringing in turn the different photographs of the scene to continue each other, that each actor of the scene recovers his mobility; he strings all his successive attitudes on the invisible movement of the film. The process then consists in extracting from all the movements peculiar to all the figures an impersonal movement abstract and simple, *movement in general,* so to speak: we put this into the apparatus, and we reconstitute the individuality of each particular movement by combining this nameless movement with the personal attitudes. Such is the contrivance of the cinematograph. And such is also that of our knowledge. Instead of attaching ourselves to the inner becoming of things, we place ourselves outside them in order to recompose their becoming artificially. We take snapshots, as it were, of the passing reality, and, as these are characteristic of the reality, we have only to string them on a becoming, abstract, uniform and invisible, situated at the back of the apparatus of knowledge, in order to imitate what there is that is characteristic in this becoming itself. Perception, intellection, language so proceed in general. Whether we would think becoming, or express it, or even perceive it, we hardly do anything else than set going a kind of cinematograph inside us. We may therefore sum up what we have been saying in the conclusion that the *mechanism of our ordinary knowledge is of a cinematographical kind.*

Of the altogether practical character of this operation there is no possible doubt. Each of our acts aims at a certain insertion of our will into the reality. There is, between our body and other bodies, an arrangement like that of the pieces of glass that compose a kaleidoscopic picture. Our activity goes from an arrangement to a re-arrangement, each time no doubt giving the kaleidoscope a new shake, but not interesting itself in the shake, and seeing only the new picture. Our knowledge of the operation of nature must be exactly symmetrical, therefore, with the interest we take in our own operation. In this sense we may say, if we are not abusing this kind of illustration, that *the cinematographical character of our knowledge of things is due to the kaleidoscopic character of our adaptation to them.*

The cinematographical method is therefore the only practical method, since it consists in making the general character of knowledge form itself on that of action, while expecting that the detail of each act should depend in its turn on that of knowledge. In order that action may always be enlightened, intelligence must always be present in it; but intelligence, in order thus to accompany the progress of activity and ensure its direction, must begin by adopting its rhythm. Action is discontinuous, like every pulsation of life; discontinuous, therefore, is knowledge. The mechanism of the faculty of knowing has been constructed on this plan. Essentially practical, can it be of use, such as it is, for speculation? Let us try with it to follow reality in its windings, and see what will happen.

I take of the continuity of a particular becoming a series of views, which I connect together by "becoming in general." But of course I cannot stop there. What is not determinable is not representable: of "becoming in general" I have only a verbal knowledge. As the letter x designates a certain unknown quantity, whatever it may be, so my "becoming in general," always the same, symbolizes here a certain transition of which I have taken some snapshots; of the transition itself it teaches me nothing. Let me then concentrate myself wholly on the transition, and, between any two snapshots, endeavor to realize what is going on. As I apply the same method, I obtain the same result; a third view merely slips in between the two others. I may begin again as often as I will, I may set views alongside of views for ever, I shall obtain nothing else. The application of the cinematographical method therefore leads to a perpetual recommencement, during which the mind, never able to satisfy itself and never finding where to rest, persuades itself, no doubt, that it imitates by its instability the very movement of the real. But though, by straining itself to the point of giddiness, it may end by giving itself the illusion of mobility, its operation has not advanced it a step, since it remains as far as ever from its goal. In order to advance with the moving reality, you must replace yourself within it. Install yourself within change, and you will grasp at once both change itself and the successive states in which *it might* at any instant be immobilized. But with these successive states, perceived from without as real and no longer as potential immobilities, you will never reconstitute movement. Call them *qualities, forms, positions,* or *intentions,* as the case may be, multiply the number of them as you will, let the interval between two consecutive states be infinitely small: before the intervening movement you will always experience the disappointment of the child who tries by clapping his hands together to crush the smoke.

The movement slips through the interval, because every attempt to reconstitute change out of states implies the absurd proposition, that movement is made of immobilities.

Philosophy perceived this as soon as it opened its eyes. The arguments of Zeno of Elea, although formulated with a very different intention, have no other meaning.

Take the flying arrow. At every moment, says Zeno, it is motionless, for it cannot have time to move, that is, to occupy at least two successive positions, unless at least two moments are allowed it. At a given moment, therefore, it is at rest at a given point. Motionless in each point of its course, it is motionless during all the time that it is moving.

Yes, if we suppose that the arrow can ever *be* in a point of its course. Yes again, if the arrow, which is moving, ever coincides with a position, which is motionless. But the arrow never *is* in any point of its course. The most we can say is that it might be there, in this sense, that it passes there and might stop there. It is true that if it did stop there, it would be at rest there, and at this point it is no longer movement that we should have to do with. The truth is that if the arrow leaves the point A to fall down at the point B, its movement AB is as simple, as indecomposable, in so far as it is movement, as the tension of the bow that shoots it. As the shrapnel, bursting before it falls to the ground, covers the explosive zone with an indivisible danger, so the arrow which goes from A to B displays with a single stroke, although over a certain extent of duration, its indivisible mobility. Suppose an elastic stretched from A to B, could you divide its extension? The course of the arrow is this very extension; it is equally simple and equally undivided. It is a single and unique bound. You fix a point C in the interval passed, and say that at a certain moment the arrow was in C. If it had been there, it would have been stopped there, and you would no longer have had a flight from A to B, but *two* flights, one from A to C and the other from C to B, with an interval of rest. A single movement is entirely, by the hypothesis, a movement between two stops; if there are intermediate stops, it is no longer a single movement. At bottom, the illusion arises from this, that the movement, *once effected,* has laid along its course a motionless trajectory on which we can count as many immobilities as we will. From this we conclude that the movement, *whilst being effected,* lays at each instant beneath it a position with which it coincides. We do not see that the trajectory is created in one stroke, although a certain time is required for it; and that though we can divide at will the trajectory once created, we cannot divide its creation, which is an act in progress and not a thing. To suppose that the moving body *is* at a point of its course is to cut the course in two by a snip of the scissors at this point, and to substitute two trajectories for the single trajectory which we were first considering. It is to distinguish two successive acts where, by the hypothesis, there is only one. In short, it is to attribute to the course itself of the arrow everything that can be said of the interval that the arrow has traversed, that is to say, to admit *a priori* the absurdity that movement coincides with immobility.

We shall not dwell here on the three other arguments of Zeno. We have examined them elsewhere. It is enough to point out that they all consist in applying the movement to the line traversed, and supposing that what is true of the line is true of the movement. The line, for example, may be divided into as many parts as we wish, of any length that we wish, and it is always the same line. From this we conclude that we have the right to suppose the movement articulated as we wish, and that it is always the same movement. We thus obtain a series of absurdities that all express the same fundamental absurdity. But the possibility of applying the movement *to* the line traversed exists only for an observer who keeping outside the movement and seeing at every instant the possibility of a stop, tries to reconstruct the real movement with these possible immobilities. The absurdity vanishes as soon as we adopt by thought the continuity of the real movement, a continuity of which every one of us is conscious whenever he lifts an arm or advances a step. We feel then indeed that the line passed over between two stops is described with a single indivisible stroke, and that we seek in vain to practice on the movement, which traces the line, divisions corresponding, each to each, with the divisions arbitrarily chosen of the line once it has been traced. The line traversed by the moving body lends itself to any kind of division, because it has no internal organization. But all movement is articulated inwardly. It is either an indivisible bound (which may occupy, nevertheless, a very long duration) or a series of indivisible bounds. Take the articulations of this movement into account, or give up speculating on its nature.

When Achilles pursues the tortoise, each of his steps must be treated as indivisible, and so must each step of the tortoise. After a certain number of steps, Achilles will have overtaken the tortoise. There is nothing more simple. If you insist on dividing the two motions further, distinguish both on the one side and on the other, in the course of Achilles and in that of the tortoise, the *sub-multiples* of the steps of each of them; but respect the natural articulations of the two courses. As long as you respect them, no difficulty will arise, because you will follow the indications of experience. But Zeno's device is to reconstruct the movement of Achilles according to a law arbitrarily chosen. Achilles with a first step is supposed to arrive at the point where the tortoise was, with a second step at the point which it has moved to while he was making the first, and so on. In this case, Achilles would always have a new step to take. But obviously, to overtake the tortoise, he goes about it in quite another way. The movement considered by Zeno would only be the equivalent of the movement of Achilles if we could treat the movement as we treat the interval passed through, decomposable and recomposable at will. Once you subscribe to this first absurdity, all the others follow.[1]

[1] That is, we do not consider the sophism of Zeno refuted by the fact that the geometrical progression $a(1 + \frac{1}{n} + \frac{1}{n2} + \frac{1}{n3} + \ldots,$ etc.)—in which a designates the initial distance between Achilles and the tortoise, and n the relation of their respective velocities—has a finite sum if n is greater than 1. On this point we may refer to the arguments of F. Evellin, which we regard as conclusive (see Evellin, *Infini et quantité*, Paris, 1880, pp. 63–97; cf. *Revue philosophique*, 11 (1881), 564–68). The truth is that mathematics, as we have tried to show in a former work, deals and can

Nothing would be easier, now, than to extend Zeno's argument to qualitative becoming and to evolutionary becoming. We should find the same contradictions in these. That the child can become a youth, ripen to maturity and decline to old age, we understand when we consider that vital evolution is here the reality itself. Infancy, adolescence, maturity, old age, are mere views of the mind, *possible stops* imagined by us, from without, along the continuity of a progress. On the contrary, let childhood, adolescence, maturity and old age be given as integral parts of the evolution, they become *real stops,* and we can no longer conceive how evolution is possible, for rests placed beside rests will never be equivalent to a movement. How, with what is made, can we reconstitute what is being made? How, for instance, from childhood once posited as a *thing,* shall we pass to adolescence, when, by the hypothesis, childhood only is given? If we look at it closely, we shall see that our habitual manner of speaking, which is fashioned after our habitual manner of thinking, leads us to actual logical deadlocks—deadlocks to which we allow ourselves to be led without anxiety, because we feel confusedly that we can always get out of them if we like: all that we have to do, in fact, is to give up the cinematographical habits of our intellect. When we say "The child becomes a man," let us take care not to fathom too deeply the literal meaning of the expression, or we shall find that, when we posit the subject "child," the attribute "man" does not yet apply to it, and that, when we express the attribute "man," it applies no more to the subject "child." The reality, which is the *transition* from childhood to manhood, has slipped between our fingers. We have only the imaginary stops "child" and "man," and we are very near to saying that one of these stops *is* the other, just as the arrow of Zeno *is,* according to that philosopher, at all the points of

deal only with lengths. It has therefore had to seek devices, first, to transfer to the movement, which is not a length, the divisibility of the line passed over, and then to reconcile with experience the idea (contrary to experience and full of absurdities) of a movement that is a length, that is, of a movement *placed upon* its trajectory and arbitrarily decomposable like it.

the course. The truth is that if language here were molded on reality, we should not say "The child becomes the man," but "There is becoming from the child to the man." In the first proposition, "becomes" is a verb of indeterminate meaning, intended to mask the absurdity into which we fall when we attribute the state "man" to the subject "child." It behaves in much the same way as the movement, always the same, of the cinematographical film, a movement hidden in the apparatus and whose function it is to superpose the successive pictures on one another in order to imitate the movement of the real object. In the second proposition, "becoming" is a subject. It comes to the front. It is the reality itself; childhood and manhood are then only possible stops, mere views of the mind; we now have to do with the objective movement itself, and no longer with its cinematographical imitation. But the first manner of expression is alone conformable to our habits of language. We must, in order to adopt the second, escape from the cinematographical mechanism of thought.

We must make complete abstraction of this mechanism, if we wish to get rid at one stroke of the theoretical absurdities that the question of movement raises. All is obscure, all is contradictory when we try, with states, to build up a transition. The obscurity is cleared up, the contradiction vanishes, as soon as we place ourselves along the transition, in order to distinguish states in it by making cross cuts therein in thought. The reason is that there is *more* in the transition than the series of states, that is to say, the possible cuts— *more* in the movement than the series of positions, that is to say, the possible stops. Only, the first way of looking at things is conformable to the processes of the human mind; the second requires, on the contrary, that we reverse the bent of our intellectual habits. No wonder, then, if philosophy at first recoiled before such an effort. The Greeks trusted to nature, trusted the natural propensity of the mind, trusted language above all, in so far as it naturally externalizes thought. Rather than lay blame on the attitude of thought and language toward the course of things, they preferred to pronounce the course of things itself to be wrong. . . .

TASKS AND SUPER-TASKS

J. F. THOMSON

JAMES F. THOMSON is Professor of Philosophy at the Massachusetts Institute of Technology.

"To complete any journey you must complete an infinite number of journeys. For to arrive from A to B you must first go from A to A', the mid-point of A and B, and thence to A'', the mid-point of A' and B, and so on. But it is logically absurd that someone should have completed all of an infinite number of journeys, just as it is logically absurd that someone should have completed all of an infinite number of tasks. Therefore it is absurd to suppose that anyone has ever completed any journey."

The argument says that to complete a journey you must do something that is impossible and hence that you can't complete a journey.

It may seem that this argument is valid; and then, since the conclusion is absurd, we must deny one of the premises. But which? Each has a certain plausibility. To some, it is more plausible that you can't complete an infinite number of journeys than that you must. These people infer the falsity of the first premiss from the truth of the second premiss and the falsity of the conclusion. To others it is more plausible that you must complete an infinite number of journeys than that you can't. These people infer the falsity of the second premiss from the truth of the first premiss and the falsity of the conclusion. The first party says 'You couldn't, but you don't need to'; the second party says 'You must, but you can'.

FROM *Analysis*, 15:1 (October 1954), by permission of Basil Blackwell, publisher, and by permission of the editor.

This division was neatly illustrated in some recent numbers of ANALYSIS. Professor Max Black[1] argued that the expression 'an infinite number of acts' was self-contradictory, and thus affirmed the second premiss. Unfortunately, he was not entirely convincing in his rejection of the first premiss. Messrs. Richard Taylor[2] and J. Watling[3] rejected Professor Black's arguments for the second premiss, and at least part of their reason for doing so was that they were impressed by the plausibility of the first premiss. Unfortunately, they were not entirely convincing in their rejection of the second.

Luckily we need not take sides in this dispute. For the argument stated above is not valid. It commits the fallacy of equivocation. There is an element of truth in each of the premisses; what the elements of truth are, it is the purpose of this paper to explain.

Let us begin by considering the second premiss. Is it conceivable that someone should have completed an infinite number of tasks? Do we know what this would be like? Let us say, for brevity, that a man who has completed all of an infinite number of tasks (of some given kind) has completed a super-task (of some associated kind). Then, do we know what a super-task is? Do we have this concept?

It is necessary here to avoid a common confusion. It is not in question whether we understand the sentence: The operation so-and-so can be performed infinitely often. On the contrary, it is quite certain that we do. But to say that some operation can be performed infinitely often is not to say that a super-operation can be performed.

Suppose (A) that every lump of chocolate can be cut in two, and (B) that the result of cutting a lump of chocolate in two is always that you get two lumps of chocolate. It follows that every lump of chocolate is infinitely divisible. Now I suppose that one of the assumptions A and B is false. For either a molecule of chocolate is a lump of chocolate, and then A is false, or it is not, in which case the result of cutting some lump of chocolate in two is not a lump of chocolate,

1 "Achilles and the Tortoise," Vol. 11, No. 5 (1951).
2 "Mr. Black on Temporal Paradoxes," Vol. 12, No. 2 (1951).
3 "The Sum of an Infinite Series," Vol. 13, No. 2 (1952).

and then B is false. But the conjunction of A and B is certainly consistent, and so it is certainly conceivable that a lump be infinitely divisible. But to say that a lump is infinitely divisible is just to say that it can be cut into any number of parts. Since there is an infinite number of numbers, we could say: there is an infinite number of numbers of parts into which the lump can be divided. And this is not to say that it can be divided into an infinite number of parts. If something is infinitely divisible, and you are to say into how many parts it shall be divided, you have $\aleph_0$ alternatives from which to choose. This is not to say that $\aleph_0$ is one of them.

And if something is infinitely divisible, then the operation of halving it or halving some part of it can be performed infinitely often. This is not to say that the operation *can have been* performed infinitely often.

The confusion that is possible here is really quite gross, but it does have a certain seductiveness. Where each of an infinite number of things can be done, e.g. bisecting, trisecting, etc. *ad inf.*, it is natural and correct to say: *You can perform an infinite number of operations.* (Cf. "you can do it seven different ways".) But it is also natural, though incorrect, to want to take the italicised sentence as saying that there is some *one* operation you can perform whose performance is completed when and only when every one of an infinite set of operations has been performed. (A super-operation). This is perhaps natural because, or partly because, of an apparent analogy. If I say "It is possible to swim the Channel" I cannot go on to deny that it is conceivable that someone *should have* swum the Channel. But this analogy is only apparent. To say that it is possible to swim the Channel is to say that there is some one thing that can be done. When we say that you can perform an infinite number of operations we are not saying that there is some one ("infinite") operation you can do, but that the *set* of operations ("finite" operations) which lie within your power is an infinite set. Roughly speaking: to speak of an infinity of possibilities is not to speak of the possibility of infinity.

So far I have just been saying that a certain inference is invalid. Suppose that we are considering a certain set of tasks

—ordinary everyday tasks—and that we have assigned numbers to them so that we can speak of Task 1, Task 2, etc. Then: given that for every n Task n is possible, we cannot straightway infer that some task not mentioned in the premiss is possible, viz. that task whose performance is completed when and only when for every n Task n has been performed. I have not been saying (so far) that the conclusion of the argument may not be true. But it seems extremely likely, so far as I can see, that the people who have supposed that super-tasks are possible of performance (e.g. Messrs. Taylor and Watling) have supposed so just because they have unthinkingly accepted this argument as valid. People have, I think, confused saying (1) it is conceivable that each of an infinity of tasks be possible (practically possible) of performance, with saying (2) that is conceivable that all of an infinite number of tasks should have been performed. They have supposed that (1) entails (2). And my reason for thinking that people have supposed this is as follows. To suppose that (1) entails (2) is of course to suppose that anyone who denies thinking (2) is committed to denying (1). Now to deny (1) is to be committed to holding, what is quite absurd, (3) that for any given kind of task there is a positive integer k such that it is conceivable that k tasks of the given kind have been performed, but inconceivable, logically absurd, that $k + 1$ of them should have been performed. But no-one would hold (3) to be true unless he had confused logical possibility with physical possibility. And we do find that those who wish to assert (2) are constantly accusing their opponents of just this confusion. They seem to think that all they have to do to render (2) plausible is to clear away any confusions that prevent people from accepting (1). (See the cited papers by Messrs. Taylor and Watling, *passim*.)[4]

I must now mention two other reasons which have led

[4] See also Mr. Taylor's criticism, *Analysis* 13:1 (1952) of J. O. Wisdom's paper, "Achilles on a Physical Race-Course," *Analysis* 12:3 (1952). I am inclined to think that Dr. Wisdom really does deny (1) and that he supposes that he is committed to this course because he wishes to deny (2).

people to suppose it obvious that super-tasks are possible of performance. The first is this. It certainly makes sense to speak of someone having performed a number of tasks. But infinite numbers are numbers; therefore it must make sense to speak of someone having performed an infinite number of tasks. But this perhaps is not so much a reason for holding anything as a reason for not thinking about it. The second is a suggestion of Russell's. Russell suggested[5] that a man's skill in performing operations of some kind might increase so fast that he was able to perform each of an infinite sequence of operations after the first in half the time he had required for its predecessor. Then the time required for all of the infinite sequence of tasks would be only twice that required for the first. On the strength of this Russell said that the performance of all of an infinite sequence of tasks was only medically impossible. This suggestion is both accepted and used by both Taylor and Watling.

Russell has the air of one who explains how something that you might think hard is really quite easy. ("Look, you do it *this* way".) But our difficulty with the notion of a super-task is not this kind of difficulty. Does Russell really show us what it would be like to have performed a super-task? Does he explain the concept? To me, at least, it seems that he does not even see the difficulty. It is certainly conceivable that there be an infinite sequence of improvements each of which might be effected in a man's skill. For any number n we can imagine that a man is first able to perform just n tasks of some kind in (say) two minutes, and then, after practice, drugs, or meditation is able to perform $n + 1$ of them in two minutes. But this is just not to say that we can imagine that someone has effected all the improvements each of which might be effected. If Russell thought it was he was making the mistake already called attention to. And otherwise his suggestion does not help. For the thing said to be possible, and to explain how a super-task is possible, are the things to be explained. If we have no difficulties with "he has effected all of an infinite number of improvements" we are not likely

[5] "The Limits of Empiricism," *Proceedings of the Aristotelian Society* 12:3 (1935–36).

to be puzzled by "He has performed an infinite number of tasks."

It may be that Russell had in mind only this. If we can conceive a machine doing something—e.g. calling out or writing down numbers—at a certain rate, let us call that rate *conceivable*. Then, there is obviously no upper bound to the sequence of conceivable rates. For any number n we can imagine a machine that calls out or writes down the first n numbers in just $2 - \dfrac{1}{2^n - 1}$ minutes. But this again is not to say that we can imagine a machine that calls out or writes down all the numerals in just 2 minutes. An infinity of possible machines is not the possibility of an infinity-machine. To suppose otherwise would again be the fallacy referred to.

So far I have only been trying to show that the reasons one might have for supposing super-tasks possible of performance are not very good ones. Now, are there any reasons for supposing that super-tasks are not possible of performance? I think there are.

There are certain reading-lamps that have a button in the base. If the lamp is off and you press the button the lamp goes on, and if the lamp is on and you press the button the lamp goes off. So if the lamp was originally off, and you pressed the button an odd number of times, the lamp is on, and if you pressed the button an even number of times the lamp is off. Suppose now that the lamp is off, and I succeed in pressing the button an infinite number of times, perhaps making one jab in one minute, another jab in the next half-minute, and so on, according to Russell's recipe. After I have completed the whole infinite sequence of jabs, i.e. at the end of the two minutes, is the lamp on or off? It seems impossible to answer this question. It cannot be on, because I did not ever turn it on without at once turning it off. It cannot be off, because I did in the first place turn it on, and thereafter I never turned it off without at once turning it on. But the lamp must be either on or off. This is a contradiction.

This type of argument refutes also the possibility of a machine built according to Russell's prescription that say writes down in two minutes every integer in the decimal ex-

pansion of π. For if such a machine is (logically) possible
so presumably is one that records the parity, o or 1, of the
integers written down by the original machine as it produces
them. Suppose the parity-machine has a dial on which either
o or 1 appears. Then, what appears on the dial after the
first machine has run through all the integers in the expansion of π?

Now what exactly do these arguments come to? Say that
the reading-lamp has either of two light-values, o ('off') and
1 ('on'). To switch the lamp on is then to add 1 to its value
and to switch it off is to subtract 1 from its value. Then the
question whether the lamp is on or off after the infinite number of switchings have been performed is a question about
the value of the lamp after an infinite number of alternating
additions and subtractions of 1 to and from its value, i.e. is
the question: What is the sum of the infinite divergent
sequence

$$+1, -1, +1, \ldots?$$

Now mathematicians do say that this sequence has a sum;
they say that its sum is $\frac{1}{2}$.[6] And this answer does not help
us, since we attach no sense here to saying that the lamp is
half-on. I take this to mean that there is no established
method for deciding *what* is done when a super-task is done.
And this at least shows that the concept of a super-task has
not been *explained*. We cannot be expected to *pick up* this
idea, just because we have the idea of a task or tasks having
been performed and because we are acquainted with transfinite numbers.

As far as I can see the argument given above about the
reading-lamp is virtually equivalent to one of Professor Black's
arguments.[7] These arguments were however rejected by
Taylor and Watling, who said that Black assumed the point
at issue by supposing that if any number of tasks have been

[6] G. H. Hardy, *Divergent Series*, Oxford University Press, 1949,
Ch. 1. There is an excellent account of the discussions this series
has provoked in Dr. Waismann's *Introduction to Mathematical
Thinking*, Frederick Ungar, New York, 1951, Ch. 10.

[7] "Achilles and the Tortoise," p. 98, para. 17.

performed some task of those performed was performed last. This assumption is, they say, exactly the assumption that if any number of tasks have been performed a finite number only have been performed. On the one hand it is not clear to me that Black actually *used* this assumption (clearly he believed it to be true, because it was what he was arguing for) and on the other hand it is clear that the question of a 'last task' is a little more complicated than Watling and Taylor supposed, just because some infinite sequences really do have last terms as well as first ones. (Thus if you could mention all the positive integers in two minutes in the way that Russell suggests you could also mention them all except 32 in two minutes; you would then have performed a super-task, but not the super-task of mentioning all the numbers; but to complete this one you would have only to mention 32, and this would be your last task.) But in any case it should be clear that no assumption about a last task is made in the lamp-argument. If the button has been jabbed an infinite number of times in the way described then there was no last jab and we cannot ask whether the last jab was a switching-on or a switching-off. But we did not ask about a last jab; we asked about the net or total result of the whole infinite sequence of jabs, and this would seem to be a fair question.

It may be instructive here to consider and take quite seriously some remarks of Mr. Watling[8] about summing an infinite convergent sequence. Mr. Watling undertook to show that if you could make all of an infinite number of additions you could compute the sum of the sequence.

$$1, \tfrac{1}{2}, \tfrac{1}{4}, \ldots,$$

that you could add the terms of this sequence together in quite literally the same way as we add together a finite number of numbers, and that you would reach the right answer. For you could add $\tfrac{1}{2}$ to 1, then add $\tfrac{1}{4}$ to the result, and so on, until all of an infinite number of additions have been made. If Mr. Watling were right about this, then of course the net result of at least one super-task would be computable by established methods, indeed by just those methods that

8 "The Sum of an Infinite Series," pp. 43 et seq.

we ordinarily use to compute the limit of the sequence of partial sums

$$1, 1\tfrac{1}{2}, 1\tfrac{3}{4}, \ldots ,$$

But is he right? There is still the difficulty of supposing that someone could have made an infinite number of additions. (The impossibility of a super-task does not depend at all on whether some vaguely-felt-to-be associated arithmetical sequence is convergent or divergent). But besides this, and partly (I think) because of it, there are special difficulties connected with what Mr. Watling says on this score. According to him, "Nothing more is required to give the sum than making every one of the additions."[9] Let us then pretend that we have a machine that does make every one of the additions; it adds $\tfrac{1}{2}$ to 1 in the first minute of its running time, adds $\tfrac{1}{4}$ to its last result in the next half-minute, and so on. Then this machine does make "every one of the additions". But does it arrive at the number 2? I do not think we can ask what number the machine arrives at, simply because it does not make a last addition. Every number computed by the machine is a number in the sequence of partial sums given above, i.e. is a value of

$$f(n) = 2 - \frac{1}{2^n - 1}$$

for some positive integral argument. But to say that the machine computes *only* numbers in this sequence ("Nothing else is required to give the sum than making every one of the additions") *and* that it computes 2 is a flat contradiction. The result of this pseudo-calculation can only be a term in the sequence of partial sums; but equally it cannot be any of these.

This may become clearer if we suppose that the machine records the results of its successive additions on a tape that runs through the machine and that the machine only has the vocabulary to print terms in the sequence of partial sums. (In particular the machine cannot print the number 2). The machine can then record the result of each of the additions that it is required to make, but it cannot record the number which is said to be 'finally' arrived at. Now Mr. Watling would perhaps wish to say that this machine does in *some* sense 'arrive' at the number 2, even though it does not record the fact. But in *what* sense? What does Mr. Watling mean by the word 'give' in the sentence quoted above from his paper? It is surely an essential feature of our notion of computation (our ordinary notion of computation) that at some point in the proceedings the answer to the sum is *read off;* we find ourselves writing down or announcing the answer and our algorithm tells us that this is the answer. It is clear how this is so when we add together some finite number of numbers. It is not at all clear from Mr. Watling's paper how or in what sense a man who has added together an infinite number of numbers can be said to *arrive* at his answer. Mr. Watling has not all explained what he means by saying that the addition of all the terms of the sequence 1, $\frac{1}{2}$, $\frac{1}{4}$, . . . would *yield* 2. And our suspicions on this score should be increased by his actual 'proof' that the number reached by adding together all the terms of an infinite convergent sequence is the number that is the limit of the sequence of partial sums; for this proof is either circular or senseless. Mr. Watling argues as follows:[10] if you start to add together the terms of the sequence to be summed, every term you add brings the sum nearer to the limit of the sequence of partial sums; therefore, when you have added together all the terms, there is no difference between the sum and the limit. This is only to say: the sequence of partial sums converges to a limit, and therefore the sum of all the terms in the original sequence *is* the limit. And here Mr. Watling has given no *independent* sense to "Sum of all the terms". He refers us to the steadily-increasing sum of the first so-many terms of the sequence; i.e. he refers to the fact that the sequence of partial sums is monotonic increasing and convergent. But this gives him no right at all to suppose that he has specified a number to be the sum of all the terms. Mr. Watling supposes, of course, that we can infer what the sum of an infinite sequence is by consideration of the relevant sequence of partial sums; as it is sometimes put, we consider the behaviour of the function that enumer-

[10] Last paragraph on p. 45.

ates the partial sums as its argument tends to infinity. And this is quite correct; we can and we do infer what is the sum of an infinite sequence in this way. But this *is* correct *only* because we usually *define* the sum of an infinite sequence to be the limit of the sequence of partial sums. Insofar as Mr. Watling relies tacitly on this his proof is circular. And otherwise I do not think that his proof can be said to show anything at all, for he gives no alternative method whereby the sum of an infinite sequence might be specified.

As far as I can see, we give a sense to the expression "sum of an infinite number of terms" by the methods that we use for computing the limits of certain sequences. There is an inclination to feel that the expression *means* something quite different; that the established method for computing limits is just the way we discover what the sum is, and that the number so discovered can be or should be specified in some other way. But I think that this is just an illusion, born of the belief that one might reach the sum in some other way, e.g. by actually adding together all the terms of the infinite sequence. And if I am correct in supposing that talk of super-tasks is *senseless*, then this kind of talk cannot *give* a sense to anything. The belief that one could add together all the terms of an infinite sequence is itself due presumably to a desire to assimilate sums of infinite sequences to sums of finite ones. This was Mr. Watling's avowed intention. "The limit of a sequence of sums has been called a sum but has not been shown to be one".[11] Mr. Watling was then trying to *justify* our practice of calling the sum of an infinite sequence a sum. Presumably this practice is due to the fact that the limit of a sequence of sums really is the limit of a sequence of *sums*. If the expression "sum of an infinite sequence" has no meaning apart from the methods we use for computing limits—methods that are, notice, *demonstrably* different from those that we use to compute the sums of finite numbers of terms—this practice *could* not be justified further. The difficulties that Mr. Watling gets into are implicit in his project.[12]

[11] P. 43.

[12] And in fact the project breaks down at once; for Mr. Watling finds it necessary to define the sum of an infinite series 'as the sum

But now, it may be said, surely it is sometimes possible to complete an infinite number of tasks. For to complete a journey is to complete a task, the task of getting from somewhere to somewhere else. And a man who completes any journey completes an infinite number of journeys. If he travels from o to 1, he travels from o to $\frac{1}{2}$, from $\frac{1}{2}$ to $\frac{3}{4}$, and so on *ad inf.*, so when he arrives at 1 he has completed an infinite number of tasks. This is virtually the first premiss in the original argument, and it certainly seems both to be true and to contradict the previous result. I think it is true but does not contradict the impossibility of super-tasks.

Let Z be the set of points along the race-course

$$0, \frac{1}{2}, \frac{3}{4}, \ldots$$

where o is the starting-point, 1 the finishing-point; suppose these on our left and our right respectively. Notice that Z is open on the right; there is no Z-point to the right of every other Z-point. Z is convergent but its limit-point 1 is not in Z. A point that is neither a Z-point nor to the left of any Z-point I shall call a point external to Z. In particular, 1 is external to Z.

Those who support the first premiss say that all you have to do to get to 1 is to occupy every Z-point from left to right in turn. Or rather they are committed to saying this; for they do say that to get to 1 it is sufficient to run all the distances in the sequence of distances $\frac{1}{2}$, $\frac{1}{4}$, . . . ; but to occupy every Z-point is to run every one of these distances, since each distance has a right-hand end-point in Z, and, conversely, every Z-point is the right-hand end of one of these distances. But put this way, in terms of points rather than distances, should not their thesis seem odd? For to have arrived at 1 you must have occupied or passed over 1. But 1 is not a Z-point. 1 is not the end-point of any of the distances: first half, third quarter. . . .

Further: suppose someone could have occupied every Z-point without having occupied any point external to Z. Where would he be? Not at any Z-point, for then there would be an unoccupied Z-point to the right. Not, for the same rea-

of all its terms in a *certain order* and with a *certain grouping'* (p. 44, my italics). But is not ordinary addition commutative?

son, between Z-points. And, ex hypothesi, not at any point external to Z. But these possibilities are exhaustive. The absurdity of having occupied all the Z-points without having occupied any point external to Z is exactly like the absurdity of having pressed the lamp-switch an infinite number of times or of having made all of an infinite number of additions.

But of course those who say that to finish your journey all you have to do is to run each of an infinite number of distances do not say in so many words that it is possible to have done what was just said to be impossible. And obviously it is possible to have occupied all the Z-points; you do this by starting off for 1 and making sure you get there. You then occupy a point external to Z; but you have occupied all the Z-points too. Now if you are given a set of tasks, and if it is impossible for you to have performed all the tasks set unless you perform a task not set or not explicitly set, should you not suppose that you are to do something you were not explicitly told to do? (If you are wearing shoes and socks and you are told to take off your socks should you not suppose that you are to take off your shoes?) So if you are told to occupy all the Z-points should you not at once proceed to 1?

But the shoes-and-socks analogy is not quite correct. To arrive at 1 you do not have to occupy all the Z-points and then do something else. If you have completed all the journeys that have end-points in Z, there is no further distance to run before arriving at 1. Arriving is not running a last distance. On the contrary, your arriving at 1 is your completing the whole journey and thus is your having completed all the infinite number of journeys (in the only sense in which this is possible). Occupying all the Z-points in turn does not get you to some point short of 1; it does not get you, in particular, to a point *next to* 1. Either occupying all the Z-points *is* getting to 1, or it is *nothing*. And this is, perhaps, obscurely noticed by those who support the first premiss. They say, "*all* you need to do is . . ." And though it would be permissible to interpret the 'all' as saying that you need not occupy any point external to Z it could also be interpreted as saying that arriving at 1 is not completing a last journey of those specified.

There is then something odd in the claim that to arrive at 1 you need only occupy all the Z-points. Take it narrowly and it is nonsense. But if we take it charitably, is it not something of a joke? For when the order "Run an infinite number of journeys!" is so explained as to be intelligible, it is seen to be the order "Run!" And indeed how could one run any distance without being at some point midway between point of departure and destination? If running to catch a bus is performing a super-task, then this super-task is, for some people at some times, *medically* possible. But *this* super-task is just a task.

If an infinite number of things are to be done, they must be done in some or other order. The order in which they are done imposes an ordering on the set of things to be done. Hence to the performance of an infinite set of tasks we assign not a transfinite cardinal but a transfinite ordinal. What is shown by the example of the lamp-switch and by the impossibility of occupying all Z-points without occupying any point external to Z is that it is impossible to have performed every task in a sequence of tasks of type ω (no last task). Now the man who runs from 0 to 1 and so passes over every Z-point may be said to have run every one of an unending sequence of distances, a sequence of type ω. But the proof that he does depends on a statement about arriving at points. Further it is completing a journey that is completing a task, and completing a journey is arriving at a point. And the sequence of points that he arrives at (or is said here to arrive at) is not a sequence of type ω but a sequence of type $\omega + 1$, (last task, no penultimate task) the sequence of the points

$$0, \tfrac{1}{2}, \ldots, 1$$

in Z's closure. So when we explain in what sense a man who completes a journey completes an infinite number of journeys, and thus explain in what sense the first premiss is true, we thereby explain that what is said to be possible by the first premiss is not what is said to be impossible by the second.

The objection to super-tasks was that we could not *say* what would be done if a super-task were done. This objection does not apply in the case of the runner; we can say, he was at o and now is at 1. But if it is sometimes possible to have performed all of an infinite sequence of tasks of type $\omega + 1$, why is it not possible to mention all the positive integers except 32 in two minutes, by Russell's prescription, and then mention 32 last? This would be performing a sequence of tasks of type $\omega + 1$. Well, here it would seem reasonable to ask about the state of a parity-machine[13] at the end of the first two minutes, i.e. immediately before the last number was mentioned. But it is obviously unreasonable to ask where the runner was when he was at the point immediately preceding his destination.

There are two points I would like to make in conclusion. There may be a certain reluctance to admitting that one does complete an infinite number of journeys in completing one journey. This reluctance would appear strongly if someone said that the concept of an open point-set like Z was *not applicable to* 'physical reality'. Such a reluctance might be lessened by the following consideration. Let Operation 1 be the operation of proceeding from o to the midpoint of o and 1. Let Operation 2 be the operation of performing Operation 1 and then proceeding from the point where you are to the midpoint of that point and 1. And in general let Operation n be the operation of performing Operation $n - 1$ and etc. Then Z is the set of points you can get to by performing an operation of the kind described. And obviously none of the operations described gets you to the point 1, hence we should expect Z not to contain its own limit-point and so to be open. Now we just cannot say *a priori* that we shall *never* have occasion to mention point-sets like Z; one might well want to consider the set of points you can get to by performing operations of this kind. So it is just wrong to say that the concept of an open point-set like Z has no application to 'physical reality' (which is I think what Black and Wisdom are saying.) But on the other hand the implicit use of the concept in the first premiss of the Zenoesque argument *is* a misleading one, and this is just what the second premiss calls attention to. Roughly speaking the argument forces us to

13 See above.

consider the *applications* of the concept of infinity. (E.g. contrast the ways in which it occurs in the propositions I called (1) and (2) at the beginning of this paper.)[14]

Secondly, it may be helpful to indicate the way in which the topic of this discussion is related to the 'mathematical solution' of the paradox, referred to by all three of the writers I have quoted. People used to raise this topic by asking *"How is it possible* for a man to run all of an infinite number of distances?" Now either they thought, or Whitehead and others thought they thought, that the difficulty of running an infinite number of distances was like the difficulty of getting to a place an infinite number of miles away. Hence Whitehead emphasised that the sequence

$$1, \tfrac{1}{2}, \tfrac{1}{4}, \ . \ . \ .$$

was convergent and had a finite sum. He also thereby pointed out a play on the word 'never'; the sequence never reaches 0, the sequence of partial sums never reaches 2. (The sequence does not contain its limit; but it is convergent, the limit exists.)[15] But though this is necessary it does not resolve all the hesitations one might feel about the premiss of the paradox. What I have been trying to show is that these hesitations are not merely frivolous, and that insofar as they spring from misunderstandings these misunderstandings are shared by those who support the 'mathematical solution'.

[14] I think it is partly this contrast that those people have in mind who claim to distinguish between the concept of a potential infinite and the concept of an actual infinite. But there are not here two concepts but two applications of one concept.

[15] This is clearly explained by Mr. Taylor, *op. cit.*, note 2.

MODERN SCIENCE AND
ZENO'S PARADOXES OF MOTION

ADOLF GRÜNBAUM

§ 1. *The Problem Posed by Zeno*

Zeno presents four pardoxes of motion. These are known respectively as the Dichotomy, the Paradox of Achilles and the Tortoise, the Arrow Paradox, and the Paradox of the Stadium. I shall devote my attention to those versions of these paradoxes which may be thought to pose problems for modern mathematical physics.

The Dichotomy and Achilles paradoxes are directed against those kinematical theories which assume that between any two instants of time there is at least one other and that between any two space points, there is at least one other. Any class of elements ordered by this kind of betweenness is said to be "dense." It is thus logically possible that diverse classes of elements are each dense with respect to their particular ordering relations of betweenness, and in the case of any one class of elements and a specified betweenness relation, we can therefore ask whether the class constitutes a dense system. Hence, it is just as significant to ask whether the points of space on a line constitute a dense system as it is to ask whether the instants of time do. By the same token, one can call the ascription of denseness to physical space into question just as one can its ascription to time.

For any given instant of a dense temporal order, there does *not* exist any *next* instant either before it or after it, since *any* two instants are separated by others, which are between them. This dense kind of betweenness is to be contrasted with the betweenness associated with a *discrete* series. In a discrete series like 1, 2, 3, . . . the elements are ordered consecutively, i.e., one *next* to the other. And if there are any elements between two others in a discrete series, their interposition is consecutive. Newtonian physics, relativity theory, and standard quantum mechanics all assume that both spatial and temporal betweenness are dense as opposed to discrete. Standard quantum theory has discretized or quantized *some* physical properties whose counterparts in classical physics were mathematically continuous. But we must be aware that standard quantum theory has *not* quantized *space* or *time*, lest it be overlooked here that the time of this theory is dense. For in standard quantum theory, every point of continuous physical space is a *potential* sharply defined position of, say, an electron, and separately, every instant of a continuous time is *potentially* the time of a physical event.[1]

By assuming that physical time is a linear mathematical continuum of instants, the modern kinematical theories assert a time interval to be an actually infinite *dense* set of elements.[2] In Bergson's view, the significance of Zeno's paradoxes of motion, whatever their intent, lies in their indictment of this mathematical assumption as resting on an assimilation of time to space. And according to James and Whitehead, Zeno's Dichotomy and his Achilles and the Tortoise do succeed in showing that the denseness postulate grafts onto time and motion an ordinal property alien to them.[3]

[1] For a detailed discussion of standard quantum mechanics in its bearing on Zeno's paradoxes of motion, see A. Grünbaum, *Modern Science and Zeno's Paradoxes,* Allen & Unwin Ltd., London, 1968, Ch. II, § 6.

[2] It is important to be aware that the spatial and temporal intervals (continua) of modern kinematics are *actually infinite* sets of punctal elements in the sense of Georg Cantor, *not* merely *potentially* infinite aggregates in Aristotle's sense. The latter are infinite merely in the sense of being infinitely divisible. Hence, in modern kinematics the members of an infinite set of non-overlapping subintervals of an interval of time or space cannot be regarded as first having to be *generated* by hypothetical division operations on the total interval.

[3] For the relevant citations from the writings of Bergson, James, Whitehead, and Weiss, cf. my "Relativity and the Atomicity of Becoming," *Review of Metaphysics,* 4 (1950), 144–60.

I shall deal critically with Zeno's Dichotomy and Achilles paradoxes in the context of modern kinematics without any historical regard to what their intent might have been. In doing so, I shall construe the Dichotomy and the Achilles as offering a *reductio ad absurdum* of the *denseness* of physical time and of motion but *not* as denying their very existence ("reality"). On this construal, the existence of *non-illusory phenomena* of physical time and motion is not in question, theory-laden though the claim of their non-illusoriness be. For this existential claim, though theory-laden, is taken to be incomparably better established than the kinematical denseness postulate invoked by dynamical theory in seeking to explain the phenomena of time and motion. Furthermore, I take it for granted that dynamical theory does explain some of the phenomena of time and motion by entailing true descriptions of them. Hence I see Zeno's Dichotomy and Achilles paradoxes as distinctively posing the following issue: does the kinematical denseness postulate entail the fact that dynamical theory *also* entails the following false consequences: (i) a physical object cannot endure through a finite time interval, (ii) a runner can never get started, and (iii) no finite space interval can ever be traversed in a finite time.

It is a corollary of my construal of the contemporary relevance of the Dichotomy and the Achilles that if the denseness postulate *did* permit the deduction of any of these false consequences—which I shall maintain it does not—then modern kinematics would have to be supplanted by a theory not suffering from this alleged defect. Far from concluding that Zeno's challenge in these two paradoxes necessitates the disavowal of the denseness postulate, I shall defend that postulate both positively and negatively as follows: (1) positively, by pointing out that the theory of physical (as distinct from *sensed*) events can give an intelligible physical meaning to the concept of a dense temporal order; this positive thesis parallels the commonly accepted claim that physical geometry can meaningfully avow the denseness of any one of the dimensions of physical space, and (2) negatively, by demonstrating against Zeno that such infinities as are deducible from denseness do not issue in any of the aforementioned false consequences, viz. do not issue in the impossibility of finite time intervals or motions.

Zeno's paradox of the Arrow has it that motion cannot be composed of immobilities. In my view, Russell has definitively disposed of this paradox if it is taken to be aimed at the assumption of the mathematical continuity of space, time, and motion.[4] More commonly, however, the Arrow is interpreted as being predicated, like the Stadium paradox, on the contrary assumption of their discreteness. I have therefore explained elsewhere[5] (i) why the Arrow and the Stadium, both interpreted as directed against the discreteness of space, time, and motion, do not pose any challenge for standard quantum mechanics, and (ii) why the refutation of the Dichotomy and Achilles which I shall offer is not rendered superfluous by standard quantum mechanics. It turns out, however, that a *cautionary lesson* can indeed be derived from the Stadium for speculations envisioning a genuinely quantized or atomic space and time.[6]

§ 2. *The Kinematical Denseness Postulate*

Since all the central issues raised by the Dichotomy and the Achilles will be seen to revolve around the denseness postulate for both space and time, our first concern will be with this postulate. I shall discuss its consistency with the remainder of kinematical theory and also the physical warrant for its temporal version. Specifically, I shall deal with the postulate in the context of the following two subtopics:

(i) Statement of some mathematical consequences of the denseness postulate for physical *space* as *prophylaxis* against errors, to be discussed in §§ 3, 4, and 5, which have been

---

[4] B. Russell, *The Principles of Mathematics,* 2d ed., W. W. Norton, New York, 1938, chs. xlii and liv, and *A History of Western Philosophy,* New York, 1945, pp. 805–6. Cf. also G. J. Whitrow, *The Natural Philosophy of Time,* London and Edinburgh, 1961, pp. 138–40.

[5] Grünbaum, *loc. cit.*

[6] *Idem.*

committed in the treatment of time and motion by mathematically literate writers on Zeno;

(ii) Statement and refutation of arguments directed specifically against the denseness of physical *time*.

The first of these two statements will be supplemented by a comparison of physical with *perceptual* space in regard to the status of the denseness postulate. And the second statement will involve the corresponding comparison for the case of time. The significant difference that will emerge between the results of these two comparisons will then serve to explain why thinkers like James and Whitehead have thought that Zeno posed a genuine problem.

Thus, § 2 will prepare the ground for showing in §§ 3, 4, and 5 that Zeno's arguments concerning time and motion are fallacious, yet inordinately subtle, highly instructive, and perennially provocative to the point of having earned for themselves the verdict: "Les arguments de Zénon d'Elée ont exercé la sagacité des plus grands penseurs de tous les temps."[7]

A. *The Denseness Postulate for Physical Space*

Within the theoretical framework of standard mathematical physics, consider a linear interval of physical space which is, say, 2 units in length. On that theory, to be such an interval logically involves being a mathematically continuous series of space points. And the *denseness* property of this kind of continuum assures that, as metricized, the interval includes, for example, a spatial progression of non-overlapping subintervals of lengths

$$1, \tfrac{1}{2}, \tfrac{1}{4}, \tfrac{1}{8}, \; \ldots$$

If there exists a total interval as postulated by the theory, then *eo ipso* there is also such a sequence of subintervals. For their existence is part and parcel of the existence of the dense actual infinity of space points constituting the total interval. In fact, if we consider *overlapping* though distinct

[7] *Larousse du XXe Siècle*, Librairie Larousse, Paris, 1933, Vol. VI, 1128. In English: The arguments of Zeno of Elea have challenged the wisdom of the greatest thinkers of every age.

subintervals as well, then there automatically exists a super-denumerable infinity of them. Therefore, there can be no question at all of first having to "generate" these subintervals by some kind of hypothetical or ideal division operation in thought. Our particular spatial progression of subintervals above may be regarded as artificial only in the sense that this particular denumerable set of subintervals has been *singled out* for consideration to the neglect of the remaining members of the superdenumerably infinite totality of all subintervals. Though artificial in this sense, the singling out of these particular non-overlapping subintervals is clearly in no way in-compatible with the *continuity* of their union, if all the sub-intervals are respectively half-open and closed on the same side.[8] Thus, it would be an error to think of the non-overlapping distinctness of our thus half-open subintervals as being incompatible with the continuity of the total interval.[9]

Being a progression, our sequence of spatial subintervals has *no last member*. Yet it would be sheer folly mathemati-cally to argue that the absence of a last subinterval in this progression warrants the conclusion that the total interval, which is known to be spatially finite, must paradoxically also be spatially infinite. I mention this folly because we shall need to see why informed people have been driven to commit the corresponding mathematical folly in the case of *time* intervals. But why is it a folly to make the allegation of para-dox in the spatial case? Though denumerably infinite in num-ber, the subintervals are of ever decreasing size such that they *all* fit into a total finite interval of length 2 both dis-tributively and collectively, i.e., any one and every one of them fits. That they fit collectively into a finite total interval is evident from the fact that *for every n*, the union of the first

---

[8] If "a" and "b" denote points, then the interval (a, b) of points x .can be closed $(a \leqq x \leqq b)$, open $(a < x < b)$ or half-open $(a \leqq x < b$ or $a < x \leqq b)$, where it is to be understood that the symbols "$<$" and "$\leqq$" have a purely ordinal meaning.

[9] For a discussion of the conditions under which the union of two or more intervals is or is not itself an interval, cf. H. Cramér, *Mathematical Methods of Statistics*, Princeton University Press, Princeton, N.J., 1946, pp. 11–12.

n of our subintervals in the progression has a length S_n less than 2 given by $S_n = 2 - \dfrac{1}{2^{n-1}}$.[10]

The metrical physical fact that all the ever-shorter subintervals of the progression collectively fit into the total interval of length 2, although the progression is unending, has an important bearing on the additivity of lengths. It shows that we are *justified* in using the standard mathematical limit definition of the arithmetic sum of the infinite sequence of length numbers

$$1, \tfrac{1}{2}, \tfrac{1}{4}, \tfrac{1}{8}, \ldots$$

to determine the length of the union of the subintervals, which is equal to the length of the total interval. Thus we see that the mathematical limit definition of the arithmetic sum of a progression of numbers is indeed appropriate to obtaining the length of the total interval of physical space from the lengths of the members of any particular set of its non-overlapping subintervals which cover the interval up to or including any end-point(s) that it may have. The limit definition of the arithmetic sum of a progression of numbers cannot, of course, be invoked *as such* to show that a *finite* interval of physical space can be the union of an unending progression of non-overlapping subintervals. But the use of this limit definition can be justified physically by showing that the lengths of physical intervals are indeed additive in the indicated sense of the arithmetic limit definition.[11]

Recalling our earlier definitions of a "closed," "open," and "half-open" interval (a, b),[12] assume now that our total interval of length 2 is closed. It is of great importance for our

[10] The sum S_n of the first n terms of the geometric progression a, ar, ar^2 . . . ar^{n-1} is given by $S_n = \dfrac{a(1-r^n)}{1-r}$. Hence in the case of our progression of lengths of subintervals, $S_n = 2 - \dfrac{1}{2^{n-1}}$.

[11] For details on the additivity of lengths, see Grünbaum, *op. cit.*, Ch. iii, § 2.

[12] See fn. 8 of this paper.

subsequent purposes to be mindful of the following set-theoretic, ordinal, and metrical facts pertaining to this interval:

(1) Even if each of the subintervals in our progression is closed, the point 2, which closes the total interval on the right, is *not* a member of *any* of the subintervals in this *unending* progression. It is therefore wholly futile and self-contradictory to conceive of the point 2 as the right end-point of the *last* subinterval in our infinite sequence of sub-intervals, a sequence that cannot possibly have a last element. If our non-overlapping subintervals are all assumed hereafter to be either closed or closed on the left side, then the point 2 is the *only* point of the total closed interval which does not belong to one of the subintervals in our progression. Hence, in that case, the total closed interval *contains* every point belonging to one of the subintervals of our progression but does not *consist* of only these points. For the total closed interval contains the rightmost point 2 as well.

(2) The interval S of all points belonging to at least one of our subintervals is identical with the half-open interval obtained by excluding the rightmost point 2 from our total initially closed interval. There is an important *ordinal* sense in which this half-open interval S "has no end" on the right side: *in virtue of spatial denseness,* there is no point *next* to the point 2 on its left, and hence S is devoid of a rightmost or "last" point. Indeed this absence of a "last" point is rendered by saying that the interval S is "open" on that side. But the failure to have an end or last point in this *ordinal* sense does *not* prevent the interval S from having the finite length 2! For the length of a finite interval (a, b) is the non-negative quantity b — a regardless of whether the interval is closed, open, or half-open. The non-existence of a last point in S fully allows the presence of the point 2 at the finite distance of 2 units from the leftmost point of S. And the set-theoretic addition of the point 2 to S at its open end would merely close this initially half-open interval without affecting its length.

It must be emphasized that the structure which scientific theory attributes to an interval of *physical* space cannot be understood as isomorphic with the elements, properties, and relations encountered in the *perceptual* space furnished by the sensory organs of the human body when we sense a line segment. A chalk line on a blackboard qualifies as "continuous" in the *sensory* sense on the strength of not exhibiting any gaps which are noticeable by means of our unaided senses: the line is *not* perceived to be an actual aggregate of distinct elements sustaining relations of linear continuity in the mathematical sense. Indeed, an interval of visual or tactile space can be sensed as an extended expanse without reference to the finite number of constituent *minima perceptibilia* (i.e. discernibly smallest distinct elements) into which it *might* be resolved. And since there is a positive (non-zero) threshold of perception, these *minima* cannot be punctal. By contrast, the interval of physical space which the theory correlates with the perceived interval is conceived as *literally* a linear mathematical continuum of points. Thus, while the interval of physical space is held to be a *dense* aggregate, its perceptual counterpart is generally *not* even an aggregate of smallest elements. And as a *potential* aggregate, the latter is not dense but discrete.

Two important results relevant to our subsequent concerns emerge from this brief comparison of physical and perceptual space: (1) A sensed expanse can be perceived as spatial *in toto* without reference to the *minima* of which it is only *potentially* an aggregate. Thus the deliverances of sensed space do *not* inevitably confront us with an aggregate whose structure is logically incompatible with the one postulated by the theory. Hence these deliverances do not militate against the immediate theoretical intelligibility of the dense linear continuum of mathematical points of physical space as the correlate of the sensed spatial interval. (2) It is a misconstrual of physical geometry to expect it to be wholly isomorphic with perceptual geometry. For by impoverishing physical geometry, the demand for such an isomorphism invites the severe curtailment of the explanatory power of physics.

B. *Statement and Refutation of Arguments against the Denseness of Physical Time*

The crucial issue posed by Zeno's Dichotomy and Achilles is the following: Can the mathematical statements made in the preceding section about the ordinal and metrical properties of a space interval and its subintervals also be made meaningfully and warrantedly about time? Specifically, can these mathematical statements also be made about (1) the *time* interval between two events at a given space point, and its subintervals, and (2) the interval of time between the start and finish of a motion through a finite spatial distance? According to thinkers such as James and Whitehead, the moral of Zeno's polemic is that the answer to each of these questions is emphatically NO. And it behooves us, at this stage of our analysis, to examine the principal reason for their contention. To do so, we must be aware that their thesis concerns not the *consistency* of the mathematical theory of motion but the *applicability* of the formal mathematics of linear continuity to time. For what they are asserting is that time does not possess the structure of the linear mathematical continuum. Hence it would be begging the question to seek to invalidate their thesis by simply *assuming* the mathematical continuity of time without argument. In particular, it would not do to try to rebut them and Zeno by simply invoking *mutatis mutandis* the ordinal and metrical results stated for physical space in § 2A.

Why do James and Whitehead deny the appropriateness of the formal mathematics of linear continuity to time? Their reasons are the following: (1) the relations of temporal order among physical events *as they actually happen* are as known to us in our conscious awareness of their coming into being, (2) occurring *now* or happening is pulsational and not punctal, as shown by the existence of a durational threshold governing our awareness of the actual occurrence of events,[13]

[13] For a very recent penetrating discussion of tachistoscopic experiments and other matters relating to the temporal threshold of awareness, see R. Efron, "The Duration of the Present," *Annals of the New York Academy of Sciences,* Vol. 138, Art. 2, 1967, pp. 713-729.

and (3) the serial order of pulsational coming into being is *not* dense but *discrete,* i.e., the temporal order of events as they actually happen exhibits *nextness* or consecutivity. Thus, James emphasizes that all processes "like motion, change, activity" which he calls "things conceived as growing"[14] as distinct from "space, past time, existing beings" which he calls "things conceived as standing"[15] must have elements which occur both successively *and* consecutively. In discussing solutions of Zeno's paradoxes of motion such as Russell's which are based on the mathematical continuum, James writes:

> On the discontinuity-theory, time, change, etc., would grow by finite buds or drops, either nothing coming at all, or certain units of amount bursting into being "at a stroke." . . . any amounts of time, space, change, etc., . . . would be composed of a finite number of minimal amounts of time, space, and change.
>
> Such a discrete composition is what actually obtains in our perceptual experience. . . .[16]

It seems to me however that Mr. Russell's statements dodge the real difficulty, which concerns the "growing" variety of infinity exclusively and not the standing variety, which is all that he envisages when he assumes the race already to have been run. . . . The real difficulty may almost be called physical, for it attends the process of *formation* of the paths. Moreover, two paths are not needed—that of either runner alone, *or even the lapse of empty time,*[17] involves the difficulty, which is that of touching a goal when an interval needing to be traversed first keeps permanently reproducing itself and getting in your way. . . . who actually *traverses* a continuum, can do so by no process continuous in the mathematical sense. Be it short or long, each point must be occupied in its due order of succession. . . . "Enu-

---

[14] William James, *Some Problems of Philosophy,* Longmans, Green, New York, 1948, p. 167.
[15] *Idem.*
[16] *Ibid.,* pp. 154–55.
[17] My italics.

meration" is, in short, the sole possible method of occupation of the series of positions implied in the famous
race. . . .[18]

. . . Such seems to be the nature of concrete experience, which changes always by sensible amounts, or
stays unchanged. The infinite character we find in it is
woven into it by our later conception indefinitely repeating the act of subdividing any given amount supposed. The facts do not resist the subsequent conceptual treatment; but we need not believe that the
treatment necessarily reproduces the operation by
which they were originally brought into existence.

The antinomy of mathematically continuous growth
is thus but one more of those many ways in which our
conceptual transformation of perceptual experience makes
it less comprehensible than ever. That being should immediately and by finite quantities add itself to being,
may indeed be something which an onlooking intellect
fails to understand; but that being should be identified
with the consummation of an endless chain of units
(such as "points"), no one of which contains any
amount whatever of the being (such as "space") expected to result, this is something which our intellect
not only fails to understand, but which it finds absurd.

. . . Better accept, as Renouvier says, the opaquely
given data of perception, than concepts inwardly absurd.[19]

. . . Does reality grow by abrupt increments of
novelty, or not? . . . The mathematical definition of
continuous quantity as "that between any two elements
or terms of which there is another term" is directly
opposed to the more empirical or perceptual notion that
anything is continuous when its parts appear as *immediate next neighbors, with absolutely nothing between*.[20]

[18] *Ibid.*, pp. 181–83.
[19] *Ibid.*, pp. 185–86.
[20] *Ibid.*, p. 187; my italics. James errs mathematically by claiming that denseness is both sufficient and necessary for linear
mathematical continuity, whereas it is only necessary.

James's thesis has been reiterated by Whitehead as follows:[21]

> . . . if we admit that "something becomes," it is easy,
> by employing Zeno's method, to prove that there can
> be no continuity of becoming.[22] There is a becoming of
> continuity, but no continuity of becoming. The actual
> occasions are the creatures which become, and they con-
> stitute a continuously extensive world. In other words,
> extensiveness becomes, but "becoming" is not itself ex-
> tensive. . . .
>
> . . . These conclusions are required by the considera-
> tion[23] of Zeno's arguments, in connection with the pre-
> sumption that an actual entity is an act of experience.[24]

In substance, James and Whitehead claim that the temporal order of occurrence of physical events is isomorphic
with the discrete order of the nows of our awareness. And
their claim raises two questions as follows:

(1) Is it true that the order of the nows of our awareness,
i.e., the order in which we perceive events as coming into
being, is discrete?

(2) Is their assertion of isomorphism among the perceptual
and physical orders of time warranted?

I shall defend an affirmative answer to the first of these
two questions. But then I shall present reasons for rejecting
the James-Whitehead thesis of isomorphism by extending the
conclusions of my article on "The Status of Temporal Becoming."[25]

It has been said by some that the James-Whitehead phenomenology of time perception simply does not accord with
actual human experience. Where, they ask, is the temporal
discreteness or atomicity in a long, drawn-out sound of constant auditory pitch or in the observed, uninterrupted move-

[21] A. N. Whitehead, *Process and Reality*, New York, 1929,
p. 53.

[22] At this point, Whitehead gives references to his own discussions of this argument.

[23] Here again Whitehead cites references to his writings.

[24] *Ibid.*, p. 105.

[25] Pp. 322 ff of this volume.

ment of a man such as Achilles? How, they ask, can the perceived contents of these phenomena be likened to the consecutive beats of the heart or claimed to be aggregates of elements which elapse *seriatim* in the manner of the ticktocks of a clock?

To this I reply in several stages as follows.

We can attend to the uniform qualitative sameness of the parts of a drawn-out sound of constant auditory pitch or to the fact that the same person (Achilles) is perceptibly present at the different places traversed by him. To be aware of the uniformity of pitch here may well involve the retrospective awareness that no sound of different pitch was heard temporally between the start and finish of the long sound. Again, in the case of a melody, we can attend to the qualitative differences in auditory pitch among its component tones. When thus attending to the *sensory* qualities of these occurrences, we may also attend *retrospectively* to such temporal features of these processes as the fact that one particular part of theirs preceded another of them. But since we may be preoccupied with other perceptual concerns, we may *not* be attending as well to the distinct *coming into being* of each of the perceived parts of these processes. Though perceptually aware that the durations of these processes exceed that of a perceived instant, we may be unmindful of the *distinct coming into being* of each of their components *as they actually happen;* indeed, in a case like that of the long sound of uniform pitch, our perception of its having components may require our attending to the coming into being of each of them. That it is easy for us *not* to attend to the coming into being of the components of a process as they are actually occurring emerges from my account[26] of coming into being in the tensed sense of occurring *now:* if I just hear a sound at a time *t*, then the sound does not qualify at *t* as coming into being or occurring *now*, unless at *t* I am judgmentally aware of the fact of my hearing it at all and of the temporal coincidence of the hearing with that awareness. Accord-

[26] See pp. 332 ff of this volume.

ingly, we can hear sounds without perceiving them as coming into being.

It now becomes clear in what sense James and Whitehead are to be understood as asserting that the comings into being of the parts of Achilles' motion or of the components of a long sound are no less discrete and pulsational than the happenings constituted by the beats of the heart. These philosophers are not claiming that the discrete becoming of processes will be apparent in all cases even if we fail to attend perceptually to the temporal order in which its components actually come into being; instead, they are asserting that if we do attend to their coming into being *as they are actually happening*, their perceived temporal order will be found to be discrete. And if their claim is construed in this way, then I regard it as correct. For it seems clear to me that *in regard to coming into being*, a stream of consciousness constituted by a long sound of constant pitch exhibits atomicity or fragmentation and elapses *seriatim* as a succession of nows no less than the tick-tocks of a clock. But a much greater effort of concentrated attention is required to perceive that discreteness in the former case than in the latter. But to ignore the becoming of the constituents of the long sound is to overlook the most striking feature yielded by our *perceptual* awareness of this process *as temporal*. Ordinally, time *as perceptually experienced* by us is the order of coming into being and thus the order of the successive nows of awareness.

Moreover, critics of the James-Whitehead phenomenology of temporal becoming must be reminded that the thesis of atomicity avowedly pertains to the becoming of temporal elements, *not* to the elements into which *past* time stretches can be resolved *retrospectively* once its constituent atomic events have already become. In regard to such elapsed stretches of time, Whitehead and James say explicitly that *retrospectively* physical theory may treat them as mathematical continua. The plausibility of the stated criticisms of the James-Whitehead phenomenology of becoming seems to derive in part from a tacit appeal to the following compound fact: (a) the deliverances of the *retrospective* awareness of past time stretches do not inevitably confront us with elements whose temporal order is logically incompatible with the denseness asserted by the mathematical theory of time, and (b) retrospective temporal awareness does not militate against theoretically treating past time stretches as dense linear continua of mathematical instants of physical time. But this tacit appeal does not score against Whitehead, since he explicitly allows for the facts on which it rests. And critics who invoke these facts are guilty of overlooking the first of the two conjuncts in Whitehead's epigram: "There is a becoming of continuity, but no continuity of becoming."

The replies I have offered to the stated objections against the atomicity of becoming now enable me to call attention to an important point. Namely, in regard to the *perceptualistic* foundation of the mathematical theory of space and time, there is a significant difference between the theoretical intelligibility of the denseness postulate for physical time, on the one hand, and for physical space on the other. Specifically, suppose that we are perceptually aware of a runner's motion as it is taking place and think of it as actually happening. Then our actual experience of its becoming—as distinct from our *retrospective* awareness of the entire motion—has the following feature: there is a first event of the motion, constituted by the runner's presence at his point of departure, a temporally *next* event right after the departure event, *consecutively* ordered temporally intermediate events, a temporally *next*-to-the-last event right before the runner's arrival at his destination, and the terminal event of the motion constituted by his arrival there. Clearly, the nextness of before and after characteristic of actual happening is inherent in the atomicity of becoming and is logically incompatible with a dense temporal order. By contrast, the confrontation of minimal elements ordered by nextness is not an ineluctable feature of spatial percepts. As we observed at the end of § 2A, a stretch of visual or tactile space can be sensed *in toto* as an extended expanse without reference to the discrete series of constituent *minima perceptibilia* into which it could be resolved. When spatial percepts are obtained via attending by sight or touch to the purely spatial extendedness of a line segment, their content is devoid of becoming. But the atomicity of the becoming of the constituent events of a motion can make itself felt even spatially: that temporal atomicity confers nextness or discreteness on the series of spatial locations corresponding to the events which become *seriatim*.

Thus, the ineluctable consecutivity of the becoming involved in the perceived elapsing of ongoing time is *not* matched by a correspondingly ineluctable discreteness of perceptual space. And *if* one insists on perceptualistic foundations, this difference renders the theoretical denseness of supposedly ongoing physical time *unintelligible* while posing no comparable obstacle to the intelligibility of the theoretical denseness of physical space. The fundamental difference in intelligibility to which I am calling attention obtains notwithstanding the fact that spatial perception is *threshold-governed* no less than temporal awareness. Nor can that difference be gainsaid by noting that in *some* respects, the spatial here is the counterpart of the temporal now. I make these claims for several reasons, as follows.

The attempt to make a dense temporal order of occurrence intelligible on the *perceptualistic* foundation of the nows of temporal awareness founders on the fact that discreteness, which is logically incompatible with denseness, is inherent in becoming. Hence the disavowal of becoming as an attribute of elementary physical events is a necessary condition for the meaningful affirmation of the denseness of physical time. By contrast, the assertion of the denseness of physical space is *not* predicated on the corresponding disavowal of some perceptualistic spatial counterpart of becoming, as follows: a hypothetical counterpart in which a discrete order of spatial loci is inherent such that each of these loci qualifies as a granular here and is a spatial counterpart of now. That our perceptual experience of time poses intellectual obstacles to the denseness postulate for physical time which are not also posed correspondingly in the case of space is patent in the light of the history of Zeno's paradoxes of motion. No mathematically literate person would claim that an avowedly finite space interval is paradoxically metrically infinite on the strength of such infinities as are entailed by its *denseness*. Specifically, suppose that someone were to claim that if there is to be a finite space interval, that interval cannot be the union of either an infinite regression or an infinite progression of subintervals. The reaction which this spatial claim elicits at once is: And why not, pray tell? But the corresponding claim for *time* intervals constitutes the heart of the conviction which Zeno's Dichotomy and Achilles paradoxes have carried perennially among mathematically literate thinkers. In short, what poses the difficulty for denseness in the case of time is not the perceptual threshold alone but rather the fact that the threshold is endemic to the cardinal perceptual feature of coming into being.[27] Accordingly, there appears to be substantial justification for the James-Whitehead contention that the order in which we perceive events as actually coming into being is discrete. Hence anyone who does insist with these philosophers on founding the theory of temporal order among physical events isomorphically on the properties of the perceptual "later than" relation among events as they come into being must indeed deny that the serial order of time can be held to be dense. But, as I showed in my article "The Status of Temporal Becoming," the coming into being of an event requires awareness of it as happening now. And the fact that a positive minimum duration is required or exceeded by each distinct bit of awareness of a happening, act of thought, or act of attention therefore has the following important consequence: *Any infinite sequence of pulses of becoming or acts of consciousness inevitably requires an infinite amount of time.* In particular, *any progression of such elements of perceptual time would require an*

[27] I am indebted to Annette Baier and Kent Bendall for having independently challenged me to defend my contention that perceptual experience has a significantly different bearing on the intelligibility of the denseness of time on the one hand, and of space, on the other. The arguments which I have presented in support of my contention are a response to the criticism implicit in the following question of theirs: Granted that spatial perception is threshold-governed no less than temporal perception, doesn't the resulting atomicity of the *minima perceptibilia* militate alike against the denseness postulate for both space and time?

infinite future, and any regression of them would have required an infinite past.

If a theory of temporal order entailing this consequence is to serve isomorphically as a basis for physics, it must do one of two things. First, it must disavow the mathematical continuity of physical time and the metrical treatment of time based upon it. Or, if the perceptualistic theory of time is to enable us to affirm intelligibly that finite stretches of physical time are infinite dense sets of instants, it can countenance only a quite restrictive physical interpretation of the denseness postulate for time. Having accepted the structure of sensed time as canonical for physics, Whitehead was driven to such a restrictive interpretation, as formulated in his previously cited epigram: "There is a becoming of continuity but no continuity of becoming."[28] Thus, his interpretation is restrictive in the Aristotelian sense of construing the infinities of the mathematical theory of time as potential ones arising from indefinite divisibility rather than as actual. And such continuity as Whitehead does allow cannot be grounded on *sensed* time by the following device: constructing a dense infinitude of instants by adapting Whitehead's spatial method of extensive abstraction to sensed durations. For Russell's avowedly merely "tentative and suggestive" attempt of 1914 to furnish such a construction is beset by (1) his own explicit doubts,[29] (2) the difficulties noted by Whitrow,[30] and (3) the logical defects by which I have shown Whitehead's method of extensive abstraction to be vitiated.[31] It would appear, there-

[28] A. N. Whitehead, *op. cit.*, p. 53.

[29] B. Russell, *Our Knowledge of the External World*, Chicago, 1914, Lecture IV, especially p. 128.

[30] G. J. Whitrow, *op. cit.*, pp. 160 and 165, especially p. 160, n. 2.

[31] Cf. A. Grünbaum, "Whitehead's Method of Extensive Abstraction," *The British Journal for the Philosophy of Science*, Vol. 4 (1954), 215–26. Commenting on this paper in his *Understanding Whitehead*, The Johns Hopkins Press, Baltimore, 1962, V. A. Lowe expressed the view (p. 79) that I "wrote finis to what is probably the most frequent reading of extensive abstraction" and adds (p. 79) "But this is a misreading of Whitehead." Whatever the merits of Lowe's exegetical contention, it does not and was not intended to impugn the validity of my critique of the views commonly attributed to Whitehead, which are the ones relevant here.

fore, that if sensed time is to be the foundation on which the theory of physical time is to be erected by construction, then an intelligible meaning cannot be given to the denseness postulate for physical time. Yet after offering such a construction, Russell invoked a dense time apropos of Zeno's Arrow paradox by writing: "when the arrow is in flight, there is . . . in fact . . . no next moment, and when once this is imaginatively realized, the difficulty is seen to disappear."[32] But in the context of the outcome of Russell's attempt to ground the world of physics on the world of sense, he has not furnished us with any intelligible foundation for *realizing imaginatively,* as he demands, that the *temporal* order of physical events is dense. For we saw that on an intuitively grounded meaning of temporal succession, there is an ineluctable feeling that if *physical* events are to *become* in temporal succession, their order of actual occurrence must be discrete, if it is to be a *temporal* order at all. And the *experienced* relation of "later than" cannot serve as a logical basis for giving physical meaning to its serial counterpart among the events of physics, since these two serial relations of "later than" belong to otherwise incompatible systems of order.

Given these consequences, it is evident that if a theory of temporal order is to justify the denseness of physical time, it must disavow as its foundation the order of coming into being, i.e., the order of the nows of awareness. But any such disavowal must satisfy two requirements: (1) its negative aspects must be justified, and (2) it must be coupled with a positive reply to the following question: In what sense can the physical events belonging to a time stretch or a motion be significantly held to succeed one another temporally, if they succeed one another densely rather than in the consecutive manner of a discrete sequence? To be positive, the answer to this question must provide a genuinely physical foundation for the relations of temporal order. But it must eschew the "later than" relation of temporal *awareness.* For what is needed is a physical meaning of temporal betweenness which involves denseness instead of entailing discrete-

[32] Russell, *Our Knowledge of the External World,* pp. 179–80.

ness. Our noting of the existence of this kind of positive answer in § 3 will enable us to cope with Zeno's challenge in
subsequent sections by showing the following: neither the
denseness of the temporal order of the constituent events of a
motion nor such non-finitary features of this process as are
entailed by this denseness property constitute obstacles to
its inception and consummation. And then it will be clear
why kinematic "how" questions about motions are *not* to be
answered on the model of the order of experienced coming
into being. Instead of appealing to the order of "nows" that
follow one another like the consecutive beats of the heart,
the specification of the kinematic "how" of a finite motion
or time interval between two given events will be satisfactory on the strength of pointing to the *dense* infinity of events
linking the two given events.

Accordingly, in order to justify the denseness of physical
time, I must first vindicate my denial of the James-Whitehead
claim that the physical time order is isomorphic with the perceived order of becoming. My disavowal of the isomorphism
they claim between the order of the nows of awareness and
the temporal order of elementary physical events has two
parts: (1) I deny that physical events as such come into
being at all and hold that they merely occur tenselessly in a
network of relations of time-like separation, and correlatively,
(2) I reject as baseless the view that physical events must
occur in the pulsational consecutive manner in which they
are perceived to come into being.[33] There is ample warrant,
I believe, for denying that coming into being is a feature of
physical events themselves. For I have argued in detail in the
article "The Status of Temporal Becoming" that the coming
into being of events, i.e., their occurrence in the present,
is a mind-dependent appearance, since belonging to the
present is a mind-dependent temporal attribute. Thus, with
respect to being mind-dependent, the coming into being of
physical events has an ontological status comparable to that

[33] As William James has noted in his *The Principles of
Psychology*, Dover Publications, New York, 1950, Vol. I, 608–10,
the sensible specious present is a duration-block or saddleback
with a certain breadth of its own rather than a knife-edge.

which physical theory—as construed by the bifurcationist view of nature—assigns to common-sense color attributes of macroscopic objects. Hence the mere fact that becoming is a feature of perceived time does not at all warrant its incorporation in the time of physics. Furthermore, note that James and Whitehead rest their claim that the temporal order of physical events is discrete rather than dense solely on the fact that perceived coming into being is pulsational and gives rise to a discrete order. But having denied the physical status of becoming, I must reject as ill-founded their thesis that physical time must be quantized just because becoming is pulsational.

Indeed, there is recent experimental evidence from psychophysics which ought to convince James and Whitehead that their thesis of isomorphism is false rather than merely ill-founded. This evidence involves phenomena of the following kind: Subthreshold effects have reportedly been used to insinuate sales messages to people despite their being too short in duration for conscious recognition. Thus, a movie theater flashed subthreshold ice-cream advertisements onto the screen during regular film showings. The result was a clear and otherwise unaccountable increase in ice-cream sales.[34] Further, Lazarus and McCleary[35] have exposed people to tachistoscopic physical stimuli at speeds too rapid for conscious identification or recognition. But persons thus exposed have been able to react autonomically to such physical stimuli by exhibiting galvanic skin responses to them. In order to contrast such autonomic responses without awareness, on the one hand, with perception on the other, these experimenters coined the term "subception" for the former. Thus, physical events which are "*subceived*"—as opposed to *perceived*—are subliminal because they are *durationally* subthreshold.

But the existence of subceived physical events would seem to show that there are physical events in our own spatio-

[34] Cf. Vance Packard, *The Hidden Persuaders*, David McKay, New York, 1957, pp. 42–43.

[35] R. S. Lazarus and R. A. McCleary, "Autonomic Discrimination without Awareness: A Study of Subception," *Psychological Review*, 58 (1951), 113–22.

temporal environment which themselves cannot be experienced by us as coming into being solely because they are durationally subthreshold. Even though these particular kinds of physical events have a stimulus impact on our bodies, our conscious experience of becoming is incompetent to furnish a reliable verdict concerning their durational properties and mode of occurrence. Hence the thesis of isomorphism would appear to become untenable in the face of these physical events. And the *atomicity* of becoming thus turns out to be expressive of an organismic feature of our kind of nervous system instead of warranting the quantization of physical time.

So much for the justification of the mere disavowal of discrete coming into being as the basis for the temporal order of physics. We are now ready to point out that there is a positive physical foundation for the claim that the time of physics is dense.

C. *The Physical Basis of the Denseness Postulate for the Time of Physics*

The key principles for a positive account of the denseness of the time of physics are the following: (1) the path of a moving classical particle is a linear continuum of spatial points, and (2) the classical particle cannot be at two different space points simultaneously. These two principles entail that for each of the densely ordered space points, there is at least one DISTINCT instant of time at which the particle is at that space point. And in the simple case of a particle that visits any given place only once, the temporal betweenness of instants will simply correspond to the DENSE spatial betweenness of points. I must omit the numerous technical details of the definition of temporal betweenness which I have given on the basis of the two stated principles.[36] But I hope that I have said enough to indicate that this definition of temporal betweenness for punctal physical events yields a dense temporal order for the following reason: it entails that for *any* two events belonging to the motion, there is a linear

[36] For a full statement of these details, see my book *Modern Science and Zeno's Paradoxes*, Ch. ii, § 2, Section C.

continuum of others temporally between them. Indeed, I hope that the two principles ingredient in my definition indicate that I have offered an *argument* for the denseness of physical time on the basis of how space and time are related in physical motion: the assumed continuity of space drives us to the continuity (and hence denseness) of time *not* because we are illegitimately "spatializing" time, as Bergson and James thought, but in virtue of our recognition of the role played by spatial continuity in the temporal process of motion. Whatever the *historical* origins of the concepts of denseness and linear mathematical continuity in human thought, denseness is an abstract type of order. And it must therefore not be overlooked, as Bergson did, that logically the attribution of denseness to time no more "spatializes" time than its ascription to space "temporalizes" space. Even if the attribution of denseness to time were shown to be false, this ascription could not then be indicted as a spatialization of time. As well say that the false ascription of denseness to the integers (with respect to magnitude) would constitute a spurious spatialization of these numbers.

It is now clear that just as Galileo recognized that a theoretically canonical appeal to such sensed attributes of physical objects as hot and cold can be scientifically stultifying, so also the discreteness of perceived coming into being can be misinvoked to encumber the event ontology of theoretical science. And now that we have overcome the objection to the physical intelligibility of temporal denseness by justifying its postulation, we have cleared the way for a defense of the following proposition: there is no more reason to infer that a temporally dense set of events must be of infinite duration in virtue of its being dense than for concluding erroneously that a spatially dense set of points must be spatially infinite on the strength of its denseness. This demonstration will involve showing in the context of the Dichotomy and the Achilles that the mathematical considerations applied to a finite *space* interval in § 2A can be *legitimately* carried over to a finite time interval, because they are fully as relevant and appropriate in the latter context.

It is already established by the positive theory of temporal denseness just outlined that (a) we are absolved from the necessity of answering "how" a succession of events can occur by exhibiting a discrete sequence of occurrence, and (b) there is no ordinal question as to "how" an interval of physical time can elapse at a given space point or in the form of a motion *despite* its denseness. On the contrary, having freed ourselves from the intellectual shackles of canonical adherence to temporal becoming, we see that the kinematic answers to such how-questions involve an appeal to the denseness of time.

§ 3. *The Dichotomy Paradox*

A. THE ARGUMENT FROM THE REGRESSION OF TIME INTERVALS

I shall disregard entirely whether the various formulations of the paradoxes of motion which have been attributed to Zeno are historically authentic. The version of each particular paradox that I shall examine critically will be one which, I believe, merits consideration in the context of modern science.

For the sake of arithmetic simplicity and without loss of generality, we shall assume in the statement of the Dichotomy that the runner is to traverse a unit space interval in unit time. If the runner is to accomplish this traversal, he must first traverse half of the interval in half the time, and, by the same token, before traversing the first half, he must traverse one-quarter of the total interval in one-quarter of the time. More generally, for *every* subinterval of length $\frac{1}{2^n}$ (n = 1, 2, 3, . . .) that he is to traverse, the runner must first traverse one-half thereof, i.e., the subinterval of length $\frac{1}{2^{n+1}}$. And thus in due temporal sequence the runner must traverse an infinite *regression* of overlapping subintervals whose lengths are given by

$$\cdots , \frac{1}{2^n} , \cdots , \frac{1}{2^3} , \frac{1}{2^2} , \frac{1}{2} .$$

The ordinal type of this kind of infinite series is denoted by "$^*\omega$." Note that there is *no first term* in this infinite regression which the runner must traverse in due temporal sequence. A corresponding sequence of time intervals has to be "survived," as it were, by any object at rest which is to endure for a unit time.

It will be recalled that as a consequence of the denseness of both the space interval and the time interval, there is no point *next* to the point of departure, and no instant of time *next* to the instant of the runner's departure. And, although there is a first punctal event of the motion process, there is no first motion: there is no first spatial subinterval of the runner's path upon which he enters after being at his starting point, and correspondingly there is no first temporal subinterval of which the instant of departure would constitute the beginning.

On the basis of these commitments of the theory of continuous motion, Zeno argues that if the runner had traversed the regression of subintervals in due temporal order, he would have required *an infinite past time:* to have accomplished the traversal, the runner would have had to be running for a past eternity and hence could never have *started* to run a finite time ago, which yet he did. But Whitehead contends that Zeno has obscured the real difficulty besetting the mathematical theory of time by irrelevantly introducing the complicating reference to space in the form of motion. In Whitehead's view, the significance of Zeno's regression in the Dichotomy is distinctively temporal but in the following *ordinal* respect: it exhibits the inability of the mathematical theory of time to make intelligible *how* any object at rest can endure for an interval of time in the face of the absence of an instant *next* to the initial instant of the interval.

Thus while Whitehead's form of the argument seeks to establish the *ordinal* unintelligibility of the mathematical theory of time, Zeno argues kinematically that there is a *metrical* paradox: though the mathematical theory of motion takes it for granted that the runner requires only a finite time for the traversal, this very theory seems to entail that he requires an infinite time. Concurring with Zeno, G. J. Whitrow wrote recently:

It is not surprising that the *application* of the principle of the infinite divisibility of time is found to be associated with logical fictions formed, strictly speaking, in violation of the law of contradiction. For the principle itself involves just such a logical fiction [i.e. self-contradiction], as is evident when Zeno's Dichotomy paradox—which he appears to have formulated for a moving body—is applied to time itself. . . . before any interval can elapse a completed infinity of overlapping sub-intervals must have elapsed. One can, therefore, either conclude that the idea of the infinite divisibility of time must be rejected, or else if one wishes to make use of the device, one must recognize that it is, strictly speaking, a logical fiction [i.e. self-contradiction].[37]

And summarizing his assessment of the cogency of Zeno's four paradoxes of motion, Whitrow concludes that the Dichotomy and the Achilles "are true paradoxes involving definite logical antinomies."[38]

My reply to Whitehead's ordinal version of the Dichotomy has already been given in § 2C, where I pointed out that a dense physical time is indeed intelligible. Hence I shall turn to the refutation of the *metrical* form of Zeno's Dichotomy argument, which was endorsed by Whitrow.[39]

Since the denseness of time is no longer at issue as such, the refutation which I am about to offer will consist in showing that such infinities as are entailed by the denseness of time do *not* paradoxically allow the deduction that a *metrically infinite* time interval is required by the runner to traverse the unit space interval. The interrelated false tacit assumptions or fallacies which have served to yield Zeno's

---

[37] G. J. Whitrow, *op. cit.*, p. 152.

[38] *Ibid.*

[39] For a reply to H. Putnam's fundamental misunderstandings and misrepresentations of my earlier writings on Zeno's paradoxes of motion in his "An Examination of Grünbaum's Philosophy of Geometry" in *Philosophy of Science*, B. Baumrin, ed., The Delaware Seminar, Vol. 2, Interscience Publishers, New York, 1963, p. 222 and pp. 222–23 n., see my book *Modern Science and Zeno's Paradoxes*, Ch. III, § 5.

paradoxical result of *metrical* infinity seem to me to arise mainly from the misguided attempt to "reach" the *first* instant of the motion by the *last* act of thought of a sequence of thoughts as follows: we begin with the contemplation of the last term of the regression of overlapping temporal subintervals of the motion which the Dichotomy singles out from the total unit time interval, and then we think *one by one* of *all* the individual members of the *regression* with a view to thus "reaching" the first instant of the motion "beyond" the regression. This attempt calls for the performance of a series of mental acts which has the form of an *infinite* progression *followed* by a last element and is said to be of ordinal type $\omega + 1$.[40] Preparatory to seeing why this misguided attempt is bound to issue in the conclusion that the unit time interval is paradoxically also metrically infinite, we must note two points as follows:

(a) Of any two of the overlapping subintervals of time in the regression, one of the subintervals—say S—temporally precedes and is included in the other—say S′—in the manner represented on the time axis diagramed here: S must have elapsed *in toto* before S′ is totally over and no part of S′ may be over before S has begun.

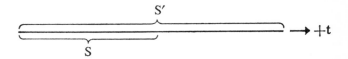

Specifically, the relations of inclusion and precedence are that every instant in S is also in S′, and there are instants in S′ later than *every* instant in S, but no instant in S′ and not also in S can precede *any* instant in S.

(b) Having just formulated the relations of inclusion and temporal precedence among the members of the regression, we are able to articulate further the previously indicated fact that in the Dichotomy the temporal order of the subintervals

[40] For relevant details on order types of infinite sets, see A. A. Fraenkel, *Abstract Set Theory*, North-Holland Publishing Co., Amsterdam, 1953, pp. 190 and 195–96.

is the reverse of the time order of the mental acts by which we think of them. Namely, the attempt to contemplate the members of the regression of subintervals one by one *begins* by letting the temporally *last* member pass in review before the mind's eye, as it were. The *second* member to "parade" in this fashion is the temporally next-to-the-last, and so on. Thus, in the case of every pair of subintervals S and S' of the regression which are such that S *immediately precedes* S', our mental act of being *aware* of S immediately *follows* our awareness of S', if our awareness encompasses both S and S' at all.

It will be recalled from § 2B that human awareness of time exhibits a positive threshold or minimum. This fact can now be seen to have a consequence of fundamental relevance to the appraisal of Zeno's Dichotomy argument. For it entails that *none* of the infinitely many temporal subintervals in the regression whose magnitude is less than the human *minimum perceptibilium* can be *experienced as elapsing* in a way that does *metrical* justice to its actual duration. In order to succeed, the attempted individual *contemplation* of all the subintervals would require a denumerable infinity of mental acts each of which requires or exceeds a positive minimum duration. *Instead of experiencing these subintervals as elapsing in a metrically faithful way, we gain our metrical impression of duration in this context from the time needed by our mental acts of contemplation and not from the respective duration numbers which we associate intellectually with the contemplated subintervals when performing these mental acts.*

Indeed, if—contrary to what is possible—we were to think of the temporal subintervals of the regression in a metrically faithful way to be elapsing *in their actual temporal order* as parts of the runner's total motion, we would need to make due allowance for the fact that all of them overlap with one another. To carry out this contemplation, we would be required to do both the following: (1) we would first think of the first *instant* of the motion, *and then* (2) despite the nonexistence in the regression of a *first subinterval* of which we could think *next* as elapsing, we would nonetheless manage to think one by one and in due temporal order of a regression of *non*-overlapping temporal subintervals of magnitudes

$$\frac{1}{2^n} - \frac{1}{2^{n+1}} \quad (n = \ldots 3, 2, 1)$$

or

$$\frac{1}{2^{n+1}} \quad (n = \ldots, 3, 2, 1)$$

This regression of non-overlapping subintervals differs from Zeno's regression of overlapping ones $\frac{1}{2^n}$ ($n = \ldots, 3, 2, 1$) by the fact that the non-overlapping subintervals are the unelapsed halves of the corresponding overlapping ones. Thus, if we were to carry out the specified contemplation and to make allowance for the overlap among Zeno's subintervals, we would be called upon to perform a sequence of mental acts of ordinal type $1 + {}^{\circ}\omega$.

The preceding considerations yield two crucial results:

1. In the case of the series of ordinal type $\omega + 1$, the successful one-by-one threshold-governed *contemplation* invited by Zeno, beginning at present with the last subinterval in the regression and encompassing all its overlapping members, would require *all infinite future time.*

2. In the case of the series of ordinal type $1 + {}^{\circ}\omega$, the futile threshold-governed attempt to think of all of the non-overlapping subintervals individually as elapsing in the actual temporal order of the runner's motion makes it *appear* that the runner must have required *all infinite past time* to have traversed the unit space interval by now. For our perceptual temporal imagination forever remains arrested within the gaping abyss that confronts it at the open end of the regression. And the compelling feeling that an infinite past time was needed to accomplish the traversal in turn insinuates the actual deducibility of this paradoxical result from the theory of motion.

No wonder then that those who are victimized by the metrical unfaithfulness of the mental act parade of the subintervals in the regression are driven to sympathize with Zeno in the manner of Max Black, who writes concerning the runner in the Dichotomy:

> To reach any point, he must first reach a nearer one. So, in order to be moving at all, Achilles must already have performed an infinite series of acts—must, as it were, have traveled along the series of points from the infinitely distant and *open* "end." This is an even more astounding feat than the one he accomplishes in winning the race against the tortoise.[41]

But the runner avowedly is called upon to traverse a regression of spatial subintervals in a corresponding regression of times *which decrease to zero* in a fixed ratio in the negative direction of time. How then does Black manage to arrive at Zeno's conclusion that (1) the runner must have succeeded in traveling from an "end" which is metrically "infinitely distant" both temporally and spatially, and that therefore (2) there was no first point whence the runner started and no first instant at which he departed, the "end" from which he traveled being "*open*"? The deduction of this metrically paradoxical conclusion is made convincing by Zeno via one or more of the following set of fallacies, each of which involves the tacit and irrelevant appeal to the threshold of our temporal awareness.

1. Let t_0 be the time of the first instant of the motion and t_1 that of the last. Zeno appeals to the relations of temporal precedence obtaining among the subintervals of his regression to emphasize that for *any* time t in the open interval $t_0 < t < t_1$, there is at least one *earlier* instant in this interval at which the runner had to be at a space point which is farther removed from his point of destination. That this much of his claim is correct is abundantly clear by reference to our regression of non-overlapping subintervals of time: any time t in the open interval $t_0 < t < t_1$ belongs to one of the subintervals of this regression, and for any such subinterval, there is a preceding subinterval containing at least one instant

[41] M. Black, *Problems of Analysis*, Routledge & Kegan Paul, London, 1954, pp. 99–100.

earlier than t. Zeno is able to make this theoretically wholesome fact perplexing by enticing us to attempt a one-by-one contemplation in thought of the sequence of ever-earlier times. For our threshold of time awareness confines our attempt at one-by-one contemplation of the sequence of ever-earlier times to a rather small finite number of the subintervals of the regression. And the thought fatigue induced by this confinement completely misleads us metrically: by tacitly appealing to our time-threshold, Zeno would have us reason that the union of the subintervals in the regression must be of infinite *duration*, just because that regression is of infinite *cardinality* and has no first member. But the finitude of the duration of the motion does not depend on the existence of a first *subinterval*, since the motion is initiated by a first *instant* and the subintervals of the regression have magnitudes permitting their union to be metrically finite. And we saw earlier that the non-existence of an instant immediately next to the first instant contributes to the theoretical intelligibility of the motion process, although the denseness of physical time is unintelligible in the context of perceived coming into being. There is therefore no warrant at all for inferring from the regression that paradoxically there could not have been a first instant at which the runner could have begun his motion in the finite past or that there can be no finite $t > t_0$ at which the runner could be beyond his point of departure. Indeed, once we recognize the misleading role of the threshold of becoming, it is apparent that Zeno's appeal to the regression to deduce the runner's need for an infinite past time is a blunder on a par with the following specious reasoning: any *finite* space interval which is open on the left side must paradoxically extend *infinitely* far to the left, because the interval has no leftmost point!

2. Zeno's argument appeals tacitly to our inability to "reach" the first instant of the motion via a thought-traversal of his regression. I therefore now turn to that facet of Zeno's fallacy. To do so, we must, of course, go beyond the subintervals of his regression in the order of temporal precedence and consider as well the first instant of the motion, which is *not* an

element of the regression of extended subintervals. We saw above that one member S of his regression temporally precedes another S′ with which it overlaps in the sense that S must have elapsed *in toto* before S′ is totally over and that no part of S′ may be over before S has begun. And now we can note that the first instant of the motion temporally precedes each and every member of the regression in the same sense in which one such member precedes another. Specifically, the first instant of the motion precedes each of the subintervals of the regression in the following sense: though the first instant belongs to every one of these assumedly closed sub-intervals, all the other instants belonging to any of the sub-intervals are later than the first instant. Hence with respect to our ordering relation of precedence, the set H comprising the first instant of the motion as well as all the members of the regression is an infinite regression *preceded* by a first element, i.e., H is of ordinal type $1 + {}^{\circ}\omega$, like the set

$$\left\{ 0, \ \ldots \ , \frac{1}{2^n} \ \ldots \ , \frac{1}{8}, \frac{1}{4}, \frac{1}{2} \right\} \quad (n = \ \ldots \ , 3, 2, 1).$$

Zeno implicitly calls on us to *start* with the temporally *last* element of our set H (i.e. the subinterval of duration $\frac{1}{2}$), and then to reach its first element (i.e. the first instant of the motion) in thought after contemplating one by one all of its members in reverse. And if we accept his unwarranted challenge to vindicate the mathematical theory of motion in this way, we are wrongly making the vindication of that theory contingent on our ability to perform a series of mental acts of ordinal type $\omega + 1$. But this is, of course, altogether precluded by the existence of the threshold governing acts of thought: in a finite time, we cannot possibly carry out the progression of mental acts required to "review" the *sub*series of H constituting the regression. In this sense, our thought cannot "get through" or spring the confines of the regression. A *fortiori* it cannot "reach" the first element of H after "going through" the regression in the required one-by-one manner.

But what follows from our threshold-based total inability to carry out the *mental* task of thus "reaching" the first instant? It does not show at all that the theory of motion entails that the runner required an infinite past time. For our failure to "reach" the first instant in the manner gratuitously required by Zeno does not entail in the context of that theory that there was no first instant at which the motion could have begun in the finite past and which preceded every one of the subintervals of the regression. Indeed, the theory shows that the entire regression of temporal subintervals was able to elapse within the finite duration of one-half of a unit of time. This fact becomes evident by reference to the regression of *non*-overlapping subintervals upon noting undisputedly that temporal subintervals are *finitely additive*: for *every* n, the sum S_n of the last n terms of the geometric series of duration numbers

$$\cdots, \frac{1}{2^{n+1}}, \cdots, \frac{1}{32}, \frac{1}{16}, \frac{1}{8}, \frac{1}{4} \quad (n = \cdots, 3, 2, 1)$$

is given by

$$S_n = \frac{1}{2} - \left(\frac{1}{2}\right)^{n+1}.$$

Hence there was time for any and every one of the non-overlapping temporal subintervals of the regression to have elapsed within one-half of a unit of time! This is, of course, exactly as it should be, since the union of all the subintervals of *this* regression is indeed identical with the half-open time interval of duration $\frac{1}{2}$ which we obtain upon leaving out the first instant of the motion from the full first temporal half of the motion.

How does Zeno attempt to sustain the paradoxical conclusion that any space point from which the runner might have started would have had to be infinitely distant from his point of destination? This conclusion depends for its plausibility on the prior fallacious deduction that the runner required an infinite past time. For how else can he argue that the non-existence of a first spatial subinterval prevents the regression of spatial subintervals from collectively fitting into the total unit space interval?

B. THE ARGUMENT FROM THE PROGRESSION OF TIME INTERVALS

So much for the version of the Dichotomy which confronts us with a *regression* of overlapping or non-overlapping subintervals of space and time. An alternative version presents us with a *progression* of non-overlapping subintervals of space and time. And this difference between the two versions makes the errors committed by Zeno in the second version sufficiently different, I believe, to warrant their being stated. Zeno calls attention to the fact that if the runner is to traverse the unit space interval in unit time, he must, among other things, successively traverse in corresponding times the progression of non-overlapping spatial subintervals whose lengths are given by the numbers

$$\frac{1}{2}, \frac{1}{4}, \frac{1}{8}, \ldots, \frac{1}{2^n}, \ldots \qquad (n = 1, 2, 3, \ldots)$$

How then, Zeno asks, can this process possibly be completed by the runner in a finite time, if its completion requires the elapsing of a progression of temporal subintervals which is endless as a consequence of the denseness postulate and whose durations are $\frac{1}{2^n}$ $(n = 1, 2, 3, \ldots)$?

It will be useful to adopt the terminology used by Vlastos[42] and to refer to the sequence of space subintervals as the "Z-sequence," to the sequence of the partial sums of their lengths as the "Z-series," to the particular subintervals of the Z-sequence as "Z-intervals," and to the running through of any of them as "making a Z-run." Vlastos notes that as commonly used, the term "run" individuates uniquely the physical action to which it applies, much as "heartbeat" does. And he points out that in *this* sense of "run," the runner's traversal of the Z-sequence could only be described as a *single* run and not as having involved $\aleph_0$ (i.e. a denumerable infinity of) "Z-runs." But clearly, in order to traverse the unit interval in one smooth and uninterrupted "run" in the ordinary sense, the runner must—among other things—traverse all the members of the Z-sequence and, in the latter sense, make $\aleph_0$ Z-"runs." In order to distinguish these two quite different uses of the noun "run," Vlastos writes "run$_a$" for the single

[42] G. Vlastos, "Zeno's Race Course," *Journal of the History of Philosophy*, 4:2 (1966), 95–108.

motion which we can perceive with our unaided senses in daily life contexts, and "run_b" for the kind relevant to the Z-sequence of kinematics.

The existence of a duration-threshold of time awareness guarantees that there is a *positive lower bound* on the duration of any run_a. And this fact enters into several of the following fallacies committed by Zeno in the second version of the Dichotomy:

1. Zeno's claim that the progression of Z-$runs_b$ requires an infinite future time is made plausible by a tacit appeal to our awareness that $\aleph_0$ $runs_a$ would indeed last forever, because there is a positive lower bound on the duration of any run_a. In the first version of the Dichotomy, the threshold governing our acts of awareness had compelled the feeling that after the first instant, a unique next event must happen in the motion, and in the present second version, there is the corresponding feeling that there must be a unique next-to-the-last event that happens before the final instant of the motion, if there is to be a final instant at all. As in the first version, the one-by-one contemplation which Zeno invites in the second version is not metrically faithful to the actual physical durations of the contemplated subintervals, which converge to zero by decreasing geometrically. And Zeno again illicitly trades on the fact that our intuitive time awareness rightly boggles at *experiencing* each of $\aleph_0$ subintervals of time as elapsing individually. But, justified though it is, this boggling cannot detract from the fact that *any and every* temporal subinterval of the motion is over by the end of one unit of time: for *every* n, the sum S_n of the first n terms of the geometric series of duration numbers

$$\frac{1}{2}, \frac{1}{4}, \frac{1}{8}, \cdot \cdot \cdot , \frac{1}{2^n}$$

is given by

$$S_n = 1 - \left(\frac{1}{2}\right)^n, \ (n = 1, 2, 3, \ldots)$$

which is less than 1. It follows that both distributively and *collectively* all $\aleph_0$ temporal subintervals of the motion elapse within one unit of time. The justification for this conclusion becomes further apparent when one becomes cognizant of the next error by which Zeno buttresses his conclusion that the runner would never reach his destination.

2. With respect to the relation of temporal precedence, the set comprising the temporal subintervals of the progression *and* the instant of the runner's arrival at his point of destination is of ordinal type $\omega + 1$. Furthermore, the instant of the runner's arrival at his destination point 1 does not belong to *any* member of the progression of temporal subintervals of durations

$$\frac{1}{2}, \frac{1}{4}, \frac{1}{8}, \cdot \cdot \cdot , \frac{1}{2^n} \cdot \cdot \cdot \qquad . \; (n = 1, 2, 3, \ldots).$$

Indeed, the instant of arrival at the point 1 is the *only* instant of the runner's total motion which does not belong to *any* of the subintervals of the progression. Thus, the closed time interval required by the runner's total motion consists of all the instants belonging to any of the subintervals of the progression *and* of the instant of arrival at the point 1: by failing to include the instant of arrival, the membership of the subintervals of the progression fails to exhaust the entire membership of the closed time interval required by the complete motion.

Zeno illicitly exploits the fact that it is *logically* impossible to find the terminal instant of the motion in any of the subintervals of the unending progression. For he appeals to this fact to lend further credence to his claim that the union of the subintervals of the progression is of infinite duration. But the logical impossibility of finding the terminal instant in any of the subintervals forming the unending progression amounts to no more than that this instant is not to be found in a time interval from which it has been excluded and which has been left half-open by its exclusion; the half-openness of the resulting time interval does *not* show that the union of the subintervals must be of infinite *duration* just because it has no terminal instant and just because the infinite progression of subintervals has no last member. For the terminal instant is the *earliest* instant *following every* instant belonging to *any* subinterval of the unending progression, while the durations of these subintervals suitably converge to zero. The non-existence in the progression of a last subinterval during which the motion would be completed does not preclude the existence of an instant later than all the subintervals which is the last instant of the motion.

This state of affairs expresses itself arithmetically in the following compound way:

(1) If the runner departs at $t = 0$, then corresponding to the non-existence of a last temporal subinterval of the motion in the progression, the respective times by which he has traversed the successive Z-intervals are given by the infinite sequence

$$\frac{1}{2}, \frac{3}{4}, \frac{7}{8}, \frac{15}{16}, \frac{31}{32}, \ldots, \frac{2^n - 1}{2^n}, \ldots \quad (n = 1, 2, 3, \ldots).$$

(2) Although the number 1 is not a member of this infinite sequence of time numbers, the arithmetic limit of this infinite sequence on the number axis is constituted by the number 1, which is the time co-ordinate of the last instant of the motion and represents the total duration of the union of the subintervals belonging to the progression.

(3) The runner traverses ever shorter subintervals of the unit race course in proportionately ever shorter subintervals of time, thereby traveling at constant speed.

What then becomes of the charge that the arithmetic theory of limits has been lifted uncritically out of the context of its legitimate application to physical space and adduced irrelevantly in an effort to refute Zeno's allegations of temporal paradox? The considerations of our present § 3 show that the mathematical apparatus of the theory of limits is ordinally and metrically no less appropriate to physical time than it is to physical space, as we saw in § 2A. Note that I have not invoked the *arithmetic* theory of limits as such to dismiss the allegation that kinematical theory entails temporal paradoxes. Instead, my contention has been that we are *justified* by the ordinal and metrical structure of physical time in applying that arithmetical theory *and* that Zeno's specific deductions of metrical contradictions in the Dichotomy are each vitiated by fallacies which I am engaged in pointing out.

The highly misleading role played by Zeno's one-by-one contemplation of the members of his progression becomes conspicuous upon noting the following fact: *it would even take us forever to contemplate one by one the progression of durationless instants which divide one temporal subinterval from the next, and yet the durational measure of this progression of instants is zero!* By the same token, the fact that our contemplation of the $\aleph_0$ subintervals would last forever is not a basis for concluding that the union of the progression of them would be of infinite duration. In summary, Zeno would have us infer that the runner can *never* reach his destination just because (1) for want of time we could never contemplate one by one *all* the subintervals of the progression and (2) for purely logical reasons, we could never find the terminal instant of the motion in any subinterval of which it is not a member, which holds for all the subintervals of the progression. But it is altogether fallacious to infer Zeno's conclusion from these two premises.

The recent literature on Zeno continues to provide illustrations of the intellectual havoc resulting from an irrelevant though tacit appeal to the fact that there is a positive lower bound on the duration of any single mental act of ours, such as conscious counting. Thus G. J. Whitrow seems to have engaged in precisely such an unwitting appeal in his endeavor to show that the denseness which we attribute to finite intervals of space cannot also be attributed to physical time without thereby generating logical antinomies. Let us quote Whitrow's defense of his thesis that attention to the distinctive elementary characteristics of time makes manifest that the infinities entailed by denseness cannot be ascribed to finite stretches of time. After stating that "we must not assume that . . . in *time,* any infinite sequence of operations can be performed,"[43] he considers the consequences of assuming

[43] Whitrow, *op. cit.,* p. 148.

that the runner (i.e. Achilles) passes through the entire progression of positions envisaged by Zeno. Whitrow invites us to assume that in so doing, the runner would number all these positions consecutively and concludes that then

. . . when he had passed through them all he would have exhausted the infinite set of positive integers by *counting*. But, however fast he counts, this feat is impossible, because no infinite set can be completely enumerated by counting: . . . although *any* member can be counted, we *cannot* count them *all*. This distinction is essentially a temporal one: at no time can we say that the operation is complete.

Acceptance of the Cantorean theory of the infinite therefore obliges us to distinguish sharply between the infinite set of positions which Zeno envisages . . . Achilles having to pass and the successive acts of passing them. Granted the possibility of regarding the former as a totality, this does not automatically assure the legitimacy of so regarding the latter. For although the former can be thought of as a static or completed infinite, the latter by its very nature can be regarded only as an indefinitely growing, dynamic, or uncompleted infinite.[44]

But Whitrow misidentifies the metrical features of the assumed process of (conscious) counting with those of traversing Zeno's progression of points in a finite interval in a manner akin to Zeno's illicit appeal to the eternity of one-by-one contemplation in the Dichotomy. For how else could Whitrow expect that the argument he gave would sustain his conclusion that the runner cannot successively have passed through the entire progression of spatial positions? To show in detail why I say this as well as to deal critically with some of the recent literature on "infinity machines," I shall now discuss some key problems pertaining to various kinds of processes that might be said to involve $\aleph_0$ "acts" or operations in specified senses.

[44] *Ibid.*, p. 148.

Ω*

§ 4. *Processes Involving an Infinite Sequence of "Acts" or Operations*

A. THE PROBLEM POSED BY SUCH PROCESSES

Hermann Weyl has initiated a discussion of the second version of the Dichotomy in which the runner's traversal of the Z-sequence is likened to a machine's completion of an infinite sequence of distinct acts of decision within a finite time interval.[45] Various authors, including some who regard the comparison as apt and others who do not, have presented difficulties that they believe to be inherent in the conception of an "infinity machine,"[46] or in any device which might be said to perform an infinite number of tasks.

In order to deal with the issues posed by Weyl and these authors, let me list under two major categories several kinds of processes which can each be held to involve, in a specified sense, an infinite sequence of "acts" or operations.

Category I

The Legato Motion. The traversal of the Z-sequence in unit time by a runner who runs continuously at uniform unit velocity. This runner will traverse the first Z-interval in $\frac{1}{2}$ of a unit of time, the second in $\frac{1}{4}$ of a unit of time, and so on. I shall refer to this process as the *"legato* Z-run."

The Staccato Motion. The traversal of the Z-sequence in unit time by a runner who runs discontinuously as follows: he takes $\frac{1}{4}$ of a unit of time to traverse the first Z-interval of length $\frac{1}{2}$ and rests for an equal amount of time; then he takes $\frac{1}{8}$ of a unit of time to traverse the second Z-interval of length $\frac{1}{4}$ and rests for an equal amount of time, and so on. I shall refer to the latter process as the *"staccato* Z-run."

Our problem will be to examine the feasibility of performing the *staccato* run in a finite time. And I shall state the

[45] Cf. H. Weyl, *Philosophy of Mathematics and Natural Science,* Princeton, 1949, p. 42.

[46] This term is introduced by Max Black in his *Problems of Analysis,* Ithaca, N.Y., p. 102.

conditions for the following conclusion: if one imagines that the two runners run parallel to one another on essentially the same race course, then the two runners depart jointly and arrive jointly at their final destination after a finite time, but the *staccato* runner traverses each Z-interval in half the time required by the *legato* runner and then waits for the latter to catch up with him before traversing the next Z-interval. And in so doing, each of the two runners traverses ever smaller space intervals in proportionately ever smaller time intervals whose successive lengths and durations each suitably converge to zero.

Category II

The π-Machine. The putative process of printing *all* of the digits 3.1415926535 . . . constituting the infinite decimal representation of π such that the first digit is printed in $\frac{1}{2}$ of a minute, the second in $\frac{1}{4}$ of a minute, the third 'n $\frac{1}{8}$ of a minute, and so on. We disregard here whether an infinite time might not be required for the more complicated process by which this progression of digits might first have been *computed seriatim* via, say, Archimedes' method of exhaustion for determining the area of a unit circle. For it suffices for our purposes that a progression of digits is to be printed as described, and, if necessary, these digits may be any digits whatever. Furthermore these $\aleph_0$ numerals might all have been inserted *simultaneously* into the printing press in a spatial arrangement to be discussed below. I shall refer to any such process as "the π printing" and to the hypothetical printing press executing it as "the π machine." And our problem will be to determine the conditions, if any, under which the π printing could be completed in 1 minute.

The Peano Machine. Let a mechanical device capable of reciting the sequence of natural numbers $n = 1, 2, 3, \ldots$ depart from the leftmost point 1 and move continuously to the right through a unit interval in 1 minute to the point 0. Now focus on the progression of points $\frac{1}{n}$ $(n = 1, 2, 3, \ldots)$ within that interval, a progression which contains the point 1 but *not* the point o. And suppose that the device might perform recitations as follows: for every one of these points $\frac{1}{n}$ ($n = 1, 2, 3, \ldots$), when reaching that point it begins to recite the number n and completes the recitation of n by the time it arrives at the next point in the progression. Thus, for every natural number n, the device takes $\frac{1}{n} - \frac{1}{n+1}$ of a minute to recite it. But in so doing, it does *not* employ the English noises which name the natural numbers; instead it employs a sequence of names whose successive lengths are governed by a restriction to be discussed below. I shall refer to this traveling number-reciting device as "the Peano machine." Our problem will be whether the prescribed names of all the natural numbers will have been recited when the Peano machine reaches the point o after 1 minute. By answering this question, we shall also have appraised Whitrow's aforementioned contention that his runner cannot exhaust all the positive integers by counting "however fast he counts."

The Thomson Lamp. There are reading lamps equipped with buttons which, if pressed, switch the lamp on when it is off and switch it off when it is on. If the lamp is off and its button is then pressed an odd number of times, the lamp will be on, but if it is pressed an even number of times, the lamp will be off. Let the lamp be off, and now suppose that the button might be pressed in such a way that the first jab requires $\frac{1}{2}$ of a minute, the second $\frac{1}{4}$ of a minute, and so on. Our problem is under what conditions, if any, the lamp button can thus be pressed to switch the lamp on and off $\aleph_0$ times within the finite time of 1 minute. Since J. F. Thomson introduced the putative process of these $\aleph_0$ on-off lamp switchings into the literature,[47] I shall refer to it as "the Thomson process." But it is to be noted that Thomson argued that the process thus named is logically impossible.

Black's Transferring Machine. Max Black has invited consideration of several processes involving $\aleph_0$ transfers of marbles:

[47] J. F. Thomson, "Tasks and Super-Tasks," *Analysis*, 15:1 (1954); see pp. 406 ff of this volume.

(a) The first process is carried out by an infinity machine called "Alpha" whose function Black describes as follows:

Let us suppose that upon our left a narrow tray stretches into the distance as far as the most powerful telescope can follow; and that this tray or slot is full of marbles. Here, at the middle, where the line of marbles begins, there stands a kind of mechanical scoop; and to the right, a second, but empty tray, stretching away into the distance beyond the farthest reach of vision. Now the machine is started. During the first minute of its operation, it seizes a marble from the left and transfers it to the empty tray on the right; then it rests a minute. In the next half-minute the machine seizes a second marble on the left, transfers it, and rests half-a-minute. The third marble is moved in a quarter of a minute, with a corresponding pause; the next in one-eighth of a minute; and so until the movements are so fast that all we can see is a gray blur. But at the end of exactly four minutes the machine comes to a halt, and now the left-hand tray that was full seems to be empty, while the right-hand tray that was empty seems full of marbles.[48]

(b) Infinity machine Beta is characterized by comparison with Alpha:

Imagine the arrangements modified as follows. Let there be only *one* marble in the left-hand tray to begin with, and let some device always return *that same marble* during the time at which the machine is resting. Let us give the name "Beta" to a machine that works in this way. From the standpoint of the machine, as it were, the task has not changed. The difficulty of performance remains exactly the same whether the task, as in Alpha's case, is to transfer an infinite series of qualitatively similar but different marbles; or whether the task, as in Beta's case, is constantly to transfer the *same* marble—a marble that is immediately returned to its original position. Imagine Alpha and Beta set to work side by side on their respec-

[48] Black, *Problems of Analysis,* p. 102.

tive tasks: every time the one moves, so does the other; if one succeeds in its task, so must the other; and if it is impossible for either to succeed, it is impossible for *each*.[49]

And Gamma functions as an accessory to Beta:

I said, before, that "some device" always restored the marble to its original position in the left-hand tray. Now the most natural device to use for this purpose is another machine—Gamma, say—working like Beta but *from right to left*. Let it be arranged that no sooner does Beta move the marble from left to right than Gamma moves it back again. The successive working periods and pauses of Gamma are then equal in length to those of Beta, except that Gamma is working while Beta is resting, and vice versa. The task of Gamma, moreover, is exactly parallel to that of Beta, that is, to transfer the marble an infinite number of times from one side to the other.[50]

I shall now discuss the various infinite processes in Categories I and II.

B. CONDITIONS FOR FINITE DURATION

The Staccato Run. The *staccato* runner at no time lags behind his *legato* colleague but is either ahead of him or abreast of him. For while running within each of the Z-intervals, the *staccato* runner's average velocity is twice that of his *legato* colleague, but his over-all average velocity for the total interval is equal to his colleague's velocity and is less than the velocity of light in *vacuo*. It follows that if the *legato* runner reaches his destination in 1 unit of time after traversing the Z-sequence, then so also does the *staccato* runner. And this conclusion has the following important consequence: given that the pauses separating the individual traversals carried out by the *staccato* runner form a geometric progression whose terms converge to zero, it is *immaterial* to

[49] Black, *op. cit.*, p. 103.
[50] *Ibid.*, p. 104.

the traversability of the total unit interval in a finite time that the process of traversal consists of $\aleph_0$ motions separated by pauses of rest instead of being one uninterrupted motion which *can be analyzed* into an infinite number of submotions. And if we wish to call the *staccato* runner's execution of the $\aleph_0$ *separate* motions "doing infinitely many things," then his performance shows that infinitely many things can be done in a finite time.[51] What could reasonably have been expected here in the way of a "proof" that the *staccato* run is *possible* is the following: a demonstration that, given the kinematical principles of the theory and the boundary conditions, the theory entails the *finitude* of the total duration of the *staccato* run. For the allegation of the impossibility of that run was based on its allegedly infinite duration. Thus, I have given a proof of the physical possibility of the *staccato* run. Of course, if the pauses between the individual traversals of the *staccato* run were all *equal*, then this run could not be carried out in a finite time, no matter how small each of the equal pauses might be.

To obviate some objections against my contention that kinematically it is physically possible for the *staccato* run to be consummated in a finite time, I call attention to several points, as follows:

[51] In thus using everyday words like "doing" and "things" in technical contexts, we are fully alerted to such confusions as misidentifying a run_b as a run_a, no less than when we use terms like "work" and "energy" in physics. I find it unedifying to be told by Max Black that "talk of an infinite series of acts performed in a finite time is illegitimate" on the grounds that "it is part of the 'grammar' of a word like 'jump' that it shall be inadmissible to speak of 'jumps' that are *indefinitely* small or *indefinitely* brief" (*Problems of Analysis*, p. 116). For when Black says that "there is a *logical absurdity* in saying that a man jumps a thousandth of an inch", he immediately goes on to trivialize this claim by adding the proviso "if the word 'jump' is understood in any of its ordinary, everyday, uses" (*ibid.*, p. 117). We need to use language to describe the physical process constituting the *staccato* runner's traversal of the total interval. And in determining whether this process can occur in a finite time as described, we need to heed the commitments of ordinary language only to the extent of guarding against being victimized or stultified by them.

(a) I was careful *not* to require my *staccato* runner to plant a flag at each of his Z-stops during the times when he suspends his motion to permit his *legato* colleague to catch up with him. For the erection of a flag at each of the $\aleph_0$ Z-stops would presumably require him to translate his own limbs and rotate the flag *each* time through a *minimum* positive distance, however small. And in that case the *staccato* runner would have to perform $\aleph_0$ *equal* spatial displacements in a *finite* time and thereby effect a spatially infinite total displacement of his own limbs and of the flags in the following manner: the successive vertical velocities of his limbs required to plant the flags consecutively would *increase boundlessly* (though *not* monotonically!) with time up to the instant at which *he comes to rest* at his destination. But such a motion has two kinematically objectionable features: (1) at the instant $t = 1$ of arrival at the destination point P, the motion violates the requirement that the *position* of a body be a continuous function of the time, since the vertical position does not approach any limit as $t \rightarrow 1$, and *a fortiori* the vertical position does not approach the point P as a limit as $t \rightarrow 1$, and (2) the fluctuating *velocity* function has an instant of *infinite discontinuity* (at the time $t = 1$), since the plot of the runner's vertical *position* against time is a function of *unbounded variation* in the time interval (0, 1) and the velocity function is unbounded in every neighbourhood of the terminal instant $t = 1$.[52]

By contrast, at $t = 1$, the *staccato* runner's *horizontal position* is a continuous function of time, and his horizontal velocities fluctuate only between the *fixed* values 0 and k. His horizontal *accelerations* do increase and decrease boundlessly as $t \rightarrow 1$, in the sense that the *same* velocity change takes place during ever shorter times. But this can reasonably be regarded as kinematically innocuous. For the horizontal *velocity* function has an instant of only *finite* discontinuity at $t = 1$ (just as the graph of a step function has points of only

[52] For a discussion of such functions, cf. E. W. Hobson, *The Theory of Functions of a Real Variable*, Vol I, Dover Publications, New York, 1957, 280, 300, 301, and 325.

finite discontinuity), while the horizontal *position* is indeed a continuous function of the time. That there are physically reasonable cases in which the position x of a particle varies continuously with time t while either the velocity or the acceleration do not, emerges from the following different case of temporally "semi-parabolic" motion along the x-axis:

$$x = t^2 \text{ for } t \geqslant 0, \text{ and } x = -t^2 \text{ for } t < 0.$$

Here both the position and velocity functions are continuous at $t = 0$, but the acceleration changes from -2 to $+2$ at that instant.

It might be asked why I gave kinematic sanction to an infinite discontinuity in the *horizontal acceleration* at $t = 1$ after having objected to the infinite discontinuity in the *vertical velocities* required to plant the flags. To this I reply: The *former* is here associated with a *continuous* time-dependence of the horizontal *position*, whereas the latter is a consequence of a *discontinuous* change in the vertical position. Thus, it can be that a given kind of discontinuity is kinematically permissible in the case of a higher-order derivative (e.g., acceleration) but not in the corresponding lower-order derivative (e.g., velocity).

(b) In view of the thresholds which govern the physiological reaction times of the *staccato* runner and his times of *conscious* execution of a set of instructions, it is clear that this runner cannot be "programed" to perform the *staccato* run in accord with the required metrical specifications, when the Z-intervals and the corresponding times of traversal become small enough to fall below his thresholds. But this fact does not vitiate my contention that, in principle, kinematically the *staccato* run as described is physically possible. For kinematic theory allows us to assume that the *staccato* runner's separate motions have the prescribed metrical properties.

(c) There *may*, of course, be specifically *dynamical*—as distinct from kinematical—difficulties in effecting the infinitude of horizontal accelerations and decelerations required by the runner's alternate starting and stopping. Thus, if we over-simplify the Newtonian treatment and consider the succession of accelerations of the body of fixed mass m from rest to a velocity of 2 units, then Newton's Second Law $F = m \dfrac{dv}{dt}$ tells us that

$$F \cdot \Delta t = m \cdot \Delta v.$$

But the successive times Δt_n ($n = 1, 2, 3, \ldots$) available for imparting the same velocity change Δv to the constant mass m converge to zero as the Z-intervals decrease. Hence the successive force values F_n have to become proportionately *indefinitely large* in order to assure the constancy of the product $F_n \cdot \Delta t_n$. And if we assume that the successive forces are given by $F_n = m \cdot a_n$ and act through distances Δx_n given by

$$\Delta x_n = \frac{1}{2} a_n \Delta t_n^2,$$

then we have

$$F_n \Delta x_n = \frac{1}{2} F_n a_n \Delta t_n^2 = \frac{1}{2m} (F_n \Delta t_n)^2.$$

But we saw that all the non-zero products $F_n \Delta t_n$ are *equal*. Hence each of the $\aleph_0$ products $F_n \cdot \Delta x_n$ has the *same* non-zero value. But this means that the total energy (work) expended by the runner in imparting the same finite velocity change Δv to his body $\aleph_0$ times is *infinite*. Thus, the runner would have required an infinite store of energy when he set out on his run. For he sustains $\aleph_0$ *uncompensated* losses of kinetic energy in the decelerations.

Let us disregard these specifically *dynamical* difficulties but be mindful of ruling out any flag-planting or other marking processes that would require *any* discontinuous change in any component of the displacement of the runner's limbs. Then I believe I have shown that kinematically it is physically possible for the *staccato* runner to reach his destination as prescribed in a finite (unit) time. Indeed he can be held to have "marked" each of the progression of the end points of the Z-intervals by the act of stopping at each one for the prescribed length of time while awaiting his *legato* colleague. If I may presume that this waiting at the Z-stops qualifies as "marking" them, then my *staccato* runner's total motion constitutes an important counterexample to one of the theses recently put forward by C. S. Chihara as part of his interesting critical response to Weyl's comparison of the Z-run with the performance of an infinity machine. Chihara believes that for *logical* reasons the difference between Achilles' mere traversal of the interval and Achilles' marking all the end points of the Z-intervals in the course of his journey determines the difference between completability and non-completability in a finite time. He says,

> . . . to give a more intuitive characterization of the difference between Achilles' journey and Achilles' task of marking the end points, in the former case we start with the task and analyze it into an infinite sequence of stages, whereas in the latter case we start with the stages and define the task as that of completing the infinite sequence of stages. To complete the journey, one must simply perform a task which can be analyzed ad infinitum, but to complete the task of marking all the end points, one must really do an infinite number of things.[53]

But, as we saw, the *staccato* runner does "really do an infinite number of things" in what is kinematically a demonstrably *finite* time. It would appear that here Chihara has misdiagnosed the source of the difference between completability and non-completability in a finite time. The *staccato* run is *not* one uninterrupted motion which can be merely *analyzed* into an infinite number of submotions, as in the case of process I, 1. Instead it consists of $\aleph_0$ motions separated by pauses of rest, and yet kinematically it is physically possible to complete it in a finite time.

The π Machine. In considering kinematically whether it is physically possible that the π machine achieve the π printing in a finite time, I must immediately stipulate that the heights from which the press descends to the paper to print

[53] C. S. Chihara, "On the Possibility of Completing an Infinite Process," *Philosophical Review*, 74 (1965), 86.

the successive digits may *not* be equal but must form a geometrically decreasing series converging to zero. In this way, I ensure that the spatial magnitude of the successive tasks does *not* remain the same while the time available for performing them decreases toward zero: just as in the case of the runners, the π machine is thereby called upon to move at only a constant average speed by traversing ever smaller distances in proportionately ever smaller times. My reason for requiring the heights of descent to converge to zero in suitable fashion becomes apparent upon recalling the analysis I gave of the flag-planting in the case of the *staccato* runner. If the heights of descent did not converge to zero, the successive velocities required for the printing would soon exceed the velocity of light and would vary with time in a manner that is kinematically objectionable even in the context of the Newtonian theory. Here, no less than in the case of the *staccato* runner, I ignore the *dynamical* problems of programing the π machine so that the successive spatially and temporally shorter descents of the press can be *triggered* as required.

I require furthermore that the widths of the successive numerals to be printed converge to zero in such a way that *all* the $\aleph_0$ digits can be printed in a horizontal line on a *finite* strip of paper. In laying down this second requirement, I blithely ignore as logically irrelevant the blurring of the digits on the paper through smudging of the ink when their widths become sufficiently small, not to speak of the need for ink droplets of width dimensions below those of an electron!

Under the fundamental restriction of my first proviso regarding the heights of descent, the π printing machine no more requires an infinite time than do either the *legato* or the *staccato* runner. And, given my second requirement concerning the widths of the successive digits, the spatial array of the $\aleph_0$ digits no more requires an infinite space than the *unending* progression of Z-intervals which collectively fit into the space of a finite unit interval: as long as the sequence 3.1415926535 . . . is printed so that the successive widths of the digits converge to zero in the manner of the Z-intervals, the question "What does this array *look like at the right end?*" receives the same kind of answer as the corresponding question about the progression of Z-intervals. We have been cautioned in § 2A against the misguided attempt to form a *visual* picture of the *open end* of a finite space interval, and we are aware that the metrically finite union of the Z-intervals is open at the right "end" as is the total space interval formed by the progression of horizontally shrinking digits. Although we cannot visually picture the *non*-existence of a rightmost point, our very characterization of the openness of the right end shows that we clearly understand in ordinal terms "what that end looks like." Just as the interval constituted by the union of the Z-intervals can be closed at the right end by the addition of a rightmost (last) point, so also, of course, can the interval formed by the horizontal cross-section of the unending π sequence.

Precisely analogous remarks apply to the time intervals that correspond to (a) the process of traversing all the Z-intervals and (b) the process of printing all the digits of π as specified. In the case of either Z-runner, we naturally tend to include in the *motion process* the event of his arrival at his destination where the runner *first* comes to rest: in so doing, we seem to be interested not only in those states of the *legato* runner in which his velocity is positive but also in the *earliest* of his states of rest. But in the case of the π printing process, there may be a tendency to include in the *printing process* only those states of the π machine belonging to the printing motion and to exclude the *earliest* subsequent event when it is no longer engaged in the printing. Thus, in virtue of our decision as to whether to include a terminal event in a given temporally finite process or not, the time interval corresponding to either Z-motion process turns out to be closed at the later end, whereas the time interval corresponding to the π printing process does not. But the exercise of our decisional option to omit from the time interval corresponding to the π printing the earliest instant following all the instants at which the press is busy printing must not be allowed to abet the following fallacious inference: drawing the conclusion that there exists no such earliest subsequent instant and that the

π printing cannot be over or completed within a finite time after its start. As well infer that the spatial interval constituted by the union of the unending progression of Z-intervals must be spatially infinite!

Let me assume that I am right in claiming that the completion of the kind of π printing process which I described is physically possible kinematically no less than the completion of the total *staccato* Z-run. Then my π printing process constitutes a further counterexample to Chihara's cited claim that an infinite number of things cannot be done in a finite time. And furthermore we see that the kind of infinite π printing process and machine I have described does not have the characteristics of the quite different kind of process and machine which Chihara invoked in support of his plea as follows:

> Granted that Thomson's argument [for the logical impossibility of the "Thomson process"] breaks down, however, I am sympathetic with his suggestion that there is something unintelligible about these hypothetical machines. The difficulty, as I see it, is not insufficiency of time, tape, ink, speed, strength or material, power, and the like, but rather the inconceivability of how the machine could actually finish its super-task. The machine would supposedly print the digits on tape, one after another, while the tape flows through the machine, say from right to left. Hence, at each stage in the calculation, the sequence of digits will extend to the left with the last digit printed being "at center." Now when the machine completes its task and shuts itself off, we should be able to look at the tape to see what digit was printed last. But if the machine finishes printing all the digits which constitute the decimal expansion of π, no digit can be the last digit printed. And how are we to understand this situation?
>
> I am not arguing that the concept of a super-machine is self-contradictory. The above difficulty can be easily avoided: one might argue that the above considerations show no more than that a super-machine would have to

be radically different from anything we now have (which, after all, should not be surprising). But even if we allow that no decisive argument has been given to show the inconceivability of such a super-machine, can we really conceive of such a machine actually finishing its computation?[54]

Suppose that I had not explicitly ruled out the equality of all the heights from which the printing press is to descend but had countenanced their equality. In that case, we can conclude the following from our discussion of the *staccato* runner: quite apart from the incompatibility of the then required super-light speeds with the special theory of relativity, these super-light *speeds* would have been *sufficient* to assure the Newtonian kinematic impossibility of the completion of the printing in a finite time. For the speeds that would be needed would not accord with the requirement that the velocity function of a body may not have an instant of infinite discontinuity, as in the above flag case. In this respect, Chihara's quoted account overlooks the relevance of speed as a sufficient condition for the unintelligibility of completability. But unless Weyl could show that the successive spatial displacements (or "tasks") performed by a machine in order to *calculate* (not just print!) seriatim the digits of π can, in principle, suitably converge to zero, my account of the π machine does sustain the conclusion reached by Chihara: Weyl was mistaken in claiming that *only* if an infinite sequence of calculations can be completed in a finite time can Achilles traverse *all* the Z-intervals.[55]

The Peano Machine. If we were to allow the use of the English names of the numbers to be recited, then there would be a number beyond which the lengths of the names—each measured by the name's syllable content—would increase boundlessly. And even if these name lengths remained the same, the "syllable-size" of the successive recitation tasks would remain the same while the time available for their performance would decrease indefinitely. In order to assure

[54] Chihara, *op. cit.*, p. 80.
[55] *Ibid.*, pp. 83 and 87.

that the average speed of the mechanical "lips" engaged in the recitation can remain constant instead of having to increase boundlessly, we would require *non*-English names of the successive numbers such that the successive distances traversed by the mechanical lips as they perform their recitations would decrease in proportion to the available time. It is quite unclear how distinctive names capable of being pronounced by the mechanical lips in accord with this stringent requirement could be generated by a rule.

Let us postpone that difficulty for the moment and turn from the modulating mechanical lips to the vibrating membrane of the mechanical voice. We note that each of the required $\aleph_0$ distinct sound-names or noises requires at least one vibration of the voice membrane. But the time available for the utterance of these successive noises converges to zero. Hence the *frequency* of the noises and also of the membrane must *increase indefinitely*. It has been suggested to me by A. Janis that the ensuing denumerable infinity of frequencies permits each natural number to be named by a sound of distinctive pitch. And it seems to me that such a pattern of noises constitutes an acceptable code language for numbers.

The energy imparted to the air particles by the vibrator is proportional to the square of the frequency and to the square of the amplitude. We can ensure, though, that the frequency pattern required by the total recitation does *not* necessitate the expenditure of an infinite amount of energy in a finite time. For although the frequencies of the membrane must increase indefinitely, we can require that the amplitudes of the successive vibrations of the total recitation decrease in such a way that the total energy expended is finite.

A decrease in the successive amplitudes is required not only on these *dynamical* grounds. For in order that the vibratory motion of the membrane be *kinematically* possible, the amplitudes of the vibrations corresponding to the successive noises must decrease and suitably converge to zero: even if the membrane executes only one vibration for each noise, the membrane would have to vibrate through an infinite total distance in a finite time, if the amplitudes of all the $\aleph_0$ noises were equal.

The assumed fulfillment of this proviso regarding the decrease in the amplitude does enable us to conclude that it is physically possible kinematically for the traveling Peano machine to complete the recitation in a finite time. Just as in the case of the π machine, there is a tendency to think of the number-recitation process as *not* including the earliest of the states of the Peano machine in which it is no longer engaged in reciting. This essentially classificatory decision on our part thus prevents the *finite* time interval required for the total recitation from being closed at its later end. But I remind the reader of the caveat I issued on this point apropos of the π machine: it should not be inferred that a time interval *must* be metrically infinite just because it is ordinally open at either the later or the earlier "end."

It is now clear why I objected at the end of § 3 to Whitrow's linking of Achilles' traversal of a progression of points in a finite time with expecting Achilles to number them all by counting. I take it that the kind of counting to which Whitrow was appealing would take the form of reciting all the natural numbers in English or performing the infinitude of threshold-governed mental acts of thinking seriatim of all of them. And we saw that either of these forms of counting would take forever. If we were to grant Whitrow that Achilles can traverse the progression of points in a unit space interval *only* if he can thus count them all, then indeed Whitrow would be warranted in concluding that Achilles cannot accomplish the traversal in a finite time. But the separate temporal analyses which I gave of the processes of traversal and of vocal or mental counting in English show that Whitrow has wrongly identified the durational features of counting with those of Achilles' traversal of the progression of Z-points.

The Thomson Lamp. In a careful and penetrating paper, P. Benacerraf has demonstrated that Thomson's attempt to establish the logical impossibility of performing the $\aleph_0$ on-off switchings by the time 1 minute has elapsed is a *non-sequitur*.[56] Let t_1 be the instant 1 minute after the start of

[56] P. Benacerraf, "Tasks, Super-Tasks, and the Modern Eleatics," *Journal of Philosophy*, 59 (1962), 765–84.

the switching process at t_0. In substance, Benacerraf makes the following points.

The information we are given is that for any time t in the interval $t_0 \leqslant t < t_1$, if the lamp is off at t, then there exists a later time in the interval at which it is on, *and* if the lamp is on at t, then there is a later instant in the interval at which it is off. Thomson infers fallaciously from the first premise that the lamp must be on at t_1 and from the second premise that it must be off at t_1, whereupon he is able to claim that the process of $\aleph_0$ on-off switchings must be logically impossible. But from these premises no conclusion follows about the state of the lamp *at time* t_1 with respect to being on or off. Although it is true that the lamp must be either on or off if it still exists at time t_1, no conclusion as to which of these two mutually exclusive situations obtains at t_1 is *deducible* from the given information: Thomson erroneously assumes it to be a matter of logic that the description of a sequence of acts of order type ω *must be determinate* with respect to the character of the outcome of a sequence of acts of order type $\omega + 1$. In so doing, he overlooks that he is insisting on deducing a conclusion about the state of affairs at an instant *following* a progression of time intervals from information pertaining *only* to the states of affairs prevailing at instants *within* the progression.

In this way, Benacerraf argued that Thomson failed to prove the logical impossibility of performing in a finite time $\aleph_0$ on-off lamp switchings whose successive durations geometrically converge to zero. Benacerraf then turns to the question of what would be involved in establishing either the logical impossibility or the logical possibility of such a process. Speaking of an infinite number of tasks as a "super-task," he writes:

To show that the concept of super-task is self-contradictory, it must be shown that there is something self-contradictory in the concept of a completed infinite series of tasks. . . . In order to show this, it would suffice, for example, to show that it is part of the meaning of "task" that nothing can be called a task that does not take some time to perform *and* that there is a lower bound on the length of time allowable for the performance of a single task.

Similarly, to show that super-tasks are not logically impossible, it would suffice to show that a correct analysis of each of the concepts involved permits their conjunction without explicit contradiction. . . . I strongly suspect that . . . there is probably no set of conditions that we can (non-trivially) state and show to be includable in a correct statement of the meaning of the expressions in question whose satisfaction would lead us to conclude that a super-task had been performed. . . . I mean only that there is no circumstance that we could imagine and describe in which we would be justified in saying that an infinite sequence of tasks had been completed.

. . . We have what appears to be a conceptual mismatch. Sequences of *tasks* do not exhibit the characteristics of sequences that lend themselves to proofs of infinity.

. . . Thomson is . . . successful in showing that arguments *for* the performability of super-tasks are invalid. [57]

Thus Benacerraf doubts the feasibility of furnishing a proof of the logical possibility of performing a super-task. Note that to his mind the issue of logical possibility raised by the $\aleph_0$ on-off switchings of Thomson's lamp in the prescribed times seems to be the following: Can a physical process thus involving $\aleph_0$ subprocesses of suitably decreasing durations be held to occur in a finite time *without* explicit contradiction, IF we *also* describe that process as constituting the performance of $\aleph_0$ "TASKS" in the *ordinary* sense of that term? But to my mind, the essential and interesting question of logical possibility within the framework of the theory arises

[57] *Ibid.*, **pp. 767–83.**

from the fact that the specified subprocesses which are collectively presumed to have occurred in a finite time constitute an infinite set of a particular ordinal type whose members must *collectively and severally satisfy certain kinematic requirements*. And I do *not* see why *this* question of logical possibility should be interlaced with the further question whether it can be shown that no contradiction is then introduced by calling the production of each of these subprocesses the performance of a "task" in the everyday sense of that term. I wish to recall the comment I made when I discussed the *staccato* run (process I, 2) à propos of Max Black's invocation of ordinary language: In considering whether it is logically possible kinematically that the $\aleph_0$ separate motions of this process occur in a finite time, we need to heed the commitments of ordinary language only to the extent of guarding against being victimized or stultified by them.

If, with Benacerraf, one disregards in this context whether "the concept of the infinite is itself self-contradictory,"[58] I cannot see that here one should demand more in the way of a "proof" of logical possibility than the provision of a kind of physical model via a kinematic description devoid of the explicit metrical contradictions which have been alleged against it.[59] Hence let us conceive in this way of "proving" kinematically whether or not the Thomson lamp can be consistently held to have carried out its $\aleph_0$ switching operations in a finite time.

Let us simplify our consideration of the problem by disregarding the question of the following electromagnetic possibility: the realizability of the conditions required for the emission of visible photons from the filament of the lamp bulb during each of $\aleph_0$ geometrically-decreasing

[58] *Ibid.*, p. 781.
[59] Benacerraf himself seems to offer this kind of "proof" of logical possibility when he writes (p. 783): "We have recognized that the shrinking genie covers all the Z-points but fails to occupy 1. . . . how could we recognize this if . . . Thomson were right and this was a contradictory notion . . . ?"

"on"-periods before t_1, and possibly at t_1 and thereafter. Instead, let any state in which the lamp circuit is merely electrically closed qualify as an "on"-state of the lamp, while an "off"-state is one in which the circuit is thus broken or open. We can therefore confine our consideration to the kinematics of the motions of the button or switch whose alternating states correspond to closed or open states of the circuit by virtue of the electrical coupling or decoupling between them.

Let the button have the form of a *rotating* little knob whose circular base has a periphery consisting of one electrically conducting and one non-conducting circular arc. Every triplet of on-off-and-on-again states will then require that any point on the periphery move circularly through a *fixed* positive distance. And since there are to be $\aleph_0$ such triplets during the time $t_1 - t_0$, any such point would have to traverse an infinite spatial distance in a finite time. As is clear from our discussion of our earlier "infinity machines," if the button is to be at rest at time t_1 or to be moving then with a particular finite velocity, even Newtonianly this arrangement would involve a kinematically impossible infinite discontinuity in the time variation of the button's velocity, quite apart from requiring relativistically prohibited superlight velocities.

Alternatively, let a button be equipped with an electrically conducting base which can close a circuit by fitting into the space between the exposed circuit elements E_1 and E_2. And let the button be depressed through a *fixed* distance d to close the circuit *every* time the lamp is to be turned on, while it is restituted upward to the same starting position to break the circuit each of the $\aleph_0$ times when the lamp is to be turned off. Then the same kinematic impossibility results.

Since Thomson imposed no restrictions on the operation of the reading lamp button other than the durations of the successive jabs, he may reasonably be presumed to have envisioned this kind of motion of the switch button and of the circuit elements. Now consider the question "What is the state of the lamp at time t_1?" Benacerraf rightly charged Thomson's deduction of *contradictory answers* to it with being fallacious. But granting our presumption as to the kind of process which Thomson envisioned, we see that this question is unanswerable for the following reason : kinematic theory *rules out* the process which is expected to issue in exactly one of the two states on or off at time t_1. Hence I must dissent from Chihara's view concerning super-machines like Thomson's lamp when he says: "Indeed the question . . . is unanswerable. But one cannot conclude that it is unanswerable because there is a contradiction in the notion of such a super-machine, since it seems quite reasonable to maintain that not enough information about the machines was supplied to answer it."[60] I dissent, because the kinematic impossibility here is, of course, not a matter of insufficient mechanical information.

Moreover, on the basis of the explicit information given by Thomson, there are certain conditions which must be satisfied by both the switch (button) and the circuit elements to make his process kinematically possible. And, as A. Janis has pointed out to me, these conditions are such that the state of the circuit at time t_1 is *predictably closed*. To see this, let us first recall the discussion of our earlier infinity machines. It is then clear that the consecutive downward and upward jabs of the switching button which· alternately close and break the circuit must produce displacements of the button whose lengths Δ x are a suitably decreasing sequence converging to zero. And we must assume that there is no electric arcing or sparking across *any* space gap Δ x, however small, between the conducting button-base, on the one hand, and the exposed circuit ends E_1 and E_2 on the other. For if there were electrical sparking-across for all Δ x equal to or less than some minimum ϵ, then the kinematic requirement that Δ x suitably converge to zero as $t{\to}t_1$ would have the following result : there would be a time

    [60] C. S. Chihara. "On the Possibility of Completing an Infinite Process," p. 80.

t_ϵ *before* t_1 such that the circuit would be electrically *closed* for all instants t belonging to the interval $t_\epsilon \leqslant t < t_1$. And this result would obviously violate Thomson's requirement that the lamp is still to be switched *off* $\aleph_0$ times during this time interval.

At time t_0, when the lamp is off, let $\dfrac{1}{2}$ be the *initial* vertical distance between the button base and the horizontal circuit-opening E_1 E_2, as shown in the diagram below, which is *not* drawn to scale. Then after the base of the button has been depressed once to close the circuit, let it be raised after each such depression *not* all the way to its initial position A but to intermediate points A_1, A_2, A_3, . . . , A*n*, . . . whose respective distance Δ x from E_1 E_2 are

$$\frac{1}{8}, \frac{1}{32}, \frac{1}{128}, \ldots \frac{1}{2^{2n+1}}, \ldots \quad (n = 1, 2, 3, \ldots).$$

Then the $\aleph_0$ circuit-closing jabs involve a sequence of downward displacements Δ x

$$\frac{1}{2}, \frac{1}{8}, \frac{1}{32}, \ldots \frac{1}{2^{2n+1}}, \ldots \quad (n = 0, 1, 2, 3, \ldots).$$

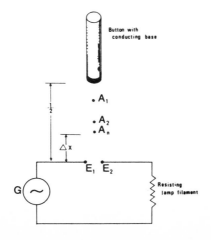

The corresponding sequence of available time intervals Δt is

$$\frac{1}{2}, \frac{1}{8}, \frac{1}{32}, \ldots \frac{1}{2^{2n+1}}, \ldots \quad (n = 0, 1, 2, 3, \ldots).$$

If all of the downward jabs were to proceed at unit velocity, then the circuit would be closed for only an instant each time during these particular time intervals. On the other hand, if only some fixed proper fraction $\frac{1}{k}$ of these available times Δt were devoted to the downward motions, then the velocity of the button would have the same value k each time, thereby satisfying the Newtonian kinematic requirement of having an upper bound during the time interval $t_0 \leqslant t < t_1$. And, if the downward motion were to start each time at the *beginning* of the time interval available for it, the lamp would be on at least for the sequence of time intervals $\Delta t \left(1 - \frac{1}{k}\right)$, i.e. at least during the time intervals

$$\frac{1}{2^{2n+1}} \left(1 - \frac{1}{k}\right) \quad (n = 0, 1, 2, 3, \ldots).$$

To conform to the requirements of the theory of relativity, the velocity k must be less than that of light in the units we are using. But even Newtonianly the button velocity would impermissibly increase boundlessly, if only *decreasing fractions* $\frac{1}{n}$ $(n = 1, 2, 3, \ldots)$ rather than a fixed proper fraction $\frac{1}{k}$ of the above decreasing time intervals Δt were granted successively for the downward motions in order to secure successive on-states of durations

$$\frac{1}{2^{2n+1}} \quad \left(1 - \frac{1}{n+1}\right) \quad (n = 0, 1, 2, 3, \ldots).$$

Turning to the $\aleph_0$ circuit-*breaking* jabs, we note that they involve a sequence of decreasing upward displacements

$$\frac{1}{8}, \frac{1}{32}, \frac{1}{128}, \ldots \frac{1}{2^{2n+1}}, \ldots \quad (n = 1, 2, 3, \ldots).$$

The corresponding sequence of decreasing time intervals Δt available to break the circuit by moving the button upward is

$$\frac{1}{4}, \frac{1}{16}, \frac{1}{64}, \ldots, \frac{1}{2^{2n}}, \ldots \quad (n = 1, 2, 3, \ldots).$$

Let $\frac{1}{k}$ be the particular fixed fraction of the available time interval Δt which is devoted each time to the button's circuit-breaking motion. Clearly $\frac{1}{k}$ 1, and the button's upward velocity v is given by $v = \frac{k}{2}$. Under the relativistic restriction that v have values less than the velocity c of light, we also have $k < 2c$, or $\frac{1}{k} > \frac{1}{2c}$, so that

$$\frac{1}{2c} < \frac{1}{k} \leqslant 1.$$

Suppose that $\frac{1}{k}$ has some value in this interval *other than* 1, and let the upward motion terminate each time at the *end* of the time interval available for it. Then the lamp will *also* be *on* during the following initial positive subintervals of the intervals available for the button's upward circuit-breaking motions

R

$$\left(1 - \frac{1}{k}\right) \quad \frac{1}{2^{2n+1}} \qquad (n = 1, 2, 3, \dots).$$

The state variable characterizing the lamp as either on or off is clearly a discrete variable by ranging over only two values rather than over a continuum of values. But we took a closed state of the circuit to be tantamount to an on-state of the lamp, while a broken state of the circuit is equivalent to an off-state of the lamp. And the positions of the button needed to close and break the circuit in the prescribed fashion must exhibit the kinematically required continuity. Therefore, $\Delta x \to 0$ as $t \to t_1$ *and* $\Delta x = 0$ at $t = t_1$, i.e., the required spatially continuous motion of the base of the switching button issues in the coincidence of the base with $E_1 E_2$ at time t_1. Hence the circuit is *predictably closed* at time t_1, i.e., the lamp must be *on* at the termination of the unit time interval $t_1 - t_0$.

Indeed there is an important respect in which the motion of the button can be understood on the model of the runner's traversal of a *progression* of Z-intervals in the Dichotomy (cf. §3, B of this chapter). The button's $\aleph_0$ downwards motions involve the traversal of a total space interval of length

$$L_d = \sum_{n=0}^{n=\infty} \frac{1}{2^{2n+1}} = \frac{4}{6}.$$

And the button's $\aleph_0$ upward motions involve a total spatial displacement of length

$$L_u = \sum_{n=1}^{n=\infty} \frac{1}{2^{2n+1}} = \frac{1}{6}.$$

But, of course, the button actually moves alternately down and up, starting at $t = t_0$ with a downward motion through the initial distance $\frac{1}{2}$. And after traversing this initial distance, it traverses *twice* each of the space intervals

$$\frac{1}{2^{2n+1}} \quad (n = 1, 2, 3, \ldots)$$

by executing first an upward and then a downward motion through the same interval. Hence the button has the task of traversing a total interval of length

$$L_d + L_u = \frac{5}{6}$$

by traversing first an interval of $\frac{1}{2}$ and then an infinite progression of subintervals

$$\frac{1}{4}, \frac{1}{16}, \frac{1}{64}, \ldots , \frac{1}{4^n}, \ldots (n = 1, 2, 3, \ldots).$$

Our mention of the runner's traversal of a progression of subintervals in the Dichotomy does *not* overlook that all of the *legato* runner's $\aleph_0$ Z-runs to his destination point are spatially in the *same* direction and proceed without velocity fluctuations, while the suitably decreasing motions of the button which terminate in a closed state of the circuit at time t_1 are $\aleph_0$ alternately *down and up* motions. Specifically, the *legato* runner's uniform motion involves only one initial acceleration of particular finite magnitude and one final deceleration of specific finite magnitude, whereas the accelerations (though *not* the velocities!) of the button increase indefinitely. And, as Wesley Salmon has noted illuminatingly, *except* for the *legato* motion, all the processes we are discussing involve indefinitely large *accelerations*. But this difference between the *legato* motion and all of the rest does not militate against a crucial similarity between them, with respect to which the completability of the latter is no less intelligible than that of the former.

For what matters is that the runner reaches his destination at time t_1 after traversing a *progression* of Z-runs, while there does not exist any last Z-run in the progression by means of which the termination of the motion could be effected. And what matters especially is that the terminal instant t_1 of the motion does *not* belong to *any* member of the progression of temporal subintervals corresponding to the $\aleph_0$ Z-runs, although *every other* instant of the motion belongs to at least one such member. In short, what matters is that the runner's arrival at his destination at time t_1 does not belong to any of the Z-runs and is surely not effected by the transversal of a non-existent *last* Z-run terminating in that arrival. Similarly, the jabbing motions form a suitably decreasing progression which issues in an on-state at time t_1, even though that on-state is *not* the terminus of any *continuously downward* jabbing motion of positive duration during which the lamp would be off. Nor can the on-state at time t_1 belong to any continuous on-state of positive duration whose first instant terminates a single continuously downward jab. Thus, if t_1 were the start of a continuous on-state of positive duration, the particular instantaneous on-state *at* t_1 would *not* be the terminus of a continuously downward jab. By contrast, within the confines of the half-open time-interval $t_0 \leqslant t < t_1$ *before* t_1, the first instant of any continuous on-state of positive duration *is* the terminus of a continuously downward jab of positive duration. And, again within the confines of that half-open interval *before* t_1, any instantaneous on-state which separates two continuous off-states is likewise the terminus of a continuously downward jabbing motion of positive duration.

These considerations will enable us to see that the production of Thomson's $\aleph_0$ on-off states would *not* be feasible under the following alternative switching arrangement even if we were to assure the finitude of the total spatial displacement of the switching button.[61] Let our modified switch button be movable through a linear space interval which is divided by a middle point into up and down, or left and

[61] I am indebted to Allen Janis for having concocted this alternative switching arrangement and for having pointed out instructively that it cannot produce Thomson's process.

right respectively. And assume that the coupling between the positions of the base of the button and the lamp circuit is such as to satisfy the following conditions: (i) when the button base is at any point in the upper (or left) segment, the circuit is open and the lamp is off, (ii) when the button base is at any point in the lower (or right) segment, the circuit is closed and the lamp is on, (iii) when the button base point coincides with the center point C in the middle, the lamp is on or off depending on whether it had arrived at C from above (left) or below (right) respectively, and (iv) if the button base is at the mid-point C at a time t, the existence of an on-state of the circuit at t requires that the button base have reached C from above (left) at or before t, and —unless a circuit-component (e.g., the lamp filament) has burnt out—the existence of an off-state at t while the base is present at C requires the base to have reached C at or before t from below (right). To assure the kinematically required finitude of the total spatial displacement of the button base during the allowed finite time $t_1 - t_0$ (1 minute), let the button base journey back and forth across C $\aleph_0$ times so as to traverse suitably decreasing distances and reach C at time t_1. After t_1, we leave the switch in the position which it attained at t_1.

Our previous considerations now enable us to assert that at time t_1, the button base *cannot* have reached C either by a continuous approach *from above* (left) or by a continuous approach *from below* (right). For this much is required if the execution of Thomson's jabbing instructions is to be *kinematically* feasible. But, in that case the posited conditions governing the coupling of the switching button to the lamp circuit entail the following conclusion: if the lamp circuit is still intact at t_1 and thereafter, then the lamp is *neither on nor off at time t_1* and thereafter. Yet if the lamp circuit still exists intact at that time, it must be either on or off. And it can easily be observed which of these two states prevails at t_1 and thereafter by looking at the lamp. Even if the lamp filament should have burned out at time t_1, we can replace the bulb by a new one at that time and observe its state thereafter. Hence if Thomson's required $\aleph_0$ on-off states of the lamp circuit are claimed to permit the endurance of the lamp circuit until and beyond the instant t_1, a contradiction is introduced by the assumption that these $\aleph_0$ states can be produced by the present *modified* switching arrangement.

Thus, in the case of the latter switching arrangement, no less than in the case of the kinematically impossible jabbing motions discussed initially, the inability to predict the state of the lamp circuit at time t_1 is not at all a matter of insufficient information. And we see that the latter impossible switching arrangement (S_2) differs from the one yielding a *predictably closed* circuit at time t_1 (S_1) as follows: in the case of S_1, on and off respectively involve coincidence and non-coincidence of the button base with E_1E_2, while the on-state at t_1 is *not* the terminus of any *continuously unidirectional* (e.g., downward or rightward) jab; but arrangement S_2 requires that the one lamp state associated with the base's center position at time t_1 and thereafter be the outcome of a continuously unidirectional jab terminating at time t_1. And precisely this is ruled out by the kinematics required for Thomson's process.

Black's Transferring Machine. For the reasons given when we discussed the other infinity machines, the marbles of Max Black's marble transferring machines would have to be so positioned and the two trays so moved (e.g. toward the line halfway between their initial separation) that the distances through which the successive marble transfers would have to be effected would decrease in proportion to the available successive times and thus would suitably converge to zero by the time the 4 minutes have elapsed. And, in that case—dynamical difficulties aside—I claim that (a) by the end of 4 minutes of Alpha's intermittent operation, the centers of mass of all the $\aleph_0$ different marbles will be to the right of the line of contact at which the left and right trays are joined at the end of 4 minutes, and (b) by the end of 4 minutes of alternate operation by Beta and Gamma, the center of mass of the single marble would be on the line of contact, and at rest there.

Max Black maintains that it is logically impossible for either machine Alpha or machine Beta (assisted by Gamma) to carry out its assigned task in a finite time. And his reasons are that there is the kinematic difficulty of a discontinuity in the position function which we just obviated by our restrictions, and also that Beta and Gamma exhibit this logical impossibility as follows:

> . . . the single marble is always returned, and each move of the machine accomplishes nothing. . . . the very act of transferring the marble from left to right immediately causes it to be returned again; the operation is self-defeating and it is logically impossible for its end to be achieved. Now if this is true for Beta, it must be true also for Alpha.

> Somebody may still be inclined to say that nevertheless when the machine Beta finally comes to rest (at the end of the four minutes of its operation) the single marble might after all be found in the right-hand tray, and this, if it happened, would *prove* that the machine's task had been accomplished.

> . . . Let it be arranged that no sooner does Beta move the marble from left to right than Gamma moves it back again.

> . . . If the result of the whole four minutes'. operation by the first machine is to transfer the marble from left to right, the result of the whole four minutes' operation by the second machine must be to transfer the marble from right to left. But there is only one marble and it must end somewhere. If it ought to be found on the right, then by the same reasoning it ought to be found on the left. But it cannot be both on the right and on the left. Hence neither machine can accomplish its task, and our description of the infinity machine involves a contradiction.[62]

We noted that under Black's conditions of a *fixed* positive separation of the two trays, there is the kinematic impossibility of a discontinuity in the position function to which he rightly calls attention. But the appreciation of *that* difficulty

[62] Black, *op. cit.*, pp. 103–5.

must not be allowed to confer acceptability on his further contention that the description of the functions of Beta and Gamma permit the deduction of contradictory conclusions regarding the spatial location of the one marble after 4 minutes. For his reasoning in support of *this* contention is vitiated by errors, some of which are analogous to those committed by Thomson and pointed out by Benacerraf.

Black says that "each move of the machine [Beta] accomplishes nothing" and that "the operation is self-defeating and it is logically impossible for its end to be achieved." He mistakenly believes here to be able to deduce that the marble does *not* end up in the right tray after 4 minutes. But the facts about the marble's transfers to which he calls attention here merely fail to sustain the conclusion that the marble does end up on the right. And he invokes the following false supposition: the assumption of the occurrence of all of Beta's prescribed one-way transfers in a finite time, if true, must enable us to *deduce* that the marble will end up on the right side at the first instant t_1 following all these transfers. If such deducibility does not obtain, Black feels entitled to conclude that Beta could not have effected the $\aleph_0$ one-way transfers in a finite time.

But Gamma's recurring return of the marble after every transfer by Beta does not provide a basis for concluding that the marble does *not* end up on the right, just as the recurring off-switchings of the Thomson lamp do not enable us to infer that the lamp will not be on at time t_1. We are given that after any *even* number of oppositely directed one-way transfers of the marble by Beta and Gamma, beginning with one from left to right, the marble will be back on the left, and after any *odd* number of such transfers it will be on the right: For any time t in the interval $t_0 \leqq t < t_1$, if the marble is on the left at t, then there exists a later time in the interval at which it is on the right, and if it is on the right at t, then there exists a later time in the interval when it is on the left. But this information does not entail where the marble would or would not be after Beta and Gamma have each carried out $\aleph_0$ one-way transfers.

Nor can the non-deducibility of the marble's location *at*

time t_1 serve to show that Beta could not have effected the $\aleph_0$ transfers in a finite time *before* t_1. The belief that if $\aleph_0$ transfers are to have taken place before t_1, the position of the marble at t_1 ought to be deducible from the information specifying its movements prior and up to the time t_1 seems to spring from the following tacit assumption: given a point at any distance d, however small, from the marble's final rest location at time t_1, there is a closed positive time interval containing t_1 as its last instant during which the marble is spatially confined to being at one of the points of the closed space interval on its path corresponding to that distance. But this tacit assumption is incompatible with the stated conditions governing the operation of Beta and Gamma, which operate alternately between trays that are a fixed distance apart during the entire interval $t_0 \leqq t < t_1$. Why then should the marble's location at time t_1 be deducible? It is indeed true that Beta's violation of Black's tacitly made assumption shows that the performance demanded from it calls for a kinematically impermissible discontinuity in the time variation of the position, as I explained when I proscribed the flag-planting by the *staccato* runner. But what are we to make of the fact that, if applicable, Black's tacit assumption would permit the deduction of the location of the marble at t_1? Surely it does not sustain the following inference: Beta could not have effected all the $\aleph_0$ transfers within 4 minutes, because the marble's location at time t_1 is *not* deducible from conditions violating Black's tacit assumption. The latter inference is a non-sequitur even though we know *independently* that its conclusion is true on the strength of the kinematically impermissible position pattern required by $\aleph_0$ transfers across a fixed distance in a finite time.

§ 5. *Achilles and the Tortoise*

Let Achilles give the tortoise a spatial head start of magnitude d, and let the tortoise move to the right at the constant velocity v while Achilles also moves right at the greater constant velocity V.

R*

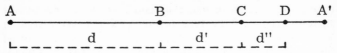

Let the simultaneous departures of Achilles and the tortoise from their respective starting points A and B occur at $T_0 = 0$. The time t_1 needed by Achilles to reach the starting point B of the tortoise is

$$t_1 = \frac{d}{V}.$$

But during t_1, the turtle moves to the point C through a distance d′ given by

$$d' = vt_1 = d\frac{v}{V}.$$

Achilles requires a time

$$t_2 = \frac{d'}{V} = \frac{d}{V} \cdot \frac{v}{V}$$

to reach the point C. But during t_2, the turtle moves to the point D through a distance d″ given by

$$d'' = vt_2 = d\frac{v^2}{V^2}.$$

And to reach D, Achilles requires a time

$$t_3 = \frac{d''}{V} = \frac{d}{V} \cdot \frac{v^2}{V^2}$$

during which the tortoise moves beyond the point D. For every space interval separating Achilles from the tortoise at a given time beginning with the latter's head start d, there is a next space interval separating them at some later time. And for every time interval during which Achilles is engaged in traversing one of these space intervals, there is a next time interval during which he must traverse the next such space interval. In general, the distance ratio of any adjacent intervals which the tortoise and Achilles traverse in the same time is, of course, given by the ratio of the respective velocities. And the initial distance d traversed by Achilles as well as his initial travel time $\frac{d}{V}$ each decrease successively geometrically by a factor of $\frac{v}{V}$.

Do these infinite progressions of space and time intervals show, as Zeno claims, that there is no instant at which Achilles comes abreast of the tortoise at a point A'? We can spare ourselves a detailed refutation of Zeno's contention that Achilles can *never* come abreast of the tortoise. For we can draw here on the results of my earlier detailed refutation of the second version of Zeno's Dichotomy as follows:

Achilles and the tortoise each separately qualify as the *legato* runner of the second version of Zeno's Dichotomy in which Zeno based his challenge on a progression of non-overlapping subintervals of space and time: Achilles is called upon to traverse an interval AA' at the velocity V, while the tortoise is required to traverse a lesser interval BA' at the lesser velocity v in the same time, and it is unproblematical for their separate *legato* runs that they have a common destination point A'. For the moment, therefore, let us consider the motion of each of them in the manner of the Dichotomy. Then our refutation of Zeno's argument in the Dichotomy enables us to claim that we have also shown the following *mutatis mutandis:*

1. Contrary to Zeno, Achilles, starting at the point A at time $T_0 = 0$ and moving at the velocity V, can reach the rendezvous point A' at a time T which is the earliest instant after a progression of decreasing time intervals whose *durations* $t_1, t_2, t_3, \ldots$ are $\dfrac{d}{V}, \dfrac{d}{V} \cdot \dfrac{v}{V}, \dfrac{d}{V} \cdot \dfrac{v^2}{V^2} \ldots$ and which converge to zero in the manner of a geometric progression. That there is such an earliest instant T is evident from the fact that for every n, the sum S_n of the first n terms of the duration numbers t_n is less than $\dfrac{d}{V - v}$. For S_n is given by the formula $S_n = \dfrac{a(1 - r^n)}{1 - r}$, and hence by

$$S_n = \dfrac{d}{V - v} [1 - \left(\dfrac{v}{V} \right)^n].$$

Since we chose $T_0 = 0$, the time co-ordinate T of this earliest instant also represents the finite duration of the union of the progression of decreasing subintervals of time, although the instant T does not belong to that union. And hence T is given by the total duration, which is the arithmetic limit

$$\lim_{n \to \infty} S_n.$$

Hence $T = \dfrac{d}{V}[1 + \dfrac{v}{V} + \dfrac{v^2}{V^2} + \ldots]$. Accordingly, $T = \dfrac{d}{V - v}$.

Clearly, this is the result we obtain directly if we use Newtonian addition of velocities and consider Achilles' motion with respect to the tortoise itself: their initial separation is d, Achilles' Newtonian velocity with respect to the turtle is $V - v$, and hence the time he requires to reach the tortoise when they are both adjacent to the point A′ on the ground is given by the quotient of these two magnitudes.

The point A′ reached by Achilles after the finite time T at the instant T is the first space point beyond a progression of decreasing space intervals whose lengths d, d′, d″ . . . are d, $d\dfrac{v}{V}$, $d\dfrac{v^2}{V^2}$, . . . and converge to zero in the manner of a geometric progression. These $\aleph_0$ space intervals collectively fit into the interval AA′. Although the union of this progression of subintervals does not contain the point A′, its length L is equal to the length of the closed space interval AA′ [cf. § 2A]. And L is given by

$$L = d[1 + \dfrac{v}{V} + \dfrac{v^2}{V^2} + \ldots] = \dfrac{d \cdot V}{V - v},$$

as expected, of course, since Achilles ran at the velocity V for a total time $\dfrac{d}{V - v}$.

2. For the tortoise, the story is the same with one exception, of course: in virtue of its head start d and departure from B rather than A at time $T_0 = o$, the progression of space intervals traversed by it begins with the interval of length d′ rather than d.

Now let us consider Achilles and the tortoise jointly and concentrate on the positions which they occupy at the *same instant* of time beginning with T_0. Then we see that the fallacy committed by Zeno in the Dichotomy when inferring that the runner can *never* reach his destination makes itself felt here as follows: Zeno infers that there is no instant T, separated by a finite time interval T from the initial instant

$T_0 = 0$, at which Achilles can come abreast of the turtle, just because there is an infinite progression of times

$$T_0, S_n, (n = 1, 2, 3, \ldots)$$

at which and between which he is not abreast of the turtle but behind it. Note that the times τ given by one of the numbers $T_0, S_n, (n = 1, 2, 3, \ldots)$ or by the numbers between them are confined to the finite, half-open time interval

$$T_0 \leqq \tau < T.$$

And hence the premise to which Zeno is entitled is that for any time τ in that half-open interval, there is a later time *in that interval* at which Achilles is not abreast of the tortoise. From this premise though, it does *not* follow that there is no instant at all after that half-open interval at which Achilles comes abreast. And indeed the premise *allows* that he comes abreast at the very first instant t thereafter!

We are now ready to appraise Whitrow's contention, previously mentioned apropos of the Dichotomy at both the beginning and end of § 3, that in his Achilles and the Tortoise, Zeno validly deduced a genuine logical antinomy.[63] I shall now state and criticize the several reasons given by Whitrow in support of his contention.

1. In the citation from him which I gave at the end of § 3, he argues that Achilles cannot pass through the entire progression of positions envisaged by Zeno on the grounds that if Achilles could, he could number them all consecutively and could then exhaust all the positive integers by counting, which is impossible. I have already discussed this argument at the end of § 3 and when dealing with the Peano machine in §4B. And there I explained why I regard Whitrow's appeal to counting as incapable of validly yielding the conclusion concerning Zeno's Achilles and the Tortoise which Whitrow believes himself to be able to derive from it.

2. Whitrow writes:

. . . on the assumption of continuity of space and time which is at issue, Achilles must go through all the points

[63] Whitrow, *op. cit.*, pp. 151–52.

of the construction *before* he can meet the tortoise, and this is the root of the difficulty. For, if Achilles goes through all these points in the way prescribed, he performs an infinite sequence of acts. *The fact that the total time-interval allotted to him for this feat has a finite measure does not automatically ensure that he can actually complete the sequence.*[64]

But his reason for thinking at all that there is a genuine difficulty here becomes apparent when he proceeds to tell us *why* Achilles' need to traverse a progression of points "is the root of the difficulty." And it turns out that this belief rests on his argument from *counting*, which we had reason to reject. He endeavors to prepare the ground for the latter argument by quoting as a "crucial question"[65] the following sentence from J. Watling: "But is not the paradox rather that we cannot understand how a man who is doing acts of a sequence and nothing else, and who is getting no nearer to having done them all, can suddenly find that he has done them all?"[66] But the immediately following sentence in Watling's paper (its concluding sentence) reads: "If this is the paradox then it arises because we believe that for any of our acts there must be an immediately preceding act and it will be in the explanation of this belief that the solution of the paradox lies."[67] The reader will recall from Sections B and C of § 2 above that I offered there an explanation of the belief mentioned here by Watling and that this explanation, coupled with the positive account of the denseness of time, renders the "how" question adduced by Whitrow impotent.

3. Whitrow writes:

Zeno may argue until he is blue in the face, but he cannot prove that Achilles will not catch the tortoise. Rather, his argument reveals that his method (and, for that

[64] *Ibid.*, p. 146.

[65] *Ibid.*, p. 147.

[66] J. Watling, "The Sum of an Infinite Series," *Analysis*, 13 (1952), 46.

[67] *Ibid.*

matter, any method) of analysing space, time, and motion raises its own problems of application. Thus, Zeno's paradox is not concerned with the question of whether Achilles does catch the tortoise but with the application to the study of motion of the hypothesis of the infinite divisibility of space and time. This hypothesis can be reconciled with the possibility of Achilles catching the tortoise, provided we introduce the further hypothesis that, as he comes indefinitely near to his quarry, he performs in the limit an infinite number of successive acts with infinite rapidity. But infinite rapidity (in the limit) means that (in the limit) these acts are simultaneous, in contradiction with their definition as successive. We thus see that, if this method of studying motion is to be of any use at all in application, we must introduce the logical fiction (self-contradiction) of an infinitely rapid succession of acts to compensate for the logical fiction that a completed infinity of successive acts can be contemplated.

. . . we require this device in order to apply the fruitful concept of infinite divisibility to the ideas of time and motion.[68]

But I am quite at a loss to understand how Whitrow reasons that any difficulty arises at all from the fact that the number of successive *steps* or "acts" performed by Achilles *per unit of time* increases boundlessly as we approach the time T when Achilles comes abreast of the tortoise. Whitrow refers to this innocuous fact ominously as involving that "in the limit" Achilles acts "with infinite rapidity." In this way, Whitrow believes himself to be adding a further complaint to his earlier allegation that a completed infinity of successive acts involves a contradiction. But, in truth, the infinite rapidity involved here is none other than that an infinite number of (suitably decreasing) steps have been taken in a finite time. And the boundlessness of the increase in the *frequency* of the steps (acts) does not detract one iota from their temporal successiveness. Even if a particle attains arbitrarily high *ve-*

locities—as in the case of the kinematically impermissible versions of the infinity machines of § 4—it does *not* follow that the particle must be at two different places simultaneously. It is true but irrelevant that if a particle is at two different places simultaneously, its *velocity* is infinite. And Whitrow simply has no case at all, because he infers quite incorrectly that "infinite rapidity (in the limit) means that (in the limit) these acts are simultaneous, in contradiction with their definition as successive."[69] The infinite rapidity mentioned by Whitrow fully allows Achilles to perform his steps (acts) in temporal succession and with the same finite velocity: as the times available for the performance of his successive acts decrease and converge to zero, the successive space intervals he is called on to traverse decrease proportionately. As we saw in § 4, the latter feature of Achilles' performance distinguished it from some of the kinematically impermissible performances assigned to hypothetical infinity machines.

Hence, even if Whitrow were right that the concept of "a completed infinity of successive acts" is self-contradictory (a "logical fiction"), he would still be plainly wrong in asserting further that the so-called "infinite rapidity" required here by kinematical theory is a compensating fiction (contradiction).

In concluding the discussion of the Dichotomy and the Achilles, I wish to call attention to a recent paper by Eugene TeHennepe[70] which shows what obscurantist ravages ordinary language philosophy can inflict on the appreciation of Zeno's challenge to kinematical theory. TeHennepe writes:

> The kernel of the paradoxes involving 'infinite' (the Achilles and the dichotomy) lies in the fact that it is paradoxical to describe a finite time or distance as an infinite series of diminishing magnitudes. Thus it seems that Achilles can never overtake the tortoise and I can never cross the room if I attempt to do so by moving half the remaining distance each time. The very barb of the

[69] *Ibid.*

[70] E. TeHennepe, "Language Reform and Philosophical Imperialism: Another Round with Zeno," *Analysis,* 23 (1963), 43–49.

paradoxes lies in this very fact: that no matter how close Achilles gets to the tortoise and how close I get to the other side of the room, there is still a remaining distance, however infinitesimal; in brief, that "close" (no matter *how* close) is never "there"! The linguistic solution to the paradoxes is simply to recognize that it is paradoxical (because contradictory) to describe a finite magnitude as an infinite series of diminishing magnitudes, and then to refuse such a description. . . .

The mathematical solution, however, is not a solution at all, but an evasion of the very point of the paradox. And for a rather obvious reason. Brief reflection on what it *means* to sum an infinite series or to say that an infinite series of diminishing magnitudes converges to a limit makes evident the definitional and thus circular or question-begging nature of solutions which rely on these means.[71]

The reasons for completely repudiating this purported "linguistic solution" to the paradoxes are implicit in this article's philosophical and mathematical discussion of the physics relevant to the Dichotomy and the Achilles.

[71] E. TeHennepe, *op. cit.*, p. 44.

BIBLIOGRAPHY

The following abbreviations are used: *A* for *Analysis; JP* for *Journal of Philosophy; M* for *Mind; P* for *Philosophy; PAS* for *Proceedings of the Aristotelian Society; PQ* for *Philosophical Quarterly; PR* for *Philosophical Review;* and *PT* for *The Problem of Time,* University of California Publications in Philosophy, 18 (1935).

SECTION I. "WHAT, THEN, IS TIME?"

Critical surveys of traditional theories of time are in: J. A. Gunn, *The Problem of Time,* George Allen & Unwin, London, 1929; and M. F. Cleugh, *Time, and Its Importance in Modern Thought,* Methuen & Co., London, 1937. L. Wittgenstein's diagnosis of Augustine's perplexities about time, which is developed by F. Waismann in the selection in this section, is to be found in Wittgenstein's books: *The Blue and Brown Books,* Basil Blackwell, Oxford, 1958, pp. 6, 26 ff., and *Philosophical Investigations,* tr. by G. E. M. Anscombe, Basil Blackwell, Oxford, 1953, pp. 42 ff. Articles in which the Wittgensteinian approach to Augustine is pursued are: O. K. Bouwsma, "The Mystery of Time (Or, The Man Who Did Not Know What Time Is)," *JP,* 51 (1954), reprinted in Bouwsma's *Philosophical Essays,* University of Nebraska Press, Lincoln, 1965; F. Waismann, "How I See Philosophy," in *Contemporary British Philosophy,* third series, H. D. Lewis, ed., George Allen & Unwin, London, 1956, especially pp. 450–53; Ronald Suter, "Augustine on Time with Some Criticisms from Wittgenstein," *Revue internationale de philosophie,* 16 (1962); and Richard M. Gale, "Some Metaphysical Statements about Time," *JP,* 60 (1963).

SECTION II. THE STATIC VERSUS THE DYNAMIC TEMPORAL

McTaggart's argument first appeared as "The Unreality of Time," *M*, 17 (1908), reprinted in his *Philosophical Studies,* Edward Arnold, London, 1934. Attempts to refute his argument through the use of the B-Theory of Time are, in addition to the D. Williams article in this section: C. D. Broad, "Time," in *Encyclopaedia of Religion and Ethics,* Charles Scribner's Sons, New York, 1922. Broad was under the influence of Russell when he wrote this article, and completely reversed his position in his subsequent writings. For a detailed account of Broad's shifting views on time see C. W. K. Mundle, "Broad's Views about Time," in *The Philosophy of C. D. Broad,* P. A. Schilpp, ed., Open Court, La Salle, Ill., 1959; R. B. Braithwaite, "Time and Change," *PAS,* Supp. Vol. 8 (1928); and D. W. Gotshalk, "McTaggart on Time," *M*, 39 (1930). Bertrand Russell developed the B-Theory of Time in his: *The Principles of Mathematics,* Cambridge University Press, Cambridge, 1903, especially pp. 458–76; *Introduction to Mathematical Philosophy,* George Allen & Unwin, London, 1919, p. 164; "The Philosophy of Logical Atomism," *Monist,* 28–29 (1918–1919) (see Lecture IV, where Russell discusses the philosophical importance of "emphatic particulars," which are later termed "egocentric particulars" in his *An Inquiry into Meaning & Truth,* W. W. Norton, New York, 1940, ch. vii). Russell's views about the reducibility of A-determinations to B-relations are developed and defended in: G. P. Adams, "Temporal Form and Existence," in *PT;* N. Goodman, *The Structure of Appearance,* Harvard University Press, Cambridge, Mass., 1951; W. V. Quine, "Mr. Strawson on Logical Theory," *M*, 62 (1953); A. J. Ayer, "Statements about the Past," in his *Philosophical Essays,* Macmillan, London, 1954; Ayer, *The Problem of Knowledge,* Macmillan, London, 1956, particularly pp. 57–58 and 179–80; and J. J. C. Smart, *Philosophy and Scientific Realism,* Routledge & Kegan Paul, London, 1963, ch. vii. Attempts to show that space and time are analogous because of the complementarity between things and events appear in: R. Taylor, "Spatial and Temporal Analogies and the

Concept of Identity," *JP*, 52 (1955), reprinted in *Problems of Space and Time*, J. J. C. Smart, ed., Macmillan, New York, 1964, which views are further elaborated on in his "Moving about in Time," *PQ*, 9 (1959); and B. Mayo, "Objects, Events, and Complementarity," *PR*, 70 (1961). Taylor's position is criticized by: N. L. Wilson, "Space, Time, and Individuals," *JP*, 52 (1955); W. J. Huggett, "Losing One's Way in Time," *PQ*, 10 (1960); J. Jarvis Thomson, "Time, Space, and Objects," *M*, 74 (1965); and J. W. Meiland, "Temporal Parts and Spatio-Temporal Analogies," *American Philosophical Quarterly*, 3 (1966). The Mayo article is criticized by F. Dretske, "Moving Backward in Time," *PR*, 71 (1962). Other writings defending the B-Theory of Time are listed under Sections III and IV of this bibliography.

Answers to McTaggart's argument employing the A-Theory of Time are: C. D. Broad, *Scientific Thought*, Kegan Paul, Trench, Trubner, London, 1923; Broad, "Reply to My Critics," in *The Philosophy of C. D. Broad*, cited earlier in full; John Wisdom, "Time, Fact and Substance," *PAS*, 29 (1928–1929); E. W. Hall, "Time and Causality," *PR*, 43 (1934); P. Marhenke, "McTaggart's Analysis of Time," in *PT*; L. S. Stebbing, "Some Ambiguities in Discussions Concerning Time," in *Philosophy and History*, R. Klibansky and H. J. Paton, eds., Clarendon Press, Oxford, 1936; E. R. Bevan, *Symbolism and Belief*, Beacon Press, Boston, 1957, ch. iv; D. Pears, "Time, Truth, and Inference," in *Essays in Conceptual Analysis*, A. G. N. Flew, ed., Macmillan, London, 1956; M. Dummett, "A Defense of McTaggart's Proof of the Unreality of Time," *PR*, 69 (1960); Richard M. Gale, "Is It Now Now?" *M*, 73 (1964). Works defending tenets of the A-Theory of Time are: R. Collingwood, "Some Perplexities about Time with an Attempted Solution," *PAS*, 26 (1925–1926); W. R. Dennes, "Time as Datum and as Construction," in *PT*; D. S. Mackay, "Succession and Duration," in *PT*; E. W. Strong, "Time in Operational Analysis," in *PT*; J. N. Findlay, "Review of Ehrenfel's *Cosmogony*," *P*, 25 (1961); Findlay, "An Examination of Tenses," in *Contemporary British Philosophy*, third series, cited earlier in full; P. F. Strawson, *Introduction to Logical Theory*, Methuen & Co., London, 1952, especially pp. 150–51; D. Y. Deshpande, "Professor Ayer on the Past," *M*, 65 (1956); W. S. Sellars, "Time and the World Order," in *Minnesota Studies in the Philosophy of Science*, III, H. Feigl, G. Maxwell, and M. Scriven, eds., University of Minnesota Press, Minneapolis, 1962, reprinted in *Science, Perception & Reality*, Humanities Press, New York, 1963; K. W. Rankin, "Order and Disorder in Time," *M*, 66 (1957); A. N. Prior, "Time After Time," *M*, 67 (1958); Prior, "Thank Goodness That's Over," *P*, 34 (1959); Prior, "Changes in Events and Changes in Things," the Lindley Lecture, University of Kansas, 1962; Stuart Hampshire, *Thought and Action*, Viking Press, New York, 1960, ch. i; M. Black, "The 'Direction' of Time," *A*, 19 (1959); Black, "Review of G. J. Whitrow's *The Natural Philosophy of Time*" in *Scientific American*, 206 (1962); L. E. Palmieri, "Empiricism and a Time-Line," *PQ*, 10 (1960); R. Taylor, "Pure Becoming," *Australasian Journal of Philosophy*, 38 (1960); David Shwayder, "The Temporal Order," *PQ*, 10 (1960); Richard M. Gale, "Dewey and the Problem of the Alleged Futurity of Yesterday," *Philosophy and Phenomenological Research*, 21 (1961); Gale, "Tensed Statements," *PQ*, 12 (1962), which article is criticized by J. J. C. Smart, "'Tensed Statements': A Comment," *PQ*, 12 (1962); by B. Mayo, "Infinitive Verbs and Tensed Statements"; and by I. Thalberg, "Tenses and 'Now'," both in *PQ*, 13 (1963), along with Gale's answer "A Reply to Smart, Mayo, and Thalberg on 'Tensed Statements'," in the same issue. A further criticism of the original Gale paper is J. Rosenberg, "Tensed Discourse and the Eliminability of Tenses," *PQ*, 16 (1966). Other articles by Gale are: "Existence, Tense and Presupposition," *Monist*, 50 (1966), and "McTaggart's Analysis of Time," *American Philosophical Quarterly*, 3 (1966). Other articles defending the A-Theory are listed under Sections III and IV. The problem of detensing language is discussed in the articles by A. Duncan-Jones, P. N. Smith, B. Mayo, and L. J. Cohen in ch. vii of *Philosophy and Analysis*, M. Macdonald, ed., Philosophical Library, New York, 1955.

The Either-Way-Will-Work Theory of Time is put forth in J. J. C. Smart, "The River of Time," in *Essays in Conceptual Analysis,* cited earlier in full, as well as in the Findlay and Smart articles included in this volume. The only philosopher who has defended the view that neither the A- nor the B-Series alone is sufficient to account for our concept of time is L. O. Mink, "Time, McTaggart and Pickwickian Language," *PQ,* 10 (1960).

SECTION III. THE OPEN FUTURE

Aristotle's discussion of future contingents, which is articulated and criticized in the Rescher and Bradley articles in this volume, has inspired a fantastic number of commentaries, criticisms, and defenses. Among these are: Cicero, *De Fato;* Ammonius, *Commentarius in Aristotelis De Interpretatione,* Adolf Busse, ed., in the Berlin Academy edition of the *Commentaria in Aristotelem Graeca,* Berlin, 1897; Boethius, *Minora Commentaria in Librum Aristotelis de Interpretatione, and Majora Commentaria . . . ,* in *Patrologiae Cursus Completus,* J. P. Migne, ed., Latin series, Vol. 64, Paris, 1891. Also, *Commentarii in Librum Aristotelis "Peri Hermēneias,"* C. Meiser, ed., Leipzig, 1877, 1880; Abū Naṣr al-Fārābī, *Alfarabi's Commentary on Aristotle's De Interpretatione,* W. Kutsch and S. Marrow, eds., Beyrouth, 1960; St. Anselm, *Tractatus de concordia praesentiae, et praedestinationis, et gratiae dei cum libero arbitrio,* Migne, ed., *Patrologia,* Latin series, Vols. 158–59; Abelard, *Dialectia,* L. M. de Rijk, ed., Assen, 1956, and "Editio super Aristotelem de Interpretatione" in *Pietro Abelardo: Scritti Filosofici,* M. dal Pra, ed., Milano, 1954; Averroes, *Commentarium Medium in Aristotelis "De Interpretatione,"* Juntine edition of *Aristotelis omnia quae extant Opera cum Averrois Cordubensis commentarii,* Venice, 1562; Albertus Magnus, *In libros II Perihermeneias* (in *Opera omnia*), A. Borgnet, ed., Vol. I, Paris, 1890, pp. 373–757; St. Thomas Aquinas, *In Libros "Perihermeneias" Exposition,* tr. by J. T. Oesterle, Marquette University Press, Milwaukee, 1962, see Lecturae 13–15; William of Ockham, "Analysis of Ockham's *Tractatus de Praedestinatione et de Praescientia Dei et de Futuris Con-*

tingentibus," in *Philosophical Writings,* sel. and ed. by Philotheus Boehner, Thomas Nelson & Sons, New York, 1957, pp. 420–41. The text of this tract was edited by Boehner in the *Franciscan Institute Publications,* Philosophy Series, no. 2, St. Bonaventure, 1945; L. Baudry, *La Querelle des Futurs Contingents,* Louvain, 1465–1475; *Textes Inédits,* Paris, 1950; Thomas Hobbes, *De Corpore,* ch. x, "Of Power and Act" in *The Metaphysical System of Hobbes,* M. W. Calkins, ed., Open Court, Chicago, 1905, pp. 76–80; C. S. Peirce, *Collected Papers,* C. Hartshorne and P. Weiss, eds., Harvard University Press, Cambridge, Mass., 1931–1958, see *passim* in Vols. III, V, VI; O. Hamelin, *Le Système d'Aristote,* Paris, 1920, 2d ed. 1931; Jan Lukasiewicz, "Three-Valued Logic" (in Polish), *Ruch Filozoficzny,* Vol. 5 (1920), pp. 169–71; Lukasiewicz, "Philosophische Bemerkungen zu mehrwertigen Systemen des Aussagenkalküls," *Comptes Rendus des Séances de la Société des Sciences et des Lettres de Varsovie,* Classe III, Vol. 23 (1930), pp. 51–77; Lukasiewicz and A. Tarski, "Untersuchungen über den Aussagenkalkül," *Comptes Rendus des Séances de la Société des Sciences et des Lettres de Varsovie,* Classe III, Vol. 23 (1930), pp. 1–21; M. Wajsberg, "Aksjomatyzacia trojwarosciowego rachunku zdan," *Comptes Rendus des Séances de la Société des Sciences et des Lettres de Varsovie,* Classe III, Vol. 24 (1931), pp. 126–48; C. A. Baylis, "Are Some Propositions Neither True nor False?" *Philosophy of Science,* 3 (1936); A. Becker, *Die Aristotelische Theorie der Moglichkeitschlüsse,* Berlin, 1933; Becker, "Bestreitet Aristotles die Gültigkeit des *Tertium non datur* für Zukunftsaussagen?" *Actes du Congrès International de Philosophie Scientifique,* VI, Paris, 1936, pp. 69–74; J. Maritain, *Introduction to Logic,* tr. by I. Choquette, Sheed & Ward, New York, 1937, pp. 97, 135–36; C. J. Ducasse, "Truth, Verifiability, and Propositions about the Future," *Philosophy of Science,* 8 (1941); D. Amand, *Fatalisme et liberté dans l'Antiquité grecque,* Louvain, 1945; J. Isaac, *Le Peri Hermeneias en Occident de Boece à Saint Thomas,* Paris, 1949; Pears, "Time, Truth, and Inference," cited earlier in full; D. Williams, "The Sea Fight Tomorrow," in *Structure, Method, and Meaning,* Paul Henle

et al., eds., Liberal Arts Press, New York, 1951. See also
L. Linsky, "Professor Donald Williams on Aristotle," *PR*, 63
(1954), and Williams' reply, "Professor Linsky on Aris-
totle," in the same issue; B. Mates, *Stoic Logic*, University
of California Publications in Philosophy, 26 (1953), 28–29;
A. N. Prior, "In What Sense Is Modal Logic Many-Valued?"
A, (1953); Prior, "Three-valued Logic and Future Con-
tingents," *PQ*, 3 (1953) (see also the review by T. Sugihara
in *The Journal of Symbolic Logic*, 19 (1954), 294). W. V.
Quine, "On a So-called Paradox," *M*, 62 (1953); G. Ryle,
"It Was to Be," in *Dilemmas*, Cambridge University Press,
Cambridge, 1954; R. J. Butler, "Aristotle's Sea Fight and
Three-valued Logic," *PR*, 64 (1955); A. N. Prior, *Formal
Logic*, Oxford University Press, Oxford, 1955, pp. 240–50;
F. Waismann, "How I See Philosophy," in *Contemporary
British Philosophy*, third series, cited earlier in full; G. E. M.
Anscombe, "Aristotle and the Sea Battle," *M*, 65 (1956).
See the review by E. J. Lemmon in *The Journal of Symbolic
Logic*, 21 (1956), 388–89; C. K. Grant, "Certainty, Neces-
sity, and Aristotle's Sea-Battle," *M*, 64 (1957); R. Taylor,
"The Problem of Future Contingents," *PR*, 66 (1957),
which is criticized by R. Albritton, "Present Truth and Fu-
ture Contingency" in the same issue; A. N. Prior, *Time and
Modality*, Clarendon Press, Oxford, 1957; H. Putnam, "Three-
valued Logic," *Philosophical Studies*, 8 (1957); Jan Lukasiewicz, *Aristotle's Syllogistic from the Standpoint of Modern
Formal Logic*, 2d ed. enl., Oxford University Press, Oxford,
1957, pp. 155–56; J. T. Saunders, "A Sea-Fight Tomorrow?"
PR, 67 (1958); J. King-Farlow, "Sea-Fights Without Tears,"
A, 19 (1959); J. Hintikka, "Necessity, Universality, and
Time in Aristotle," *Ajatus*, 20 (1959); Hintikka, "The Once
and Future Sea Fight," *PR*, 73 (1964); R. J. Butler, a review of *Saunders* (1958), *Bradley* (reprinted in this book),
and *Wolff* (1960) in *The Journal of Symbolic Logic*, 25
(1960), 343–45; R. Montague, "Mr. Bradley on the Future,"
M, 59 (1960); C. Strang, "Aristotle and the Sea Battle,"
M, 69 (1960); P. Wolff, "Truth, Futurity and Contingency," *M*, 69 (1960); R. M. Gale, "Endorsing Predictions," *PR*, 70 (1961); Gale, "Can a Prediction 'Become

True'?" *Philosophical Studies*, 13 (1962); W. and M. Kneale, *The Development of Logic*, Oxford University Press, Oxford, 1962; A. J. Ayer, "Fatalism," *The Concept of a Person and Other Essays*, Macmillan, London, 1963; Z. Jordan, "Logical Determinism," *Notre Dame Journal of Formal Logic*, 4 (1963); N. Rescher, "An Interpretation of Aristotle's Doctrine of Future Contingency and Excluded Middle," in *Studies in the History of Arabic Logic*, University of Pittsburgh Press, Pittsburgh, 1963; Rescher, "Aristotle's Theory of Modal Syllogisms and Its Interpretation" in *The Critical Approach to Science and Philosophy*, M. Bunge, ed., Free Press, London, 1964; and N. Pike, "Divine Omniscience and Voluntary Action," *PR*, 74 (1965). The above articles by Lukasiewicz, Pears, Ryle, Prior, Butler, Taylor, Gale, Jordan, and Rescher defend Aristotle's doctrine of future contingents by employing certain tenets of the A-Theory of Time; while the articles by Ducasse, Williams, and Quine criticize Aristotle from the standpoint of the B-Theory of Time.

The Master Argument of Diodorus, which is taken up in the Rescher article in this book, is commented on by: E. Zeller, "Ueber den *Kyrieuon* des Megarikers Diodorus," *Sitzungsberichte der Königlichen Akademie der Wissenschaften zu Berlin*, Berlin, 1882; N. Hartmann, "Der Megarische und der Aristotelische Möglichkeitsbegriff," *Sitzungsberichte der Preussischen Akademie der Wissenschaften*, philosophisch-historische Klasse, Jahrgang, 1937; V. Goldschmidt, *Le system stoicien et l'idee de temps*, Paris, 1953; B. Mates, *Stoic Logic*, cited earlier in full; S. Sambursky, "On the Possible and the Probable in Ancient Greece," *Osiris*, 12 (1956); Prior, "Diodorus and Modal Logic," *PQ*, 8 (1958); S. Sambursky, *Physics of the Stoics*, Macmillan, New York, 1959; O. Becker, "Zur Rekonstruction des *Kyrieuōn Logos* des Diodorus Kronos," *Erkenntnis und Verantwortung: Festschrift für Theodor Litt*, J. Derbolav and F. Nicolin, eds., Düsseldorf, 1960; Pierre-Maxime Schuhl, *Le Dominateur et les possibles*, Paris, 1960; W. and M. Kneale, *The Development of Logic*, cited earlier in full; Hintikka, "Aristotle and the 'Master Argument' of Diodorus," *American Philosophical Quarterly*, 1 (1964); and N. Rescher, *Tem-*

poral Modalities in Arabic Logic, Supp. Series of *Foundations of Language,* Dordrecht, 1967.

Taylor's piece on "Fatalism" has evoked the following literature: J. T. Saunders, "Professor Taylor on Fatalism," *A,* 23 (1962); B. Aune, "Fatalism and Professor Taylor," *PR,* 71 (1962); R. Taylor, "Fatalism and Ability," *A,* 23 (1962); P. Makepeace, "Fatalism and Ability, II," *ibid.;* Saunders, "Fatalism and Linguistic Reform," *ibid.;* R. Abelson, "Taylor's Fatal Fallacy," *PR,* 72 (1963); R. Sharvy, "A Logical Error in Taylor's 'Fatalism'," *A,* 23 (1962); Saunders, "Fatalism and the Logic of 'Ability'," *A,* 24 (1963); Taylor, "A Note on Fatalism," *PR,* 72 (1963); Sharvy, "Tautology and Fatalism," *JP,* 61 (1964); S. Cahn, "Fatalistic Arguments," *ibid.;* Taylor, "Comment," *ibid.;* Saunders, "Fatalism and Ordinary Language," *JP,* 62 (1965); and Diodorus Cronus (Richard Taylor), "Time, Truth and Ability," *A,* 25 (1965).

Discussions of Dummett's problem concerning whether a cause can be later than its effect are found in: M. Dummett and A. Flew, "Can an Effect Precede Its Cause?" (symposium), *PAS,* Supp. Vol. 28 (1954); M. Black, "Why Cannot an Effect Precede Its Cause?" *A,* 16 (1956); A. Flew, "Effects Before Their Causes? Addenda and Corrigenda," *A,* 16 (1956); M. Scriven, "Randomness and the Causal Order," *A,* 17 (1957); A. J. Ayer, *The Problem of Knowledge,* cited earlier in full; D. F. Pears, "The Priority of Causes," *A,* 17 (1957); Flew, "Causal Disorder Again," *A,* 17 (1957); R. M. Chisholm and R. Taylor, "Making Things to Have Happened," *A,* 20 (1960); S. Gorovitz, "Leaving the Past Alone" (a criticism of Dummett's "Bringing About the Past") *PR,* 73 (1964); and R. M. Gale, "Why a Cause Cannot Be Later Than Its Effect," *Review of Metaphysics,* 19 (1965). Also to be consulted on this topic are the articles by Flew and Ducasse in *The Philosophy of C. D. Broad,* cited earlier in full.

Mayo's thesis that future, unlike past, individuals cannot be identified is defended in some form by the following persons: C. S. Peirce, *Collected Papers,* C. Hartshorne and P. Weiss, eds., Vol. IV (1933), #172, and also Vol. II

(1932), ##146–48, and Vol. V (1934), #447; Broad, *Scientific Thought,* cited earlier in full, p. 77; G. Ryle, "It Was to Be," cited earlier in full; Prior, *Time and Modality,* cited earlier in full; Prior, "Identifiable Individuals," *Review of Metaphysics,* 13 (1960); J. Margolis, "Statements about the Past and Future," *PR,* 72 (1963); and R. M. Gale and I. Thalberg, "The Generality of Predictions," *JP,* 62 (1965). The following pieces have been critical of the generality of predictions thesis: P. T. Geach, *Reference and Generality,* Cornell University Press, Ithaca, N.Y., 1962, p. 29; and A. J. Ayer, *The Concept of a Person and Other Essays,* cited earlier in full, pp. 249–50.

Section IV. Human Time

Works expounding or criticizing some version of the doctrine of the "specious present" (which is taken up in the article by Mabbott in this volume) are: W. James, *The Principles of Psychology,* Henry Holt, New York, 1890, Vol. I; W. P. Montague, "A Theory of Time Perception," in *The Ways of Things,* pp. 363–81; E. Husserl, *The Phenomenology of Internal Time-Consciousness,* ed. by M. Heidegger and tr. by J. S. Churchill, Indiana University Press, Bloomington, Ind., 1964; Broad, *Scientific Thought,* cited earlier in full; L. E. Akeley, "The Problem of the Specious Present and Physical Time," *JP,* 22 (1925); C. D. Broad, *An Examination of McTaggart's Philosophy,* Cambridge University Press, Cambridge, 1938, Part II, vol. I, pp. 281 ff.; Mabbott, "The Specious Present," *M,* 64 (1955); P. Fraisse, *The Psychology of Time,* tr. by J. Leith, Eyre and Spottiswoode, 1964.

Grünbaum's thesis that temporal becoming is psychological or mind-dependent is also espoused by: B. Russell, "On the Experience of Time," *Monist,* 25 (1915); R. M. Blake, "On Mr. Broad's Theory of Time," *M,* 34 (1925); Braithwaite, "Time and Change," cited earlier in full; A. S. Eddington, *The Nature of the Physical World,* Macmillan, New York, 1928; Eddington, *Space, Time, and Gravitation,* Cambridge University Press, Cambridge, 1920; H. Weyl, *Philosophy of Mathematics and Natural Science,* based on a tr. by Olaf

Helmer, Princeton University Press, Princeton, N.J., 1949; H. Bergmann, *Der Kampf um das Kausalgesetz in der jüngsten Physik,* F. Vieweg and Son, Braunschweig, 1929; C. J. Ducasse, *Nature, Mind, and Death,* Open Court, La Salle, Ill., 1951; A. Grünbaum, *Philosophical Problems of Space and Time,* Alfred A. Knopf, New York, 1963. Those who have argued that becoming is not mind-dependent are: C. D. Broad, "Time and Change," *PAS,* Supp. Vol. 8 (1928); H. Reichenbach, "Die Kausalstruktur der Welt und der Unterschied von Vergangenheit und Zukunft," *Berichte der Bayerischen Akademie München, Mathematisch-Naturwissenschaftliche Abteilung* (November 1925); P. Marhenke, "McTaggart's Analysis of Time," cited earlier in full; L. S. Stebbing, "Some Ambiguities in Discussions Concerning Time," cited earlier in full; H. Reichenbach, *The Direction of Time,* University of California Press, Berkeley, 1956; M. Capek, *The Philosophical Impact of Contemporary Physics,* D. Van Nostrand, Princeton, N.J., 1961; and G. J. Whitrow, *The Natural Philosophy of Time,* Thomas Nelson & Sons, London and Edinburgh, 1961. Some philosophers, using H. Reichenbach's treatment of tensed verbs as token-reflexive words in his *Elements of Symbolic Logic,* Macmillan, New York, 1947, have argued that becoming is subjective because A-determinations involve a reference to the subject qua language-user: among the defenders of this view are Ayer, *The Problem of Knowledge,* and Smart, *Philosophy and Scientific Realism,* both cited earlier in full. Those who have argued that tensed verbs are not token-reflexive are: Wisdom, "Time, Fact, and Substance," cited earlier in full; Broad, *An Examination of McTaggart's Philosophy,* cited earlier in full; F. B. Ebersole, "Verb Tenses as Expressors and Indicators," *A,* 12 (1952); J. Jorgensen, "Some Reflections of Reflexivity," *M,* 62 (1953); Findlay, "An Examination of Tenses," cited earlier in full; K. W. Rankin, "Referential Identifiers," *American Philosophical Quarterly,* 1 (1964); R. M. Gale, "The Egocentric Particular and Token-Reflexive Analyses of Tense," *PR,* 73 (1964); and Gale, "Pure and Impure Descriptions," *Australasian Journal of Philosophy,* 1966.

Some of the significant treatments of time by existentialists are: M. Heidegger, *Kant and the Problem of Metaphysics,* tr. by J. S. Churchill, Indiana University Press, Bloomington, Ind., 1962; Heidegger, *Being and Time,* tr. by J. Macquarrie and E. Robinson, Harper & Row, New York, 1962; Jean-Paul Sartre, *Being and Nothingness,* tr. by H. Barnes, Philosophical Library, New York, 1956; and M. Merleau-Ponty, *Phenemenology of Perception,* tr. by C. Smith, Routledge & Kegan Paul, London, 1962.

For a detailed bibliography of B. L. Whorf's writings see *Language, Thought, and Reality,* J. B. Carroll, ed., Massachusetts Institute of Technology Press, Cambridge, Mass., 1956.

SECTION V. ZENO'S PARADOXES OF MOTION

For a discussion of the historical Zeno and the subsequent treatments of his paradoxes see: F. Cajori, "The History of Zeno's Arguments on Motion," *American Mathematical Monthly,* 23 (1915); Cajori, "The Purpose of Zeno's Arguments on Motion," *Isis,* 3 (1920–1921); *Zeno of Elea,* text, with tr. and notes by H. D. P. Lee, Cambridge University Press, Cambridge, 1936; C. B. Boyer, *The Concepts of the Calculus,* Hafner, New York, 1949; G. Vlastos, "Zeno's Race Course," *Journal of the History of Philosophy,* 4 (1966); Vlastos, "Zeno," in *The Encyclopedia of Philosophy,* P. Edwards, ed., Collier, New York, 1967; and W. C. Salmon's Introduction to *Zeno's Paradoxes,* Salmon, ed., Bobbs-Merrill, New York, 1967.

What I have termed the "Metaphysical Replies" to Zeno are in: H. Bergson, *Time and Free Will,* tr. by R. L. Pogson, George Allen & Unwin, London, 1910; Bergson, *An Introduction to Metaphysics,* tr. by T. E. Hulme, G. P. Putnam's Sons, New York, 1912; W. James, *Some Problems of Philosophy,* Longmans, Green, London, 1911; A. N. Whitehead, *Process and Reality,* Macmillan, New York, 1929; A. Edel, "Aristotle's Theory of the Infinite," New York, 1934, not publ.; J. O. Wisdom, "Why Achilles Does Not Fail to Catch the Tortoise," *M,* 50 (1941); A. P. Ushenko, "Zeno's Paradoxes," *M,* 55 (1946); H. R. King, "Aristotle and the

Paradoxes of Zeno," *JP,* 46 (1949). Criticisms of these various metaphysical replies are in: A. O. Lovejoy, "The Problem of Time in Modern French Philosophy," *PR,* 21 (1912); R. M. Blake, "The Paradoxes of Temporal Process," *JP,* 23 (1926); G. Santayana, *Winds of Doctrine,* Charles Scribner's Sons, New York, 1926; B. Russell, *A History of Western Philosophy,* Simon & Schuster, New York, 1945, chapter on "Bergson"; A. Grünbaum, "Relativity and the Atomicity of Becoming," *Review of Metaphysics,* 4 (1950).

The problem of completing an infinite number of tasks, which is central to the Thomson article, is discussed by the following authors: Weyl, *Philosophy of Mathematics and Natural Science,* cited earlier in full; H. B. Smith, "Mr. Blake and the Paradox of Zeno," *JP,* 34 (1923); Max Black, "Achilles and the Tortoise," *A,* 11 (1951), reprinted with new comments and other articles on Zeno in *Problems of Analysis,* Cornell University Press, Ithaca, N.Y., 1954; R. Taylor, "Mr. Black on Temporal Paradoxes," *A,* 12 (1951); J. O. Wisdom, "Achilles on a Physical Race Course," *A,* 13 (1952); Taylor, "Mr. Wisdom on Temporal Paradoxes," *A,* 13 (1952); L. E. Thomas, "Achilles and the Tortoise," *A,* 13 (1952); A. Grünbaum, "Messrs. Black and Taylor on Temporal Paradoxes," *A,* 13 (1952); J. Watling, "The Sum of an Infinite Series," *A,* 13 (1952); J. M. Hinton and C. B. Martin, "Achilles and the Tortoise," *A,* 14 (1954); G. Ryle, "Achilles and the Tortoise," in *Dilemmas,* cited earlier in full; D. S. Shwayder, "Achilles Unbound," *JP,* 52 (1955); G. E. L. Owen, "Zeno and the Mathematicians," *PAS,* 58 (1957–1958); Whitrow, *The Natural Philosophy of Time,* cited earlier in full; P. Benacerraf, "Tasks, Super-tasks, and the Modern Eleatics," *JP,* 59 (1962); E. TeHennepe, "Language Reform and Philosophical Imperialism: Another Round with Zeno," *A,* 23 (1963); C. S. Chihara, "On the Possibility of Completing an Infinite Process," *PR,* 74 (1965); and Vlastos, "Zeno's Race Course," cited earlier in full.

For a discussion of the mathematical continuum and its relevance to Zeno's paradoxes see: B. Russell, *The Principles of Mathematics,* cited earlier in full; Russell, *Our Knowledge of the External World,* Open Court, Chicago, 1914.